The Best of
Peter Drucker
on Management

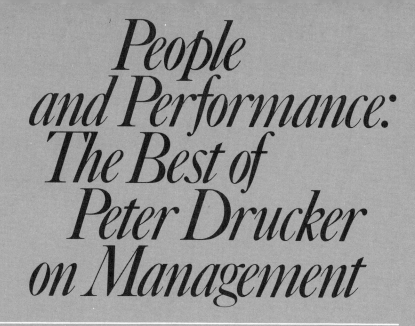

People and Performance: The Best of Peter Drucker on Management

Peter F. Drucker

How to Use This Book
Definitions of Key Terms

by Oscar Tivis Nelson, Jr.
Vanderbilt University

HARPER & ROW, PUBLISHERS
New York Hagerstown Philadelphia San Francisco London

Sponsoring Editors: Raleigh Wilson and William Eastman
Project Editor: Kathleen Murray
Designer: Howard S. Leiderman
Production Supervisor: Kewal Sharma
Compositor: Telecki Publishing Services

Art Studio: J & R Technical Services Inc.

Library of Congress Cataloging in Publication Data

Drucker, Peter Ferdinand, 1909—
    People and performance.

    Includes index.
    1. Management. I. Title.
HD31.D774   658.4   76-51792
ISBN 0-06-166400-6

Acknowledgments

Grateful acknowledgment is made to the publishers for permission to reprint the material specified:

"Fifty Years of Management — A Look Back and A Look Forward," Paper No. 60 — W-46 (part of the report "Ten Years' Progress in Management, 1950–1960"). Reprinted with permission of the American Society of Mechanical Engineers.

"The Delusion of Profits," from the *Wall Street Journal*, February 5, 1975. Reprinted with permission of the *Wall Street Journal* © 1976 Dow Jones & Company, Inc. All Rights Reserved.

"Managing Capital Productivity," from the *Wall Street Journal*, July 24, 1975. Reprinted with permisssion of the *Wall Street Journal* © 1976 Dow Jones & Company, Inc. All Rights Reserved.

"New Templates for Today's Organizations," from the *Harvard Business Review*, January-February, 1974. Reprinted with permission of the *Harvard Business Review*. Copyright © 1973 by the President and Fellows of Harvard College; all rights reserved.

"How to Be an Employee," from *Fortune*, May 1952. Reprinted with permission of *Fortune* Magazine.

"Managing the Knowledge Worker," from the *Wall Street Journal*, November 7, 1975. Reprinted with permission of the *Wall Street Journal* © 1976 Dow Jones & Company, Inc. All Rights Reserved.

"What The Computer Will Be Telling You," reprinted by permission from *Nation's Business*, August, 1966. Copyright © 1966 by *Nation's Business*, Chamber of Commerce of the United States.

"Multinationals and Developing Countries: Myths and Realities." Reprinted by permission from *Foreign Affairs*, October 1974. Copyright © 1974 by Council on Foreign Relations, Inc.

Preface

Of all the subjects taught in college, management may well be the one most closely related to the needs and aspirations of students and their future prospects. Nine out of every ten young people attending college will become employees in organizations, for it is primarily in organizations that there are opportunities to apply knowledge to performance and that one gets paid for being educated. Indeed, it is only because we have learned, these last hundred years, to build and to structure organizations that we can offer opportunities and jobs to millions of educated people. And organizations are held together, directed, and made to function by managers and management. Whether in a business or hospital, in a school system or the county highway department, whether as trainees or the "big boss" — employees work with managers. And a very large number of today's students will themselves become managers during their working life, many fairly soon after leaving school.

Whether today's students will be able to grow, to achieve, and to fulfill themselves in their future working lives thus depends heavily on having enough understanding of management to make the organization a tool for attaining their individual ends. And whether they can achieve, accomplish, and succeed depends equally heavily on their ability to practice management successfully themselves.

Management in today's society of organizations is both a liberal art and professional preparation. It is — or should be —a basic means to personal growth, personal fulfillment, and self-enrichment. It is at the same time preparation for adult work responsibility and performance.

Management, among all the subjects in the college curriculum, offers the widest scope and appeals to a great many interests, abilities, and temperaments. It offers the intellectual stimulus of rigorous analysis, of careful diagnosis, and of problem-solving. But management is also people. Indeed, the specific job of the manager is to make the strengths of people productive and their weaknesses irrelevant. And "people" means community and teams, personality and temperament, relationships and communications, shared vision and conflict — and, above all, the thrill of achievement and the enjoyment of human diversity. Finally management works in society and culture. It thus deals with values and beliefs, with ethical choices and responsibilities, with goals and the means of attaining them.

That students today are aware of the importance of management as a subject of study and as an opportunity in their future is attested to by the steady rise of enrollments in management courses. But students often find it difficult to relate themselves to these courses. Few students have yet worked in an organization at all, let alone as managers. Most have yet to experience management firsthand, have yet to see and feel what an organization is like and how the beast behaves, and what it is like both to have and to be a "boss." In medicine we can take the students to the patient's sickbed. But we can't bring into the classroom the state's motor vehicle department or a company — not even a small one. We cannot easily give students the "clinical exposure" that would show them that principles of management deal with real people in real situations, that the dilemmas and decisions of managers entail real risks and have real consequences, and that mangerial controls are not just figures on paper, but espouse values, mold commitment to work and results, and direct behavior.

This selection from my writings on management deals with the major dimensions of management: as a person's craft and as a tool for achievement; as an intellectual discipline in its own right; as people working alone and working together; as society's organ for the performance of vital social tasks; and as an integrating, synthesizing function in a complex and changing world. But above all, this selection aims at giving students the thrill of management, the feel of an experience that is otherwise still ahead of them. While concerned with ideas, concepts, and general rules (the only things one can learn systematically and in a course), all the chapters in this book have been developed out of many years of practice as advisor to, and diagnostician for, managements in organizations — businesses from the very biggest to the smallest, and from old-established ones to fledglings barely hatched; governments and government agencies of large countries, such as the United States, Canada, and Japan, to state governments, cities, and small towns; and numerous public-service institutions such as museums, hospitals, libraries, universities, and charitable foundations. In turn the selections brought together in this volume have been tested for their effectiveness by a great many practitioners — that is, managers in organizations — and have been found by them to be effective in application. An additional criterion was that writings included be of proven effectiveness in the classroom — that is, writings experienced teachers in a host of different colleges and schools have used repeatedly and found effective, and writings their students have found readable, accessible, and enjoyable.

There are six section to this book. Section One discusses what management is. Why do we have management and managers? How did management emerge and develop? And what is management concerned with, what are its tasks, and what are its dimensions?

Section Two deals with what a manager is. What does he or she do? What specifically is the work that distinguishes the manager from the chemist, the salesperson, the accountant, the nurse, or the dietician?

Section Three turns to what is being managed and asks what a business (or a public-service institution, such as a hospital) is. What are its realities? What are its tasks? And what has to be done to enable it to perform and to contribute?

Section Four is concerned with organization and structure — with identifying the work needed and placing it in relation to the entire organization and to all its individual parts; with the ways we can design organizations and with the strengths and limitations of each design principle, but also with such special structural problems as the innovative organization and the multinational corporation.

Section Five focuses on people and their work. What do we know about work and working? What do we know about people in jobs, their needs, their aspirations, and their problems? What does today's student have to know to be effective and satisfied as an employee tomorrow? And what do organizations have to know — and to learn — to make truly productive that high-grade but expensive resource, the "knowledge worker" (today's educated young adult)?

Finally, in Section Six management and organization are looked at from the outside, from society and culture. What are the manager's opportunities and responsibilities in a society of organizations for the quality of life, for the social impacts of their institutions, and for the problems of society? What are the ethics of social responsibility?

The emphasis throughout this book is on people and performance. For this is what management is all about. Indeed, if there is one right way to define management it is as the work and function that enables people to perform and to achieve.

Peter F. Drucker

Claremont, California
New Years Day 1977

How to Use This Book

At some point, every student of management "discovers" Peter Drucker. It is widely realized that Drucker has a number of insights of broad applicability. Writing in a lucid style and using multiple examples from well-known companies, Drucker facilitates the acceleration of the student's study of the field of management. At the same time, Drucker's ideas always return to the unity of the management task and thus help the learner integrate numerous areas that might otherwise be left as fragments. Finally, Drucker is the philosopher of management: while laying out the geography of the management terrain and conveying in a most readable style what is known about management, he also gives the reader a view of the most important imponderables and of the points that demand new knowledge. In so doing, he places management squarely in historical perspective and emphasizes the value issues central to the future of management as a discipline and practice. These characteristics make Peter Drucker's works important tools for the student of management — be he or she a beginning student or an advanced practitioner.

Drucker's books and other publications are numerous. Thus to date the student of management has been drawn to many items in utilizing Drucker's work in his or her study of management. *People and Performance: The Best of Peter Drucker on Management* was designed specifically for the student of management, making the book useable in a number of ways as a part of an organized study of the discipline and practice of management:

1. as an introduction to the field of management, placing the need for management thought in a historical perspective and giving a view of the conceptual advances of earlier times, and how these relate to present circumstances
2. as a companion to studying the management functions, processes, and problems using one of the best current textbooks on management

3. as a base for the discussion of a number of managerial issues facing today's and to-morrow's managers and society

Ideally, a program of study by a class would focus on each of these. At the outset Part One could be used to give the student an introduction to the study of management. Chapter 1, "Why Managers?" Chapter 2, "Management: Its Roots and Its Emergence," "Chapter 3, "Management: A Look Backward and a Look Forward," Chapter 4, "The Dimensions of Management," and Chapter 5, "The Challenges of Management," would provide a solid base on which to proceed to the detailed study of managerial functions and processes. The Ford Motor Company story in Chapter 1 is used to show why management is required by the large, complex institution. The development of a society of institutions, first in business and now in many areas, is recounted in Chapter 2. In the third chapter, the basic themes of management thought are elaborated. In Chapters 4 and 5, the central dimensions of the management job and the conceptual foundations of the management boom are set forth. With this background and other introductory readings such as the introductory chapters of a management text, the student is ready to begin the study of managerial functions and processes that are central to the study of management.

The study of the management functions, processes, and problems could be handled quite effectively using one of the best management texts available in conjunction with *People and Performance.* These texts are excellent in their coverage of the basic concepts and theories available to be applied in each of the functional or process areas. However, because of limitations on book length and the difficulty of the task, they do less than an ideal job in integrating these various ideas into an overall view of the management task. Drucker's work, however, considers each of the basic areas *and* does a notable job of conceptualizing the unity of the managerial task. Thus, in considering each subunit of management, the materials in the text and the parallel portions of *People and Performance* could be assigned and discussed together. Prior to this parallel study, students should read and discuss Chapter 6, "Managers and Their Work," Chapter 10, "What Is a Business?" Chapter 11, "Business Realities," and Chapter 12, "Managing a Business: The Sears Story." The Sears story is an especially effective tool to use in learning about the unity of management, the requirement that multiple and varied contributions be molded into a central thrust for the organization. Following the study of managerial functions and processes, students could well return to a consideration of how these functions and processes come together in specific jobs. The discussion of middle management positions in Chapter 8, "From Middle Management to Knowledge Organization," especially such positions as product manager or quality control manager, could be a useful focal point for this discussion. (The table that follows is a guide to the use of *People and Performance* in conjunction with one of the mangement texts. Corresponding chapters should be studied and discussed in parallel.)

After acquiring an appreciation for the powerful tools available to solve problems in a number of areas, it is important that the student develop an appreciation for the challenges that demand new approaches. *People and Performance* is an effective resource to use in channeling the discussion of the issues which reflect these challenges. Chapter 3, "Management: A Look Backward and a Look Forward," gives an overview of these issues:

1. new challenges for top management
2. internal problems of manageability
3. social and political problems (social responsibility isssues)
4. the legitimacy of management
5. the development of a management theory that can be applied to multinational firms as well as to organizations in developing countries (the world-wide scope of management)

Later chapters outline much of the current dialogue regarding each of these areas requiring new developments. In addition, Drucker, being the philosopher of management that he is, gives his own perspective. Thus the student gets both a formulation of each problem area and at least one view of how to proceed and thus should be prepared to develop his or her own view.

Peter Drucker's writings have always been among the most useful and thought-provoking available. However, their diversity and the fact that they appeared in so many different publications made it difficult for the student of management to use them readily in a concentrated study of management. However, with the publication of *People and Performance: The Best of Peter Drucker on Management*, the student now has a volume that brings Drucker's thoughts together in one place in a manner that will allow them to be used effectively in a concentrated study of management. Best results are likely to be obtained using *People and Performance* in conjunction with a management textbook. Drucker's work provides the core of introductory work and of material on the issues ahead while parallel assignments would cover the managerial functions and processes and mold them into a unified view of management. Whatever adaptation of this approach is used, Drucker's readable exposition is likely to remain one of the most interesting and useful avenues to enhanced understanding of management thought and practice.

Oscar Tivis Nelson, Jr.

CHAPTERS OF *PERFORMANCE AND PEOPLE* CORRELATED WITH CURRENT MANAGEMENT TEXTBOOKS

CHAPTER NUMBERS

	Donnelly, Gibson, and Ivancevich, *Fundamentals of Management* (Business Publications, 1975)	Haynes and Massie, *Management* (Prentice-Hall, 1969)	Hodgetts, *Management: Theory, Process, and Practice* (Saunders, 1975)	Koontz and O'Donnell, *Management* (McGraw-Hill, 1976)	Massie and Douglas, *Managing: A Contemporary Introduction* (Prentice-Hall, 1973)	Newman, Summer, and Warren, *The Process of Management* (Prentice-Hall, 1972)	Sisk, *Management and Organization* (Southwestern, 1973)
Part ONE WHAT IS MANAGEMENT?							
1 Why Managers?	1						1
2 Management: Its Roots and Its Emergence	2, 6		1, 2	1, 2		1	2
3 Management: A Look Backward and a Look Forward	12	1, 2	3, 4		1, 2		
4 The Dimensions of Management							
5 The Challenges of Management		11-12, 15-16, 17,18	7	3, 4, 5	12	3	4-5
Part TWO WHAT IS A MANAGER?							
6 Managers and Their Work	1		5, 6				7
7 Management by Objectives and Self-Control	5	5, 6, 11,12, 13,14	15, 19, 7,9	7	11, 12, 16		3, 4-5, 20-22
8 From Middle Management to Knowledge Organization		7, 8		19, 20			
9 Staffing for Excellence				21, 22	13	10	19, 6
Part THREE WHAT IS A BUSINESS?							
10 What Is a Business?							
11 Business Realities			7	4, 6, 8, 10, 11	19		
12 Managing a Business: The Sears Story	3	30	7		18		4-5
13 The Power and Purpose of Objectives			19	7	11	17, 18, 19	
14 The Delusion of Profits							
15 Managing Capital Productivity	5	15,16, 17,18	7, 9	28, 29	12, 16	25	20-22
16 Managing the Public Service Institution		11-14		10,11			4-5, 20-22

CHAPTERS OF *PERFORMANCE AND PEOPLE* CORRELATED WITH CURRENT MANAGEMENT TEXTBOOKS

CHAPTER NUMBERS

	Donnelly, Gibson, and Ivancevich, *Fundamentals of Management* (Business Publications, 1975)	Haynes and Massie, *Management* (Prentice-Hall, 1969)	Hodgetts, *Management: Theory, Process, and Practice* (Saunders, 1975)	Koontz and O'Donnell, *Management* (McGraw-Hill, 1976)	Massie and Douglas, *Managing: A Contemporary Introduction* (Prentice-Hall, 1973)	Newman, Summer, and Warren, *The Process of Management* (Prentice-Hall, 1972)	Sisk, *Management and Organization* (Southwestern, 1973)
Part FOUR ORGANIZING AND MANAGING FOR PERFORMANCE							
17 The Innovative Organization	11	29, 11, 12	7, 22		8, 12, 19, 22	16, 19	4, 5 / 20-22
18 New Templates for Today's Organizations	5 / 4	13, 14	9	12-18	16 / 6	5, 6	10, 11
19 The Building Blocks of Organization	10	5, 6 / 7, 8	8, 18		6	7, 9 / 2	12, 13
20 ...And How They Join Together	13, 14		10	9	9, 10	11-15	8
21 The Multinational Corporation	17	11-12, 27-28	7, 21	10, 11	12, 19	16, 28, 29	4, 5
Part FIVE HOW CAN MANAGERS USE THE STRENGTHS OF PEOPLE?							
22 Is Personnel Management Bankrupt?			6		3, 4		9, 11
23 What We Know About Work, Working, and Workers	6, 7	9, 10	13, 14	23, 24 25, 28	5, 15	20, 25	15, 16, 18
24 Worker and Working: Theories and Reality	8, 9	19-24				8	
25 How to Be an Employee	15, 16	13-14	12	26	14	10, 22, 23	17
26 Managing the Knowledge Worker	5	25-26	9	30	16	4	20-22
27 What the Computer Will Be Telling You	12		16	27, 28, 29	7	6	7
Part SIX MANAGEMENT IN SOCIETY AND CULTURE							
28 Management and the Quality of Life		3	20			14	
29 Social Impacts and Social Problems	17	11, 12, 29	7, 17	4 / 8	17, 20, 21		4-5
30 The Limits of Social Responsibility	5	4 / 13-14	9 / 20		12 / 16		20-22
31 The Ethics of Responsibility							3
32 Multinationals and Developing Countries: Myths and Realities		27-28		5			

Contents

PART ONE   WHAT IS MANAGEMENT?

      Chapter 1   Why Managers? 3
      Chapter 2   Management: Its Roots and Its Emergence, 9
      Chapter 3   Management: A Look Backward and a Look Forward, 18
      Chapter 4   The Dimensions of Management, 27
      Chapter 5   The Challenges of Management, 36

PART TWO   WHAT IS A MANAGER?

      Chapter 6   Managers and Their Work, 47
      Chapter 7   Management by Objectives and Self-Control, 60
      Chapter 8   From Middle Management to Knowledge Organization, 71
      Chapter 9   Staffing for Excellence, 79

PART THREE   WHAT IS A BUSINESS?

      Chapter 10   What Is a Business? 87
      Chapter 11   Business Realities, 100
      Chapter 12   Managing a Business: The Sears Story, 108
      Chapter 13   The Power and Purpose of Objectives, 115
      Chapter 14   The Delusion of Profits, 122
      Chapter 15   Managing Capital Productivity, 126
      Chapter 16   Managing the Public Service Institution, 131

PART FOUR   *ORGANIZING AND MANAGING FOR PERFORMANCE*

Chapter 17   *The Innovative Organization, 145*
Chapter 18   *The Templates for Today's Organizations, 164*
Chapter 19   *The Building Blocks of Organizations . . . , 176*
Chapter 20   *. . . And How They Join Together, 187*
Chapter 21   *The Multinational Corporation, 194*

PART FIVE   *HOW CAN MANAGERS USE THE STRENGTHS OF PEOPLE?*

Chapter 22   *Is Personnel Management Bankrupt? 223*
Chapter 23   *What We Know About Work, Working, and Worker, 234*
Chapter 24   *Worker and Working: Theories and Reality, 248*
Chapter 25   *How to Be an Employee, 261*
Chapter 26   *Managing the Knowledge Worker, 271*
Chapter 27   *What the Computer Will Be Telling You, 276*

PART SIX   *MANAGEMENT IN SOCIETY AND CULTURE*

Chapter 28   *Management and the Quality of Life, 287*
Chapter 29   *Social Impacts and Social Problems, 298*
Chapter 30   *The Limits of Social Responsibility, 312*
Chapter 31   *The Ethics of Responsibility, 320*
Chapter 32   *Multinationals and Developing Countries: Myths and Realities, 329*

Definitions of Key Terms, 341
Index, 357

What Is Management?

Part One

Why Managers?

Chapter 1

Managers, the Basic Resource of a Business, the Scarcest, Most Expensive, and Most Perishable
The Ford Story: A Controlled Experiment in Mismanagement
The Lesson of the Ford Story
Management Precedes Ownership
Management Was Designed for Large, Complex Business; It Did Not Evolve From Small Business That Grew Large
Management. "Change of Phase" Rather Than Adaptation
Management an Autonomous Function, Not a Delegated One

*M*anagers are the basic resource of the business enterprise. In a fully automated factory — such as already exist in a few places, modern oil refineries for instance — there may be a few highly skilled technicians and professionals, but almost no other workers at all. But there will be managers! In fact, there will be many more managers than there used to be in yesterday's factory filled with semi-skilled machine operators. Where the foreman on the assembly line supervises fifty people, managers in automated plants rarely have more than two or three people on their team — and each of them has greater autonomy, more responsibility and far more decision-making power than the foreman in the traditional mass-production plant.

Managers are the most expensive resource in most businesses — and the one that depreciates the fastest and needs the most constant replenishment. It takes years to build a management team; but it can be depleted in a short period. The number of managers as well as the capital investment each manager represents — both in the investment of society's capital in his education (which runs upward of $40,000 for each college graduate) and in the employer's direct investment in the managerial job (which in the U.S. today ranges from $50,000 to $500,000 for each managerial job, dependent on industry and function, e.g., whether in the research lab, in manufacturing or in accounting) — are bound to increase steadily as they have increased in the past half century. Parallel with this will go an increase in the demands of the enterprise on the ability of its managers. Today's manager, even at a fairly low level, is, for instance, expected to know a good deal both about analytical and quantitative methods, and about human behavior; both were "advanced" subjects less than a generation ago. These demands have doubled in every generation; there is no reason to expect a slowing down of the trend during the next decades.

How well managers manage and are managed determines whether business goals will be reached. It also largely determines how well the enterprise manages worker and work. For the workers' attitude reflects, above all, the attitude of their management. It directly mirrors management's competence and structure. The workers' effectiveness is determined largely by the way they are being managed.

During the last quarter century managers everywhere have subjected themselves to a steady barrage of exhortations, speeches, and programs in which they tell each other that their job is to manage the people under them, urge each other to give top priority to that responsibility, and furnish each other with much advice and many expensive gadgets for "downward communications." But I have yet to sit down with a manager, at any level or job, who was not primarily concerned with upward relations and upward communications. Every vice-president feels that relations with the president are the real problem. And so on down to the first-line supervisor, the production foreman, or chief clerk, all of whom are quite certain that they could get along with their people if only the "boss" and the personnel department left them alone.

This is not a sign of the perversity of human nature. Upward relations are properly a manager's first concern. To be a manager means sharing in the responsibility for the performance of the enterprise. A person who is not expected to take this responsibility is not a manager. And the individual contributors, the research engineer, the tax accountant, the field salesperson, who are expected to take such responsibility for the results and performance of the enterprise are, in effect, managers even though they are not "bosses," have no subordinates and manage only themselves.

The Rise, Decline and Rebirth of Ford

The story of Henry Ford, his rise and decline, and of the revival of his company under his grandson, Henry Ford II, has been told so many times that it has passed into folklore. The story is

- that Henry Ford, starting with nothing in 1905, had built fifteen years later the world's largest and most profitable manufacturing enterprise;
- that the Ford Motor Company, in the early twenties, dominated and almost monopolized the American automobile market and held a leadership position in most of

the other important automobile markets of the world;
- that, in addition, it had amassed, out of profits, cash reserves of a billion dollars or so;
- that, only a few years later, by 1927, this seemingly impregnable business empire was in shambles. Having lost its leadership position and barely able to stay a poor third in the market, it lost money almost every year for twenty years or so, and remained unable to compete vigorously right through World War II; and
- that in 1944 the founder's grandson, Henry Ford II, then only twenty-six years old and without training or experience, took over, ousted his grandfather's cronies in a palace coup, brought in a totally new management team and saved the company.

But it is not commonly realized that this dramatic story is far more than a story of personal success and failure. It is, above all, what one might call a controlled experiment in mismanagement.

The first Ford failed because of his firm conviction that a business did not need managers and management. All it needed, he believed, was the owner with his "helpers." The only difference between Ford and most of his contemporaries in business, in the U.S. as well as abroad, was that Henry Ford stuck uncompromisingly to his convictions. The way he applied them – e.g., by firing or sidelining any one of his "helpers," no matter how able, who dared act as a "manager," make a decision, or take action without orders from Ford – can only be described as a test of a hypothesis that ended up by fully disproving it.

In fact, what makes the Ford story unique – but also important – is that Ford could test the hypothesis, in part because he lived so long, and in part because he had a billion dollars to back his convictions. Ford's failure was not the result of personality or temperament but first and foremost a result of his refusal to accept managers and management as necessary and as grounded in task and function rather than in "delegation" from the "boss."

GM – The Countertest

In the early twenties, when Ford set out to prove that managers are not needed, Alfred P. Sloan, Jr., the newly appointed president of General Motors, put the opposite thesis to the test. GM at that time was almost crushed by the towering colossus of the Ford Motor Company and barely able to survive as a weak number two. Little more than a financial speculation, stitched together out of small automobile companies that had been for sale because they could not stand up to Ford's competition, GM did not have one winning car in its line, no dealer organization, and no financial strength. Each of the former owners was allowed autonomy, which in effect meant that he was allowed to mismanage his former business his own way. But Sloan thought through what the business and structure of GM should be and converted his undisciplined barons into a management team. Within five years GM had become the leader in the American automobile industry and has remained the leader ever since.

Twenty years after Sloan's success, Henry Ford's grandson put Sloan's hypothesis to the test again. The Ford Motor Company by then was nearly bankrupt: the entire billion dollars of cash assets it had held in the early twenties had been poured into paying for the deficits since. As soon as young Henry Ford II took over in 1946, he set out to do for his company what Sloan had done for GM two decades earlier. He created a management structure and a management team. Within five years the Ford Motor Company regained its potential for growth and profit, both at home and abroad. It became the main competitor to General Motors and even outstripped GM in the fast-growing European automobile market.

The Lesson of the Ford Story

The lesson of the Ford story is that managers and management are the specific need of the business enterprise, its specific organ, and its basic structure. We can say positively that enterprise cannot do without managers. One cannot argue that management does the owner's job by delegation. Management is needed not only because the job is too big for any one person to do alone, but because managing an enterprise is something essentially different from managing one's own property.

Henry Ford failed to see the need to change to managers and management because he believed that a large and complex business enterprise "evolves" organically from the small one-man shop. Of course, Ford started small. But the growth brought more than a change in size. At one point quantity turned into quality. At one point Ford no longer ran "his own business." The Ford Motor Company had become a *business enterprise,* that is, an organization requiring different structure and different principles — an organization requiring managers and management.

Legally, management is still seen as delegation from ownership. But the actual doctrine that is slowly evolving is that management precedes and indeed outranks ownership, at least in the large enterprise. Even total ownership of such an enterprise is dependent on proper management. If the owner does not subordinate himself to the enterprise's need for management, his ownership — while legally unrestricted — will in fact be curtailed, if not taken away from him.

This idea was probably first laid down as an emerging legal doctrine by the U. S. Air Force in the early fifties in dealing with Howard Hughes and the Hughes Aircraft Company. Hughes owned the company, lock, stock, and barrel. He refused to let professional managers run it and insisted on running it himself the way Ford, thirty years earlier, had run the Ford Motor Company. Thereupon the Air Force, the company's main customer, gave Hughes an ultimatum: either you put your shares into a trust and let professional management take over, or we put the company into bankruptcy and force you out altogether. Hughes retained ownership title through one of his foundations but relinquished control entirely.

The next case also concerns Howard Hughes. As all but complete owner of one of America's major airlines, TWA, he, it is alleged, subordinated TWA's interests to those of other companies of his. For an owner this is perfectly legitimate behavior; he is supposed to do with his property as he pleases. But TWA management sued Hughes for $150 million in damages. It lost the suit only in 1973 in the Supreme Court — having won it in two lower courts — on a technicality; the Supreme Court ruled that this was a matter for the Civil Aeronautics Board over which the ordinary courts had no jurisdiction. But the principle that even the owner has to act as a manager, at least in a large company, was not disputed.

Genetically, so to speak, management did not evolve out of the small owner-managed firm and as a result of its growth. From its very beginning, management was designed for enterprises that were large and complex.

The large American railroad which covered vast distances — and which wrestled with the complex interplay between the engineering task of building a railbed, the financial task of raising very large sums of capital, and the political-relations tasks of obtaining charters, land grants, and subsidies — was the first enterprise that can be called "managed." Indeed, the management structure designed shortly after the Civil War for the first long-distance and transcontinental American railroads has essentially remained unchanged to this day. In continental Europe, at about the same time, management was designed for the first banks founded expressly to be national rather than local banks. And in faraway Japan, the builders of the so-called "Zaibatsu" (the great business groups) of the Meiji Period — Mitsui, Sumitomo, and Iwasaki's successors at Mitsubishi — using traditional Japanese approaches in a new manner, also fashioned a management system for the large and complex enterprise.

It was not until thirty or forty years later, some time around the turn of the century, that the concept of management was transferred from the enterprise that started out large to the enterprise that had grown large. At about that time, Andrew Carnegie and John D. Rockefeller, Jr., introduced management into the steel and petroleum industries respectively. A little later still, Pierre S. du Pont restructured the family company (E.I. du Pont de Nemours & Co.) and gave it a management, both to make it capable of growth and to preserve family control. The management structure Pierre du Pont built in his family company between 1915 and 1920 became, a few years later, the starting point for the General Motors structure of "professional management" after the du Ponts had acquired control of the near-bankrupt and floundering automotive conglomerate and had put Alfred P. Sloan, Jr., in as president.

Management as a "Change of Phase"

The change from a business which the "boss" can run with "helpers" to a business enterprise that requires a management is what the physicists call a "change of phase" such as the change from fluid to solid. It is a leap from one state of matter, from one fundamental structure, to another. Sloan's example shows that the change can occur within one and the same organization. But Sloan's restructuring of GM also shows that the job can be done only if basic concepts, basic principles, and individual vision are changed radically.

One can compare the business which the older Ford tried to run and the business which Sloan designed to two different kinds of organisms — the insect, which is held together by a tough, hard skin, and the vertebrate animal, which has a skeleton. The English biologist D'Arcy Thompson showed that animals supported by a hard skin can reach only a certain size and complexity. Beyond this, a land animal has to have a skeleton. Yet the skeleton has not genetically evolved out of the hard skin of the insect; it is a different organ with different antecedents. Similarly, management becomes necessary when a business reaches a certain size and complexity. But management, while it replaces the "hard-skin" structure of the owner, is not its successor. It is, rather, its replacement.

When does a business reach the stage at which it has to shift from "hard skin" to "skeleton"? The line lies somewhere between 300 and 1,000 employees in size. More important, perhaps, is the increase in complexity of the business; when a variety of tasks have all to be performed in cooperation, synchronization, and communication, a business needs managers and a management. Otherwise, things go out of control; plans fail to turn into action; or, worse, different parts of the plans get going at different speeds, different times, and with different objectives and goals, and the favor of the "boss" becomes more important than performance. At this point the product may be excellent, the people able and dedicated. The boss may be — indeed often is — a man of great ability and personal power. But the business will begin to flounder, stagnate, and soon go downhill unless it shifts to the "skeleton" of managers and management structure.

Henry Ford wanted no managers. But the only result was that he mismanaged, misdirected, and misorganized his company and stunted or broke management people. The only choice for an institution is between management and mismanagement. But managers are inevitable. And the job of management cannot be evaded. Whether it is being done right or not will determine largely whether the enterprise will survive and prosper or decline and ultimately fall.

Management: Its Roots and Its Emergence

Chapter 2

The Society of Institutions
From 1900 to 1970
The Employee Society
Management: The Organ of Institutions
From Business Society to Pluralist Society
Why Business Management Has to Be the Focus
The Roots and History of Management

*D*uring the last fifty years, society in every developed country has become a society of institutions. Every major social task, whether economic performance or health care, education or the protection of the environment, the pursuit of new knowledge or defense is today being entrusted to big organizations, designed for perpetuity and managed by their own managements. The performance of modern society — if not the survival of each individual — increasingly depends on the performance of these institutions.

Only seventy-five years ago such a society would have been inconceivable. In the society of 1900 the family still served in every single country as the agent of, and organ for, most social tasks. Institutions were few and small. The society of 1900, even in the most highly institutionalized countries, still resembled the Kansas prairie. There was one eminence, the central government. It loomed very large on the horizon — not because it was large but because there was nothing else around it. The rest of society was diffused in countless molecules: small workshops, small schools, the individual professionals — whether doctors or lawyers — practicing by themselves, the farmers, the craftsmen, the neighborhood retail stores, and so on. There were the beginnings of big business — but only the beginnings. And what was then considered a giant business would strike us today as very small indeed.

The octopus which so frightened the grandparents of today's Americans, Rockefeller's giant Standard Oil Trust, was split into fourteen parts by the U.S. Supreme Court in 1911. Thirty years later, on the eve of America's entry into World War II, every single one of these fourteen Standard Oil daughters had become at least four times as large as the octopus when the Supreme Court divided it — in employment, in capital, in sales, and in every other aspect. Yet, among these fourteen there were only three major oil companies — Jersey Standard, Mobil, and Standard of California. The other eleven were small to fair-sized, playing little or no role in the world economy and only a limited role in the U.S. economy.

While business has grown in these seventy years, other institutions have grown much faster. There was no university in the world before 1914 that had much more than 6,000 students — and only a handful that had more than 5,000. Today the university of 6,000 students is a pygmy; there are even some who doubt that it is viable. The hospital, similarly, has grown from a marginal institution to which the poor went to die into the center of health care and a giant in its own right — and also into one of the most complex social institutions around. Labor unions, research institutes, and many others have similarly grown to giant size and complexity.

In the early 1900s the citizens of Zurich built themselves a splendid City Hall, which they confidently believed would serve the needs of the city for all time to come. Indeed, it was bitterly attacked as gross extravagance, if not as megalomania. Government in Switzerland has grown far less than in any other country in the world. Yet the Zurich City Hall long ago ceased to be adequate to house all the offices of the city administration. By now, these offices occupy ten times or more the space that seventy-five years ago seemed so splendid — if not extravagant.

The Employee Society

The citizens of today in every developed country are typically employees. They work for one of the institutions. They look to the institutions for their livelihood. They look to the institutions for their opportunities. They look to the institutions for access to status and function in society, as well as for personal fulfillment and achievement.

The citizens of 1900, if employed, worked for a small family-type operation; the small pop-and-mom store employing a helper or two; the family household; and so on. And of course, the great majority of people in those days, except in the most highly industrialized countries — such as Britain or Belgium — worked on the farm.

Our society has become an employee society. In the early 1900s people asked, "What do you do?" Today they tend to ask, "Whom do you work for?"

And management is the specific organ of the new institution, whether business enterprise or university, hospital or armed service, research lab or government agency. If institutions are to function, managements must perform.

The word "management" is a singularly difficult one. It is, in the first place, specifically American and can hardly be translated into any other language, not even into British English. It denotes a function but also the people who discharge it. It denotes a social position and rank but also a discipline and field of study.

But even within the American usage, management is not adequate as a term, for institutions other than business do not speak of management or managers, as a rule. Universities or government agencies have administrators, as have hospitals. Armed services have commanders. Other institutions speak of executives, and so on.

Yet all these institutions have in common the management function, the management task, and the management work. In all of these there is a group of people whose function it is to "manage," and who have legal power and responsibility as managers. In all of them there is the same task: making the institution perform. And in all of them this requires doing specific work: setting objectives, goals and priorities; organizing; staffing; measuring results; communicating and decision making; and so on. All these institutions require management. And in all of them, management is the effective, the active, organ.

The institution itself is, in effect, a fiction. It is an accounting reality, but not a social reality. When this or that government agency makes this ruling or this decision, we know perfectly well that it is some people within the agency who make the ruling or the decision and who act for the agency and as the effective organ of the agency. When we speak of General Electric closing a plant, it is not, of course, General Electric that is deciding and acting, it is a group of managers within the company.

Georg Siemens, who built the Deutsche Bank into the European continent's leading financial institution in the decade between 1870 and 1880, once said, "Without management, a bank is so much scrap, fit only to be liquidated." Without institution there is no management. But without management there is no institution. Management is the specific organ of the modern institution. It is the organ whose performance determines the performance and even the survival of the institution.

Management Is Professional

We further know that management is independent of ownership, rank, or power. It is objective function and ought to be grounded in the responsibility for performance. It is professional — management is a function, a discipline, a task to be done; and managers are the professionals who practice this discipline, carry out the functions, and discharge these tasks. It is no longer relevant whether the manager is also an owner; ownership is incidental to the main job which is to manage.

From Business Society to Pluralist Society

Society in the Western world *was* a business society — seventy-five years ago. Then business was, indeed, the most powerful of all institutions — more powerful even than some governments. Since the turn of the century, however, the importance of business has gone down steadily — not because business has become smaller or weaker, but because the other institutions have grown so much faster. Business is no longer the singularly important institution in society; the other institutions have grown to be equally, or more, important. Society has become pluralist.

In the United States in the 1970s, no businessman compares in power or visibility with the tycoons of 1900, such as J. P. Morgan, John D. Rockefeller, or — a little later — Henry Ford. Few people today even know the names of the chief executive officers of America's biggest corporations; the names of the tycoons were household words. Not even the largest corporation today can compare in power and even in relative wealth with those tycoons who could hold the U.S. government for ransom.

The power of business has been displaced. No business today — in fact, no business in American history — has a fraction of the power that today's big university has. By granting or denying admission or the college degree, the university grants or denies access to jobs and livelihoods. Such power no business — and no other institution — ever had before in American history. Indeed, no earlier institution would ever have been permitted such power.

In the United States of 1900, almost the only career opportunity open to the young and ambitious was business. Today there are untold others, each promising as much (or more) income, and advancement as rapid, as a career in business.

Around the turn of the century, whatever of the gross national product did not go to the farmer went in and through the private business economy. The nonbusiness service institutions, beginning with government, accounted probably for no more than 10 percent of the nonfarm gross national product of the United States at the turn of the century and up till World War I. Today, while farming has largely become a business, more than half of the gross national product goes to or through service institutions which are not businesses and which are not held accountable for economic performance.

Well over a third of the gross national product in the United States today goes directly to governments, federal, state, and local. Another 3 to 5 percent goes to nongovernmental schools, that is, private and parochial, including the nongovernmental colleges and universities. Another 5 percent of GNP, that is, two-thirds of the total health-care bill, is also nongovernmental, but also nonbusiness. On top of this, there is a great variety of not-for-profit activities, accounting maybe for another 2 to 5 percent of gross national product. This adds up to 50 or perhaps as much as 60 percent of the GNP which does not go to the business sector but to, or through, public-service institutions.

Indeed, while the current crop of radicals may talk of the big-business society, their actions show a keen awareness that business is not the dominant institution. Every period of public unrest since the end of the Napoleonic Wars began with uprisings against business. But the revolt against authority that swept the developed countries in the sixties centered in the institutions — especially the university — which were most esteemed by yesterday's radicals and which were, so to speak, the good guys of organization thirty or forty years ago.

The nonbusiness, public-service institutions do not need management less than business. They may need it more.

There is a growing concern with management in nonbusiness institutions.

Among the best clients of the large American management consulting firms these last ten or fifteen years have been government agencies such as the Department of Defense, the City of New York, or the Bank of England. When Canada in the late sixties first created a unified military service, with army, navy, and air force all combined, the first conference of Canadian generals and admirals was not on strategy; it was on management. The venerable orders of the Catholic Church are engaged in organization studies and in management development, with the Jesuits in the lead.

An increasing number of students in advanced management courses are not business executives but executives from hospitals, from the armed services, from city and state governments, and from school administrations. The Harvard Business School even runs an increasingly popular advanced management course for university presidents.

The management of the nonbusiness institutions will indeed be a growing concern from now on. Their management may well become the central management problem— simply because the lack of management of the public-service institution is such a glaring weakness, whether municipal water department or graduate university.

And yet, *business management is the exemplar.* And any book on management, such as this one, has to put management in the center.

Why Business Management Has to Be the Focus

One reason is history. Business enterprise was the first of the modern institutions to emerge. From the beginning, that is, from the emergence of the railroads as large businesses in the late nineteenth century, business enterprise was unmistakably a new and different institution rather than an outgrowth of older ones, as were apparently government agency, university, hospital, and armed service. There was, of course, concern about management in these institutions. But until recently it was sporadic and undertaken usually in connection with an acute problem and confined to it. But the work on management in business and industry was from the beginning meant to be generic and continuous.

Another reason why the study of management to this day has primarily been a study of business management is that so far the economic sphere alone has measurements both for the allocation of resources and for the results of decisions. Profitability is not a perfect measurement; no one has even been able to define it, and yet it is a measurement, despite all its imperfections. None of the other institutions has measurements so far. All they have are opinions — which are hardly an adequate foundation for a discipline.

The most important reason for focusing on business management is that it is the success story of this century. It has performed within its own sphere. It has provided economic goods and services to an extent that would have been unimaginable to the generation of 1900. And it has performed despite world wars, depressions, and dictatorships.

The achievement of business management enables us today to promise — perhaps prematurely (and certainly rashly) — the abolition of the grinding poverty that has been mankind's lot through the ages. It is largely the achievement of business management that advanced societies today can afford mass higher education. Business both produces the economic means to support this expensive undertaking and offers the jobs in which knowledge can become productive and can be paid for. That we today consider it a social flaw and an imperfection of society for people to be fixed in their opportunities and jobs by class and birth — where only yesterday this was the natural and apparently inescapable condition of mankind — is a result of our economic performance, that is, of the performance of business management. In a world that is politically increasingly fragmented and obsessed by nationalism, business management is one of the very few institutions capable of transcending national boundaries.

The multinational corporation brings together in a common venture management people from a great many countries with different languages, cultures, traditions, and values, and unites them in a common purpose. It is one of the very few institutions of our world that is not nationalistic in its world view, its values, and its decisions; but truly a common organ of a world economy that, so far, lacks a world polity, that is, a transnational political community or transnational political institutions.

It is also business management to which our society increasingly looks for leadership in respect to the quality of life. Indeed, what sounds like harsh criticism of business management tends often to be the result of high, perhaps unrealistically high, expectations based on the past performance of business management. "If you can do so well, why don't you do better?" is the underlying note.

This book will discuss performance in the nonbusiness service institution and I will stress again and again that managing the service institution is likely to be the frontier of management for the rest of this century. But the foundation of any work on management has to be business management.

The emergence of management may be the pivotal event of our time, far more important than all the events that make the headlines. Rarely, if ever, has a new basic institution, a new leading group, a new central function, emerged as fast as has management since the turn of the century. Rarely in human history has a new institution proven indispensable so quickly. Even less often has a new institution arrived with so little opposition, so little disturbance, so little controversy. And never before has a new institution encompassed the globe as management has, sweeping across boundaries of race and creed, language and traditions, within the lifetime of many men still living and at work.

Today's developed society, without aristocracy, without large landowners, even without capitalists and tycoons, depends for leadership on the managers of its major institutions. It depends on their knowledge, on their vision, and on their responsibility. In this society, management — its tasks, its responsibilities, its practices — is central: as a need, as an essential contribution, and as a subject of study and knowledge.

The Roots and Early History of Management

Some writers seem to believe that the "management boom" of the post-World-War-II years invented, or at least discovered, management. Management, both as a practice and as a field of thought and study, has a long history. Its roots go back almost two hundred years.

Management, one might say, was discovered before there was any management to speak of. The great English economists, from Adam Smith (1723–1790) to David Ricardo (1772–1823) to John Stuart Mill (1806–1873), including their successor and antagonist, Karl Marx (1818–1883), knew no management. To them the economy was impersonal and objective. As a modern exponent of the classical tradition, the Anglo-American Kenneth Boulding (b. 1910) phrases it, "Economics deals with the behavior of commodities, rather than with the behavior of men." Or, as with Marx, impersonal laws of history were seen to dominate. Man can only adapt. Man can, at best, optimize what the economy makes possible; at worst, he impedes the forces of the economy and wastes resources. The last of the great English classical economists, Alfred Marshall (1842–1924), did indeed add management to the factors of production, land, labor, and capital. But this was a half-hearted concession. Management was still, even to Marshall, an extraneous factor, rather than central.

From the beginning there was a different approach which put the manager into the center of the economy and which stressed the managerial task of making resources productive. J. B. Say (1767–1832), perhaps the most brilliant economist produced by France — or for that matter by continental Europe — was an early follower of Adam Smith and the propagandist for *The Wealth of Nations* in France. But in his own works the pivot is not the factors of production. It is the entrepreneur — a word Say coined — who directs resources from less productive into more productive investments and who thereby creates wealth. Say was followed by the "utopian socialists" of the French tradition, especially François Fourier (1772–1837) and that eccentric genius, the Comte de Saint-Simon (1760–1825). At that time there were no large organizations and no managers, but both Fourier and Saint-Simon anticipated developments and "discovered" management before it actually came into being. Saint-Simon in particular saw the emergence of organization. And he saw the task of making resources productive and of building social structures. He saw managerial tasks.

It is for their stress on management as a separate and distinct force, and one which can act independently of the factors of production as well as of the laws of history, that Marx vehemently denounced the French and gave them the derisory name of "utopians." But it is the French — and above all, Saint-Simon — who, in effect, laid down the basic approaches and the basic concepts on which every socialist economy has actually been designed. No matter how much the Russians today invoke the name of Marx, their spiritual ancestor is Saint-Simon.

In America too management was early seen as central. Alexander Hamilton's (1757–1804) famous "Report on Manufactures" starts out with Adam Smith, but then Hamilton gave emphasis to the constructive, purposeful, and systematic role of management. He saw in management, rather than in economic forces, the engine of economic and social development; and in organization, the carrier of economic advance. Following him, Henry Clay (1777–1852) with his famous "American system" produced what might be called the first blueprint for systematic economic development.

A little later, a Scottish industrialist, Robert Owen (1771–1858), actually became the first manager. In his textile mill in Lanark, Owen, in the 1820s, first tackled the problems of productivity and motivation, of the relationship of worker to work, of worker to enterprise, and of worker to management — to this day key questions in management. With Owen, the manager emerges as a real person, rather than as an abstraction, as in Say, Fourier, Saint-Simon, Hamilton, and Clay. But it was a long time before Owen had successors.

The Emergence of Large-Scale Organization

What had to happen first was the rise of large-scale organization. This occurred simultaneously — around 1870 — in two places. In North America the transcontinental railroad emerged as a managerial problem. On the continent of Europe, the "universal bank" — entrepreneurial in aim, national in scope, and with multiple headquarters — made traditional structures and concepts obsolete, and required management.

One response was given by Henry Towne (1844—1924) in the United States, especially in his paper *"The Engineer as Economist."* Towne outlined what might be called the first program for management. He raised basic questions: effectiveness as against efficiency; organization of the work as against the organization of the plant community, that is, of the workers; value set in the marketplace and by the customer as against technical accomplishment. With Towne begins the systematic concern with the relationship between the tasks of management and the work of management.

At roughly the same time, in Germany, Georg Siemens (1839—1901), in building the Deutsche Bank into the leading financial institution of continental Europe, first designed an effective top management, first thought through the top-management tasks, and first tackled the basic problems of communications and information in the large organization.

In Japan, Eiichi Shibusawa (1840—1931), the Meiji statesman turned business leader, in the seventies and eighties first raised fundamental questions regarding the relationship between business enterprise and national purpose, and between business needs and individual ethics. He tackled management education systematically. Shibusawa envisioned the professional manager first. The rise of Japan in this century to economic leadership is largely founded on Shibusawa's thought and work.

A few decades later, in the years before and after the turn of the century, all the major approaches to modern management were fashioned. Again the developments occurred independently in many countries.

In the 1880s Frederick W. Taylor (1856—1915), the self-taught American engineer, began the study of work. It is fashionable today to look down on Taylor and to decry his outmoded psychology, but Taylor was the first man in the known history of mankind who did not take work for granted, but looked at it and studied it. His approach to work is still the basic foundation. And, while Taylor in his approach to the worker was clearly a man of the nineteenth century, he started out with social rather than engineering or profit objectives. What led Taylor to his work and provided his motivation throughout was first the desire to free the worker from the burden of heavy toil, destructive of body and soul. And then it was the hope to break the Iron Law of wages of the classical economists (including Marx) which condemned the worker to economic insecurity and to enduring poverty. Taylor's hope — and it has largely been fulfilled in the developed countries — was to make it possible to give the laborer a decent livelihood through increasing productivity of work.

Around the same time in France, Henri Fayol (1841—1925), head of a coal mine which for its time was a very large company, first thought through organization structure and developed the first rational approach to the organization of enterprise: the functional principle. In Germany, Walther Rathenau (1867—1922), whose early training had been in a large company (the German equivalent of the General Electric Company, AEG, founded by his father, Emil [1838–1915], but developed in large part under the supervision of Georg Siemens), asked: "What is the place of the large enterprise in a modern society and in a modern nation? What impact does it have on both? And, what are its fundamental contributions and its fundamental responsibilities?" Most present questions of the social responsibilities of business were first raised and thought through by Rathenau in the years before World War I. Also in Germany, at the same time, the new discipline of *Betriebswissenschaft*, literally the "science of enterprise," was developed by such men as Eugen Schmalenbach (1873–1955). The management sciences developed since — managerial accounting, operations research, decision theory, and so on — are largely extensions, though in the main, unconscious ones, of the *Betriebswissenschaft* of those years before World War I. And in America, German-born Hugo Muensterberg (1863–1916) first tried to apply the social and behavioral sciences, and especially psychology, to modern organization and management.

Management:
A Look Backward
and a Look Forward

Chapter 3

*The Pioneers of Management Laid Its Foundation Without Realizing
       What It Was*
The Six Basic Management Themes
Top Management: Once Taken for Granted but Now Must Be Explored
*Internal Problems: Limits of Manageability, Decision-Making: Manage-
       rial and Entrepreneurial, Integrating People and Things*
*Social Problems: Knowledge Workers Displacing Laborers, Effective-
       ness Displacing Efficiency*
What Gives Management Its Authority?
The Exploding Management Universe

*A*mong the forerunners of management in the nineteenth century was Robert Owen, who is still outstanding in the depth of his insight and the courage of his convictions. He is still, a hundred and fifty years after his model experiment in New Lanark — the bankrupt Scottish textile mill which he turned in a few years into a highly successful business and into a model of human relations and plant organization — one of the most "progressive" managers and well up with the best of them today. But there was also Saint-Simon, the Frenchman, Owen's contemporary, who first saw the importance of the entrepreneur as the creator of wealth. There were, in the second half of the century, the Japanese. Confronted with the need to excel in the techniques and economics of the West and yet desirous to maintain the social and cultural values of their own old and rich tradition, the Japanese were the first to think seriously about the social responsibility *and function* of the manager. Finally toward the end of the century, there was an American, Henry Towne, with his emphasis on the wealth-creating contribution of knowledge and on the sharing of managerial experience.

These pioneers were by no means without influence.

Owen, to be sure, was so far ahead of his time as to have no imitators. New Lanark was a sensation; it never became an example. For a few years it was a popular tourist attraction; but, while there were many princes and crowned heads among the sightseers, the author has not heard of a single businessman who went there to find out what Owen was doing.

Saint-Simon, by contrast, was tremendously effective. To this day the basic philosophy and structure of management on the European continent bears his stamp, especially in its emphasis upon the difference between the "entrepreneur," that is, the bearer of financial risk, and the manager. Indeed, though Saint-Simon's name is anathema to any good Marxist, Russian industry is organized on his concepts rather than on those of Karl Marx. Similarly Towne had profound influence upon the basic structure of management and enterprise in the United States. He may only have codified what already existed, but certainly the structure of American management to this day mirrors Towne's concept that the function of business enterprise is to use systematic knowledge in order to create economic value. The Japanese, finally, may have had the most important impact of all the earlier thinkers. By enabling a nonwestern country to become modern and industrial and yet to remain, in essentials, a nonwestern country with its own tradition and culture, they not only broke the western monopoly on economic and technical advance, but also created the foundation for today's explosion of economic development. In many, and especially in its constructive, aspects, the modern world is their creation.

And yet this is the prehistory of management, rather than its history proper. For there was one thing lacking in all these pioneers, namely, a realization that there was "management" as a distinct field, "managing" as a distinct kind of work, and "managers" as a distinct group and function. When we read their insights today, we are struck by them. But then we know something that their contemporaries did not know; we read something into these works that simply was not in them. Each of these pioneers found a nugget of pure gold but dropped it again, unaware of its value.

The Seven Basic Management Themes

This new insight, this new concept of managing as something specific, suddenly arose around 1910. In the ten years between 1910 and 1920, the decade of the first World War, every single one of the great themes of management is struck. Every single one of the seven basic approaches to the study of managing and management was developed then. And almost anything we have done since then, in theory as well as in practice, is only variation and extension of the themes first heard during that decade.

Management, as a specific discipline, as a specific kind of work, as a specific function in society and economy, was developed, almost entirely, within the past fifty years.

Taylor's "Principles and Methods of Scientific Management" appeared in 1911. Together with his famous testimony before a Congressional Committee a year later, it converted what had been a technique into an organized, systematic, teachable approach to the study of work and of its rational organization. Almost at the same time Elihu Root, reorganizing the United States Army, and Henri Fayol, reorganizing a French mining company, established the counterpart to Taylor's study of the individual task within a work force. They established the systematic study of organization to determine what tasks have to be performed. And at roughly the same time the Germans, especially Schmalenbach, developed *Betriebswissenschaft*; namely, the systematic study of the individual transactions which together make up the total economic results of an enterprise.

These three approaches look at enterprise and its management in isolation. But in the years after 1910, we also developed, for the first time, approaches that looked upon enterprise and management in society and economy. In 1911 — at the same time at which Taylor's "Principles and Methods of Scientific Management" appeared — Schumpeter in Austria published his "Theory of Economic Development" which, for the first time, raised the question of the role of the manager in a modern expanding economy. Such recent "discoveries" as innovation, marketing, or long-range planning were all anticipated in this book. In the years before World War I, Walther Rathenau in Germany first concerned himself with the impact of large organization on modern society and with the responsibility of management in a modern society. His concern was echoed in the United States, in the closing years of World War I, by Henry Gantt.

The question of the individual in the plant community and the industrial organization was the first of the management themes struck — it was Robert Owen's main concern. It was, however, the last one to be tackled by modern management thinking. It was not raised again until World War I, most effectively perhaps by Elton Mayo, then still in Australia.

These themes have been the major themes of management ever since:

- the systematic study of work;
- the systematic study of organization;
- the systematic study of effort and results;
- managerial and entrepreneurial economics;
- managerial analysis, i.e., managerial accounting;
- the social position and responsibility of management;
- the human relations of an industrial society and the place of the individual in it.

The New Themes

Each of these approaches was developed quite independently. Each has, essentially, remained separate to this day. Each has made great advances, especially during the last decade.

Can these different approaches remain different much longer? Or are we fast reaching the point where we need what, so far, we have not achieved: a unified discipline of management?

There is no doubt that we will have to learn — and learn fast — to consider these different approaches not as different disciplines, not even as different points of view, but simply as different pieces in the same tool box, every one of which is needed to do the job.

And so every manager — and above all, every student who aspires to become a manager — better learn to use all these approaches to management as his tools.

But there are also new tasks for which the tools the pioneers fashioned are not enough and may not even be appropriate. What are these tasks? We might perhaps distinguish them by major categories.

The Problem of Top Management: Beginning to Explore It

First, we find ourselves suddenly confronted with the amazing fact that we have always taken *top management* for granted, to the point where we know little about it.

Actually the situation with respect to our knowledge of top management, that is, with respect to our knowledge regarding the unifying, determining and deciding organ of enterprise and management, is even more confused. In the traditional approaches which focus on the function of enterprise in economy and society — the Rathenau line of concern with social responsibility or the Schumpeter line of concern with managerial and entrepreneurial economics — top management is the only thing that is seen. The enterprise itself is seen practically as an extension of top management. We know today that things are not so simple. The organization, even in a small business, is a good deal more than the extension of top management. We know, for instance, that the basic problem in the decision-making function of top management is not to make the decision itself. It is not even to get the "facts" about the decision. The basic problem is how to make a decision effective in and through the organization.

But, on the other hand, the approaches which deal with enterprise and management in isolation, the approaches that lead back to Taylor, Fayol, and Schmalenbach, respectively, do not see top management at all. These approaches are static — in the way in which a microscopic slide of cell tissue is static. This, of course, gives them the great analytical power they have. But it means that they are incapable of distinguishing between what is relevant and what is not; incapable, above all, of distinguishing between the decisions that mean life and death for an enterprise, and those that have to do with marginal efficiencies. These approaches quite properly point out that even the healthiest organization can die as a result of malfunction of the smallest, least observed operation. What they completely overlook is that even the healthiest organization in which everything functions properly cannot live, let alone perform, unless it has a different, a separate, and effective governing organ. They do not see top management either, in other words.

The function, organization, and work of the people at the head of an enterprise is the unexplored continent of management.

It is, at the same time, the most crucial question that faces us in practice as well as in theory. That there is reason to be dissatisfied with our present state of knowledge, no one, I think, will doubt. At least I know no top management of a large enterprise anywhere — in the United States, in Europe, or in the East — which is not in a state of continuous reorganization, of continuous questioning, of continuous dissatisfaction with what we know and can do today.

One question in the top management area is of particular importance: *The selec-*

tion of the successors to today's top management people. It is precisely because of the great success of management that this has become a critical question. For this success has made management of the large company a social and economic resource and power far beyond the individual company. A great deal more than the dividends of the stockholders, the price of the stock, or even the jobs of the company's employees hinges today on the questions: Who should succeed today's top management people? By what criterion should they be selected and by whom? In what manner and through what processes? Who will hold them accountable and remove them if they are found wanting? It is doubtful that anyone, whether in management practice or in management theory, can give satisfying answers to these questions.

Internal Problems

The next group of tasks ahead deals with basic internal problems of enterprise and management. First, we are becoming aware of the *problem of manageability.*

There are, in all likelihood, limits beyond which an enterprise becomes too big to be managed, and particularly too complex to be managed. These limits may well be capable of being pushed outward by such new developments as organized information and decisions systems in the business, systematic business research, and systematic organization of self-governing businesses within the large enterprise. But there is, in all likelihood, a limit even to this.

In addition, there is the question whether every kind of activity and every kind of business really belongs in the large business enterprise.

Business enterprise is only one of the large power centers which have grown up in modern society. Modern government and labor unions have become major centers of power. But business is distinct in that there are both large and small units existing, working, and competing side by side.

This is obviously a unique strength — perhaps as important for the maintenance of a free society as the realization that society need not explode in the inevitable class war between the very many destitute and the very few rich. But it also presupposes some understanding of what kind of activity is best performed within a large business, and what had better be left to the small one. This, too, is a problem of manageability. On this, too, we so far can only ask a question, and cannot, so far, even define it properly, let alone answer it.

Another major area is that of *decision making.* During the past thirty years this has become a central focus of research and thought. For the first time we believe that decision making can be made rational to some extent. At the very least, we can define the nonrational elements within it.

One problem that is still ahead of us — one that cannot be tackled within any one of the traditional approaches to management — is that of distinguishing between "decision" and "decision." We do not speak of a "decision" that two and two make four; we call it the "right answer." In a good deal of modern decision theory, especially as applied to managerial decisions, we talk of "decisions" when there is actually only one right answer. This applies to all problems where the job is to restore or maintain the operation at a preset level. These are the routine decisions — these we understand. But we understand them precisely because they are not decisions.

Then we have a whole group of decisions which I would call managerial in that they deal with the allocation of existing resources, especially people. Here there is no right answer. Here, in other words, there is already risk. But here there is still a range of optimal solutions, each with a definable risk or balance of risks. Here, obviously, belong all the "decisions" on inventory levels and on inventory location which are the favorite exercises of the quantitative "management scientists." And again these are not really decisions. These also are not, usually, the decisions which make a difference between survival and death of an enterprise.

But as to those last ones, the *entrepreneurial decisions,* we know very little. Here there is obviously no one right answer. There is not even a range of optima. There is only the ability to take the right risk — the ability, in other words, to innovate and change the trend rather than follow it or anticipate it. This, too, requires strict and rigorous mental discipline. But it is a very different kind of decision, requiring very different kinds of "facts," and having very different impact from either routine or managerial decisions. Above all in this, the only true critical decision, the aim is not to eliminate risk, indeed not even to minimize it, but to make the enterprise capable of taking bigger risks — but the right ones.

Finally, still within this area of basic internal tasks within the enterprise, we now have to bring together "management science" dealing with things, and "management science" dealing with people. Unless we succeed in integrating into one process of analysis, into one thought concept, into one act of decision, the understanding of objective, impersonal, that is, physical or economic phenomena, and the understanding of and concern with people, their development, their needs and desires, their dignity and personality, we will have no discipline of management. We cannot keep these two apart any longer, we cannot engineer data processing through a computer without thinking through who is to make what use of the data and why. We cannot, conversely, think through the role, function, and position of an individual in the organization without reference to objective, economic, impersonal contribution, and performance. So far we cannot do this — so far these two approaches are still separate, if not even incompatible.

Social and Political Problems

A unified approach is needed for the new great tasks in respect to the *social and political problems of enterprise and management.*

During the past thirty years Towne's deep insight of nearly a century ago — that knowledge is the wealth-creating resource — has borne fruit. Everywhere the professionally trained individual is becoming the real "labor force" — in cost as well as in numbers, let alone in contribution. The "laborer" of yesterday with whom Owen was concerned first and whose work Taylor first analyzed, is rapidly becoming a thing of the past in modern industry. Work is increasingly being done by people with high education, contributing knowledge and working with their minds.

We still tend to think of two classes in industrial society; i.e., "manager" and "workers." This idea is not only dangerous, it is rapidly becoming completely fallacious. The majorities of a modern industrial society are essentially the professional people who work, as nonmanagers, but also as nonlaborers, who are middle class though employed, and who see themselves as "part of management" without being "managers," and as "workers" without, in the slightest degree, considering themselves "proletarians" let alone exploited.

This is the social reality of the twentieth century — and its social problem. Economically these people are not a problem. In that sense we can say that we have overcome the nineteenth-century "social question." We know, at least, that it cannot be solved through any of the nineteenth-century prescriptions. But it can be solved through the unique twentieth-century prescription of economic development based upon high investment in knowledge and in the people who bring knowledge to work.

The position of these people, however, we do not yet fully understand. Nor do we know how to manage them, that is, how to make their knowledge, their efforts, their contribution effective in the performance of the whole. This is a problem which few, if any, of the founding fathers of management could have foreseen, it is a problem that only arose because they were so successful. But as problems of success usually are, this is a more difficult, at least a much more subtle, problem than any they tackled.

There is one more, and an equally important consequence of this tremendous shift in the social structure of industrial society. "Productivity" is beginning to have a different meaning and to require completely different approaches and concepts. We have had, especially in the past fifteen years, a great manay "productivity centers" all over the world. What we will need from now on are, increasingly, *"effectiveness centers"*: that is, organized efforts to make fully effective and productive the new workers, the knowledge worker, the employed middle-class professional.

This, too, is a task for analysis and for careful study of the work. But it is different work. And both the approach and the tools will have to vary. For the manual workers' productivity consisted in increasing output per hour or per dollar spent by organizing their task and their motion. For the "knowledge workers" the question is less how much they produce than whether they direct their attentions to the right "product." It is effectiveness rather than efficiencey that characterizes their economic contribution. And efficiency itself in the knowledge worker is much less a matter of the individual doing more, as it is a matter of the group doing better. These are new things. So far none of us, whether we be Americans or Russians or Europeans or Japanese, know how to do this.

We are, in respect to the work that is typical, characteristic, and wealth-producing in an industrial society, in exactly the situation we were in in respect to manual work before Taylor. We need a new Taylor — though a very different one, not an engineer looking upon the human being with the analogy of the well-designed mechanical implement in mind, but the "systems thinker" looking upon human beings in a group as living, organic, moving parts of a whole where the whole has to be effective — and where effectiveness above all consists in doing the things that are really important instead of frittering away time and energy in doing things, no matter how well and how "efficiently," that are not primarily contributing to performance and to results. Here is one of our major frontiers.

The Problem of Management's Authority

And then there is the great political question of the *legitimacy of management.* On what ground does management base its authority? That management is not and need not be based on exploitation and force — that, in other words, the Marxist interpretation of history is not "scientific," let alone "inevitable" — even the Marxists today probably know. But it is not enough for a leading group not to be exploiter and usurper. It needs a ground for its power. It needs a code of responsibility and a focus of accountability.

It is not too relevant whether ownership and control have really split asunder, or whether there is still, substantially, control by ownership in modern industry. The fact of the matter is that management, as a function, has peeled off from the legal title to property ownership. Managing has to be performed, and performed professionally, objectively, and in the interest of the enterprise rather than in that of the owners, no matter whether the business is "owned" by one man, by the government, or by the anonymous multitudes of millions who have a diluted stake in the enterprise through insurance policies or future pension claims. It is also quite irrelevant how much power management really has. For there is no doubt that management has to have a considerable amount of authority to discharge its function, even on the strictest interpretation of managerial authority and responsibility.

And such power always must be anchored in a social value, in an ethical concept and in a rational accountability, to be socially and politically legitimate power. We need management, this we no longer dispute. We also know that management is only one group having power in a modern society — in sharp contrast to the belief, common in managerial circles thirty years ago, that management should or could be the "power elite."

But we do not know how management's authority can be rooted, how it can be limited, and where those limits should be drawn. Here is a central task awaiting the student of management — a task, essentially of political theory, but one that cannot be tackled without a great deal of knowledge and understanding of management, its concerns, its functioning, its economics, organization, and philosophy.

The Exploding Management Universe

There is an entirely different, and perhaps even more compelling reason why we are at the end of the seventy-year period during which separate approaches to the study of management could, profitably, be pursued. *Management has become world-wide.* It is needed the most in those countries that do not have a managerial tradition, in the "under-developed" countries, primarily of nonwestern tradition and non-European population.

In the West management was a function and an organ which developed fairly late in the process of economic development. Certainly the consciousness of such a function developed very late — and so did the leadership group of "managers." In the underdeveloped countries, however, management is the central resource of development, and managers the central engine of development.

Management as a supernational function and discipline also goes back a good long time. It is sixty years now since, as a result of World War I, two men founded the International Management Movement: the American, Herbert Hoover, the mining engineer turned statesman, and the Czech, Thomas Masaryk, the philosopher-historian turned statesman.

But essentially, up until recently, management was seen as a phenomenon of the "developed" countries. And, by and large, despite the exception of Japan, this was seen as being confined to the "western" world, that is, essentially to countries peopled by nations of European stock.

Today, as no one needs to be reminded, this is simply no longer so. This is the greatest event, perhaps, in the short history of management. It is also the event that makes the greatest demand on our knowledge of management and on the dedication of managers.

Above all, it demands a unified approach to management as a discipline and to managing as a kind of work. We face today, all over the world, a demand for people capable of doing the work of a manager — in tremendous numbers and possessing ability, knowledge, and integrity of a high order.

These past seventy years were the first seventy years of management, the years during which we developed a recognition of the discipline, the function and the work, and the first approaches toward rational understanding and professional competence. They were also the years during which we developed management education. Indeed, the first school to be called a "School of Business Administration," the Harvard Business School, will soon celebrate its seventieth birthday.

This, the childhood and adolescence of management, is now at an end. If nothing else, the tremendous challenge of a world engulfed by the rising tide of human expectations demands of us a unified approach to management and the development of something that can be learned, can be taught — and, above all, can be admired and can give inspiration.

"Management" is the catalyst which makes possible rapid economic and social development in freedom and with human dignity. The alternative is no longer the primitive society without development — and perhaps with an occasional brief glimpse of human freedom and dignity. The alternative is rapid economic development through terror, through tyranny, through debasing the person to a nonentity in the inhuman machine of total society.

The world-wide cry for economic development is in large measure the result of the management achievement. But this achievement also transformed management and, above all, the tasks it has to fulfill. What is needed now cannot be satisfied by technical excellence alone, but also not alone by moral responsibility or human relations. From now on "management science" and "scientific management," "managerial economics," and "human relations" will have to be made one in the theory as well as in the practice of management.

The Dimensions of Management

Chapter 4

Management Is an Organ
It Exists Only in Contemplation of Performance
The Three Primary Tasks: Economic Performance; Making Work Pro-
ductive and the Worker Achieving; Managing Social Impacts and
Social Responsibilities
The Time Dimensions
Administration and Entrepreneurship
Efficiency and Effectiveness
Optimization and Innovation
The Specific Work of Management: Managing Managers
Focus on Tasks

Business enterprises — and public-service institutions as well — are organs of society. They do not exist for their own sake, but to fulfill a specific social purpose and to satisfy a specific need of society, community, or individual. They are not ends in themselves, but means. The right question to ask in respect to them is not, What are they? but, What are they supposed to be doing and what are their tasks?

Management, in turn, is the organ of the institution. It has no function in itself, indeed, no existence in itself. Management divorced from the institution it serves is not management.

What people mean by bureaucracy, and rightly condemn, is a management that has come to misconceive itself as an end and the institution as a means. This is the degenerative disease to which managements are prone, and especially those managements that do not stand under the discipline of the market test. To prevent this disease, to arrest it, and, if possible, to cure it, must be a first purpose of any effective manager — but also of an effective book on management.

The question, What is management? comes second. First we have to define management in and through its tasks.

There are three tasks, equally important but essentially different, which management has to perform to enable the institution in its charge to function and to contribute:

- fulfilling the specific purpose and mission of the institution, whether business enterprise, hospital, or university;
- making work productive and the worker achieving;
- managing social impacts and social responsibilities.

Purpose and Mission: First Dimension

An institution exists for a specific purpose and mission, a specific social function. In the business enterprise this means economic performance.

With respect to this first task, the task of specific performance, business and non-business institutions differ. In respect to every other task, they are similar. But only business has economic performance as its specific mission. It is the definition of a business that it exists for the sake of economic performance. In all other institutions — hospital, church, university, or armed services — economics is a restraint. In business enterprise economic performance is the rationale and purpose.

The emphasis of this book is on business enterprise and the task of economic performance. While by no means the only task to be discharged in society, it is a priority task, because all other social tasks — education, health care, defense, and the advancement of knowledge — depend on the surplus of economic resources, i.e., profits and other savings, which only successful economic performance can produce. The more of these other satisfactions we want, and the more highly we value them, the more we depend on economic performance of business enterprise.

Business management must always, in every decision and action, put economic performance first. It can justify its existence and its authority only by the economic results it produces. A business management has failed if it fails to produce economic results. It has failed if it does not supply goods and services desired by the consumer at a price the consumer is willing to pay. It has failed if it does not improve, or at least maintain, the wealth-producing capacity of the economic resources entrusted to it. And this, whatever the economic or political structure or ideology of a society, means responsibility for profitability.

The first definition of business management is that it is an economic organ, the specifically economic organ of an industrial society. Every act, every decision, every deliberation of management, has economic performance as its first dimension.

Productive Work and Worker Achievement: Second Dimension

The second task of management is to make work productive and the worker achieving.

Business enterprise (or any other institution) has only one true resource: people. It performs by making human resources productive. It accomplishes its performance through work. To make work productive is, therefore, an essential function. But at the same time, these institutions in today's society are increasingly the means through which individual human beings find their livelihood, find their access to social status, to community and to individual achievement and satisfaction. To make the worker achieving is, therefore, more and more important and is a measure of the performance of an institution. It is increasingly a task of management.

Organizing work according to its own logic is only the first step. The second and far more difficult one is making work suitable for human beings — and their logic is radically different from the logic of work. Making the worker achieving implies consideration of the human being as an organism having peculiar physiological and psychological properties, abilities, and limitations, and a distinct mode of action. It implies consideration of the human resource as human beings and not as things, and as having — unlike any other resource — personality, citizenship, control over whether they work, how much and how well, and thus requiring responsibility, motivation, participation, satisfaction, incentives and rewards, leadership, status, and function.

Management, and management alone, can satisfy these requirements. For workers, whether machine tenders or executive vice-presidents, must be satisfied through their achievement in work and job — that is, within the enterprise; and management is the activating organ of the enterprise.

Social Impacts and Social Responsibilities: Third Dimension

The third task of managing is the social impacts and the social responsibilities of the enterprise. None of our institutions exists by itself and is an end in itself. Every one is an organ of society and exists for the sake of society. Business is no exception. Free enterprise cannot be justified as being good for business. It can be justified only as being good for society.

The first new institution to emerge after antiquity, the first institution of the West, was the Benedictine monastery of the sixth century. It was not founded to serve community and society, however. On the contrary, it was founded to serve exclusively its own members and to help them toward their own salvation. Therefore, Saint Benedict removed his monastery from human society and into the wilderness. He was not particularly afraid that his monks would yield to the temptations of the world. He saw a greater danger: that they would be concerned with the world, take responsibility for it, try to do good, and be forced to take leadership.

Unlike the Benedictine monastery, every one of our institutions today exists to contribute outside of itself, to supply and satisfy nonmembers. Business exists to supply goods and services to customers, rather than to supply jobs to workers and managers, or even dividends to stockholders. The hospital does not exist for the sake of doctors and nurses, but for the sake of patients whose one and only desire is to leave the hospital cured and never come back. The school does not exist for the sake of teachers, but for the students. For a management to forget this is mismanagement.

No institution can, therefore, exist outside of community and society as the Benedictine monastery, unsuccessfully, tried. Psychologically, geographically, culturally, and socially, institutions must be part of the community.

To discharge its job, to produce economic goods and services, the business enterprise has to have impacts on people, on communities, and on society. It has to have power and authority over people, e.g., employees, whose own ends and purposes are not defined by and within the enterprise. It has to have impact on the community as a neighbor, as the source of jobs and tax revenue, but also of waste products and pollutants. And, increasingly, in our pluralist society of organizations, it has to add to its fundamental concern for the quantities of life, i.e., economic goods and services, concern for the quality of life, that is, for the physical, human, and social environment of modern man and modern community.

This dimension of management is inherent in the work of managers of *all* institutions. University, hospital, and government agency equally have impacts, equally have responsibilities — and by and large have been far less aware of them, far less concerned with their human, social, and community responsibilities than business has. Yet, more and more, we look to business management for leadership with regard to the quality of life. Managing social impacts is, therefore, becoming a third major task and a third major dimension of management.

These three tasks always have to be done at the same time and within the same managerial action. It cannot even be said that one task predominates or requires greater skill or competence. True, business performance comes first — it is the aim of the enterprise and the reason for its existence. But if work and worker are mismanaged there will be no business performance, no matter how good the chief executive may be in managing the business. Economic performance achieved by mismanaging work and workers is illusory and actually destructive of capital even in the fairly short run. Such performance will raise the costs to the point where the enterprise ceases to be competitive; it will, by creating class hatred and class warfare, make it impossible in the end for the enterprise to operate at all. And, mismanaging social impacts eventually will destroy society's support for the enterprise and with it the enterprise as well.

Each of these three tasks has a primacy of its own. Managing a business has primacy because the enterprise is an economic institution; but making work productive and workers achieving has importance precisely because society is not an economic institution and looks to management for the realization of basic beliefs and values. Managing the enterprise's social impacts has importance because no organ can survive outside the body which it serves; and the enterprise is an organ of society and community.

In these areas also, there are neither actions nor results except of the entire business (or university, or hospital, or government agency). There are no "functional" results and no "functional" decisions. There is only business investment and business risk, business profit and business loss, business action or business inaction, business decision and business information. It is not a plant that pollutes; it is Consolidated Edison of New York, the Union Carbide Corporation, the paper industry, or the city's sewers.

Yet, work and effort are always specific. There is tension, therefore, between two realities: that of performance and that of work. To resolve this tension, or at least to make it productive, is the constant managerial task.

The Time Dimension

One complexity is ever-present in every management problem, every decision, every action — not, properly speaking, a fourth task of management, and yet an additional dimension: time.

Management always has to consider both the present and the future; both the short run and the long run. A management problem is not solved if immediate profits are purchased by endangering the long-range health, perhaps even the survival, of the company. A management decision is irresponsible if it risks disaster this year for the sake of a grandiose future. The all too common case of the great leader in management who produces startling economic results while running the company but afterward leaves behind nothing but a sinking hulk is an example of irresponsible managerial action and of failure to balance present and future. The immediate economic results are actually fictitious and are achieved by paying out capital. In every case where present and future are not both satisfied, where their requirements are not harmonized, or at least balanced, capital, that is, wealth-producing resource, is endangered, damaged, or destroyed.

Today we are particularly conscious of the time dimension in respect to the long-range impact of short-run economic decisions on the environment and on natural resources. But the same problem of harmonizing today and tomorrow exists in all areas, and especially with respect to people.

The time dimension is inherent in management because management is concerned with decisions for action. And action always aims at results in the future. Anybody whose responsibility it is to act — rather than to think or to know — commits himself to the future.

There are two reasons why the time dimension is of particular importance in management's job, and of particular difficulty. In the first place, it is the essence of economic and technological progress that the time span for the fruition and proving out of a decision is steadily lengthening. Edison, in the 1880s, needed two years or so between the start of laboratory work on an idea and the start of pilot-plant operations. Today it may well take Edison's successors fifteen years. A half century ago a new plant was expected to pay for itself in two or three years; today, with capital investment per worker twenty times that of 1920, the payoff period often runs to ten or twelve years. A human organization, such as a sales force or management group, may take even longer to build and to pay for itself.

The second peculiar characteristic of the time dimension is that management — almost alone — has to live always in both present and future.

A military leader, too, knows both times. But traditionally he rarely had to live in both at the same time. During peace he knew no "present"; the present was only a preparation for the future war. During war he knew only the most short-lived "future"; he was concerned with winning the war at hand. Everything else he left to the politicians.

That this is no longer true in an era of cold wars, near wars, and police actions may be the single most important reason for the crisis of military leadership and morale that afflicts all armed services today. The military today lives neither in "peace" nor in "war"; it lives in something we call "defense," which is a state of preparedness akin closely to what was "all-out war" yesterday but aimed not at "winning" but at preventing actual conflict. As a result, military objectives and military planning in the traditional sense no longer apply. Both assumed a sharp conflict between present and future, rather than the profound ambiguity of the modern political and military world.

But management always must do both. It must keep the enterprise performing in the present — or else there will be no enterprise capable of performing in the future. And it has to make the enterprise capable of performance, growth, and change in the future. Otherwise it has destroyed capital — that is, the capacity of resources to produce wealth tomorrow.

The only thing we know about the future is that it is going to be different. There may be great laws of history, great currents of continuity operating over whole epochs. But within time spans of conscious decision and action — time spans of years rather than centuries — in which the managers of any institution operate, the uncertainty of the future is what matters. The long-run continuity is not relevant; and anyhow, it can be discerned only in retrospect and only in contemplation of history, of how it came out.

For the manager the future is discontinuity. And yet the future, however different, can be reached only from the present. The greater the leap into the unknown, the stronger the foundation for the takeoff has to be. The time dimension endows the managerial decision with its special characteristics. It is the act in which the manager integrates present and future.

Administration and Entrepreneurship: Another Dimension

There is another dimension to managerial performance. The manager always has to *administer*. He has to manage and improve what already exists and is already known. But he also has to be an *entrepreneur*. He has to redirect resources from areas of low or diminishing results to areas of high or increasing results. He has to slough off yesterday and to render obsolete what already exists and is already known. He has to create tomorrow. Managing always embraces both, concern for getting the most out of what already exists, and creating a very different tomorrow that makes obsolete what already exists.

In the ongoing business markets, technologies, products, and services exist. Facilities and equipment are in place. Capital has been invested and has to be serviced. People are employed and are in specific jobs, and so on. The *administrative* job of the manager is to *optimize* the yield from these resources.

This, we are usually told, especially by economists, means *efficiency*, that is, doing better what is already being done. Efficiency means focus on costs. But the optimizing approach should focus on *effectiveness*. Effectiveness focuses on opportunities to produce revenue, to create markets, and to change the economic characteristics of existing products and markets. It asks not, How do we do this or that better? It asks, Which of the products really produce extraordinary economic results or are capable of producing them? Which of the markets and/or end uses are capable of producing extraordinary results? It then asks, To what results should, therefore, the resources and efforts of the business be allocated so as to produce extraordinary results rather than the "ordinary" ones which is all efficiency can possibly produce?

This does not deprecate efficiency. Even the healthiest business, the business with the greatest effectiveness, can well die of poor efficiency. But even the most efficient business cannot survive, let alone succeed, if it is efficient in doing the wrong things, that is, if it lacks effectiveness. No amount of efficiency would have enabled the manufacturer of buggy whips to survive.

Effectiveness is the foundation of success — efficiency is a minimum condition for survival *after* success has been achieved. Efficiency is concerned with doing things right. Effectiveness is doing the right things.

Efficiency concerns itself with the input of effort into *all* areas of activity. Effectiveness, however, starts out with the realization that in business, as in any other social organism, 10 or 15 percent of the phenomena — such as products, orders, customers, markets, or people — produce 80 to 90 percent of the results. The other 85 to 90 percent of the phenomena, no matter how efficiently taken care of, produce nothing but costs (which are always proportionate to transactions, that is, to busy-ness).

The first administrative job of the manager is, therefore, to make effective the very small core of worthwhile activities which is capable of being effective. At the same time, he neutralizes (if he does not abandon) the very large penumbra of transactions: products or staff activities, research work or sales efforts, which, no matter how well done, will not yield extraordinarily high results (whether they represent the realized opportunities of the past, mere busy-ness, or unfulfilled hopes and expectations of the past, that is, the mistakes of yesterday).

The second administrative task is to bring the business all the time a little closer to the full realization of its potential. Even the most successful business works at a low efficiency as measured against its potential — the economic results that could be obtained were efforts and resources marshaled to produce the maximum yield they are inherently capable of.

This task is not innovation; it actually takes the business as it is today and asks, What is its *theoretical optimum?* What inhibits attainment thereof? Where (in other words) are the limiting and restraining factors that hold back the business and deprive it of the full return on its resources and efforts?

One basic approach — offered here by way of illustration only — is to ask the question: What *relatively minor changes* in product, technology, process, market, and so on, would significantly improve or alter the economic characteristics and results of this business? (This is similar to the vulnerability analysis of the modern systems engineers.)

In making steel, these vulnerabilities — the factors that hold the economic results of the steel industry way below the theoretical potential of industry and process — might, for instance, be the need, in present steel technology, to create high heats three times, only to quench them three times. For the most expensive thing to produce are temperatures, whether hot or cold. In mass communications, the economic vulnerability of the print medium is the need for personal delivery of a low-priced uniform product, such as the daily paper or the magazine. TV has much less impact for most products. But because there is mass-delivery through the electronic tube, the cost per message is so much lower — despite the incredible cost of producing a commercial and the equally incredible cost of 30 seconds of prime viewing time — that the economic results are vastly more advantageous for the mass advertiser. In life insurance, to give one more example, a central vulnerability might be the high cost of the individual sale. A way to overcome this vulnerability and to realize the potential of the business somewhat more fully might be either statistical selling — elimination of the expensive personal selling efforts — or enrichment of the sales channel, for instance, by selling financial planning (including all other investment instruments), rather than only life insurance.

These examples are cited to show that a relatively minor change does not necessarily have to be easy to make. In fact, we may not know how to do it. But it is still minor, for the business would remain essentially as it is now, yet would have different economic results. And while the illustrations show clearly that these changes may require innovation, they are not, in themselves, innovations. They are primarily modifications of the existing business.

At the same time, inherent in the managerial task is entrepreneurship: making the business of tomorrow. Inherent in the task is innovation.

Making the business of tomorrow starts out with the conviction that the business of tomorrow will be and must be different. But it also starts out — of necessity — with the business of today. Making the business of tomorrow cannot be a flash of genius. It requires systematic analysis and hard, rigorous work *today* — and that means by people in today's business and operating within it.

The specific job of entrepreneurship in business is to make today's business capable of making the future, of making itself into a different business. It is the specific job of entrepreneurship in the going business to enable today's already existing — and especially today's successful — business to remain existing and to remain successful in the future.

Success cannot, one might say, be continued forever. Businesses are, after all, creations of man which have no true permanence. Even the oldest businesses are creations of recent centuries. But a business enterprise must continue beyond the lifetime of the individual or of the generation to be capable of producing its contributions to economy and to society. The perpetuation of a business is a central entrepreneurial task — and ability to do so may well be the most trenchant and definitive test of a management.

The Work of the Manager

Each of these tasks and dimensions has its own skills, its own tools, its own requirements. But the total management task requires their integration. And this too requires specific work and its specific tool. The tool is management; and the work is managing managers.

The tasks — economic performance; making work productive and the worker achieving; managing social impact and social responsibilities; and doing all this in a balance between the demands of today and the demands of tomorrow — are things in which the public at large has a stake. The public has no concern with — and only mild interest in — what managers have to do to accomplish their tasks. It rightly is concerned with performance. But managers must be concerned with the means to the accomplishment of their tasks. They must be concerned with managerial jobs, with the work of managers, with the skills they need, and with their organization.

Any book of management that does not begin with the tasks to be performed misconceives management. Such a book sees management as something in itself, rather than as a means to an end. It fails to understand that management exists only in contemplation of performance. It treats management as an independent reality, whereas management is an organ which derives existence, identity, and justification from the function it serves. The focus must be on the tasks.

To start out discussing management with the work of the manager or with managerial organization — as most books on management do — is the approach of the technocrat, who soon degenerates into a bureaucrat. But it is even poor technocracy. For, as will be stressed again and again in this book, management work, management jobs, and management organization are not absolutes, but are determined and shaped by the tasks to be performed. "Structure follows strategy" is one of the fundamental insights we have acquired in the last twenty years. Without understanding the mission, the objectives, and the strategy of the enterprise, managers cannot be managed, organizations cannot be designed, managerial jobs cannot be made productive.

The Challenges
of Management

Chapter 5

The Management Boom and Its Conceptual Foundations
The Need for New Knowledge in the Foundation Areas
The Productivity Need
Beyond Decentralization
The Need for a New Model
From Personnel Management to the Leadership of People
The New Demands
The Entrepreneurial Manager
Multi-Institutional Management
Knowledge and Knowledge Worker
Multinational and Multicultural Management
Management and the Quality of Life
Management's New Role

*F*rom the end of World War II to the early seventies, the entire world experienced what the Japanese graphically called a "management boom." There were seven conceptual foundations to the management boom: (1) scientific management of work as the key to productivity; (2) decentralization as a basic principle of organization; (3) personnel management as the orderly way of fitting people into organization structures (which included such things as job descriptions, appraisals, wage and salary administration, but also "Human Relations"); (4) manager development to provide today for the management needs of tomorrow; (5) managerial accounting as the foundation for decision-making; (6) marketing; (7) finally, there was long-range planning.

36

Each of the seven was practiced successfully well before the management boom got going. The management boom, in other words, refined, added, modified — but created little. It made accessible to managers everywhere what, up to then, had been the well-kept secret of a few experts. It made into general practice what, till then, had been the rare exception.

The Need for New Knowledge in the Foundation Areas

By the late sixties or early seventies it was becoming clear that the knowledge on which the management boom was founded no longer sufficed. Even in most of the foundation areas there emerged needs for new knowledge, particularly with respect to productivity, organization design and structure, and the management of people. Scientific management could no longer deliver increased productivity. In every country there was a productivity crisis resulting in severe inflationary pressures.

In retrospect it is becoming apparent that the great productivity increases of the post-World War II period in Western Europe and Japan were only partially the result of better management. The main cause was the movement of very large numbers of people from areas and employments of low productivity, e.g., marginal subsistence farming in Sicily, in Spain, and in Japan's mountainous north, into high-productivity employment in industry. Without such massive migration the productivity gains of these growth areas would probably have been quite modest. But these migrations are over. In Western Europe the limit of absorptive capacity for guest workers has clearly been reached. In Japan there is not much population left in marginal farming. From now on productivity gains in these countries will have to be achieved by making existing workers more productive in existing jobs.

At the same time the demands of economic performance that can be satisfied only through higher productivity are escalating. Affluence, for instance, everybody "knew" (and many still believe) would greatly reduce the demand for economic performance. Once we knew how to produce material goods, the demand on the economic function in society would surely lessen. Instead we are confronted with a rising tide of human expectations. When President Kennedy coined this phrase in the early sixties, he had in mind the explosive growth of demands for economic rewards and satisfactions on the part of the poor, the underdeveloped countries of the world. But affluence has released a similar rising tide of human expectations among the remaining poor of the developed countries, whether American Negro or Sicilian peasant. And the affluent themselves are escalating their demands for economic performance faster than their own capacity to perform. The educated young people, contrary to the headlines in the popular press, show little sign of diminished demand for the traditional economic goods and services. They show, in addition, an insatiable appetite for new services and new satisfactions — for education, for health care, for housing, or for leisure.

Equally new, and perhaps even more costly, is the demand for a clean environment. It too was a luxury until now.

Every one of these new expectations and demands requires massive economic efforts. Every one of them absorbs economic resources on a grand scale. Every one of them presupposes, above all, an economic surplus beyond anything the economy has ever produced before. To satisfy these demands requires, in other words, a far higher level of productivity.

We know what is needed. First, the traditional approach focuses on only one factor of productivity: labor. But productivity is the output of all three factors of production: land, labor, and capital, in balance. Even in respect to the productivity of labor, we have taken only the first step: the analysis of individual pieces of work. We need to understand the principles of production so as to put work together into the most productive process. And we need to harmonize the very different requirements and logics of work and worker.

Beyond Decentralization

Decentralization is the best principle of organization design *where it fits*. But the specifications for its application are fairly stringent. It fits the business for which it was originally designed: manufacturing, with distinct markets for distinct product lines. It fits few nonmanufacturing businesses perfectly or even adequately. And it does not fit manufacturing businesses such as the process industries (e.g., aluminum or steel), where the same process produces a variety of products with an infinity of overlapping markets.

As a result of our experience we are looking at new — and so far still largely experimental — design principles: the task force team; simulated decentralization; the systems organization. They are far from satisfactory, so far. But their emergence bespeaks a great need for new models of organization design.

We know that the model which the management boom took to be the universal one is only a partial model, and in fact no longer the ruling model. The management boom was, in all areas, based on work done in and with manufacturing companies, companies that essentially had one product or one product line, operated within one national market, and which predominantly employed manual labor. The model, in other words, was General Motors.

Increasingly the dominant institutions to be managed and organized, even in the business field, are not manufacturing companies, not single-product companies operating in one country or one market alone, not companies employing primarily manual labor. They are businesses in the service industries — banking or retail businesses, and nonbusinesses such as hospitals and universities. They are multiproduct, multitechnology, multimarket businesses. They are multinational businesses. And increasingly, the central human resources are not manual workers — skilled or unskilled — but knowledge workers: company presidents but also computer programmers; engineers, medical technologists, hospital administrators, salesmen and cost accountants; teachers, and the entire employed educated middle class, which has become the center of population gravity in every developed country. In other words, the model of yesterday is becoming less and less pertinent. But we do not, so far, have a new model.

From Personnel Management to the Leadership of People

Finally, we know that we will have to go beyond personnel management. We will have to learn to lead people rather than to contain them.

Our traditional approaches fall into three categories. In part they are philanthropic: the desire to look after the needs, the housing, the health care, the welfare of people who cannot look after themselves. In part the traditional approaches are procedural: to handle in an orderly fashion the recurrent chores connected with the employment of people. In large measure, finally, the traditional approaches aim at preventing and curing trouble; they see in people, above all, potential threats.

The traditional approaches are needed. They are, however, not enough. Beyond them we will have to learn to look on people as resource and opportunity rather than as problem, cost, and threat. We will have to learn to lead rather than to manage, and to direct rather than to control.

The New Demands

While in important areas the old approaches and the old knowledge have been outgrown, demands have appeared in entirely new areas which only a few people at the start of the management boom even perceived, let alone studied. Some of the fundamental assumptions on which the management boom based itself — the assumptions of all the work on management during the past century — are being put into doubt by new developments demanding new vision, new work, and new knowledge.

The Entrepreneurial Manager

For three-quarters of a century management has meant primarily managing the established, going business. Entrepreneurship and innovation, while mentioned in many management books, were not seen as central from 1900 till today. From now on, management will have to concern itself more and more with creating the new in addition to optimizing the already existing. Managers will have to become entrepreneurs, will have to learn to build and manage innovative organizations.

We face a period of innovation such as the one in which the modern industrial economy was born in the last half of the nineteenth century. Then, in the fifty years between the end of America's Civil War and the outbreak of World War I, a new major invention made its appearance on average every fifteen or eighteen months. Each soon spawned new businesses and entirely new industries. Practically all the industries that we consider "modern" today, including aircraft and electronics, grew out of these inventions of the late nineteenth and early twentieth centuries. Economic growth right through the period of reconstruction after World War II was carried primarily by technologies that had been fully developed by the time World War I broke out, and by the four large industries built on these technologies: steel, the automobile, scientific agriculture, and organic chemistry. Now we face another period of major technological change in which the thrust of economic and industrial development will come from industries based on new, twentieth-century technologies and their development.

In sharp contrast to the late nineteenth century, much of the new technology will have to be developed and, above all, will have to be applied in and by already existing businesses. In the late nineteenth century the archetype was the inventor, an Edison or an Alexander Graham Bell, who worked by himself, at most with a few assistants. Even then successful application of an invention very rapidly led to the emergence of an enterprise. But it was not the enterprise that had to generate the new. These days increasingly it will be the existing, often large organization to which we will have to look for innovation — for the simple reason that both the trained people and the money needed to develop the new are concentrated in existing and usually large organizations. Management will therefore have to learn to run, at one and the same time, an existing managerial organization and a new innovative organization.

The need for social innovation may be even greater than for technical innovation. Social innovation has played as large a part in social and economic change and development as technical innovation. The needs of our society — the need for rapid social and economic development in the poor two-thirds of the world; the needs of our big cities; the needs of the environment; the need for productivity in education and health care — all these are opportunities for social innovation by business and business managers. They are opportunities for the entrepreneur, and as such offer challenges to, and make demands on the knowledge, the skill, the performance of management.

Multi-Institutional Management

The management boom was a boom in *business* management, and most management work of the preceding century centered in managing a business.

Now we know, however, that all our institutions need management.

This would have been heresy only a few years ago. Running a business and administering a public-service institution, e.g., a hospital, were then seen as being poles apart. The mission and purpose of an institution does indeed make a basic difference. Nothing is less likely to cure the managerial ills of the public-service institution than the attempt to make its management "businesslike." But then, an investment banking firm also requires management that is different from that of a steel mill or of a department store. And the manager in public-service institutions faces the same tasks as the manager in a business: to perform the function for the sake of which the institution exists; to make work productive and the worker achieving; to manage the institution's social impacts and to discharge its social responsibilities. These are managerial tasks. Public-service institutions equally face the challenge of innovation, and have to manage growth, diversity, and complexity. And we do know, as said before, that a central management need is to make the nonbusiness, the service institution, manageable and managed for performance.

Knowledge and Knowledge Worker

A primary task of management in the developed countries in the decades ahead will be to make knowledge productive. The manual worker is yesterday — and all we can fight on that front is a rearguard action. The basic capital resource, the fundamental investment, but also the cost center of a developed economy, are the knowledge workers who put to work what they have learned in systematic education, that is, concepts, ideas, and theories, rather than the person who puts to work manual skill or muscle.

Taylor put knowledge to work to make the manual worker productive. His industrial engineer was one of the first knowledge workers employed in the manufacturing process. But Taylor himself never asked the question, What constitutes "productivity" with respect to the industrial engineer who applies "scientific management"? As a result of Taylor's work, we could define what productivity is with respect to the manual worker; we still cannot answer what productivity is with respect to the industrial engineer, or to any other knowledge worker. The measurements which give us productivity for the manual worker, such as the number of pieces turned out per hour or per dollar of wage, are irrelevant if applied to the knowledge worker. There are few things as useless and unproductive as the engineering department which with great dispatch, industry, and elegance turns out the drawings for an unsalable product. Productivity with respect to the knowledge worker is, in other words, primarily quality.

One thing is clear: making knowledge productive will bring about changes in job structure, careers, and organizations as drastic as those which resulted in the factory from the application of scientific management to manual work. The entrance job — that is, the job that first introduces the man or woman with high formal education to the adult world of work and experience — will have to be changed drastically to enable the knowledge worker to become productive. For it is abundantly clear that knowledge cannot be productive unless the knowledge workers find out who they are, what kind of work they are fitted for, and how they work best. There can be no divorce of planning from doing in knowledge work. On the contrary, knowledge workers must be able to do their own planning. Present entrance jobs, by and large, do not make this possible. They are based on the assumption — valid to some extent for manual work but quite inappropriate to knowledge work — that an outside expert such as the industrial engineer or the work-study specialist can objectively determine the one best way for any kind of work to be done. For knowledge work, this is simply not true. There may be one best way, but it is heavily conditioned by the individual and not entirely determined by physical, or even mental, characteristics of the job. It is temperamental as well.

Multinational and Multicultural Management

There is need for business managements to be multinational. Economically the world, and especially the developed world, has become one market. And the underdeveloped, the poor, countries differ from the developed ones only in their inability to afford what they would like to have. In terms of its demands, its appetites, and its economic values, the whole world has become one global shopping center, however divided it may be politically. The multinational enterprise which optimizes productive resources, market opportunities, and talents beyond and across national boundaries is thus a normal, indeed a necessary, response to economic reality.

But all these developments introduce complexity into management well beyond what earlier generations had to deal with. For management is also a culture and a system of values and beliefs. It is also the means through which a given society makes productive its own values and beliefs. Management may well be considered the bridge between a civilization that is rapidly becoming worldwide and a culture which expresses divergent traditions, values, beliefs, and heritages. Management must become the instrument through which cultural diversity can be made to serve the common purposes of mankind. At the same time, management increasingly is not being practiced within the confines of one national culture, law, or sovereignty but multinationally. Indeed, management is becoming an institution — so far, almost the only one — of a genuine world economy.

Management, we now know, has to make productive the values, aspirations, and traditions of individuals, community, and society for a common productive purpose. If management does not succeed in putting to work the specific cultural heritage of a country and of a people, social and economic development is unlikely to take place. This is, of course, the great lesson of Japan — and the fact that Japan managed, a century ago, to put to work her own traditions of community and human values for the new ends of a modern industrialized state explains why Japan succeeded while every other nonwestern country has so far failed. Management will have to be considered both a science and a humanity, both a statement of findings that can be objectively tested and validated, and a system of belief and experience.

Within the individual country, especially the developed country, business is rapidly losing its exceptional status as we recognize that it is the prototype of the typical, universal, social form, the organized institution requiring management. Beyond the national boundary, however, business is rapidly acquiring the same exceptional status it no longer has within the individual developed country. Beyond the national boundary, business is rapidly becoming the exception, and the one institution which expresses the reality of a world economy and of a worldwide knowledge society.

We need to learn how to harmonize in one institution and in one management both the need for managerial unity across national boundaries, that is, in a common world economy, and the need for cultural diversity.

Management and the Quality of Life

Because our society is rapidly becoming a society of organizations, all institutions, including business, will have to hold themselves accountable for the quality of life and will have to make fulfillment of basic social values, beliefs, and purposes a major objective of their continuing normal activities rather than a social responsibility that restrains or that lies outside of their normal main functions. Institutions will have to learn to make the quality of life compatible with their main tasks. In the business enterprise this means that the attainment of the quality of life will have to be considered an opportunity to be converted by management into profitable business.

This will apply increasingly to fulfillment of the individual. It is the organization which is today our most visible social environment. The family is private rather than communal — not that this makes it any less important. The community is increasingly in the organization. It will be the job of management to make the individual's values and aspirations contribute to organizational energy and performance. It will simply not be good enough to be satisfied — as industrial relations and even human relations traditionally have been — with satisfaction, that is, with the absence of discontent. Perhaps one way to dramatize this is to say that we may, within another ten years, become far less concerned with manager development as a means of adapting the individual to the demands of the organization and far more with management development to adapt the organization to the needs, aspirations, and potential of the individual.

We also know that management creates economic and social development. Economic and social development is the *result* of management.

Wherever we have contributed only the economic factors of production, especially capital, we have not achieved development. In the few cases where we have been able to generate management energies we have generated rapid development. Development, in other words, is a matter of human energies rather than of economic wealth. And the generation and direction of human energies is the task of management. Management is the mover and development is a consequence.

More important even than the new tasks, however, may be management's new role. Management is fast becoming the central resource of the developed countries and the basic need of the developing ones. From being the specific concern of business, i.e., the economic institution of society, management and managers are becoming the distinctive organs of developed society. What management is and what managers do will, therefore — and properly — become increasingly a matter of public concern rather than a matter for the experts. Management will increasingly be concerned as much with the expression of basic beliefs and values as with the accomplishment of measurable results. It will increasingly stand for the quality of life of a society as much as for its standard of living.

There are many new tools of management the use of which we will have to learn, and many new techniques. There are a great many new and difficult tasks. But the most important change for management is that the aspirations and values and the very survival of society in the developed countries will come to depend on the performance, the competence, the earnestness, and the values of their managers. The task of the next generation is to make productive for individual, community, and society the new organized institutions of our new pluralism. And that is, above all, the task of management.

What Is a Manager?

Part Two

Managers and Their Work

Chapter 6

The Traditional Definition of a Manager
Its Inadequacy
The Career Professional
Defining a Manager by Function Rather Than Power
Title, Function, and Pay of the Career Professional
Defining Management's Job
The Work of the Manager
Information: The Tool of the Manager
The Manager's Resource: People
What Makes a Manager?

*W*hat characterizes a manager? And what defines a manager?

The words "manager" and "management" are slippery, to say the least. They are untranslatable into any other language. In British English they do not have the meaning they have in the United States. And even in American usage, their meaning is far from clear.

The word "manager" has no exact counterpart in German, French, Spanish, Italian, or Russian; yet the words used in these languages are as imprecise and elusive as "manager" is in American. Most people, when asked what they mean by "manager," will reply "a boss." But when the sign over the shoeshine stand in an airport reads "John Smith, Manager," everybody (at least in America) knows that this means that Mr. Smith is not the boss, i.e., not the proprietor, but a hired hand with a minimum of authority and a salary just above that of the workers who shine the shoes.

Early in the history of management a manager was defined as someone who "is responsible for the work of other people." This served a useful purpose at the time. It distinguished the manager's function from that of the "owner." It made clear that managing was a specific kind of work which could be analyzed, studied, and improved systematically. The definition focused on the essentially new, large and permanent organization emerging to perform the economic tasks of society.

Yet, the definition is not at all satisfactory. In fact it never was. From the beginning, there were people in the enterprise, often in responsible positions, who were clearly management and yet did not manage, that is, who were not responsible for the work of other people. The treasurer of a company, the person responsible for the supply and use of money in the business, may have subordinates and in that sense be a manager in terms of the traditional definition. But clearly, the treasurer himself does most of the treasurer's job. He works with the company's underwriters, with the financial community and so on. He is an "individual contributor," rather than a manager. But he is a member of top management.

Also, the definition focuses on the tools for the task rather than on the task itself. The man in charge of market research in a company may have a large number of people reporting to him and is thus a manager in the traditional sense. But it really makes no difference to his function and contribution whether he has a large staff, a small staff, or no staff at all. The same contribution in terms of market research and market analysis can well be made by a man to whom no one reports. He may even make a greater contribution when he is not forced to spend a great deal of his time with subordinates and on their work. He thus may make market research more effective in the business, better understood by his associates in management, and more firmly built into the company's basic business decisions and into its definition of what "our business is and should be."

In line with the traditional definition of a manager as a person who "is responsible for the work of others" we should talk of a "manager of market researchers." Instead, we always talk of a "manager of market research." This common usage is right in its intuitive understanding of what the responsibility of the managerial position is and should be, and how the person who occupies the position should be measured.

The traditional definition has become increasingly inappropriate and a bar to effective management, effective organization, and true performance.

The most rapidly growing group in any organization, especially in today's business enterprise, are people who are management, in the sense of being responsible for contribution to and results of the enterprise. However, they are clearly not managers in that they are not, as a rule, the bosses and responsible for the work of other people. The most rapidly growing group in business enterprise today are individual professional contributors of all kinds who work by themselves (perhaps with an assistant and a secretary) and yet have impact on the company's wealth-producing capacity, the direction of its business, and its performance.

Such people are not to be found only in research work, though it was here that they first emerged as a distinct group. The senior chemist in the laboratory has major responsibility and makes major decisions, many of them irreversible in their impact. But so also does the person who works out and thinks through the company's organization and designs managerial jobs. Here also belongs the senior cost accountant who determines the definition and allocation of costs. By defining the measurements for management, the cost accountant, in effect, largely decides whether a certain product will be kept or will be abandoned. In this same category are the people charged with the development and maintenance of quality standards for a company's products, the people working on the distributive system through which the company's products are brought to the market, and the advertising director, who may be responsible for the basic promotion policy of a company, its advertising message, the media it uses, and the measurements of advertising effectiveness.

The traditional definition is responsible, in large measure, for the fact that the individual professional contributor presents a problem within the structure and a problem to himself or herself. The title, pay, function and opportunities of the professional contributor are confused, ambiguous, and a cause of dissatisfaction and friction. Yet the number of these career professionals is increasing fast.

There needs to be greater flexibility in assigning people within the management group — to task forces, teams, and other organizational units which do not fit the traditional concept of a "line organization," that is, an organization in which one member is the boss, while the others are subordinates.

Managers in the traditional sense will have to be able to move into situations where they are not superiors, indeed, into situations where they are the "juniors" to nonmanagers on a team or a task force. Conversely, career professionals without managerial function or title in the traditional sense will have to be able to be team leaders or task force leaders. The traditional separation between managers and nonmanagers will increasingly become a hindrance and inappropriate.

The New Definition of a Manager

It is necessary and urgent that we think through what really defines a manager and who should be considered management.

The first attempt at solving the problem, made in the early 1950s, supplemented the definition of the manager with a new definition of an "individual professional contributor" with "parallel paths of opportunity" for both. This made it possible to pay a person properly for "professional" work rather than make higher pay dependent upon promotion into a "manager's" job, that is, into a position of responsibility for the work of others.

Yet this formula has not fully solved the problem. The companies that have adopted it report that the individual professional contributor is only slightly less dissatisfied than before. The professional contributor remains convinced that true opportunities for advancement exist only, or at least primarily, within the administrative structure, and that one has to become a "boss" to "get ahead." Above all, the separation of the managerial world into two groups serves to emphasize the inferiority of those who do their own work as compared with those responsible for the work of others. The emphasis is still on power and authority rather than on responsibility and contribution.

Outside of the U.S. the problem may be even worse. In Japan there are no career opportunities at all for the individual contributor. Seniority forces a Japanese to become an administrator — as a result of which, for instance, the ablest journalists are forced to stop writing and the ablest scientists in the research labs to become "research managers" and to stop researching.

Any analysis which does not start out from the traditional definition but looks at the work itself will come to the conclusion that the traditional definition of a manager as one responsible for the work of others emphasizes a secondary, rather than a primary, characteristic.

As we will see, one can define the work of a manager as planning, organizing, integrating, and measuring. Career professionals — e.g., a market researcher who works alone or a senior cost accountant — also have to plan, to organize, and to measure their results against their objectives and expectations. They also have to integrate their work with the work of other people in the organization. They have to integrate their work into that of the unit of which they are a part. Above all, if they are to have results, they have to integrate "sideways," that is, with the people in other areas and functions who have to put their work to use.

To be sure, "managers" have to integrate "downwards," that is, with the work of the people who report to them — which is what the traditional definition stresses. The most important relation areas in which managers have to integrate the work of their unit, if it is to have any results, is, however, sideways — that is, with people over whom they have no managerial control.

The essence of the first-line supervisor's job in the plant or office is the management of the people who report to him or her. Upward or sideways relations are secondary on that level. Yet common usage does not consider the first-line supervisor a manager. We speak of supervisors as "members of management," implying that they should be managers but really are not, or only marginally so. The reason is, of course, that first-line supervisors, whether in the factory or in the office, are not commonly expected to take much responsibility for their contribution and results. They are expected to deliver according to objectives set for them by others — in the typical mass-production plant this is all they possibly can or should do. This makes the supervisor's job ambiguous and difficult. But the fact that we are reluctant to call the supervisor a manager, even though the job fits the traditional definition better than the jobs of people who hold higher and much more important positions in the executive hierarchy, only demonstrates that the definition accentuates the secondary, rather than the primary.

It would, therefore, seem appropriate to stress that the first criterion in identifying those people within an organization who have management responsibility is not command over people. *It is responsibility for contribution. Function rather than power has to be the distinctive criterion and the organizing principle.*

But what should these people be called? Many organizations have experimented with new definitions or have tried to give old terms a new meaning. Perhaps the best thing is not to coin a new term, but to follow popular usage which speaks of the "management group." Within the management group, there will be people whose function includes the traditional managerial function, responsibility for the work of others. There will be others who do not carry this responsibility within their specific assignment. And there will be a third group which is somewhat ambiguous and in-between, people whose job is that of team leader or task force captain, or people who combine the function of advisor to top management and the "conscience" of a business in a certain area, with supervisory and administrative responsibility over a staff in a given area. This is not a neat, let alone a perfect, solution. In every organization there are people who are true specialists and who, while anything but rank-and-file workers, do not see themselves as part of management either. They want to remain specialists and are not, fundamentally, much concerned with the whole of which they are a part. Their allegiance is to their technical or professional skill, rather than to their organization. The psychologist within a personnel department sees himself or herself as a professional — that is, a member of the world of that particular academic specialty — rather than as an executive of this or that company (or even as a faculty member of this or that university). And so does the computer specialist.

Conversely, in many traditions other than the American, there are people who fully accept the responsibility for their contribution but are not deemed managers, or part of management, even though they may be responsible for the work of others. An example is the German *Meister*, the highly skilled worker who has risen to leadership within his craft, who is in most cases the true "boss" within his craft area, and who yet considers himself a skilled worker rather than a manager. He corresponds, in many ways, to the noncommissioned officer in the military, the long-serving master sergeant, for instance, who within his own area, e.g., supply, is the real "boss," but who will never become an officer and does not expect to be one.

Yet though fuzzy, to define the management group by function and responsibility enables us to work out the relationship between the manager and the career professional.

The Career Professional

Career professionals — and particularly the specialists — need a manager. Their major problem is the relation of their area of knowledge and expertise to the performance and results of the entire organization. Career professionals therefore have a major problem of communication. They cannot be effective unless their output becomes the input of other people. But their output is ideas and information. This requires that the users of their output understand what they are trying to say and to do. But, by the nature of their task, they will be tempted to use their own specialized jargon. Indeed, in many cases, they are fluent only in their own jargon. It is the job of the manager to make the specialists realize that they cannot become effective unless they are understood, and that they cannot be understood unless they try to find out the needs, the assumptions, and the limitations of their "customers," the other people (also, often, specialists in their own areas) within the organization. It is the manager who has to translate the objectives of the organization into the language of the specialist, and the output of the specialist into the language of the intended user. It is the manager, in other words, on whom the specialists depend for the integration of their output into the work of others.

Yet while career professionals need a manager to be effective, the manager is not their boss. The manager is their "guide," their "tool," and their "marketing arm." The manager is the channel through which the career professionals, and especially the true specialists, can direct their knowledge, their work, and their capacities toward joint results, and through which in turn, they find out the needs, the capacities, and the opportunities of the enterprise of which they are members.

In one way, indeed, the true career professionals will and should be the "superiors" of their manager. The career professional must be the "teacher" and the "educator." It is the career professional's job to teach management, to raise its vision, to show new opportunities, new horizons, new and more demanding standards. In that sense, career professionals should be expected to be the senior in their relationships to their managers and, indeed, to managers within the organization. If they do not take the responsibility for leadership within their area of expertise and knowledge they are not true career professionals. They are instead subordinate "technicians."

Title, Function, and Pay of the Career Professional

The thorny problems of title, function, and pay of managers and career professionals cannot be completely solved. But they can be deprived, in substantial measure, of their capacity to disturb and to misdirect.

Traditionally, there has been only one line of advancement in organizations; a worker could acquire higher pay and status by becoming a manager. As a result, a good many people who deserved recognition and reward did not receive them. Or, in order to give recognition and reward, people who neither wanted to manage nor were competent in doing so were put into management positions.

This system is inappropriate to the reality of today's organization, and especially of today's business enterprise. People should be able to move freely from one kind of work to the other as they advance. We should therefore have a system of rank and title that differentiates clearly between a person's function and his or her standing within the organization.

In the military services the separation between rank and function has long been routine. If a man is a Major that establishes his rank. But it does not tell us whether he is in command of a battalion — that is, a manager — or whether he works in the Pentagon as a researcher — that is, as an individual professional contributor. His rank is Major; but his functional title, Battalion Commander or Communications Specialist, describes his assignment.

It might make sense to call all members of the management group executives and to have only four ranks within an organization: junior executive; executive; senior executive; and corporate executive. Then one could have a system of rank which cuts across the distinction between managerial and nonmanagerial positions. One could, then, describe a person's position, whether it be Senior Engineer — Heat Treating, or Manager — Cost Control, and separate thereby rank and function. Such a system is more likely to succeed than a system that tries to build "parallel ladders."

The traditional definition of a manager also implies that the manager, being the superior, must get more money than the workers who report to him or her and who are considered "inferiors." This makes sense on the assembly line and in clerical work. It is also appropriate for the junior knowledge workers who are not yet career professionals and who are not expected to take full responsibility for their objectives and contribution.

But it makes little sense for the true professionals, that is, for the people who are considered to be the leaders in their field within an enterprise and the pacesetters within their area. For them, the right rules are those that apply to "performers," whether in the arts or in sports.

No one finds it strange that the star baseball player gets more money than his coach or even the team's manager. Nobody is surprised that the prima donna gets more for one appearance than the opera manager may earn in the entire year. It is clearly understood by everybody that the top-flight athlete or the outstanding singer needs a manager — and yet their contributions are different and justify differential payment as a result of which, the organizationally "subordinate" receives more money than the "superior," that is, the manager.

There is even an instructive business precedent for this. When Pierre S. du Pont and Alfred P. Sloan, Jr., first attempted, in 1920, to bring order into the chaos of the General Motors Company, they set the same salary for the heads of the operating divisions as for the president, Pierre du Pont. But, at his own request, Sloan received substantially less as the operating vice-president to whom the division heads reported. The manager of a unit composed of career professionals or specialists will, of course, receive more money than most of the men in the unit, but it should not be considered unusual, let alone undesirable, for one or two "stars" of the group to receive more money than the manager. This can apply just as well to sales personnel; a star salesperson should be expected to make more money than the regional sales manager. It should apply in the research laboratory, and in all other areas where performance depends on individual skill, effort, and knowledge.

There should be no distinction between members of the management group who are managers and those who are career professionals in the demands made on them. The managers differ from the other professionals only in having one extra dimension to their responsibility and performance. The difference between the market research manager with a staff of fifty people and the market researcher who does the same job without any staff is in means rather than in contribution, let alone in function. Both should be held to the same demand. Both are "management" and "managers."

What Is Management's Job?

A manager has two specific tasks. Nobody else in the business enterprise discharges these tasks. And everyone charged with them works as a manager.

The manager has the task of creating a true whole that is larger than the sum of its parts, a productive entity that turns out more than the sum of the resources put into it. One analogy is the conductor of a symphony orchestra, through whose effort, vision and leadership individual instrumental parts that are so much noise by themselves become the living whole of music. But the conductor has the composer's score and only interprets it. The manager is both composer and conductor.

This task requires the manager to bring out and make effective whatever strength there is in his or her resources — and above all in the human resources — and neutralize whatever there is of weakness. This is the only way in which a genuine whole can ever be created.

It requires the manager to balance and harmonize the three major functions of business enterprise: managing a business, managing managers and managing worker and work. A decision or action that satisfies a need in one of these functions by weakening performance in another weakens the whole enterprise. One and the same decision or action must always be sound in all three areas.

The task of creating a genuine whole also requires that the manager in each and every act consider simultaneously the performance and results of the enterprise as a whole and the diverse activities needed to achieve synchronized performance. It is here, perhaps, that the comparison with the orchestra conductor fits best. A conductor must always hear both the whole orchestra and, for example, the second oboe. Similarly, a manager must always consider both the over-all performance of the enterprise and, say, the market-research activity needed. By raising the performance of the whole, the manager creates scope and challenge for market research. By improving the performance of market research, the manager makes possible better over-all business results. The manager must continuously ask two double-barreled questions in one breath: What better business performance is needed and what does this require of what activities? And: What better performance are the activities capable of and what improvement in business results will it make possible?

The second specific task of managers is to harmonize in every decision and action the requirements of the immediate and long-range future. Managers cannot sacrifice either without endangering the enterprise. They must, so to speak, keep their noses to the grindstone while lifting their eyes to the hills — which is quite an acrobatic feat. Or, to vary the metaphor, they can neither afford to say: "We will cross this bridge when we come to it," nor "It's the next hundred years that count." They not only have to prepare for crossing distant bridges — they have to build them long before they get there. And if a manager does not take care of the next hundred days, there will be no next hundred years; indeed, there may not even be a next five years. Whatever managers do should be sound in expediency as well as in basic long-range objective and principle. And where they cannot harmonize the two time dimensions, they must at least balance them. Managers must carefully calculate the sacrifice they impose on the long-range future of the enterprise to protect its immediate interests, or the sacrifice they make today for the sake of tomorrow. Managers must limit either sacrifice as much as possible. And they must repair the damage it inflicts as soon as possible. A manager lives and acts in two time dimensions, and is responsible for the performance of the whole enterprise and of his or her component.

The Work of the Manager

Every manager does many things that are not managing and may spend much time on them. A sales manager makes a statistical analysis or placates an important customer. A foreman repairs a tool or fills in a production report. A manufacturing manager designs a new plant layout or tests new materials. A company president works through the details of a bank loan or negotiates a big contract — or spends dreary hours presiding at a dinner in honor of long-service employees. All these things pertain to a particular function. All are necessary, and have to be done well.

But they are apart from that work which every manager does whatever the manager's function or activity, or rank and position, work which is common to all managers and peculiar to them. The best proof is that we can apply to the job of the manager the systematic analysis of Scientific Management. We can isolate that work which a person does because he or she is a manager. We can divide it into the basic constituent operations. And a person can improve his or her performance as a manager by improving the performance of these constituent motions.

There are five such basic operations in the work of the manager. Together they result in the integration of resources into a living and growing organism.

A manager, in the first place, *sets objectives*. A manager: Determines what the objectives should be; Determines what the goals in each area of objectives should be; Decides what has to be done to reach these objectives; And makes the objectives effective by communicating them to the people whose performance is needed to attain them.

Secondly, a manager *organizes*. A manager: Analyzes the activities, decisions and relations needed. Classifies the work; Divides it into manageable activities; Further divides the activities into manageable jobs; Groups these units and jobs into an organization structure; And selects people for the management of these units and for the jobs to be done.

Next a manager *motivates and communicates*. A manager makes a team out of the people that are responsible for various jobs. A manager forms the team in one or more of several ways; Through the practices with which he or she manages; Through relationships with the people managed; Through incentives and rewards for successful work; Through promotion policy; And through constant communication, both from the manager to subordinates, and from the subordinates to the manager.

The fourth basic element in the work of the manager is *the job of measurement*. The manager establishes measuring yardsticks — and there are few factors as important to the performance of the organization and of everyone in it. A manager sees to it that there are measurements available to everyone in the organization; that the measurements are focused on the performance of the whole organization, and at the same time focused on the work of the individual and help the individual to do it. A manager analyzes performance, appraises it and interprets it. And again, as in every other area of their work, managers communicate both the meaning of the measurements and their findings to superiors as well as to subordinates.

Finally, a manager *develops people*. How well or how poorly subordinates develop themselves in their work depends directly on the way a manager manages. A manager: Directs people or misdirects them; Brings out what is in them or stifles them; Strengthens their integrity or corrupts them; Trains them to stand upright and strong or deforms them.

Every manager does these things — knowingly or not. A manager may do them well, or may do them wretchedly, but always does them.

Every one of these categories can be divided further into sub-categories, and each of the sub-categories could be discussed in a book of its own. The work of the manager, in other words, is complex. And every one of its categories requires different qualities and qualifications.

Setting objectives, for instance, is a problem of balances: a balance between business results and the realization of the principles a manager believes in; a balance between the immediate needs of the business and those of the future; a balance between desirable ends and available means. Setting objectives therefore requires analytical and synthesizing ability.

Organizing, too, requires analytical ability. For it demands the most economical use of scarce resources. But it deals with human beings; and therefore it also stands under the principle of justice and requires integrity. Both analytical ability and integrity are similarly required for the development of people.

The skill needed for motivating and communicating, however, is primarily social. Instead of analysis, integration and synthesis are needed. Justice dominates as the principle, economy is secondary. And integrity is of much greater importance than analytical ability.

Measuring requires again first and foremost analytical ability. But it also requires that measurements be used to make self-control possible. To use them to control people from outside and above, that is, to dominate them, is to abuse measurements. It is the common violation of this principle that largely explains why measurement is the weakest area in the work of the manager today. And as long as measurements are abused as a tool of "control" (as long, for instance, as measurements are used as a weapon of an internal secret policy that supplies audits and critical appraisals of a manager's performance to the boss without even sending a carbon copy to the manager) measuring will remain the weakest area in the manager's performance.

Setting objectives, organizing, motivating and communicating, measuring and developing people are formal, classifying categories. Only a manager's experience can bring them to life, concrete and meaningful. But because they are formal, they apply to every manager and to everything a manager does. They can therefore be used by all managers to appraise their own skill and performance, and to work systematically on improving themselves and their performance as managers.

Being able to set objectives does not make someone a manager, just as ability to tie a small knot in confined space does not make a person a surgeon. But without the ability to set objectives, it is not possible to be an adequate manager, just as it is not possible to be a good surgeon without the ability to tie small knots. And as a surgeon's knot-tying skill improves and he becomes a better surgeon, a manager who improves his or her skills and performance in all five categories becomes a better manager.

Information: The Tool of the Manager

The manager has a specific tool: information. A manager does not "handle" people; but instead motivates, guides, organizes people to do their own work. The tool — the only tool — to do all this is the spoken or written word or the language of numbers. It does not matter whether the manager's job is engineering, accounting or selling. To be effective a manager must have the ability to listen and to read, and the ability to speak and to write. Managers need skill in getting their thinking across to other people as well as skill in finding out what other people are after.

Of all the skills needed, today's manager possesses least those of reading, writing, speaking and figuring. One look at what is known as "policy language" in large companies will show how illiterate we are. Improvement is not a matter of learning faster reading or public speaking. Managers have to learn to know language, to understand what words are and what they mean. Perhaps most important, they have to acquire respect for language as our most precious gift and heritage. The manager must understand the meaning of the old definition of rhetoric as "the art which draws men's heart to the love of true knowledge." Without ability to motivate by means of the written and spoken word or the telling number, a manager cannot be successful.

How a Manager Uses Time

Everybody has the problem of time; for of all resources it is the scarcest, the most perishable and the most elusive. But the manager must solve what is a common problem in very specific ways.

Managers are forever pursuing some glittering panacea for their time problem: a course in faster reading, a restriction of reports to one page, a mechanical limitation of interviews to fifteen minutes. All such panaceas are pure quackery and, in the end, a waste of time. It is, however, possible to guide managers toward an intelligent allocation of their time.

Managers who know how to use time well achieve results by planning. They are willing to think before they act. They spend a great deal of time on thinking through the areas in which objectives should be set, a great deal more on thinking through systematically what to do with recurrent problems.

Most managers spend a large amount of time — in small driblets — on attempts to appraise the performance and quality of the people who work under them. Good time users do not. Instead, they systematically appraise their people once a year. As the result of a few hours' work, they then have the answers for all the decisions — concerning someone's salary or promotion or work assignment — on which judgment is required.

Good time users do not spend a great deal of time on the modification engineering of their products. They sit down once a year — for a few days perhaps — and work out with their sales and manufacturing departments the basic policy, the objectives and the rules for the necessary modifications, determining then how much of it there should be — and assign the engineering workload in advance to the job. In their eyes it is no praise to say: "This year we managed to get through this inventory crisis, thanks to the experience we had acquired last year." If they have a recurrent crisis, they spend the time to find out what causes it so as to prevent its repetition. This may take time, but in the long run it saves time.

The good time users among managers spend many more hours on their communications up than on their communications down. They tend to have good communications down, but they seem to obtain these as an effortless by-product. They do not talk to their subordinates about their problems, but they know how to make the subordinates talk about theirs. They are, for instance, willing to spend a great deal of their time on a half-yearly Manager Letter, in which each subordinate sets down his or her job objectives, plans, and how the superior helps or hampers the job. They may spend a whole day every six months with each of their ten or twelve subordinates going carefully over the Manager Letter — and as a result they do not have to worry much in between about their communications down.

The manager who utilizes time well also spends a great deal of time considering the boss's problems, and on thinking how to contribute to the success of the boss, of the whole activity and of the business. A manager takes responsibility, in other words, for the boss's job — considering this a part of the job of being a manager. As a result, such a manager seems to need no extra time for clearing up the messes that result from a confusion of objectives and viewpoints.

The Manager's Resource: People

The manager works with a specific resource: people. And the human being is a unique resource requiring peculiar qualities in whoever attempts to work with it.

For human beings, and human beings alone, cannot be "worked." A relationship between two people is never a relationship between a person and a "thing" to be used as a passive "resource." Legally the slave was a "chattel," i.e., a thing. But slavery affected the master just as much as it did the slave. It is in the nature of a human relationship that it changes both parties — whether they are man and wife, father and child, or manager and the people managed.

A human being is not "worked"; a human being is "developed." And the direction this development takes decides whether the human being — both as a person and as a resource — will become more productive or cease, ultimately, to be productive at all. This applies, as cannot be emphasized too strongly, not alone to the man or woman who is being managed, but also to the manager. Whether a manager develops subordinates in the right direction, helps them to grow and become bigger and richer persons, will directly determine whether that manager will develop, will grow or wither, become richer or become impoverished, improve or deteriorate.

One can learn certain skills in managing people, for instance, the skill to lead a conference or to conduct an interview. One can set down practices that are conducive to development — in the structure of the relationship between manager and subordinate, in a promotion system, in the rewards and incentives of an organization. But when all is said and done, developing people still requires a basic quality in the manager which cannot be created by supplying skills or by emphasizing the importance of the task. It requires integrity of character.

There is tremendous stress these days on liking people, helping people, getting along with people, as qualifications for a manager. These alone are never enough. In every successful organization there is one boss who does not like people, does not help them, does not get along with them. Cold, unpleasant, demanding, this boss often teaches and develops more people than anyone else. Bosses like this often command more respect than the most likable person ever could. They demand exacting workmanship of themselves as well as of their subordinates. They set high standards and expect that they will be lived up to. They consider only what is right and never who is right. And though usually themselves quite brilliant, they never rate intellectual brilliance above integrity in others. The manager who lacks these qualities of character — no matter how likeable, helpful, or amiable, no matter even how competent or brilliant — is a menace and should be adjudged "unfit to be a Manager."

It may be argued that every occupation — the doctor, the lawyer, the grocer — requires integrity. But there is a difference. The manager lives with the people he or she manages; the manager decides what their work is to be; the manager directs their work, trains them for it, appraises it and, often, decides their future. The relationship of merchant and customer, professional and client requires honorable dealings. Being a manager, though, is more like being a parent, or a teacher. And in these relationships honorable dealings are not enough; personal integrity is of the essence.

We can now answer the question: Does it require genius, or at least a special talent, to be a manager? Is being a manager an art or an intuition? The answer is: "No." What a manager does can be analyzed systematically. What a manager has to be able to do can be learned (though perhaps not always taught). Yet there is one quality that cannot be learned, one qualification that the manager cannot acquire but must bring with him. It is not genius; it is character.

What Makes a Manager?

The standard definition is that someone is a manager if he or she is in charge of other people and their work. This is too narrow. The first responsibility of a manager is upward: to the enterprise because the manager is an organ of the enterprise. Nevertheless, both upward and downward relations are essential to the performance of a manager: relations with superiors and fellow-managers, and relations and responsibilities to subordinates.

Another definition — though one that is usually implied rather than spelled out — is that importance defines the manager. But in the modern enterprise no one group is more essential than another. The worker at the machine, and the professional employee in the laboratory or the drafting room, are as necessary for the enterprise to function as is the manager. This is the reason why all members of the enterprise have to have the managerial vision. It is not importance but function that differentiates the various groups within the enterprise.

The most common concept of what defines the manager is rank and pay. This is not only wrong, but it is destructive. Even today we find incidentally, so-called rank-and-file workers who have higher incomes than the majority of managers; there are model makers in the automobile industry, for instance, whose annual income exceeds $35,000 and who are yet considered workers and are indeed members of the union's bargaining unit. And unless we can pay professional contributors adequately, can give them promotional opportunities as individual contributors, and can provide for them the status, dignity and self-respect of the true professional, we will simply not be able to manage their ever-increasing numbers.

Altogether the idea that rank and pay define the manager is not much more than a fallacious analogy from the individual proprietor of yesterday to the manager of today's business enterprise.

Who is a manager can be defined only by that person's function and by the contribution he or she is expected to make. And the function that distinguishes the manager above all others is the function no one but the manager can perform. The one contribution a manager is uniquely expected to make is to give others vision and ability to perform. It is vision and moral responsibility that, in the last analysis, define the manager.

Management by Objectives and Self-Control

Chapter 7

The Forces of Misdirection
Workmanship: A Necessity and a Danger
Misdirection by the Boss
What Should the Objectives Be?
Management by "Drives"
How Should Managers' Objectives Be Set and by Whom?
Self-control through Measurements
The Proper Use of Reports and Procedures
A Philosophy of Management

*A*ny business enterprise must build a true team and weld individual efforts into a common effort. Each member of the enterprise contributes something different, but they must all contribute toward a common goal. Their efforts must all pull in the same direction, and their contributions must fit together to produce a whole — without gaps, without friction, without unnecessary duplication of effort.

Business performance therefore requires that each job be directed toward the objectives of the whole business. And in particular each manager's job must be focused on the success of the whole. The performance that is expected of the manager must be derived from the performance goals of the business, the manager's results must be measured by the contribution they make to the success of the enterprise. Managers must know and understand what the business goals demand of them in terms of performance, and their superiors must know what contribution to demand and expect of them — and must judge them accordingly. If these requirements are not met, managers are misdirected. Their efforts are wasted. Instead of team work, there is friction, frustration, and conflict.

Management by objectives requires major effort and special instruments. For in the business enterprise managers are not automatically directed toward a common goal. On the contrary, business, by its very nature, contains three powerful factors of misdirection: in the specialized work of most managers; in the hierarchical structure of management; and in the differences in vision and work and the resultant insulation of various levels of management.

A favorite story at management meetings is that of the three stonecutters who were asked what they were doing. The first replied: "I am making a living." The second kept on hammering while he said: "I am doing the best job of stonecutting in the entire county." The third one looked up with a visionary gleam in his eyes and said: "I am building a cathedral."

The third man is, of course, the true "manager." The first man knows what he wants to get out of the work and manages to do so. He is likely to give a "fair day's work for a fair day's pay." But he is not a manager and will never be one.

It is the second man who is a problem. Workmanship is essential; without it no work can flourish; in fact, an organization demoralizes if it does not demand of its members the most scrupulous workmanship they are capable of. But there is always a danger that the true workers, the true professionals, will believe that they are accomplishing something when in effect they are just polishing stones or collecting footnotes. Workmanship must be encouraged in the business enterprise. But it must always be related to the needs of the whole.

The majority of managers in any business enterprise are, like the second man, concerned with specialized work. True, the number of functional managers should always be kept at a minimum, and there should be the largest possible number of "general" managers who manage an integrated business and are directly responsible for its performance and results. Even with the utmost application of this principle the great bulk of managers will remain in functional jobs, however. This is particularly true of the younger people.

A person's habits as a manager, and therefore his or her vision and values, will as a rule be formed through the functional and specialized work they do. And it is essential that functional specialists develop high standards of workmanship, that they strive to be "the best stonecutters in the county." For work without high standards is dishonest. It corrupts managers. It corrupts subordinates. Emphasis on, and drive for, workmanship produces innovations and advances in every area of management. That managers strive to do "professional personnel management," to run "the most up-to-date plant," to do "truly scientific market research," to "put in the most modern accounting system," or to do "perfect engineering" must be encouraged.

But this striving for professional workmanship in functional and specialized work is also a danger. It tends to direct a manager's vision and efforts away from the goals of the business. The functional work becomes an end in itself. In far too many instances the functional manager no longer measures his or her performance by its contribution to the enterprise, but only by his or her own professional criteria of workmanship. The functional manager tends to appraise subordinates by their craftsmanship, to reward and to promote them accordingly. Such managers resent demands made on them for the sake of business performance as interference with "good engineering," "smooth production," or "hard-hitting selling." The functional manager's legitimate desire for workmanship becomes, unless counterbalanced, a centrifugal force which tears the enterprise apart and converts it into a loose confederation of functional empires, each concerned only with its own craft, each jealously guarding its own "secrets," each bent on enlarging its own domain rather than on building the business.

This danger will be greatly intensified by the technological changes now under way. The number of highly educated specialists working in the business enterprise is bound to increase tremendously. And so will the level of workmanship demanded of these specialists. The tendency to make the craft or function an end in itself will therefore be even more marked than it is today. But at the same time the new technology will demand much closer coordination between specialists. And it will demand that functional managers even at the lowest management level see the business as a whole and understand what it requires of them. The new technology will need both the drive for excellence in workmanship and the consistent direction of managers at all levels toward the common goal.

The hierarchical structure of management aggravates the danger. What the "boss" does and says, even the boss's most casual remarks, habits, and mannerisms, tend to appear to his or her subordinates as calculated, planned, and meaningful.

"All you ever hear around the place is human-relations talk; but when the boss calls you on the carpet it is always because the costs are too high; and when it comes to promoting someone, the plums always go to those who do the best job filling out accounting-department forms." This is one of the most common tunes, sung with infinite variations on every level of management. It leads to poor performance — even in cutting the costs. It also expresses loss of confidence in, and absence of respect for, the company and its management.

Yet the manager who so misdirects subordinates does not intend to do so, although it is a universal problem. Let's take for example, Bob Michalak, an upper-level manager in a steel mill. He genuinely considers human relations to be the most important task of his plant managers. But he talks about cost control because he feels that he has to establish himself with his men as a "practical man," or because he thinks that he shows familiarity with their problems by talking their "shop." He stresses the accounting-department forms only because they annoy him as much as they do his men — or he may just not want to have any more trouble with the comptroller than he can help. But to his subordinates these reasons are hidden; all they see and hear is the question about the costs, the emphasis on forms.

The solution to this problem requires a structure of management which focuses both the manager's and the boss's eyes on what the job — rather than the boss — demands. To stress behavior and attitudes — as does a good deal of current management literature — cannot solve the problem. It is likely instead to aggravate it by making managers self-conscious in their relationships. Indeed, everyone familiar with business today has seen situations in which a manager's attempt to avoid misdirection through changing his or her behavior has converted a fairly satisfactory relationship into a nightmare of embarrassment and misunderstanding.   The manager has become so self-conscious as to lose all easy relationship with his or her subordinates.   And the subordinates in turn react with: "So help us, the old bird has read a book; we used to know what was wanted of us, now we have to guess."

Differences in Levels of Management

The misdirection that can result from the difference in concern and function between various levels of management is illustrated by this story.   I call it "the mystery of the broken washroom door."

> The newly appointed comptroller of a railroad in the Northwest noticed, when going through the accounts, that extraordinarily large sums were spent each year for the replacement of broken doors in passenger stations. He found that washroom doors in small stations were supposed to be kept locked, with the key obtainable from the ticket agent on request.   For economy reasons the agent was only issued one key per door — a long-defunct president had decreed this economy measure and had preened himself on thus saving the company two hundred dollars at one stroke.   Hence when a customer walked off without returning the key — as happened all the time — the agent had a locked door on his hands and no means of opening it.   To get a new key made — cost twenty cents — was, however, regarded as a "capital expenditure"; and agents could make capital expenditures only with the approval of the Superintendent of Passenger Service at company headquarters, which it took six months to obtain. "Emergency repairs," however, an agent could make on his own and pay for out of his cash account.   There could be no clearer emergency than a broken washroom door — and every small station has an ax!

This may seem the height of absurdity.   But every business has its "broken washroom doors," its misdirections, its policies, procedures, and methods that emphasize and reward wrong behavior, penalize or inhibit right behavior.   In most cases the results are more serious than an annual twenty-thousand-dollar bill for washroom doors.

This problem, too, cannot be solved by attitudes and behavior; for it is rooted in the structure of the enterprise.   Nor can it be solved by "better communications"; for communications presuppose common understanding and a common language, and it is precisely that which is usually lacking.

> It is no accident that the old story of the blind men meeting up with an elephant on the road is so popular among management people.   For each level of management sees the same "elephant" — the business — from a different angle of vision.   The production foreman, like the blind man who felt the elephant's leg and decided that a tree was in his way, tends to see only the immediate production problems.   Top management — the blind man feeling the trunk and deciding a snake bars his way — tends to see only the enterprise as a whole; it sees stockholders, financial problems, altogether a host of highly abstract relations and figures.   Operating management — the blind man feeling the elephant's belly and thinking himself up against a landslide — tends to see things functionally.   Each level needs its particular vision; it could not do its job without it.   Yet, these visions are so different that people on different levels talking about the same thing often do not realize it — or, as fre-

quently happens, believe that they are talking about the same thing, when in reality they are poles apart.

An effective management must direct the vision and efforts of all managers toward a common goal. It must insure that individual managers understand what results are demanded of them. It must insure that superiors understand what to expect of each of their subordinate managers. It must motivate each manager to maximum efforts in the right direction. And while encouraging high standards of workmanship, it must make them the means to the end of business performance rather than ends in themselves.

What Should the Objectives of a Manager Be?

Each manager, from the "big boss" down to the production supervisor or the chief clerk, needs clearly spelled-out objectives. These objectives should lay out what performance each managerial person's own unit is supposed to produce. They should lay out what contribution the manager and the manager's unit are expected to make to help other units obtain their objectives. Finally, they should spell out what contribution the manager can expect from other units toward the attainment of his or her own objectives. Right from the start, in other words, emphasis should be on teamwork and team results.

These objectives should always derive from the goals of the business enterprise. In one company, I have found it practicable and effective to provide even a supervisor with a detailed statement of not only his or her own objectives but those of the company and of the manufacturing department. Even though the company is so large as to make the distance between the individual supervisor's production and the company's total output all but astronomical, the result has been a significant increase in production. Indeed, this must follow if we mean it when we say that the supervisor is "part of management." For it is the definition of a manager that in what managers do they take responsibility for the whole — that, in cutting stone, they "build a cathedral."

The objectives of all managers should spell out their contribution to the attainment of company goals in *all areas* of the business. Obviously, not every manager has a direct contribution to make in every area. The contribution which marketing makes to productivity, for example, may be very small. But if a manager and his or her unit are not expected to contribute toward any one of the areas that significantly affect prosperity and survival of the business, this fact should be clearly brought out. For managers must understand that business results depend on a balance of efforts and results in a number of areas. This is necessary both to give full scope to the craftsmanship of each function and specialty, and to prevent the empire-building and clannish jealousies of the various functions and specialties. It is necessary also to avoid overemphasis on any one key area.

To obtain balanced efforts the objectives of all managers on all levels and in all areas should also be keyed to both short-range and long-range considerations. And, of course, all objectives should always contain both the tangible business objectives and the intangible objectives for manager organization and development, worker performance and attitude, and public responsibility. Anything else is shortsighted and impractical.

Management by "Drives"

Proper management requires balanced stress on objectives, especially by top management. It rules out the common and harmful business malpractice: management by "crisis" and "drives."

There may be companies in which management people do not say: "The only way we ever get anything done around here is by making a drive on it." Yet, "management by drive" is the rule rather than the exception. That things always collapse into the *status quo ante* three weeks after the drive is over, everybody knows and apparently expects. The only result of an "economy drive" is likely to be that messengers and typists get fired, and that $35,000 executives are forced to do $150-a-week work typing their own letters. And yet many managements have not drawn the obvious conclusion that drives are, after all, not the way to get things done.

But over and above its ineffectiveness, management by drive misdirects. It puts all emphasis on one phase of the job to the inevitable detriment of everything else.

> "For four weeks we cut inventories," a case-hardened veteran of management by crisis once summed it up. "Then we have four weeks of cost-cutting, followed by four weeks of human relations. We just have time to push customer service and courtesy for a month. And then the inventory is back where it was when we started. We don't even try to do our job. All management talks about, thinks about, preaches about, is last week's inventory figure or this week's customer complaints. How we do the rest of the job they don't even want to know."

In an organization which manages by drives people either neglect their job to get on with the current drive, or silently organize for collective sabotage of the drive to get their work done. In either event they become deaf to the cry of "wolf." And when the real crisis comes, when all hands should drop everything and pitch in, they treat it as just another case of management-created hysteria.

Management by drive is a sure sign of confusion. It is an admission of incompetence. It is a sign that management does not know how to plan. But, above all, it is a sign that the company does not know what to expect of its managers — that, not knowing how to direct them, it misdirects them.

How Should Managers' Objectives Be Set and by Whom?

By definition, managers are responsible for the contribution that their component makes to the larger unit directly above and eventually to the entire enterprise. Managerial performance aims upward rather than downward. This means that the goals of each manager's job must be defined by the contribution he or she has to make to the success of the larger unit of which they are a part. The job objectives of district sales managers should be defined by the contribution they and their district sales forces have to make to the sales department. The objectives of the general manager of a decentralized division should be defined by the contribution his or her division has to make to the objectives of the parent company.

This requires all managers to develop and set their own objectives for themselves and their units. Higher management must, of course, reserve the power to approve or disapprove these objectives. But their development is part of a manager's responsibility; indeed, it is a manager's first responsibility. It means, too, that every manager should responsibly participate in the development of the objectives of the higher unit of which his or her unit is a part. To "give a manager a sense of participation" (to use a pet phrase of the "human relations" jargon) is not enough. Being a manager demands the assumption of genuine responsibility. Precisely because their aims should reflect the objective needs of the business, rather than merely what individual managers want, they must commit themselves to their aims with a positive act of assent. They must know and understand the ultimate business goals, what is expected of them and why, what they will be measured against and how. There must be a "meeting of minds" within the entire management of each unit. This can be achieved only when each of the contributing managers is expected to think through what the unit objectives are, is led, in other words, to participate actively and responsibly in the work of defining them. And only if lower managers participate in this way can a higher manager know what to expect of them and make exacting demands.

This is so important that some of the most effective managers I know go one step further. They have each of their subordinates write a "manager's letter" twice a year. In this letter to his or her superior, each manager first defines the objectives of the superior's job and of their own job as they see them. For example, manager Jane Smith sets down the performance standards which she believes are being applied to her. Next, she lists the things she must do herself to attain these goals — and the things within her own unit she considers the major obstacles. She lists the things her superior and the company do that help her and the things that hamper her. Finally, she outlines what she proposes to do during the next year to reach her goals. If her superior accepts this statement, the "manager's letter" becomes the charter under which the manager operates.

This device, like no other I have seen, brings out how easily the unconsidered and casual remarks of even the best "boss" can confuse and misdirect. One large company has used the "manager's letter" for ten years. Yet almost every letter still lists as objectives and standards things which completely baffle the superior to whom the letter is addressed. And whenever the superior asks: "What is this?" the answer is: "Don't you remember what you said last spring going down with me in the elevator?"

The "manager's letter" also brings out whatever inconsistencies there are in the demands made on a manager by his or her superior and by the company. Does the superior demand both speed and high quality when only one or the other is practical? And what compromise is needed in the interest of the company? Does the superior demand initiative and judgment of his managers but also that they obtain approval before they do anything? Does the superior ask for their ideas and suggestions but never uses them or discusses them? Does the company expect a small engineering force to be available immediately whenever something goes wrong in the plant, and yet bend all its efforts to the completion of new designs? Does it expect a manager to maintain high standards of performance but forbid that same manager to remove poor performers? Does it create the conditions under which people say: "I can get the work done as long as I can keep the boss from knowing what I am doing?"

These are common situations. They undermine spirit and performance. The "manager's letter" may not prevent them. But at least it brings them out in the open, shows where compromises have to be made, objectives have to be thought through, priorities have to be established, behavior has to be changed.

As this device illustrates: managing managers requires special efforts not only to establish common direction, but to eliminate misdirection. Mutual understanding can never be attained by "communications down," can never be created by talking. It can result only from "communications up." It requires both the superior's willingness to listen and a tool especially designed to make lower managers heard.

Self-control through Measurements

The greatest advantage of management by objectives is perhaps that it makes it possible for managers to control their own performance. Self-control means stronger motivation: a desire to do the best rather than just enough to get by. It means higher performance goals and broader vision. Even if management by objectives were not necessary to give the enterprise the unity of direction and effort of a management team, it would be necessary to make possible management by self-control.

So far I have not talked of "control" at all; I have talked of "measurements." This was intentional. For "control" is an ambiguous word. It means the ability to direct oneself and one's work. It can also mean domination of one person by another. Objectives are the basis of "control" in the first sense; but they must never become the basis of "control" in the second, for this would defeat their purpose. Indeed, one of the major contributions of management by objectives is that it enables us to substitute management by self-control for management by domination.

That management by self-control is highly desirable will hardly be disputed in America or in American business today. Its acceptance underlies all the talk of "pushing decisions down to the lowest possible level," or of "paying people for results." But to make management by self-control a reality requires more than acceptance of the concept as right and desirable. It requires new tools and far-reaching changes in traditional thinking and practices.

To be able to control their own performance, managers need to know more than what their goals are. They must be able to measure their performance and results against the goal. It should indeed be an invariable practice to supply managers with clear and common measurements in all key areas of a business. These measurements need not be rigidly quantitative; nor need they be precise. But they have to be clear, simple, and rational. They have to be relevant and direct attention and efforts to where they should go. They have to be reliable — at least to the point where their margin of error is acknowledged and understood. And they have to be, so to speak, self-announcing, understandable without complicated interpretation or philosophical discussion.

Each manager should have the information needed to measure his or her own performance and should receive it soon enough to make any changes necessary for the desired results. And this information should go to the manager and not to the superior. It should be the means of self-control, not a tool of control from above.

This needs particular stress today, when our ability to obtain such information is growing rapidly as a result of technological progress in information gathering and synthesis. Up till now information on important facts was either not obtainable at all, or could be assembled only so late as to be of little but historical interest. This former inability to produce measuring information was not an unmixed curse. For while it made effective self-control difficult, it also made difficult effective control of managers from above; in the absence of information with which to control them, managers had to be allowed to work as they saw fit.

Our new ability to produce measuring information will make possible effective self-control; and if so used, it will lead to a tremendous advance in the effectiveness and performance of management. But if this new ability is abused to impose control on managers from above, the new technology will inflict incalculable harm by demoralizing management, and by seriously lowering the effectiveness of managers. And care must be taken to keep controls within a proper overall perspective, else what will happen is that managers will run their units not to obtain the best performance but to obtain the best showing of the control-measurement information.

This should not be misunderstood as advocacy of low performance standards or absence of control. On the contrary, management by objectives and self-control is primarily a means to obtain standards higher than are to be found in most companies today. And every manager should be held strictly accountable for the results of his or her performance.

But what managers do to reach these results they — and only they — should control. It should be clearly understood what behavior and methods the company bars as unethical, unprofessional or unsound. But within these limits managers must be free to decide what they must do. And only if they have all the information regarding their operations can they fully be held accountable for results.

The Proper Use of Reports and Procedures

Management by self-control requires complete rethinking concerning our use of reports, procedures, and forms.

Reports and procedures are necessary tools. But few tools can be so easily misused, and few can do as much damage. For reports and procedures, when misused, cease to be tools and become malignant masters.

There are three common misuses of reports and procedures. The first is the all too common belief that procedures are instruments of morality. They are not; their principle is exclusively that of economy. They never decide what should be done, only how it might be done most expeditiously. Problems of right conduct can never be "proceduralized" (surely the most horrible word in the bureaucrat's jargon); conversely, right conduct can never be established by procedure.

The second misuse is to consider procedures a substitute for judgment. Procedures can work only where judgment is no longer required, that is, in the repetitive situation for whose handling the judgment has already been supplied and tested. Our civilization suffers from a superstitious belief in the magical effect of printed forms. And the superstition is most dangerous when it leads us into trying to handle the exceptional, nonroutine situation by procedure. In fact, it is the test of a good procedure that it quickly identifies the situations that, even in the most routine of processes, do not fit the pattern but require special handling and decision based on judgment.

But the most common misuse of reports and procedures is as an instrument of control from above. This is particularly true of those that aim at supplying information to higher management — the "forms" of everyday business life. As only one of thousands of examples, let us take another look at the case of Bob Michalak, the steel-mill manager. He has to fill out twenty forms to supply accountants, engineers, or staff people in the central office with information he himself does not need. As a result the man's attention is directed away from his own job. The things he is asked about or required to do for control purposes come to appear to him as reflections of what the company wants of him, become to him the essence of his job; while resenting them, he tends to put effort into these things rather than into his own job. Eventually, his boss, too, is misdirected, if not hypnotized, by the procedure.

> A large insurance company, a few years ago, started a big program for the "improvement of management." To this end it built up a strong central-office organization concerned with such things as renewing policies, claim settlement, selling costs, sales methods, etc. This organization did excellent work — top management learned a lot about running an insurance company. But actual performance has been going down ever since. For the managers in the field spend more and more time filling out reports, less and less doing their work. Worse still, they soon learned to subordinate performance to a "good showing." Not only did performance go to pieces — spirit suffered even more. Top management and its staff experts came to be viewed by the field managers as enemies to be outsmarted or at least kept as far away as possible.

Similar stories exist *ad infinitum* — in every industry and in companies of every size.

Reports and procedures should be kept to a minimum, and used only when they save time and labor. They should be as simple as possible.

> One of our leading company presidents tells the following story on himself. Thirty years ago he bought for his company a small independent plant in Los Angeles. The plant had been making a profit of $250,000 a year; and it was purchased on that basis. When going through the plant with the original owner — who stayed on as plant manager — the president asked: "How do you determine your pricing?" "That's easy," the former owner answered; "we just quote ten cents per thousand less than your company does." "And how do you control your costs?" was the next question. "That's easy," was the answer; "we know what we pay for raw materials and labor and what production we ought to get for the money." "And how do you control your overhead?" was the final question. "We don't bother about it."
>
> Well, thought the president, we can certainly save a lot of money here by introducing our thorough controls. But a year later the profit of the plant was down to $125,000; sales had remained the same and prices had remained the same; but the introduction of complex procedures had eaten up half the profit.

Every business should regularly find out whether it needs all the reports and procedures it uses. At least once every five years every form should be put on trial for its life. I once had to recommend an even more drastic measure to clear up a situation in which reports and forms, luxuriating like the Amazon rain forest, threatened to choke the life out of an old established utility company. I suggested that all reports be suspended simultaneously for two months, and only those be allowed to return which managers still demanded after living without them. This cut reports and forms in the company by three quarters.

Reports and procedures should focus only on the performance needed to achieve results in the key areas. To "control" everything is to control nothing. And to attempt to control the irrelevant always misdirects.

Finally, reports and procedures should be the tool of the person who fills them out. They must never themselves become the measure of that person's performance. If Jane Smith fills out forms, she must never be judged by the quality of the production forms she fills out — unless she be the clerk in charge of these forms. She must always be judged by her production performance. And the only way to make sure of this is by having her fill out no forms, make no reports, except those she needs herself to achieve performance.

A Philosophy of Management

What the business enterprise needs is a principle of management that will give full scope to individual strength and responsibility, and at the same time give common direction of vision and effort, establish team work and harmonize the goals of the individual with the common welfare.

The only principle that can do this is management by objectives and self-control. It makes common welfare the aim of every manager. It substitutes for control from outside the stricter, more exacting, and more effective control from the inside. It motivates managers to action not because somebody tells them to do something or talks them into doing it, but because the objective needs of their tasks demand it. Managers act not because somebody wants them to but because they themselves decide that they have to — they act, in other words, freely.

The word "philosophy" is tossed around with happy abandon these days in management circles. I have even seen a dissertation, signed by a vice-president, on the "philosophy of handling purchase requisitions" (as far as I could figure out "philosophy" here meant that purchase requisitions had to be in triplicate). But management by objectives and self-control may legitimately be called a "philosophy" of management. It rests on a concept of the job of management. It rests on an analysis of the specific needs of the management group and the obstacles it faces. It rests on a concept of human action, human behavior, and human motivation. Finally, it applies to all managers, whatever their level and function, and to any business enterprise whether large or small. It insures performance by converting objective needs into personal goals. And this is genuine freedom, freedom under the law.

From Middle Management to Knowledge Organization

Chapter 8

Middle Management's Predicted Demise
And the Middle Management Boom
The Needed Correction
The Danger of Overstaffing
Where the Growth Occurred
The Emergence of the Knowledge Professional
The New Middle Manager: Middle Rank but Top-Management
        "Impacts"
The Knowledge Organization
Middle-Management Job Design
The Need for Clear Decision Authority
Top Management's Role in the Knowledge Organization
Middle Managers: "Juniors" and "Colleagues" Rather than
        "Subordinates"

*I*n the early fifties when computer and automation were the headline makers, the imminent demise of middle management was widely predicted. By 1980, we were told by a number of experts, middle management would have disappeared. All decisions would be made by the computer or by top management on the basis of a "total information system."

Very few predictions have been disproven so fast and so completely. At the very time the predictions were being widely publicized, the middle-management boom began.

And it kept going for twenty years. Indeed, the fifties and the sixties might have been called the era of middle management. No other group in the work force, in all developed countries, has been growing as fast.

Here are some examples from manufacturing, that is, from the economic sector where automation has been most widely applied and where computers have become as commonplace, at least in big companies, as smokestacks were a few generations ago. One of the large American automobile companies recently built a major manufacturing plant to turn out the entire production of a new model. It was the company's first major automotive plant since 1949, when a similar plant, designed for a similar production volume, was opened. The number of rank-and-file employees, both blue-collar and clerical, is almost one-third less than that of the earlier plant — the result, however, of normal increases in productivity rather than of a shift of the process to automation. The top-management group in the new plant is about the same size. But the middle-management group, that is, the group that is paid more than a general supervisor and less than the plant's general manager, is almost five times the size of the middle-management group in the 1949 plant.

Another manufacturing company — a producer of a wide range of industrial components — grew between 1950 and 1970 from a sales volume of $10 million to one of $100 million. In terms of units the growth was fivefold. During this period of rapid expansion, the top-management group grew from three men to five. Rank-and-file employment grew from 1,000 to 4,000. The middle-management ranks, again defined by salary, grew from 14 to 235 — that is, almost seventeen times — and this does not include sales personnel.

These examples actually understate the growth rate of middle management. During the period in which middle management was expected to disappear, the center of economic gravity and growth shifted to industries that have a much higher ratio of middle managers in their employ than have the industries which dominated the business scene in 1950. The symbol of economic dynamism in the United States economy of 1970 was no longer General Motors. It was IBM. And at IBM, or at any other computer manufacturer, the middle group is far bigger than in traditional manufacturing industries such as automobile or steel. The same is true of the pharmaceutical companies which grew so rapidly in the twenty years between 1950 and 1970.

Outside of manufacturing industries the growth has been even more rapid. It has been particularly pronounced in the nonbusiness service institutions. The prototype is the hospital.

Top management in the hospital — however one defines it — has not grown. There is still the hospital administrator, perhaps with an assistant, in the larger hospital. In the community hospitals there are trustees and a medical director. Rank-and-file employment in terms of number of employees per patient day has gone down rather than up. It is in the kitchen, in maintenance, and in the other rank-and-file areas that hospitals have become somewhat less labor-intensive. But the middle ranks — technicians, engineers, accountants, psychologists, and social workers — have exploded. They have grown at least fourfold — in some big teaching hospitals even faster.

The Needed Correction

Growth at fast rates always overshoots the target. It is bound to be disorderly and wasteful. There is overstaffing because it is the fashion to go in for this or that activity whether needed or not. There is overstaffing because times are good and it is easier to accede to a demand for more people than to fight it. And in such a period of explosive growth no one pays much attention to the organization of the work. Yet expansion of such magnitude is always qualitative change rather than mere additional quantity. If the work and its organization are not studied and changed, waste, duplication of effort, and organizational obesity follow.

The middle-management boom therefore had to lead, like any other boom, to a "middle-management depression." At the first significant economic setback there had to be a sharp correction. This came in the United States with the 1970/71 recession, although the reaction was mild: it consisted of a sharp two-year curtailment of college recruiting for management and professional positions, with very few layoffs of middle-management people already on the payroll (except in the particularly distressed aerospace and defense industries).

Such a reaction, however painful, is fundamentally healthy. It always goes too far, of course. But at least it forces management to think through what the work is and what it needs. Such thinking is particularly important with respect to middle-management work. There are few areas where overstaffing does as much damage as in the middle-management group. It costs a great deal more than money. It costs performance and motivation.

The Danger of Overstaffing

Knowledge work — that is, the specific work of middle managers — should always be demanding. It should be lean, and err, if at all, on the side of understaffing. An overstaffed middle-management organization destroys motivation. It destroys accomplishment, achievement, and satisfaction. In the end, it destroys performance.

The middle-management boom and the resulting overstaffing, especially in larger companies, did indeed undermine morale and motivation. Overstaffing is a main reason for the dissatisfaction and disenchantment of so many of the young middle-rank people, managers and career professionals, whom business, governments, school systems, and hospitals recruited in such large numbers during the fifties and sixties. They are well paid and well treated; but there is not enough for them to do, not enough challenge, not enough contribution, not enough accomplishment, and too much sheer busyness. There are too many bodies busily "interacting" with each other rather than doing their own work. When the able young educated people, e.g., the brightest graduates of the leading American business schools, are asked to explain their growing preference for a job in a small company or in the medium-sized city administration, they always say, "At least I'll have something to do."

The first lesson is to keep the middle ranks lean. "What really needs to be done?" is the first question. And the second and equally important one is "What no longer needs to be done and should be cut back or cut out?" The first lesson is the *need for weight control.*

In particular this means that a new middle-management activity should, as a rule, be sanctioned only if an old one is sloughed off or, at least, pruned back. The middle-management budget needs to be constantly watched to make sure that good, performing people are allocated to opportunities, to results, and to making the future rather than wasted on problems, busyness, and on defending the past.

What needs even more thought and attention is, however, the work of middle management and its organization: The expansion of the middle ranks not only produced a qualitative change — it was itself produced by a change in the nature of the middle-management function.

Middle management will, it is safe to predict, continue to expand. But future growth will have to be directed, controlled, managed. It will have to be based on an understanding of the changing nature of middle management and of the resulting need for change in function, relationship, and structure.

Where the Growth Occurred

The middle management of forty years ago has not disappeared. Rather it has grown, and quite substantially. There are today proportionately more plant managers around, more district sales managers, and more branch managers in banks than there were before World War II.

But the real growth of middle-rank people in management jobs has been in manufacturing engineers and process specialists; in tax accountants and market analysts; in product and market managers; in advertising and promotion specialists. It has been in a host of functions which, a generation ago, were hardly known. The new middle managers are the knowledge professionals.

The traditional middle manager is essentially a commander of men and women. The new middle manager is essentially a supplier of knowledge. The traditional middle manager has authority downward, over subordinates. The new middle manager essentially has responsibility sideways and upward, that is, to people over whom he or she exercises no command authority.

Above all, the job of traditional middle managers was largely routine. They did not make decisions. They carried them out. At the most, they implemented the decisions and adapted them to local conditions. Their job was to keep running a system that they had neither designed nor were expected to alter.

This underlay, of course, the traditional definition of a manager as someone who is responsible for the work of others rather than responsible for his or her own work. It also underlay the traditional social structure of management outside the U.S. and Japan, especially in Europe.

In the United States and Japan top management has traditionally been recruited from middle management, that is, from people who worked their way up in the business. In European countries this was not the pattern. In England there was — and to some extent still is — a tremendous gulf between managers and "the board," that is, top management. Even in large companies the board was until recently recruited from people who had never discharged operating management functions, if not from people who had never worked in a business, such as distinguished former public servants. In Holland top management, even in the large and professionally managed companies, rarely comes out of operations. In the large French company all positions in top and senior management are typically held by graduates of the *Grandes Écoles*. Most of them, especially top-management people, make their careers in government and then move directly into senior management jobs in business. Operating managers who come up in the business are normally considered unfit for top jobs, even if they are university graduates. The Germans tend to draw a sharp line between *Führung*, i.e., top management, and *Leitung*, operating management.

The Decision Impact of the New Middle Manager

But as the new middle people are knowledge professionals, their actions and decisions are intended to have direct and major impact on the business, its ability to perform, and its direction.

Here are some fairly typical examples.

The product manager in companies such as Procter & Gamble's soap and detergent business, in Unilever's food business, or in the radio and TV business of Philips of Holland, is definitely middle management by rank and compensation. The product manager has no command authority. The work is being carried out by people who report to their respective functional bosses, the manufacturing manager, the sales manager, the head of the chemical and development laboratories, and so on. But the product manager is held responsible for the development, the introduction, and the performance of a product in the marketplace. The product manager also: decides very largely whether a new product should indeed be developed; decides what its specifications should be; determines its price; decides where and how to test-market it; and decides the sales goals. The product manager does not have any direct command authority and cannot issue an order, but does directly control a major determinant of performance and success for a branded consumer product, the advertising and promotion budget.

The quality control engineer in a machine tool company also has no command authority and no subordinates. But the quality control engineer decides the design and structure of the manufacturing process by setting quality control standards which largely decide the costs of the manufacturing process and the performance of the manufacturing plant. The manufacturing manager or the plant manager does indeed make the decisions. But the quality control engineer can veto them.

The tax accountant also has no command, can give no orders, and often has no subordinates except a secretary. Yet, in effect, the tax accountant has a veto power over even top-management decisions by rendering opinions on the tax consequences of a course of action which often determine both what a company can do and how it must do it.

The product manager of Procter & Gamble, the quality engineer, and the tax accountant are not "line" managers. But neither are they "staff." Their function is not advice and teaching. They do "operating" work. Yet they have top-management impacts even though they are not top management in rank, compensation, or function.

To be sure, they cannot make some of the key decisions — what our business is and what it should be; what its objectives are; what the priorities are and should be; where to allocate key resources of capital and people. But even with respect to these decisions they contribute the essential knowledge without which the key decisions cannot be made, at least not effectively. And the key decisions cannot become effective unless these new middle managers build them into their own knowledge and work on their own responsibility and on their own authority. Earlier it was argued that knowledge professionals are managers even though no one reports to them. Now we see that in their impacts and responsibilities they are top management even though they may be five or six organizational levels down.

The Knowledge Organization

Middle management has not disappeared, as was predicted. Indeed not even the traditional middle manager has disappeared. But yesterday's middle management is being transformed into tomorrow's *knowledge organization.*

This requires restructuring individual jobs, but also restructuring the organization and its design. In the knowledge organization the job, all the way down to the lowest professional or managerial level, has to focus on the company's objectives. It has to focus on contribution, which means that it has to have its own objectives. It has to be organized according to assignment. It has to be thought through and structured according to the flow of information both to and from the individual position. And it has to be placed into the decision structure. It can no longer be designed, as was the traditional middle-management job, in terms of downward authority alone. It has to be recognized instead as multidimensional.

Traditionally, middle-management jobs have been designed narrowly. The first concern has been with the limits on a middle manager's authority. In the knowledge organization we will instead have to ask, "What is the greatest possible contribution this job can make?" The focus will have to shift from concern with authority to stress on responsibility.

The Need for Clear Decision Authority

The knowledge organization demands clear decision authority. It demands clear thinking through what decision belongs where. The knowledge organization is far more complex than the simple "line" organization it is replacing. Unless decision authority is clearly spelled out, the knowledge organization will tend to become confused.

The knowledge organization is also designed to take greater risks. Operating no longer is a "routine" in which the norms are clear. It is a decision-making organization rather than one that has no other function than to keep the machinery running at a known speed and for known results. Things, therefore, will go wrong, and in unexpected ways. And unless authority to change the decision is built into the decision itself, malfunction is bound to result.

A major pharmaceutical company decided to introduce seven new products in one year — twice as many as the company had ever introduced before in a single year. An elaborate multinational strategy was worked out in year-long sessions of task forces assembled from all functions, all levels, and all major territories. Some products were to be introduced first into European markets, some into the American market, some first with general practitioners of medicine, others with specialists or in hospitals. When the products were brought out, however, the two which had been considered the weakest unexpectedly developed into best sellers. But the two supposedly strongest products ran into unforeseen troubles which sharply slowed down their growth. In working out the strategy, no one had asked, "If things do not work out as planned, who is going to be responsible for changing the plan?" As a result, there were endless reports, endless studies, endless meetings — and no action. In the end, the company lost much of the benefit of its accomplishments. The two products that had shown unexpected success did not receive the support needed to exploit their acceptance by the medical profession. Competitors who moved in with near-imitations were therefore able to reap most of the harvest. Clinical testing and marketing efforts on the two products that had run into unexpected difficulties should either have been cut back sharply or should have been raised sharply. Everyone saw that; but no one had the authority to make the decision.

In the knowledge organization of the new middle management any program, any project, and any plan will have to ask and answer the question "Who has the authority to change the plan?" And this will lead to far greater devolution of authority to middle people than even the American middle management tradition ever envisaged. Even line managers will need more rather than less authority in the knowledge organization. Line managers must also be part of the decision and understand what it implies. They must be given authority commensurate to their responsibility — and this is not knowledge authority, but command authority. Or, if in any area they cannot be given command authority which their task — and their people — require, it must be perfectly clear, above all to line managers, where the command authority lies.

Top Management's Role in the Knowledge Organization

In the knowledge organization, top management can no longer assume that the "operating people" do as they are being told. It has to accept that the middle ranks make genuine decisions. But the operating organization can also no longer assume that it can do its job in isolation from top management. It must understand the top-management decisions. Indeed middle management in the knowledge organization must take responsibility for "educating" top management. Top management must understand what the knowledge organization tries to do, what it is capable of doing, and where it sees the major opportunities, the major needs, the major challenges to the enterprise. Finally, middle management must insist that top management make decisions on what the business is and what it should be, on objectives, strategies, and priorities. Otherwise the middle ranks cannot do their own job.

Top management needs to know the knowledge organization and to understand it. It needs to establish communication with it. The traditional assumption that the people in top management know the middle manager's job because they have been through it is no longer going to be valid. Even the people who have risen into top management through the middle-management organization can no longer expect to have been exposed directly to more than a small sample of the functional work of the knowledge organization. And some of the most important areas of middle management will no longer pre-pare and test a person for top-management positions.

Indeed the most capable men and women in such areas will not even want to get into top-management work but will prefer to stay in their specialty. The computer spe-cialist wants, as a rule, to stay within that specialization and work on information and in-formation technology. Equally, most researchers want to stay in research, whether in physical and technical fields, in research on people, or in economic research.

Middle managers in knowledge organizations can no longer be taken for granted and be treated with condescension as people who, after all, do only routine tasks and only carry out and implement top-management decisions and orders. If it wants to be effec-tive, top management therefore needs to establish team work with, and communications from and to, the knowledge organization.

The most important "public" in the knowledge organization for top management — and the one that most needs a relationship to top management — are the younger and highly specialized knowledge workers. They are least likely to understand what top man-agement is trying to do, least likely to see the business whole, least likely to focus them-selves on company objectives and performance. Yet they are likely, because of their knowledge, to have impact early in their careers. In any business of any size or com-plexity the top-management group needs to organize its relationship to these younger knowledge professionals.

Each member of the top-management team might sit down a few times a year with a group of younger knowledge people and say to them, "I have no agenda. I have nothing I want to tell you. I am here to listen. It is your job to tell me what you think we in top management need to know about your work and how you think we can make it most productive. It is your job to tell me where you see the problems and opportunities for this company and to tell me what we in top management do to help you in your job and what we do that hampers you. I shall insist on only one thing: that *you* have done *your* homework and that you take seriously your responsibility to inform and to educate."

But altogether in the knowledge organization it becomes a top-management job to mobilize, to organize, to place, and to direct knowledge. Knowledge people — and that means managers and career professionals in today's organization — cannot be seen and treated as inferiors. They are middle in rank, pay, authority. But they are juniors and colleagues rather than subordinates.

"Management" means, in the last analysis, the substitution of thought for brawn and muscle, of knowledge for folkways and superstition, and of cooperation for force. It means the substitution of responsibility for obedience to rank, and of authority of per-formance for authority of power. The knowledge organization, therefore, is what man-agement theory, management thinking, management aspirations have been about, all along. But now the knowledge organization is becoming accomplished fact. The tremen-dous expansion of managerial employment since World War II converted the middle ranks into knowledge professionals — that is, people paid for putting knowledge to work and to make decisions based on their knowledge which have impact on performance capacity, results, and future directions of the whole enterprise. The task of making these new knowledge people in the middle ranks truly effective and achieving has barely begun. It is a central task in managing managers.

Staffing for Excellence

Chapter 9

Effective Staffing Aims to Build on Strength, Not to Avoid Weakness
The Idea Is to Make Employees' Strengths Effective, Their Weaknesses
Irrelevant
Avoiding the Trap of Staffing to Suit Personality: Make Sure the Job Is
Well Designed; Make Each Job Demanding and Big; To Get
Strength Often Means Tolerating Weaknesses
How to Manage the Boss

*E*ffective managers make strength productive. They know that they cannot build on weakness. To get results, they use all the available strengths — of associates, of superiors, and their own strengths. To make strength productive is the unique purpose of organizations.

The manager first encounters the challenge of strength in staffing. The effective manager fills positions and promotes on the basis of what a man or woman can do, making staffing decisions not to minimize weaknesses, but to maximize strength. President Lincoln, when told that General Grant, his new commander-in-chief, was fond of the bottle, is reported to have said: "If I knew his brand, I'd send a barrel or so to some other generals." After a childhood on the Kentucky and Illinois frontier, Lincoln assuredly knew all about the bottle and its dangers. But of all the Union generals, Grant alone had proved consistently capable of winning campaigns. Grant's appointment was the turning point of the Civil War. It was an effective appointment because Lincoln chose his general for his ability to win battles, not for the absence of a weakness.

Lincoln learned this the hard way, however. Before he chose Grant, he had appointed in succession three or four generals whose main qualifications were their lack of major weaknesses.

In sharp contrast, Robert E. Lee had staffed the Confederate forces from strength. Every one of his generals was a man of obvious and monumental weaknesses. But these failings Lee considered — rightly — to be irrelevant. Each of them had one area of real strength, and it was only this strength that Lee utilized and made effective.

One of his generals, the story goes, had disregarded orders and completely upset Lee's plans — and not for the first time. Lee, who normally controlled his temper, blew up in a towering rage. When he had simmered down, one of his aides asked respectfully, "Why don't you relieve him of his command?" Lee, it is said, turned around in complete amazement, looked at the aide and said, "What an absurd question — he performs."

Effective Staffing Aims to Build on Strength, Not to Avoid Weakness

The executive who is concerned with what a person cannot do rather than with what that person can do, and therefore tries to avoid weakness rather than make strength effective, is probably a weak executive. Such an executive probably sees strength in others as a threat. But no executive has ever suffered because of subordinates who were strong and effective.

Effective executives know that their subordinates are paid to perform, not to please their superiors. It does not matter how many tantrums a temperamental soprano or tenor throws as long as they bring in the customers.

Effective executives never ask, "How does he get along with me?" Their question is "What does he contribute?" It is always, "What can she do uncommonly well?" They look for excellence in a major area, and not for performance that simply gets by all around. The executive who does not first ask, "What can a person do?" is bound to accept far less than that person can really contribute. The executive thereby excuses nonperformance in advance. The really "demanding" boss — and all effective executives are demanding bosses in one way or another — always starts out with what a person should be able to do well — and then demands that that person do it.

Building against weakness frustrates the purpose of organization. But one can so structure an organization that the weaknesses become a personal blemish outside of, or at least beside, the work and accomplishment. A good tax accountant, for example John Jones, might be greatly hampered in private practice by an inability to get along with people. But in an organization he can be set up in an office of his own and shielded from contact with others: One can make his strength effective, his weakness irrelevant. The executive who understands that it is his or her job to enable John Jones to do his tax accounting has no illusions about Jones's ability to get along with people.

All this is obvious. Why, then, is it not done all the time?

The main reason is that the immediate task of the executive is not to place a man or woman. It is to fill a job. The tendency is therefore to start out with the job, and then look for someone to fill it. It is only too easy to be misled this way into looking for the "least misfit" — the one person who leaves least to be desired. And this invariably results in mediocrity.

The widely advertised "cure" for this is to structure jobs to fit the personalities available. But this cure is worse than the disease — except perhaps in a very small and simple organization. Jobs have to be objective, determined by task rather than personality.

One reason for this is that every change in the definition, structure, and position of a job within an organization sets off a chain reaction. Jobs in an organization are interdependent and interlocked. One cannot change everybody's work and responsibility just because one has to replace a single person in a single job: It results in a dozen people being uprooted and pushed around in order to accommodate the one person.

But there is a subtler reason for insistence on impersonal, objective jobs. It is the only way to provide the organization with the human diversity it needs. Structuring jobs to fit personality is almost certain to lead to favoritism and conformity. No organization can afford either. It needs equity and impersonal fairness in its personnel decisions or else it will either lose its good people or destroy their incentive.

Avoiding the Trap of Staffing to Suit Personality

How, then, do effective executives staff for strength without stumbling into the opposite trap of building jobs to suit personality?

By and large, they follow three rules:

1. They do not start out with the assumption that jobs are created by nature or by God. They know that they have been designed by highly fallible people. And they are therefore forever on guard against the "impossible" job.

    Such jobs are common. They usually look exceedingly logical on paper — but they cannot be filled. One qualified candidate after the other is tried. None does well. Six months or a year later, the job has defeated the candidate. Why? It was probably created to accomodate an unusual person and tailored to his or her idiosyncrasies. It usually calls for a mixture of temperaments rarely found in one person. Such a job becomes "undoable."

    The rule is simple: Any job that has defeated two or three candidates in succession, even though each had performed well in previous assignments, must be assumed unfit for human beings. It must be redesigned.

    Every text on marketing concludes, for instance, that sales management belongs with advertising and promotion under the same marketing executive. The experience of large manufacturers of branded and mass-marketed consumer goods has been, however, that this job is impossible. Such a business needs high effectiveness both in field selling, i.e., moving goods, and in advertising and promotion, i.e., moving people. These appeal to different personalities rarely found in one person.

    The effective executive therefore first makes sure that the job is well designed. And if experience suggests otherwise, the effective executive does not hunt for a genius to do the impossible but instead redesigns the job. This executive knows that the test of organization is not genius. It is its capacity to make common people achieve uncommon performance.

2. The second rule for staffing from strength is to make each job demanding and big. A job should challenge people to bring out their strengths.

This, however, is not the policy of most large organizations. They tend to make the job small — which would make sense only if people were designed and machined for specific performance at a given moment. Yet not only do we have to fill jobs with people as they come. The demands of any job above the simplest are also bound to change, and often abruptly. The "perfect fit" then rapidly becomes the misfit. But if the job is big and demanding to begin with, it will enable an incumbent to rise to the new demands of a changed situation.

This rule applies to someone's first job in particular because that is where a person's strengths should have a chance to find full play. For a beginner like Jane Jones, for example, in her first job the standards are set by which she will guide and measure herself the rest of her career. Till she entered her first adult job she never had a chance to perform. All one can do in school is to show promise. Performance is possible only in real work, whether in a research lab, in teaching, in business, or a government agency. Both for a beginner like Jane and for the rest of the organization, her colleagues and superiors, the most important thing to find out is what she really can do.

It is equally important for her to find out as early as possible whether she is indeed in the right place, or even in the right kind of work. A young person who has the right strength for one organization may be a total misfit in another, which from the outside looks the same.

This not only holds for different kinds of organizations. It also holds for organizations of the same kind. I have yet to see two large businesses which have the same values and stress the same contributions. A happy and productive faculty member at one university may become lost, unhappy, and frustrated at another.

Young people in first jobs should ask the question at some point: "Am I in the right work and in the right place?" But they cannot ask this question, let alone answer it, if the beginning job is too small, too easy, and designed to offset their lack of experience rather than bring out what they can do.

The young person whose job is too small to challenge and test his or her abilities either leaves or declines rapidly into premature middle age, soured, cynical, unproductive. Executives everywhere complain that many young men and women with fire in their bellies turn so soon into burned-out sticks. These executives have only themselves to blame: They quenched the fire by making the job too small.

3. The effective executive knows that to get strength one has to put up with weaknesses.

The effective executive will therefore ask: "Does this candidate have strength in *one* major area? And is this strength relevant to the task? If this person achieves excellence in this one area, will it make a significant difference?" If the answer is "yes," the executive will appoint the candidate.

Effective executives are above all intolerant of the argument: "I can't spare Jack Jones; I'd be in trouble without him." They have learned that there are only three explanations for an "indispensable person" like Jack Jones. He is actually incompetent and can survive only if he is carefully shielded from demands; his strength is misused to bolster a weak superior; or his strength is misused to delay tackling a serious problem, if not to conceal its existence.

In every one of these situations, the "indispensable person" *should be moved* — and soon. Otherwise one only destroys whatever strengths he may have.

One chief executive decided to move automatically anyone whose boss described him or her as indispensable. "This either means," the executive said, "that I have a weak superior or a weak subordinate — or both. Whichever of these, the sooner we find out, the better."

Altogether it must be an unbreakable rule to promote the person who, by the test of performance, is best qualified for the job to be filled. All arguments to the contrary — "She is indispensable"... "He won't be acceptable to the people there"... "We never put anyone in there without field experience" — should be given short shrift. Not only does the job deserve the best person; the person of proven performance has earned the opportunity. Staffing the opportunities instead of the problems not only creates the most effective organization; it also creates enthusiasm and dedication.

Conversely, it is the duty of the executive to remove anyone — especially any manager — who consistently fails to perform with high distinction. To let such a failure stay on corrupts the others. It is grossly unfair to his or her subordinates, and to the whole organization. Above all, it is senseless cruelty to that person. People in situations like this — and again, especially managers — realize they are inadequate, whether or not they admit it to themselves.

Superiors have responsibility for the work of others. They also have power over the careers of others. Making strengths productive is therefore much more than an essential of effectiveness. It is a moral imperative, a responsibility of authority and position. Superiors owe it to their organizations to make the strength of every subordinate as productive as it can be. But even more, they owe it to subordinates as human beings to help them get the most out of whatever strength they may have. Organizations must serve individuals through their strengths, regardless of their limitations and weaknesses.

How to Manage the Boss

I have yet to find a manager, whether in business, government or any other institution, who did not say: "I have no great trouble managing my subordinates. But how do I manage my boss?" It is actually remarkably easy: make the strengths of the boss productive.

One does not do so by toadying to the boss. The effective executive accepts that the boss is human (something that intelligent young subordinates often find hard to do). The boss is human and therefore has strengths as well as limitations. Trying to build on the boss's weaknesses will be as frustrating and as stultifying as trying to build on the weaknesses of a subordinate. The effective executive therefore asks: "What can my boss do really well?" "What has he done really well?" "What does my boss need to get from me to perform?" "What does she need to know to use her strength?" The effective executive does not worry too much about what the boss cannot do.

The effective executive also knows that the boss, being human, has ways of being effective and looks for these ways.

We are all experts on other people and see them much more clearly than they see themselves. To make the boss effective is therefore usually fairly easy. But it requires building on strength to make weaknesses irrelevant. Few things make executives as effective as building on the strengths of their superior.

What Is a Business?

Part Three

What Is a Business?

Chapter 10

Business Created and Managed by People, Not by Forces
The Fallacy of Profit Maximization
Profit: An Objective Condition of Economic Activity, Not Its
    Rationale
The Purpose of a Business: To Create a Customer
The Two Entrepreneurial Functions: Marketing and Innovation
The Marketing Revolution in America
Marketing Not a Specialized Activity
Consumerism, the "Shame of Marketing"
From Selling to Marketing
The Enterprise as the Organ of Economic Growth and Development
Innovation as an Economic Function
As a Dimension of the Total Business
The Productive Utilization of All Wealth-Producing Resources
What Is Productive Labor?
Knowledge, Time, Product-Mix, Process-Mix, and Organization
    Structure as Factors in Productivity
Making Knowledge Productive
The Functions of Profit
Profit as a Social Responsibility
How Much Profit Is Required?

A business enterprise is created and managed by people, not by forces. Economic forces set limits to what management can do. They create opportunities for management's action. But they do not by themselves determine what a business is or what it does. Nothing could be sillier than the oft-repeated assertion that "management only adapts the business to the forces of the market." Management not only has to find these forces, it has to create them.

Another conclusion is that a business cannot be defined or explained in terms of profit. Asked what a business is, the typical business man or business woman is likely to answer, "An organization to make a profit." The typical economist is likely to give the same answer. This answer is not only false, it is irrelevant.

The prevailing economic theory of business enterprise and behavior, the maximization of profit — which is simply a complicated way of phrasing the old saw of buying cheap and selling dear — may adequately explain how a particular entrepreneur operates. But it cannot explain how any business enterprise operates, nor how it should operate. The concept of profit maximization is, in fact, meaningless.

Contemporary economists realize this; but they try to salvage the theorem. Joel Dean, one of the most brilliant and fruitful of contemporary business economists, still maintains the theorem as such. But this is how he defines it:

> Economic theory makes a fundamental assumption that maximizing profits is the basic objective of every firm. But in recent years, profit maximization has been extensively qualified by theorists to refer to the long run; to refer to management's rather than to owner's income; to include non-financial income such as increased leisure for high-strung executives and more congenial relations between executive levels within the firm; and to make allowance for special considerations such as restraining competition, maintaining management control, warding off wage demands and forestalling anti-trust suits. The concept has become so general and hazy that it seems to encompass most of men's aims in life.
>
> This trend reflects a growing realization by theorists that many firms, and particularly the big ones, do not operate on the principle of profit maximizing in terms of marginal cost and revenues. . . .[1]

A concept that has "become so general and hazy that it seems to encompass most of men's aims in life" is not a concept. It is another way of saying, "I don't know and I don't understand." A theorem that can be maintained only by declaring almost everything to be an exception has surely ceased to have meaning or usefulness.

The danger in the concept of profit maximization is that it makes profitability appear a myth. Anyone observing the discrepancy between the theory of profit maximization and the reality, as portrayed by Joel Dean, would be justified in concluding that profitability does not matter — the conclusion actually reached by John Kenneth Galbraith in *The New Industrial State*.[2]

Profit and profitability are, however, crucial — for society even more than for the individual business. Yet profitability is not the purpose of, but a limiting factor on, busi-

[1] Joel Dean, *Managerial Economics* (Prentice-Hall, 1951), p. 28.
[2] Houghton Mifflin, 1967.

ness enterprise and business activity. Profit is not the explanation, cause, or rationale of business behavior and business decisions, but the test of their validity. If archangels instead of business people sat in directors' chairs, they would still have to be concerned with profitability, despite their total lack of personal interest in making profits. This applies with equal force to those far from angelic individuals, the commissars who run Soviet Russia's business enterprises, and who have to run their businesses on a higher profit margin than the wicked capitalists of the West.

The first test of any business is not the maximization of profit but the achievement of sufficient profit to cover the risks of economic activity and thus avoid loss.

The root of the confusion is the mistaken belief that the motive of people in business — the so-called profit motive — is an explanation of their behavior or their guide to right action. Whether there is such a thing as a profit motive at all is highly doubtful. It was invented by the classical economists to explain the economic reality which their theory of static equilibrium could not explain. There has never been any evidence for the existence of the profit motive. We have long since found the true explanation of the phenomena of economic change and growth which the profit motive was first put forth to explain.

It is irrelevant for an understanding of business behavior, profit, and profitability whether there is a profit motive or not. That Jim Smith is in business to make a profit concerns only him and the Recording Angel. It does not tell us what Jim Smith does and how he performs. We do not learn anything about the work of prospectors hunting for uranium in the Nevada desert by being told that they are trying to make a fortune. We do not learn anything about the work of heart specialists by being told that they are trying to make a livelihood, or even that they are trying to benefit humanity. The profit motive and its offspring, maximization of profits, are just as irrelevant to the function of a business, the purpose of a business, and the job of managing a business.

In fact, the concept is worse than irrelevant: it does harm. It is a major cause for the misunderstanding of the nature of profit in our society and for the deep-seated hostility to profit which are among the most dangerous diseases of an industrial society. It is largely responsible for the worst mistakes of public policy which are squarely based on the failure to understand the nature, function, and purpose of business enterprise. And it is in large part responsible for the prevailing belief that there is an inherent contradiction between profit and a company's ability to make a social contribution. Actually, a company can make a social contribution only if it is highly profitable. To put it crudely, a bankrupt company is not likely to be a good company to work for, or likely to be a good neighbor and a desirable member of the community — no matter what some sociologists of today seem to believe to the contrary.

The Purpose of a Business

To know what a business is we have to start with its purpose. Its purpose must lie outside of the business itself. In fact, it must lie in society since business enterprise is an organ of society. There is only one valid definition of business purpose: *to create a customer*.

Markets are not created by God, nature, or economic forces but by the people who manage a business. The want a business satisfies may have been felt by customers before they were offered the means of satisfying it. Like food in a famine, it may have dominated the customers' lives and filled all their waking moments, but it remained a potential want until the action of business people converted it into effective demand. Only then are there customers and a market. The want may have been unfelt by potential customers; people — the potential customers — did not know that they wanted Xerox machines or computers until these became available. There may have been no want at all until business action created it — by innovation, by credit, by advertising, or by the ability to sell. In every case, it is business action that creates the customer.

It is the customer who determines what a business is. It is the customer alone whose willingness to pay for a good or for a service converts economic resources into wealth, things into goods. What the business thinks it produces is not of first importance — especially not to the future of the business and to its success. What customers think they are buying, what they consider value, is decisive — it determines what a business is, what it produces, and whether it will prosper. And what customers buy and consider value is never a product. It is always utility, that is, what a product or service does for them. And what is value for customers is, as we shall see, anything but obvious.

Customers are the foundation of a business and keep it in existence. They alone give employment. To supply the wants and needs of consumers, society entrusts wealth-producing resources to the business enterprise.

The Two Entrepreneurial Functions

Because its purpose is to create a customer, the business enterprise has two — and only these two — basic functions: marketing and innovation. Marketing and innovation produce results; all the rest are "costs."

Marketing is the distinguishing, unique function of the business. A business is set apart from all other human organizations by the fact that it *markets* a product or a service. Neither church, nor army, nor school, nor state does that. Any organization that fulfills itself through marketing a product or a service is a business. Any organization in which marketing is either absent or incidental is not a business and should never be managed as if it were one.

The first man in the West to see marketing clearly as the unique and central function of the business enterprise, and the creation of a customer as the specific job of management, was Cyrus H. McCormick (1809–1884). The history books mention only that he invented a mechanical harvester. But he also invented the basic tools of modern marketing: market research and market analysis, the concept of market standing, pricing policies, the service salesman, parts and service supply to the customer, and installment credit. He had done all this by 1850, but not till fifty years later was he first widely imitated even in his own country.

The revolution of the American economy since 1900 has in large part been a marketing revolution. However, creative, aggressive, pioneering marketing is still far too rare in American business. Fifty years ago the typical attitude of American business toward marketing was "the sales department will sell whatever the plant produces." Today it is increasingly, "It is our job to produce what the market needs." However deficient in exe cution, the attitude has by itself changed our economy as much as any of the technical innovations of this century.

Marketing is so basic that it cannot be considered a separate function (i.e., a separate skill or work) within the business, on a par with others such as manufacturing or personnel. Marketing requires separate work, and a distinct group of activities. But it is, first, a central dimension of the entire business. It is the whole business seen from the point of view of its final result, that is, from the customer's point of view. Concern and responsibility for marketing must, therefore, permeate all areas of the enterprise.

Among American manufacturing companies the outstanding practitioner of the marketing approach may well be IBM; and IBM is also the best example of the power of marketing. IBM does not owe its meteoric rise to technological innovation or product leadership. It was a Johnny-come-lately when it entered the computer field, without technological expertise or scientific knowledge. But while the technological leaders in the early computer days, Univac, GE, and RCA, were product-focused and technology-focused, the punch-card sales people who ran IBM asked: "Who are the customers? What is value for them? How do they buy? And, what do they need?" As a result, IBM took over the market.

From Selling to Marketing

Despite the emphasis on marketing and the marketing approach, marketing is still rhetoric rather than reality in far too many businesses. "Consumerism" proves this. For what consumerism demands of business is that it actually market. It demands that business start out with the needs, the realities, the values of the customer. It demands that business define its goal as the satisfaction of customer needs. It demands that business base its reward on its contribution to the customer. That after twenty years of marketing rhetoric consumerism could become a powerful popular movement proves that not much marketing has been practiced. Consumerism is the "shame of marketing."

But consumerism is also the opportunity of marketing. It will force businesses to become market-focused in their actions as well as in their pronouncements.

Above all, consumerism should dispel the confusion which largely explains why there has been so little real marketing. When managers speak of marketing, they usually mean the organized performance of all selling functions. This is still selling. It still starts out with "our products." It still looks for "our market." True marketing starts out with the customers' demographics, their realities, their needs, their values. It does not ask, "What do we want to sell?" It asks, "What do customers want to buy?" It does not say, "This is what our product or service does." It says, "These are the satisfactions, values, and needs the customers look for."

Indeed, selling and marketing are antithetical rather than synonymous or even complementary.

There will always, one can assume, be need for some selling. But the aim of marketing is to make selling superfluous. The aim of marketing is to know and understand customers so well that the product or service fits them and sells itself.

Ideally, marketing should result in customers who are ready to buy. All that should be needed then is to make the product or service available, i.e., logistics rather than selling, and statistical distribution rather than promotion. We may be a long way from this ideal. But consumerism is a clear indication that the right motto for business management should increasingly be, "from selling to marketing."

The Enterprise as the Organ of Economic Growth and Development

Marketing alone does not make a business enterprise. In a static economy there are no business enterprises. There are not even businessmen. The middleman of a static society is a broker whose compensation is a fee, or a speculator who creates no value.

A business enterprise can exist only in an expanding economy, or at least in one which considers change both natural and acceptable. And business is the specific organ of growth, expansion, and change.

The second function of a business is, therefore, *innovation* – the provision of different economic satisfactions. It is not enough for the business to provide just any economic goods and services; it must provide better and more economic ones. It is not necessary for a business to grow bigger; but it is necessary that it constantly grow better.

Innovation may result in a lower price – the datum with which the economist has been most concerned, for the simple reason that it is the only one that can be handled by quantitative tools. But the result may also be a new and better product, a new convenience, or the definition of a new want.

The most productive innovation is a *different* product or service creating a new potential of satisfaction, rather than an improvement. Typically this new and different product costs more – yet its overall effect is to make the economy more productive.

The antibiotic drug costs far more than the cold compress which is all yesterday's physician had to fight pneumonia. The computer costs far more than an adding machine or a punch-card sorter, the typewriter far more than a quill pen, the Xerox duplicator far more than a copy press or even a mimeograph copier. And, if and when we get a cancer cure, it will cost more than even a first-class funeral.

The price of the product is thus only one measurement of the value of an innovation, or of the economic process altogether. We may relate price to unit output, i.e., price of a drug to the saving it produces in days of hospital stay and in added years of working life. But even that is hardly adequate. We really need a value measurement. What economic value does innovation give the customer? The customer is the only one to judge; and the customer alone knows his or her economic reality.

Innovation may be finding new uses for old products. A sales person who succeeds in selling refrigerators to Eskimos to prevent food from freezing would be as much of an innovator as someone who had developed brand-new processes or invented a new product. To sell Eskimos a refrigerator to keep food from getting too cold is actually creating a new product. Technologically there is, of course, only the same old product; but economically there is innovation.

Above all, innovation is not *invention.* It is a term of economics rather than of technology. Nontechnological innovations – social or economic innovations – are at least as important as technological ones.

However important the steam engine was as an invention, two nontechnological innovations have had as much to do with the rise of modern economy: the mobilization of purchasing power through bank credit, and the application of probability mathematics to the physical risks of economic activity, that is, insurance. The innovation of limited liability and the subsequent development of the publicly owned limited-liability company were of equal importance. And installment credit (or as the British call it more accurately, hire purchase) has equal impact. It makes it possible to pay for the means to increase production out of the future fruits of the investment. It thus enabled the American farmer in the nineteenth century to buy the implements that made him productive and to pay for them after he had obtained the larger crop at lower cost. And this also makes installment credit a powerful dynamo of economic development in today's poor, under-developed countries.

In the organization of the business enterprise innovation can no more be considered a separate function than marketing. It is not confined to engineering or research but extends across all parts of the business, all functions, all activities. It cannot be confined to manufacturing business. Innovation in distribution has been as important as innovation in manufacturing; and so has been innovation in an insurance company or in a bank.

The leadership in innovation with respect to product and service has traditionally been focused in one functional activity which is responsible for nothing else. This has been particularly true for businesses with heavy engineering or chemical technology. In an insurance company, too, a special department charged with leadership responsibility for the development of new kinds of coverage may be in order; and there might well be other such departments charged with innovation in the organization of sales, the administration of policies, and the settling of claims. Yet another group might work on innovation in investing the company's funds. All these are the insurance company's business.

But the best way to organize for systematic, purposeful innovation is as a business activity rather than as functional work. At the same time, every managerial unit of a business should have responsibility for innovation and definite innovation goals. It should be responsible for contributing to innovation in the company's product or service; in addition, it should strive consciously to advance the art in the particular area in which it is engaged: selling or accounting, quality control or personnel management.

Innovation can be defined as the task of endowing human and material resources with new and greater wealth-producing capacity. Innovation is particularly important for developing countries. These countries have the resources. They are poor because they lack the capacity to make these resources wealth-producing. They can import technology. But they have to produce their own social innovations to make imported technology work.

To have realized this was the great strength of the founders of modern Japan a century ago. They deliberately kept their country dependent on the West's technology — a dependence that remained until very recently. But they channeled their energies and those of their people into social innovations that would enable their country to become a strong modern society and economy and yet retain its distinct Japanese character and culture.

Innovation is thus crucial to economic development. Indeed, economic development is, above all, an entrepreneurial task.

Managers must convert society's needs into opportunities for profitable business. That, too, is a definition of innovation. It needs to be stressed today, when we are so conscious of the needs of society, schools, health-care systems, cities, and environment. These needs are not too different in kind from those which the nineteenth-century entrepreneur converted into growth industries — the urban newspaper and the streetcar; the steel-frame skyscraper and the school textbook; the telephone and pharmaceuticals. The new needs similarly demand the innovating business.

The Productive Utilization of Wealth-Producing Resources

The enterprise must utilize wealth-producing resources to discharge its purpose of creating a customer. It is, therefore, charged with productive utilization of these resources. This is the administrative function of business. In its economic aspect it is called productivity.

Everybody these last few years has been talking productivity. That greater productivity — better utilization of resources — is both the key to a high standard of living and the result of business activity is not news. And we should realize by now that the scourge of modern economics, uncontrolled inflation, is a deficiency disease caused by inadequate productivity. But we actually know very little about productivity; we are, indeed, not yet able to measure it.

Productivity means that balance between *all* factors of production that will give the greatest output for the smallest effort. This is quite different from productivity per worker or per hour of work; it is at best distantly and vaguely reflected in such traditional standards.

These standards are still based on the eighteenth-century tenet that manual labor is, in the last resort, the only productive resource; manual work the only real effort. The standards still express the mechanistic fallacy — of which Marx, to the permanent disability of Marxian economics, was the last important dupe — that all human achievement could eventually be measured in units of muscle effort. Increased productivity in a modern economy is never achieved by muscle effort. It is always the result of doing away with muscle effort, of substituting something else for the laborer. One of these substitutes is, of course, capital equipment, that is, mechanical energy.

At least as important, though unnoticed until very recently, is the increase in productivity achieved by replacing manual labor, whether skilled or unskilled, by knowledge, resulting in a shift from laborers to knowledge workers, such as managers, technicians, and professionals.

A little reflection will show that the rate of capital formation, to which economists give so much attention, is a secondary factor. Someone must plan and design the equipment — a conceptual, theoretical, and analytical task — before it can be installed and used. The basic factor in an economy's development must be the rate of "brain formation," the rate at which a country produces people with imagination and vision, education, and theoretical and analytical skills.

However, the planning, design, and installation of capital equipment is only a part of the increase in productivity through the substitution of brain for brawn. At least as important is the contribution made through the direct change of the character of work from one requiring the manual labor, skilled and unskilled, of many people, to one requiring theoretical analysis and conceptual planning without any investment in capital equipment.

This contribution first became evident in the 1950s in the analysis of the productivity gap between American and European industry. Studies — e.g., by the Stanford Research Institute and by the Organization for Economic Cooperation (OEC) — showed clearly that the productivity differential between Western Europe and the United States was not a matter of capital investment. In many European industries productivity was as much as two-thirds below that of the corresponding American industry, even though capital investment and equipment were equal. The only explanation was the lower proportion of managers and technicians and the poor organization structure of European industry with its reliance on manual skill.

In 1900 the typical manufacturing company in the United States spent probably no more than $5 or $8 on managerial technical and professional personnel for every $100 in direct-labor wages. Today there are many manufacturing industries where the two items of expenditure are equal — even though direct-labor wage rates have risen proportionately much faster. Outside of manufacturing, transportation, and mining, e.g., in distribution, finance, insurance, and the service industries (that is, in two-thirds of the American economy), the increase in productivity has been caused primarily by the replacement of labor by planning, brawn by brain, sweat by knowledge.

The greatest opportunities for increasing productivity are surely to be found in knowledge work itself, and especially in management. The vocabulary of business — especially of accounting — in relation to productivity has become so obsolete as to be misleading. What the accountant calls productive labor is manual workers tending machines, who are actually the least productive labor. What the accountant calls nonproductive labor — all the people who contribute to production without tending a machine — is a hodgepodge. It includes pre-industrial, low-productivity brawn labor like sweepers; some traditional high-skill, high-productivity labor like toolmakers; new industrial high-skill labor like maintenance electricians; and industrial high-knowledge personnel like supervisors, industrial engineers, and quality control personnel. Finally, what the accountant lumps together as overhead — the very term reeks of moral disapproval — contains what should be the most productive resource, the managers, researchers, planners, designers, innovators. It may also, however, contain purely parasitical, if not destructive, elements in the form of high-priced personnel needed only because of malorganization, poor spirit, or confused objectives, that is, because of mismanagement.

We need a concept of productivity that considers together all the efforts that go into output and expresses them in relation to their result, rather than one that assumes that labor is the only productive effort. But even such a concept — though a big step forward — would still be inadequate if its definition of effort were confined to the activities measurable as visible and direct costs, that is, according to the accountant's definition of, and symbol for, effort. There are factors of substantial, if not decisive, impact on productivity that never become visible cost figures.

First there is knowledge — our most productive resource if properly applied, but also the most expensive one, and totally unproductive, if misapplied. Knowledge workers are, of necessity, high-cost workers. Having spent many years in school, they also represent a very high social investment.

Then there is time — our most perishable resource. Whether people and machines are utilized steadily or only half the time will make a difference in their productivity. There is nothing less productive than idle time of expensive capital equipment or wasted time of highly paid and able people. Equally unproductive may be cramming more productive effort into time than it will comfortably hold — for instance, the attempt to run three shifts in a congested plant or on old or delicate equipment.

The most productive — or least productive — time is that of the managers themselves. Yet it is usually the least known, least analyzed, least managed of all factors of productivity.

Productivity is also a function of the product mix, the balance between various combinations of the same resources. As every manager should know, differentials in the market values of various combinations are rarely proportional to the efforts that go into making up the combinations. Often there is barely any discernible relationship between the two. A company turning out a constant volume of goods with unchanging materials and skills requirements and a constant amount of direct and indirect labor may reap fortunes or go bankrupt, depending on the product mix. Obviously this represents a considerable difference in the productivity of the same resources — but not one that shows in costs or can be detected by cost analysis.

There is also an important factor which I would call "process mix." Is it more productive for a company to buy or to make it, to assemble its product or to contract out the assembly process, to market under its own brand name through its own distributive organization or to sell to independent wholesalers using their own brands? What is the company good at? What is the most productive utilization of its specific knowledge, ability, experience, reputation?

Not every management can do everything, nor should any business necessarily go into those activities which seem objectively to be most profitable. Every management has specific abilities and limitations. Whenever it attempts to go beyond these, it is likely to fail, no matter how inherently profitable the venture.

People who are good at running a highly stable business will not be able to adjust to a mercurial or a rapidly growing business. People who have grown up in a rapidly expanding company will, as everyday experience shows, be in danger of destroying the business should it enter upon a period of consolidation. People good at running a business with a foundation in long-range research are not likely to do well in high-pressure selling of novelties or fashion goods. Utilization of the specific abilities of the company and its management and observance of these specific limitations is an important productivity factor. Conglomerates may optimize the productivity of capital, but they will have rather low productivity — and inherently poor results — in other equally important areas.

Finally, productivity is vitally affected by organization structure and by the balance among the various activities within the business. If a lack of clear organization causes managers to waste their time trying to find out what they are supposed to do rather than doing it, the company's scarcest resource is being wasted. If top management is interested only in engineering (perhaps because that's where all the top managers came from) while the company needs major attention to marketing, it lacks productivity; the resulting damage will be greater than could be caused by a drop in output per worker hour.

These factors are additional to the factors accountants and economists usually consider, namely, productivity of labor, capital, and materials. They are, however, fully as important.

We therefore not only need to define productivity so as to embrace all these factors affecting it, but also need to set objectives that take all these factors into account. We must develop yardsticks to measure the impact on productivity of the substitution of capital for labor, and of knowledge for both — and means to distinguish between creative and parasitical overhead, and to assess the impact on productivity of time utilization, product mix, process mix, organization structure, and the balance of activities.

Not only does individual management need adequate concepts and measurements for productivity, the economy needs them. Their lack is the biggest gap in our economic statistics and seriously weakens all economic policy. It frustrates our attempts to fight depression and inflation alike.

The Functions of Profit

Profit is not a cause but a result — the result of the performance of the business in marketing, innovation, and productivity. It is a needed result, serving essential economic functions. Profit is, first, the test of performance — the only effective test, as the communists in Russia soon found out when they tried to abolish it in the early twenties (though they coyly called it the capital fund and avoided the "bad" word profit until well into the 1950s).

Profit has a second function which is equally important. It is the premium for the risk of uncertainty. Economic activity, because it is activity, focuses on the future; and the one thing that is certain about the future is its uncertainty, its risks. The word "risk" itself is said to mean "earning one's daily bread" in the original Arabic. It is through risk-taking that business people earn their daily bread. Because business activity is economic it always attempts to bring about change. It always saws off the limb on which it sits; it makes existing risks riskier or creates new ones.

The future of economic activity is a long one; it can take fifteen or twenty years for basic decisions to become fully effective, and for major investment to pay off. "Lengthening the economic detour" has been known for a hundred years to be a prerequisite for economic advance. Yet while we know nothing about the future, we know that its risks increase in geometric progression the farther ahead we commit ourselves to it.

Profit and profit alone can supply the capital for tomorrow's jobs, both for *more* jobs and for *better* jobs.

Again it is a definition of economic progress that the investment needed to create new and additional jobs increases.

Today's accountants or engineers do not make a better living than grandfather on the farm because they work harder. They work far less hard. Nor do they deserve a better living because they are better people than grandfather. They are the same kind of human being as grandfather was, and grandfather's grandfather before him. Today's accountants or engineers can be paid so much more and yet work so much less hard because the capital investment in them and their jobs is infinitely greater than that which financed grandfather's job. In 1900, when grandfather started, capital investment per American farmer was at most $5000. To create the accountant's or the engineer's job, society first invests at least $50,000 in capital and expenses for school and education. And then the employer invests another $25,000 to $50,000 per job. All of this investment that makes possible both additional and better jobs has to come out of the surplus of economic activity, that is, out of profits.

And finally profit pays for the economic satisfactions and services of a society, from health care to defense, and from education to the opera. They all have to be paid for out of the surplus of economic production, that is, out of the difference between the value produced by economic activity and its cost.

People in business these days tend to be apologetic about profit. This is a measure of the dismal job they have done explaining profit — above all to themselves. For there *is* no justification and no rationale for profit as long as one talks the nonsense of profit motive and profit maximization.

No apology is needed for profit as a necessity of economy and society. On the contrary, what business people should feel guilty about, what they should feel the need to apologize for, is failure to produce a profit appropriate to the economic and social functions which profit, and only profit, can develop.

Walther Rathenau (1867–1922), the German executive, statesman, and social philosopher, who thought more deeply than any other Westerner of his time about the social responsibility of business, proposed replacing the word profit with responsibility. Profit, to be sure, is not the whole of business responsibility; but it is the first responsibility. The business that fails to produce an adequate profit imperils both the integrity of the resources entrusted in its care and the economy's capacity to grow. It is untrue to its trust.

At the very least, business enterprise needs a *minimum* of profit: the profit required to cover its own future risks, the profit required to enable it to stay in business and to maintain intact the wealth-producing capacity of its resources. This required minimum profit affects business behavior and business decision — both by setting limits and by testing their validity. Management, in order to manage, needs a profit objective at least equal to the required minimum profit, and yardsticks to measure its profit performance against this requirement.

What, then, is managing a business? It follows from the analysis of business activity as the creation of a customer through marketing and innovation that managing a business must always be entrepreneurial in character. There is need for administrative performance. But it follows the entrepreneurial objectives. Structure follows strategy.

It also follows that managing a business must be a creative rather than an adaptive task. The more a management creates economic conditions or changes them rather than passively adapts to them, the more it manages the business.

But an analysis of the nature of a business also shows that management, while ultimately tested by performance alone, is a rational activity. Concretely this means that a business must set objectives that express what is desirable of attainment rather than (as the maximization-of-profit theorem implies) aim at accommodation to the possible. Once objectives have been set by fixing one's sights on the desirable, the question can be raised what concessions to the possible have to be made. This requires management to decide what business the enterprise is engaged in, and what business it should be engaged in.

Business Realities

Chapter 11

To Create Time Today for Future Activity, Today's Job Must Be Done
Better
Three Inseparable Dimensions: Make the Present Business Effective,
Identify and Realize Its Potential, Prepare Now for Changes in
the Future
Results and Resources of a Business Exist Outside It
Results Come from Opportunities; Resources Should Go to
Opportunities
Leadership in Providing Value to a Customer
Executives Spend Too Much Time Today on What Happened Yesterday
Misallocation: Most Results Derive from Few Events; Most Costs Yield
Few Results

*T*hat managers give neither sufficient time nor sufficient thought to the future is a universal complaint. It is a recurrent theme in their working day and in the articles and in the books on management.

It is a valid complaint. Managers should spend more time and thought on the future of their business. They also should spend more time and thought on a good many other things, their social and community responsibilities for instance. Both they and their business pay a stiff penalty for these neglects. The neglect of the future is only a symptom; executives slight tomorrow because they cannot get ahead of today. That too is a symptom. The real disease is the absence of any foundation of knowledge and system for tackling the economic tasks in business.

Today's job takes all the manager's time, as a rule; yet it is seldom done well. Few managers are greatly impressed with their own performance in the immediate tasks. They feel themselves caught in a "rat race," and managed by whatever is dumped into their "in" tray. They know that crash programs which attempt to "solve" this or that particular "urgent" problem rarely achieve right and lasting results. And yet, they rush from one crash program to the next. Worse still, they know that the same problems recur again, no matter how many times they are "solved."

Before thinking of tackling the future, a manager must be able therefore to dispose of the challenges of today in less time and with greater impact and permanence. For this a systematic approach is needed to today's job.

Three Dimensions of the Economic Task

There are three different dimensions to the economic task: (1) The present business must be made effective; (2) its potential must be identified and realized; (3) it must be made into a different business for a different future. Each task requires a distinct approach. Each asks different questions. Each comes out with different conclusions. Yet they are inseparable. All three have to be done at the same time: today. All three have to be carried out with the same organization, the same resources of people, knowledge, and money, and in the same entrepreneurial process. The future is not going to be made tomorrow; it is being made today, and largely by the decisions and actions taken with respect to the tasks of today. Conversely, what is being done to bring about the future directly affects the present. The tasks overlap. They require one unified strategy. Otherwise, they cannot really get done at all.

To tackle any one of these jobs, let alone all three together, requires an understanding of the true realities of the business as an economic system, of its capacity for economic performance, and of the relationship between available resources and possible results. Otherwise, there is no alternative to the "rat race." This understanding never comes ready-made; it has to be developed separately for each business. Yet the assumptions and expectations that underlie it are largely common. Businesses are different, but business is much the same, regardless of size and structure, of products, technology and markets, of culture and managerial competence. There is a common business reality.

There are actually two sets of generalizations that apply to most businesses most of the time: one with respect to the results and resources of a business, one with respect to its efforts. Together they lead to a number of conclusions regarding the nature and direction of the entrepreneurial job.

Most of these assumptions will sound plausible, perhaps even familiar to most people in business, but few people ever pull these assumptions together into a coherent whole. Few draw action conclusions from them, no matter how much each individual statement agrees with their experience and knowledge. As a result, few managers base their actions on these, their own assumptions and expectations.

Results and Resources Exist Outside a Business

Neither results nor resources exist inside the business. Both exist outside. There are no profit centers within the business; there are only cost centers. The only thing one can say with certainty about any business activity, whether engineering or selling, manufacturing or accounting, is that it consumes efforts and thereby incurs costs. Whether it contributes to results remains to be seen.

Results depend not on anybody within the business nor on anything within the control of the business. They depend on somebody outside — the customer in a market economy, the political authorities in a controlled economy. It is always somebody outside who decides whether the efforts of a business become economic results or whether they become so much waste and scrap.

The same is true of the one and only distinct resource of any business: knowledge. Other resources, money or physical equipment, for instance, do not confer any distinction. What does make a business distinct and what is its peculiar resource is its ability to use knowledge of all kinds — from scientific and technical knowledge to social, economic, and managerial knowledge. It is only in respect to knowledge that a business can be distinct, can therefore produce something that has a value in the market place.

Yet knowledge is not a business resource. It is a universal social resource. It cannot be kept a secret for any length of time. "What one person has done, another can always do again" is old and profound wisdom. The one decisive resource of business, therefore, is as much outside the business as are business results.

Indeed, business can be defined as a process that converts an outside resource, namely knowledge, into outside results, namely economic values.

Results from Opportunities: Resources to Opportunities

Results are obtained by exploiting opportunities, not by solving problems. All one can hope to get by solving a problem is to restore normality. All one can hope, at best, is to eliminate a restriction on the capacity of the business to obtain results. The results themselves must come from the exploitation of opportunities.

Resources, to produce results, must be allocated to opportunities rather than to problems. Needless to say, one cannot shrug off all problems, but they can and should be minimized.

Economists talk a great deal about the maximization of profit in business. This, as countless critics have pointed out, is so vague a concept as to be meaningless. But "maximization of opportunities" is a meaningful, indeed a precise, definition of the entrepreneurial job. It implies that effectiveness rather than efficiency is essential in business. The pertinent question is not how to do things right but how to find the right things to do, and to concentrate resources and efforts on them.

Leadership Position and Results

Economic results are earned only by leadership, not by mere competence. Profits are the rewards for making a unique, or at least a distinct, contribution in a meaningful area; and what is meaningful is decided by market and customer. Profit can only be earned by providing something the market accepts as value and is willing to pay for as such. And value always implies the extra which makes one product stand out, the distinction which gives it that elusive quality of leadership. The genuine monopoly, which is as mythical a beast as the unicorn (save for politically enforced, that is, governmental monopolies of which the cartel of the Petroleum Exporting countries is perhaps the outstanding example), is the one exception.

This does not mean that a business has to be the giant of its industry nor that it has to be first in every single product line, market, or technology in which it is engaged. To be big is not identical with leadership. In many industries the largest company is by no means the most profitable one, since it has to carry product lines, supply markets, or apply technologies where it cannot do a distinct, let alone a unique job. The second spot, or even the third spot, is often preferable, for it may make possible that concentration on one segment of the market, on one class of customer, on one application of the technology, in which genuine leadership often lies. In fact, the belief of so many companies that they could — or should — have leadership in everything within their market or industry is a major obstacle to achieving it; it makes these companies splinter their resources — and performance demands their concentration.

But a company which wants economic results has to have leadership in *something* of real value to a customer or market. It may be in one narrow but important aspect of the product line, it may be in its service, it may be in its distribution, or it may be in its ability to convert ideas into salable products on the market speedily and at low cost.

Unless it has such leadership position, a business, a product, a service, becomes marginal. It may seem to be a leader, may supply a large share of the market, may have the full weight of momentum, history, and tradition behind it. But the marginal is incapable of survival in the long run, let alone of producing profits. It lives on borrowed time. It exists on sufferance and through the inertia of others. Sooner or later, whenever boom conditions abate, it will be squeezed out.

Any leadership position is transitory and likely to be short-lived. No business is ever secure in its leadership position. The market in which the results exist, and the knowledge which is the resource, are both generally accessible. No leadership position is more than a temporary advantage. What this really means is that profits result only from the innovator's advantage and therefore disappear as soon as the innovation has become routine. In business (as in a physical system) energy always tends toward diffusion. Business tends to drift from leadership to mediocrity. And the mediocre is three-quarters down the road to being marginal. Results always drift from earning a profit toward earning, at best, a fee which is all competence is worth.

It is, then, the manager's job to reverse the normal drift. It is the manager's job to focus the business on opportunity and away from problems, to re-create leadership and counteract the trend toward mediocrity, to replace inertia and its momentum by new energy and new direction.

Efforts Within the Business and Their Cost

The second set of assumptions deals with the *efforts within the business and their cost.*

What exists is getting old. To say that most managers spend most of their time tackling the problems of today is euphemism. They spend most of their time on the problems of yesterday. Managers spend more of their time trying to unmake the past than on anything else.

This, to a large extent, is inevitable. What exists today is of necessity the product of yesterday. The business itself — its present resources, its efforts and their allocation, its organization as well as its products, its markets and its customers — expresses necessarily decisions and actions taken in the past. Its people, in the great majority, grew up in the business of yesterday. Their attitudes, expectations, and values were formed at an earlier time; and they tend to apply the lessons of the past to the present. Indeed, every business regards what happened in the past as normal, with a strong inclination to reject as abnormal whatever does not fit the pattern.

No matter how wise, forward-looking, or courageous the decisions and actions were when first made, they will have been overtaken by events by the time they become normal behavior and the routine of a business. No matter how appropriate the attitudes were when formed, by the time their holders have moved into senior, policy-making positions, the world that made them no longer exists. Events never happen as anticipated; the future is always different. Just as generals tend to prepare for the last war, the people in business always tend to react in terms of the last boom or of the last depression. What exists is therefore always aging. Any human decision or action starts to get old the moment it has been made.

It is always futile to restore normality; "normality" is only the reality of yesterday. The job is not to impose yesterday's normal on a changed today; but to change the business, its behavior, its attitude, its expectations — as well as its products, its markets, and its distributive channels — to fit the new realities.

What exists is likely to be misallocated. Business enterprise is not a phenomenon of nature but one of society. In a social situation a very small number of events *at one extreme* — the first 10 per cent to 20 per cent at most — account for 90 per cent of all results; whereas the great majority of events accounts for only 10 per cent or so of the results. This is true in the market place: a handful of large customers out of many thousands produce the bulk of orders; a handful of products out of hundreds of items in the line produce the bulk of the volume; and so on. It is true of sales efforts: a few sales people out of several hundred always produce two-thirds of all new business. It is true in the plant: a handful of production runs account for most of the tonnage. It is true of research: the same few people in the laboratory are apt to produce nearly all the important innovations.

It also holds true for practically all personnel problems: the bulk of the grievances always comes from a few places or from one group of employees, as does the great bulk of absenteeism, of turnover, of suggestions under a suggestion system, of accidents. As studies at the New York Telephone Company have shown, this is true even in respect to sickness.

The implications of this simple statement about normal distribution are broad.

It means, first: while 90 per cent of the results are being produced by the first 10 per cent of events, 90 per cent of the costs are incurred by the remaining and resultless 90 per cent of events. In other words, results and costs stand in inverse relationship to each other.

A second implication is that resources and efforts will normally allocate themselves to the 90 per cent of events that produce practically no results. They will allocate themselves to the number of events rather than to the results. In fact, the most expensive and potentially most productive resources (i.e., highly trained people) will misallocate themselves the worst. For the pressure exerted by the bulk of transactions is fortified by the individual's pride in doing the difficult — whether productive or not. This has been proved by every study. Let me give some examples:

A large engineering company prided itself on the high quality and reputation of its technical service group, which contained several hundred expensive engineers. They were indeed first-rate. But analysis of their allocation showed clearly that while they worked hard, they contributed little. Most of them worked on the "interesting" problems —especially those of the very small customers — problems which, even if solved, produced little business. The automobile industry was the company's major customer and accounted for almost one-third of all purchases. But few technical service people had within memory set foot in the engineering department or the plant of an automobile company. "General Motors and Ford don't need me; they have their own people" was their reaction.

Similarly, in many companies, sales people are misallocated. The largest group of sales people (and the most effective ones) are usually put on the products that are hard to sell, either because they are yesterday's products or because they are also-rans which managerial vanity desperately is trying to make into winners. Tomorrow's important products rarely get the sales effort required. And the product that has sensational success in the market, and which therefore ought to be pushed all out, tends to be slighted. "It is doing all right without extra effort, after all" is the common conclusion.

Research departments, design staffs, market development efforts, even advertising efforts have been shown to be allocated the same way in many companies — by transactions rather than by results, by what is difficult rather than by what is productive, by yesterday's problems rather than by today's and tomorrow's opportunities.

A third and important implication is that revenue money and cost money are rarely the same money stream. Most business people see in their mind's eye — and most accounting presentations assume — that the revenue stream feeds back into the cost stream, which then, in turn, feeds back into the revenue stream. But the loop is not a closed one. Revenue obviously produces the wherewithal for the costs. But unless management constantly works at directing efforts into revenue-producing activities, the costs will tend to allocate themselves by drifting into nothing-producing activities, into sheer busy-ness.

In respect then to efforts and costs as well as to resources and results the business tends to drift toward diffusion of energy.

There is thus need for constant reappraisal and redirection; and the need is greatest where it is least expected: *in making the present business effective.* It is the present in which a business first has to perform with effectiveness. It is the present where both the keenest analysis and the greatest energy are required. Yet it is dangerously tempting to keep on patching yesterday's garment rather than work on designing tomorrow's pattern.

A piecemeal approach will not suffice. To have a real understanding of the business, the manager must be able to see it in its entirety. The manager must be able to see its resources and efforts as a whole and to see their allocation to products and services, to markets, customers, end-users, to distributive channels. The manager must be able to see which efforts go onto problems and which onto opportunities, and also must be able to weigh alternatives of direction and allocation. Partial analysis is likely to misinform and misdirect. Only the over-all view of the entire business as an economic system can give real knowledge.

Concentration is the key to economic results. Economic results require that managers concentrate their efforts on the smallest number of products, product lines, services, customers, markets, distributive channels, end-uses, and so on, that will produce the largest amount of revenue. Managers must minimize the amount of attention devoted to products which produce primarily costs because, for instance, their volume is too small or too splintered.

Economic results require that staff efforts be concentrated on the few activities that are capable of producing significant business results.

Effective cost control requires a similar concentration of work and efforts on those few areas where improvement in cost performance will have significant impact on business performance and results — that is, on those areas where a relatively minor increase in efficiency will produce a major increase in economic effectiveness.

Finally, human resources must be concentrated on a few major opportunities. This is particularly true for the high-grade human resources through which knowledge becomes effective in work. And, above all it is true for the scarcest, most expensive, but also potentially most effective of all human resources in a business: managerial talent.

No other principle of effectiveness is violated as constantly today as the basic principle of concentration. This, of course, is true not only of businesses. Governments try to do a little of everything. Today's big university tries to be all things to all people, combining teaching and research, community services, consulting activities, and so on. But business — especially large business — is no less diffuse.

Not long ago it was fashionable to attack American industry for "planned obsolescence." And it has long been a favorite criticism of industry, especially American industry, that it imposes "deadening standardization." Unfortunately industry is being attacked for doing what it should be doing and fails to do.

Large United States corporations pride themselves on being willing and able to supply any specialty, to satisfy any demand for variety, even to stimulate such demands. Any number of businesses boast that they never of their own free will abandon a product. As a result, most large companies end up with thousands of items in their product line — and all too frequently fewer than twenty really sell. However, these twenty or fewer items have to contribute revenues to carry the costs of the 9999 non-sellers.

Indeed, the basic problem of United States competitive strength in the world today may be product clutter. If properly costed, the main lines in most of our industries prove to be fully competitive, despite our high wage rate and our high tax burden. But we fritter away our competitive advantage in the volume products by subsidizing an enormous array of specialties, of which only a few recover their true cost. In electronics, for instance, the competition of the Japanese portable transistor radio rests on little more than the Japanese concentration on a few models in this one line — as against the uncontrolled excess of barely differentiated models in the United States manufacturers' lines.

We are similarly wasteful in this country with respect to staff activities. Our motto seems to be: "Let's do a little bit of everything" — personnel research, advanced engineering, customer analysis, international economics, operations research, public relations, and so on. As a result, we build enormous staffs, and yet do not concentrate enough effort in any one area.

Similarly, in our attempts to control costs, we scatter our efforts rather than concentrate them where the costs are. Typically the cost-reduction program aims at cutting a little bit — say, 5 or 10 per cent — off everything. This across-the-board cut is at best ineffectual; at worst, it is apt to cripple the important, result-producing efforts which usually get less money than they need to begin with. But efforts that are sheer waste are barely touched by the typical cost-reduction program; for typically they start out with a generous budget.

These are the business realities, the assumptions that are likely to be found valid by most businesses at most times, the concepts with which the approach to the entrepreneurial task has to begin.

That these are only assumptions should be stressed. They must be tested by actual analysis; and one or the other assumption may well be found not to apply to any one particular business at any one particular time. Yet they have sufficient probability to provide the foundation for the analysis the executive needs to understand his business. They are the starting points for the analysis needed for all three of the entrepreneurial tasks: making effective the present business; finding business potential; and making the future of the business.

The small and apparently simple business requires this understanding just as much as does the big and highly complex company. Understanding is needed as much for the immediate task of effectiveness today as it is for work on the future, many years hence. It is a necessary tool for any managers who take seriously their entrepreneurial responsibility. And it is a tool which can neither be fashioned for them nor wielded for them. They must take part in making it and using it. The ability to design and develop this tool and the competence to use it should be standard equipment for business managers.

Managing a Business: The Sears Story

Chapter 12

What Is a Business and How Is It Managed?
How Sears, Roebuck Became a Business
Rosenwald's Innovations
Inventing the Mail-Order Plant
General Wood and Sears's Second Phase
Merchandise Planning and Manager Development
Sears's Third Phase: From Selling to Buying to Procurement
Class Markets and Mass Markets
The Challenges Ahead

*T*here is no better illustration of what a business is and what managing it means than one of America's most successful enterprises: Sears, Roebuck and Company.

With sales in excess of $10 billion, Sears is the largest retailer in the world. It is by far the most profitable retail business anywhere and altogether one of the most profitable companies in the American economy, by any yardstick. Only Marks & Spencer in Great Britain can compare with Sears in terms of success. But, Marks & Spencer is not only much smaller — barely one-tenth of Sears, it also admittedly owes much of its success, especially in its earlier years, to imitating Sears.

Sears, Roebuck has also been a major growth company, even though its industry, the retail business, is, of course, old and well established, and totally lacking in the glamour of high technology or scientific innovation. No other business in America, not even

General Motors, has shown such a consistent and sustained growth pattern since before the turn of the century.

Sears is also a political phenomenon that deserves study. In an age of consumerism, Sears would seem to be a prime target for consumer attacks. Yet there has been no or little criticism. Sears controls, through majority ownership, or through ownership of a substantial minority of the stock, the manufacturers of 60 per cent of the merchandise it sells. It would seem a prime target for antitrusters and a glaring example of concentration of economic power. Yet there has never been mention of an antitrust investigation of Sears, let alone an antitrust suit.

The typical case studied in business schools is a case of failure, or at least of problems. But one can learn more from successes. It is far more important to know the right thing to do than to know what to avoid doing.

Sears became a business around the turn of the century with the realization that the American farmers represented a separate and distinct market. Separate because of their isolation, which made existing channels of distribution virtually inaccessible to them; distinct because of their specific needs, which, in important respects, were different from those of the city consumer. While the farmer's purchasing power was individually low, it represented a tremendous, almost untapped, buying potential in the aggregate.

To reach farmers, a new distribution channel had to be created. Merchandise had to be produced to answer their needs and wants. It had to be brought to them at low price, and with a guarantee of regular supply. Farmers had to be given a warranty of reliability and honesty on the part of the supplier, since their physical isolation made it impossible for them to inspect merchandise before delivery or to obtain redress if cheated.

To create Sears, Roebuck as a business required analysis of customer and market, and especially of what the farmer considered "value." Furthermore, it required major innovation in a number of distinct areas.

First, it demanded systematic "merchandising," that is, the finding and developing of sources of supply for the particular goods the farmers needed, in the quality and quantity they needed and at a price they could pay. Second, it required a mail-order catalog capable of serving as adequate substitute for the shopping trips to the big city the farmers could not make. For this reason, the catalog had to become a regular publication, rather than an announcement of spectacular bargains at irregular intervals. It had to break with the entire tradition of selling by mail and learn not to high-pressure the farmers into buying by exaggerated claims, but to give them a factual description of the goods offered. The aim had to be to create permanent customers by convincing them of the reliability of the catalog and of the company behind it; the catalog had to become the "wish book" for the farmer.

Third, the age-old concept of *caveat emptor* had to be changed to *caveat vendor* — the meaning of the famous Sears policy of "your money back and no questions asked." (Customers, I am given to understand, actually return less merchandise to Sears than to most of the large American department stores — it's the basic policy and what it expresses that makes the difference.)

Fourth, a way had to be found to fill large quantities of customer orders cheaply and quickly. Without the mail-order plant, conduct of the business would have been physically impossible.

Finally, a human organization had to be built — and when Sears, Roebuck started to become a business, most of the necessary human skills were not available. There were, for instance, no buyers for this kind of operation, no accountants versed in the new requirements of inventory control, no artists to illustrate the catalogs, no clerks experienced in the handling of a huge volume of customer orders.

Richard Sears gave the company his name. He understood the needs of the customer; and he brilliantly improvised to satisfy these needs. But it was not he who made Sears, Roebuck into a business enterprise. In fact, Richard Sears's own operations could hardly be called a business. He was a shrewd speculator, buying up distress-merchandise and offering it, one batch at a time, through mail advertising. Every one of his deals was a complete transaction in itself which, when finished, liquidated itself and the business with it. Sears might have made a lot of money for himself. But his way of operating could have never founded a business, let alone perpetuated it. Indeed his success almost bankrupted him as it pushed his company far beyond the limit of his managerial capacity. His company was about to go under when he sold it to a total outsider, the Chicago clothing merchant Julius Rosenwald (1862–1932).

Between 1895, when he took control, and 1905, when the Chicago mail-order plant was opened, Rosenwald made a business enterprise out of Sears. He analyzed the market, began the systematic development of merchandise sources, and invented the regular, factual mail-order catalog and the policy of "satisfaction guaranteed or your money back." He built the productive human organization, and gave management people a maximum of authority and full responsibility for results. Later he gave every employee an ownership stake in the company, bought for the employee out of profits. Rosenwald is the father not only of Sears, Roebuck but of the distribution revolution which has changed the world economy in the twentieth century and which is so vital a factor in economic growth.

Only one basic contribution to the early history of Sears was not made by Rosenwald. The Chicago mail-order plant was designed by Otto Doering in 1903. Five years before Henry Ford's it was the first modern mass-production plant, complete with the breakdown of all work into simple repetitive operations, with an assembly line, conveyor belt, standardized, interchangeable parts — and, above all, with planned plant-wide scheduling. (There is a persistent legend at Sears that Henry Ford, before he built his own first plant, visited and carefully studied the then brand-new Sears mail-order plant.)

On these foundations, Sears had grown by the end of World War I into a national institution; its "wish book" was the only literature, besides the Bible, to be found in many farm homes.

The next phase of the Sears story begins in the mid-twenties. Just as the first chapter was dominated by one man, Julius Rosenwald, the second chapter was dominated by another, General Robert E. Wood (1879–1969). When Wood joined Sears, the original Sears market was changing rapidly. Farmers were no longer isolated; the automobile enabled them to go to town and shop there. They no longer formed a distinct market but were, largely thanks to Sears, rapidly modifying their way of life and their standard of living to conform to those of the urban middle class.

At the same time a vast urban market had come into being that was, in its own way, as isolated and as badly supplied as the farmer had been twenty-five years earlier. The low-income groups in the cities had outgrown both their subsistence standards and their distinct lower-class habits. They were acquiring the money and the desire to buy the same goods as the middle and upper classes. The country was rapidly becoming one big homogeneous market — but the distribution system was still one of separate and distinct class markets.

Wood had made this analysis even before he joined Sears. Out of it came the decision to switch Sears's emphasis to retail stores — equipped to serve both the motorized farmer and the city population.

A whole series of innovations had to be undertaken to make this decision viable. To the finding of sources of supply and to the purchase of goods from them, merchandising had to add two new major functions; the design of products and the development of manufacturers capable of producing these products in large quantity. Class-market products — for instance, refrigerators in the twenties — had to be redesigned for a mass market with limited purchasing power. Suppliers had to be created — often with Sears money and Sears-trained management — to produce these goods. This also required another important innovation: a basic policy for the relations between Sears and its suppliers, especially those who depended on the company's purchases for the bulk of their business. Merchandise planning and research and the systematic building of hundreds of small suppliers capable of producing for a mass market had to be invented. They were as basic to mass distribution in Sears's second phase as mail order and catalogs were in its first, and they were as distinct a contribution to the American economy.

Retail selling also meant getting store managers. Mail-order selling did not prepare a person for the management of a retail store. The greatest bottleneck for the first ten or fifteen years of Sears's retail operation — almost until World War II — was the shortage of managers. The most systematic innovations had to be in the field of manager development; and the Sears policies of the thirties became the starting point for all the work in manager development now going on in industry.

Expansion into retail selling also meant radical innovations in organization structure. Mail-order selling is highly centralized; retail stores cannot be run from headquarters two thousand miles away. They must be managed locally. Only a few mail-order plants were needed to supply the country; Sears today has over a thousand stores, each with its own market in its own locality. A decentralized organization structure, methods of managing a decentralized company, measuring the performance of store managers, and maintaining corporate unity with maximum local autonomy — all these had to be devised to make retail selling possible. And new compensation policies had to be found to reward store managers for performance.

Finally, Sears had to innovate in store location, architecture, and physical arrangement. The traditional retail store was unsuited for the Sears market. It was not just a matter of putting the Sears store on the outskirts of the city and of providing it with an adequate parking lot. The whole concept of the retail store had to be changed. In fact, few people even at Sears realize how far this innovation has gone and how deeply it has influenced the shopping habits of the American people as well as the physical appearance of our towns. The suburban shopping center which appeared in the fifties as a radical innovation in retail selling is but a logical extension of the concepts and methods developed by Sears during the thirties.

The basic decisions underlying the expansion into retail stores were taken in the mid-twenties; the basic innovations had been made by the early thirties. This explains why Sears's volume of business and its profits grew right through the Depression and World War II.

In 1954 General Wood retired, though he retained influence in the company for another ten years. No other long-term dominant chief executive has emerged to replace him. Since Wood's retirement Sears has been run by a small team of men, a chairman, a president, and an executive vice-president. Without exception, these members of the top team retire after five to seven years in office rather than, like Rosenwald or Wood, holding power for twenty or thirty years.

The changes these successor managements brought about are almost as profound as those wrought by Rosenwald and Wood. They also redefined Sears's business. Under General Wood, Sears was moving from being a seller to being a buyer. Under his successors, Sears has redefined itself as a maker for the American family. Increasingly the emphasis is on Sears as the informed, responsible producer who designs for the American family the things it needs and wants. Today Sears's capital investment probably centers in the manufacturing plants it owns and controls — even though retail-store expansion has been pursued vigorously.

Sears again and again changed the definition of its market in line with the shifting patterns of the American population. Rosenwald made available mass goods to a new, emerging mass market. Wood made available to this mass market what earlier had been class-market goods, e.g., kitchen appliances. In the last twenty years Sears has shifted to a view of the American market in which there is no class market any more; it now operates on the assumption that the American middle class is, in its economic behavior, actually an upper class. Sears has thus greatly widened its product scope. Of course, Sears still carries appliances in its stores — and they probably are still the largest-selling product category. Sears has, however, also become the world's biggest diamond merchant, one of the country's biggest booksellers, and a large buyer and seller of original art objects, such as drawings, prints, and paintings.

General Wood has taken Sears into automobile insurance, which he rightly considered just as much an automobile accessory as brake lining or windshield wipers. His successors have added property insurance of all kinds. They have added a mutual fund to serve the new mass-capital market. They have gone into the travel business, and so on. In other words, Sears no longer defines its business as goods. It is defined as the needs, wants, and satisfactions of the American middle-class family.

Julius Rosenwald and, far more aggressively, General Wood had moved into controlling key manufacturers as the only way to make sure of the quality Sears needed, of the quantities its tremendous distribution system required, and of the lowest possible price for the customers. This is still the rationale given at Sears for ownership or control of manufacturing sources. But it would probably be more correct to describe the source relationship of Sears, Roebuck of today as procurement rather than as buying. The emphasis has steadily shifted toward a long-range strategy which anticipates what tomorrow's American family will be and what it will require, and then designs and develops the appropriate products or services. Sears today may be the first truly marketing-focused manufacturing business in the U.S., practicing what most manufacturing businesses so far only preach, that is, the total marketing approach. To this marketing strategy, focused on creating the sources of supply rather than on selling products to the public, Sears owes both its tremendous growth in sales and its profitability.

Yet Sears today faces new challenges which will require innovation and strategic thinking fully as much as the developments of the past.

From the beginning Sears has been keenly aware of basic population trends in the United States. Wood's favorite management tool was a "little black book" full of population statistics and population projections. Julius Rosenwald, too, had built his business on population analysis and population trends. The Sears policy, all along, has been to find the majority market and to convert it into a true mass market.

There may be a market shift ahead in America, and Sears may not be strategically positioned for it. By the late 1970s the young educated families, whose breadwinners make their living as knowledge workers, have come to dominate the American market. Even if Sears can transfer to them the special relationship it has had with their parents, the blue-collar workers of the big industrial cities, Sears does not make, buy, or sell in the same areas in which their needs may be greatest and their spending likely to go up the fastest. Sears is still primarily thing-focused, primarily a maker, buyer, and seller of manufactured goods. The young educated families have a healthy appetite for goods; but in their spending behavior and values, they are upper-upper rather than upper class, even if their incomes are only average. This means that the major growth areas in their budgets may not be goods but information and education, health care, travel and leisure, reliable financial advice and services, and guidance on job and career choices. These, too, are wants and needs of the American family; these, too, are areas in which the American family needs an informed and responsible buyer. But these, by and large, are not areas in which Sears has established itself as the responsible maker and buyer.

Sears, further, has always looked upon its market as homogeneous. Sears has not been bothered by the fact that minority segments of the market were not its customers. Neither the very poor nor the very rich shop at Sears. But it has been taken for granted that the bulk of the population buys the same merchandise, considers the same things of value, and altogether shares a common economic profile and a common economic psychology. This may no longer be true. There are signs that the American market is fragmenting into a number of big segments with significant differences in buying behavior and economic values between them. For such a development, Sears would seem to be quite unprepared.

Sears began in the forties to expand beyond the American frontier, into Canada, then into Latin America. In the sixties it went into Spain. It has acquired minority interests in retail stores in other European countries. There are persistent rumors that it plans to expand into Japan. But so far, Sears is still an American rather than a multinational business. It will have to face up to a difficult and risky decision. If it stays American, it faces the serious possibility of a steady slowdown in its growth and profitability as nongoods become increasingly important in the family budget of the American middle class. If it decides to become truly multinational, Sears would have to choose in what countries and markets the Sears mass-marketing approach can make the greatest contribution. It would then have to think through what policies — from store design to merchandising to the structure of the relationship to foreign countries, their governments, their manufacturers, their investors — this would require. And Sears would undoubtedly have to learn to apply the same basic approaches and principles quite differently in different markets and different cultures.

If Sears wants to maintain its leadership position and its capacity to grow, it faces major new challenges and may have to redefine what its business is, where its markets are, and where innovations are needed.

The right answers are always obvious in retrospect. The basic lesson of the Sears story is that the right answers are likely to be anything but obvious *before* they have proven themselves. "Everybody knew" around 1900 that to promise "satisfaction guaranteed or your money back" could bring only financial disaster to a retailer. "Everybody knew" around 1925 that the American market was sharply segmented into distinct income groups, each buying different things in different places. "Everybody knew" — as late as 1950 — that the American consumer wanted to shop downtown, and so on.

Even more important as a lesson from the Sears story is the knowledge that the right answers are not the result of brilliance or of "intuition." Richard Sears had both — and failed. The right answers are the result of asking the right questions. And this in turn requires hard, systematic work to understand what a business is and what "our" business is.

The Power
and Purpose
of Objectives

Chapter 13

Social Revolution as Business Purpose and Mission
The Concentration Decision
The Objectives: Marketing; Innovation; Key Resources; Productivity;
  Social Responsibilities
Profit as Result Rather Than as Goal
Converting Objectives into Work Assignments
The Lessons
Specifications for Objectives
Objectives Needed in All Survival Areas
The Eight Areas of Objectives
The Basis for Work and Assignments
Objectives and Measurements
The Use of Objectives

*O*ne company in the Western world can be compared with Sears, Roebuck: Marks &
Spencer. It might even be slightly ahead in growth of sales and profits over a long period
of years.

Like Sears, Marks & Spencer is a chain retailer. It opened its first penny bazaar in
1884, or just about the time Richard Sears made his first mail-order offer of cheap but reliable watches to the Midwestern farmer. By 1915 the company was building variety stores.
It has been growing fast ever since. Its most spectacular growth period, however, was the
ten years between 1963 and 1972 — a period in Britain's economic history which was

characterized by "stagflation," i.e., inflationary stagnation, rather than growth. During this difficult period Marks & Spencer more than doubled its sales volume (from £184 million to £463 million, or in U.S. dollars, $460 million to $1,100 million at the rate of exchange then). Profits were up just as fast, from £22 million to £54 million ($55 million to $135 million). Equally remarkable was the profit margin — almost 12 percent on sales before taxes — which is double what any other retail merchant (except Sears) would consider fully satisfactory.

Social Revolution as Business Mission

By the mid-twenties the four brothers-in-law (Simon Marks, Israel Sieff, Harry Sacher, and Norman Laski) who had built the penny bazaars of 1915 into a major chain of variety stores owned a successful business. They might have been satisfied to rest on their laurels and to enjoy their considerable wealth. Instead they decided — following a trip to America by Simon Marks in 1924 in the course of which he carefully studied Sears, Roebuck — to rethink the purpose and mission of their business. The business of Marks & Spencer, they decided, was not retailing. It was social revolution.

Marks & Spencer redefined its business as the subversion of the class structure of nineteenth-century England by making available to the working and lower-middle classes upper class goods of better than upper-class quality, and yet at prices the working and lower-middle-class customer could well afford.

Marks & Spencer was by no means alone in the England of the twenties in seeing a major opportunity in the rapid social changes of the post-World War I period. What made Marks & Spencer unique and successful, however, was its conversion of the definition of "what our business is, and should be" into clear, specific operationally effective and multiple *objectives.*

This required first a decision as to what to concentrate on, that is, a *basic strategy objective.*

Marks & Spencer had been a variety store chain like many others, offering a large assortment of products which had nothing in common except low price. Now the company decided to concentrate on wearing apparel (to which it soon added household textiles such as towels and draperies).

This was a rational decision. In the England of that time dress was still highly class-determined and the most visible of all class distinctions. Yet all of Europe, after World War I, had become fashion conscious. At the same time mass-production facilities for good-quality but inexpensive fabrics and clothes had come into being, in large part as a result of the huge demand for uniforms during World War I. New textile fibers, such as rayon and acetate, were coming on the market. There was still, however, no mass-distribution system in England for well-designed, up-to-date, and inexpensive clothing for the masses.

Within a few years the new Marks & Spencer had become the leading clothing and textile distributor in England, a position held ever since. By 1972 clothing sales accounted for a full three-quarters of total Marks & Spencer volume, i.e., for £327 million (roughly $800 million).

After World War II the same thinking was applied to a new major product category: food. During World War II the English people, formerly known for their dogged resistance to any innovation in eating, learned to accept new foods. Marks & Spencer's food business accounted, in 1972, for the remaining one-fourth of its sales.

From having been a successful variety chain in the early twenties, and even in the early thirties, Marks & Spencer purposefully changed itself into a highly distinct "specialty" marketer — maybe the largest in the world.

The Objectives

The concentration decision then enabled the company to set specific *marketing* objectives. The decision enabled it to decide who its customer was and should be; what kind of store it needed and when; what pricing policy to follow; and what market penetration to aim at.

The next area which Marks & Spencer tackled was that of *innovation objectives.* The clothing and textiles Marks & Spencer needed did not exist at the time. Marks & Spencer started out with quality control, like any other large retailer. But it rapidly built its quality-control laboratories into research, design, and development centers. It developed new fabrics, new dyestuffs, new processes, new blends, and so on. It developed designs and fashions. Finally, it went out and looked for the right manufacturer, whom it often had to help get started — for the existing old-line manufacturers were for obvious reasons none too eager to throw in their lot with the brash upstart who tried to tell them how to run their business. And when, after World War II, the company moved into prepared and processed foods, bakery goods, and dairy products, it applied the same innovative approach to a new industry.

Marks & Spencer set innovation goals in marketing. It pioneered, for instance, in consumer research in the early thirties, when such work was still so new that Marks & Spencer had to develop the needed techniques. (General Motors had a consumer research activity well before 1929. I doubt that this was known to Marks & Spencer, however; it was not generally known even within the American automobile industry.)

Marks & Spencer set objectives for the supply and development of key resources. It early copied and adapted the Sears program for recruiting, training, and developing managers. It set objectives for the systematic development of financial resources, and measurements to control the utilization of these resources. And it set objectives for the development of its physical facilities, that is, for retail stores.

Hand in hand with these objectives for resources went objectives for their productivity. Marks & Spencer had originally taken its measurements and controls from America. In the twenties and early thirties it began to set its own objectives for continuously improving the productivity of key resources.

As a result, Marks & Spencer has a singularly high productivity of capital — surely one of the keys to its success. Unnoticed, by and large — but fully as important — is the productivity of the Marks & Spencer retail store, which exceeds, to my knowledge, anything to be found anyplace else, including even Sears, Roebuck or Kresge, the acknowledged store-management virtuosi of the American retail scene.

Up till the late twenties the expansion of Marks & Spencer had been achieved primarily by opening new stores. Since the thirties Marks & Spencer's expansion has been achieved primarily by making each store more productive and by raising sales per square foot of selling space. Marks & Spencer, measured by the number of its stores, is still a medium sized chain — there are only 250 stores (Sears for instance has a thousand and so does J.C. Penny). The stores themselves are not large, even by English standards; the average selling area is only 20,000 square feet per store. (The large American supermarket, by comparison, goes up to 100,000 square feet.) Yet these small stores sell something like $4 million apiece a year, which is many times what even highly successful retail stores of other companies do. The only explanation is continual upgrading of volume per store, that is, upgrading of merchandise, display, and sales per customer. Store selling space is the controlling resource of a retail merchant; Marks & Spencer's success in raising its utilization was central to its performance.

Marks & Spencer set objectives for its social responsibilities, and especially for areas of major impact: its own work force and its suppliers. It introduced staff managers (actually, they were referred to as "staff manageresses" because they were all women) into its stores to look after the employees, to take care of personal problems, and to make sure employees are treated with intelligence and compassion. Personnel management remains the job of the store manager. The staff manager was set up to be the "people conscience" of the company.

Similarly Marks & Spencer developed objectives for its relations with its suppliers. The more successfully a supplier works with Marks & Spencer, the more dependent upon the company the supplier will be. To safeguard the supplier against exploitation by the company became a concern of the company's management. It set out to develop a "putting out" system which, unlike its pre-industrial predecessor of early eighteenth-century England, would not impoverish and make the supplier less secure but would, on the contrary, enrich and give the supplier security.

Profit: A Result, Not a Goal

But what about a profit objective? The answer is that there has never been one. Profit goals have been anathema at Marks & Spencer. Obviously the company is highly profitable and highly profit conscious. But it sees profit not as an objective but as a requirement of the business, that is, not as a goal but as a need. Profit, in the Marks & Spencer view, is the *result* of doing things right rather than the purpose of business activity. It is, above all, determined by what is necessary to attain company objectives. Profitability is a measurement of how well the business discharges its functions in serving market and customer. Above all, it is a restraint; unless profit is adequate to cover the risks, a company will not be able to attain its objectives.

I do not know how conscious Marks & Spencer's top management was in the early years, the late twenties and early thirties, of the full import of the decisions they then made. There was probably no master plan. But the young key executives who were brought into the firm in those years to take on new jobs such as innovation or the development of productivity objectives and standards were fully aware that their company had committed itself to a definition of what its business was — and they knew what the definition entailed. They were highly conscious of the company's social and business objectives. They knew what these objectives meant to each of them individually in terms of performance goals, performance standards, and demands for their own contribution.

Marks & Spencer from the start converted objectives into work assignments. It thought through what results and contributions were needed in each objectives area. It assigned responsibility for these results to someone and held that person accountable. And it measured performance and contribution against the objectives.

The Lessons

The Marks & Spencer story reaffirms the central importance of thinking through "what our business *is* and what it *should* be." But it also shows that this, by itself, is not enough. The basic definition of the business and the definition of its purpose and mission have to be translated into objectives. Otherwise they remain insight, good intentions, and brilliant epigrams which never become achievement.

The Marks & Spencer story brings out the specifications for objectives, which are listed below.

1. Objectives must be derived from "what our business is, what it will be, and what it should be." They are not abstractions. They are the action commitments through which the mission of a business is to be carried out, and the standards against which performance is to be measured. Objectives, in other words, are the *fundamental strategy of a business.*

2. Objectives must be *operational.* They must be capable of being converted into specific targets and specific assignments. They must be capable of becoming the basis, as well as the motivation, for work and achievement.

3. Objectives must make possible *concentration* of resources and efforts. They must winnow out the fundamentals among the goals of a business so that the key resources of people, money, and physical facilities can be concentrated. They must, therefore, be selective rather than encompass everything.

4. There must be *multiple objectives* rather than a single objective.

   Much of today's lively discussion of management by objectives is concerned with the search for the "one right objective." This search is not only likely to be unproductive; it does harm and misdirects.

   To manage a business is to balance a variety of needs and goals. And this requires multiple objectives.

5. Objectives are needed in all areas on which the survival of the business depends. The specific targets, the goals in any objective area, depend on the strategy of the individual business. But the areas in which objectives are needed are the same for all businesses, for all businesses depend on the same factors for their survival.

   A business must first be able to create a customer. There is, therefore, need for a *marketing objective.* Businesses must be able to innovate or else their competitors will obsolesce them. There is need for an *innovation objective.* All businesses depend on the three factors of production of the economist, that is, on the *human resource,* the *capital resource,* and *physical resources.* There must be objectives for their supply, their employment, and their development. The resources must be employed productively and their productivity has to grow if the business is to survive. There is a need, therefore, for *productivity objectives.* Business exists in society and community and, therefore, has to discharge social responsibilities, at least to the point where it takes responsibility for its impact upon the environment. Therefore objectives in respect to the *social dimensions* of business are needed.

Finally, there is need for *profit* — otherwise none of the objectives can be attained. They all require effort, that is, cost. And they can be financed only out of the profits of a business. They all entail risks; they all, therefore, require a profit to cover the risk of potential losses. Profit is not an objective but it is a requirement that has to be objectively determined in respect to the individual business, its strategy, its needs, and its risks. Instead of asking: how much profit do we aspire to? a business needs to ask: how much profit is needed to cover the costs of capital, the risks of the business and the demands of survival in all objectives areas?

Objectives, therefore, have to be set in these eight key areas:

- marketing;
- innovation;
- human organization;
- financial resources;
- physical resources;
- productivity;
- social responsibility;
- profit requirements;

Objectives in these key areas enable us to do five things: to organize and explain the whole range of business phenomena in a small number of general statements; to test these statements in actual experience; to predict behavior; to appraise the soundness of decisions while they are still being made; and to let managers on all levels analyze their own experience and, as a result, improve their performance.

The Basis for Work and Assignments

Objectives are the basis for work and assignments.

They determine the structure of the business, the key activities which must be discharged, and, above all, the allocation of people to tasks. Objectives are the foundation for designing both the structure of the business and the work of individual units and individual managers.

Objectives are always needed in all eight key areas. The area without specific objectives will be neglected. Unless we determine what shall be measured and what the yardstick of measurement in an area will be, the area itself will not be seen.

The measurements available for the key areas of a business enterprise are still haphazard by and large. We do not even have adequate concepts, let alone measurements, except for market standing. For something as central as profitability we have only a rubber yardstick; and we have no real tools at all to determine how much profitability is necessary. In respect to innovation and, even more, to productivity, we hardly know more than that something ought to be done. In the other areas — including physical and financial resources — we are reduced to statements of intentions; we do not possess goals and measurements for their attainment.

However, enough is known about each area to give a progress report at least. Enough is known for each business to go to work on objectives.

How to Use Objectives

We know one more thing about objectives: how to use them.

If objectives are only good intentions they are worthless. They must degenerate into work. And work is always specific, always has — or should have — clear, unambiguous, measurable results, a deadline and a specific assignment of accountability.

But objectives that become a straitjacket do harm. Objectives are always based on expectations. And expectations are, at best, informed guesses. Objectives express an appraisal of factors that are largely outside the business and not under its control. The world does not stand still.

The proper way to use objectives is the way an airline uses schedules and flight plans. The schedule provides for the 9 A.M. flight from Los Angeles to get to Boston by 5 P.M. But if there is a blizzard in Boston that day, the plane will land in Pittsburgh instead and wait out the storm. The flight plan provides for flying at 30,000 feet and for flying over Denver and Chicago. But if the pilot encounters turbulence or strong headwinds he will ask flight control for permission to go up another 5,000 feet and to take the Minneapolis-Montreal route. Yet no flight is ever operated without schedule and flight plan. Unless 97 percent or so of its flights proceed on the original schedule and flight plan — or within a very limited range of deviation from either — a well-run airline gets another operations manager who can do the job.

Objectives are not fate; they are direction. They are not commands; they are commitments. They do not determine the future; they are means to mobilize the resources and energies of the business for the making of the future.

The Delusion of Profits

Chapter 14

The Essential Fact about Profit: It Does Not Exist
Profit Represents Cost of Capital, Cost against Risk, and Cost of
Future Jobs and Pensions

*M*ost people in business don't seem to know the first thing about profit and profitability. And what they say to each other as well as to the public about profit and profitability inhibits both business action and public understanding.

For the essential fact about profit is that there is no such thing. There are only costs.

What is called "profit" and reported as such in company accounts is genuine and largely quantifiable cost in three respects: as a genuine cost of a major resource, namely capital; as a necessary insurance premium for the real — and again largely quantifiable — risks and uncertainties of all economic activity; and as cost of the jobs and pensions of tomorrow. The only exception, the only true "surplus," of revenue over costs is a genuine monopoly profit such as that now being exacted by the governments of the oil exporting countries (especially the Arabs) through OPEC, i.e., the Organization of Petroleum Exporting Countries.

Cost of Capital

All economists have known for 200 years that there are "factors of production," that is, three necessary resources: labor, "land" (i.e., physical resources), and capital. And all of us should have learned in the last 10 years that there are no "free" resources. They all have a cost. Indeed, the economists are way ahead of most business people in their understanding and acceptance of a genuine "cost of capital." Some of them have worked out elegant methods both for determining the cost of capital and for measuring the performance of a business in earning it.

We know that in the post-World War II period, until the onset of global inflation in the mid-'60s, the cost of capital in all developed countries of the Free World ran somewhat above 10 percent a year (it is almost certainly much higher in Communist economies). The cost of capital is what a user has to pay in order to obtain money. It varies little, by the way, between different legal forms, e.g., between money lent as a loan, money raised by selling bonds, and money obtained by selling shares. What determines the cost of capital are in part what economists call its "true cost" — which probably runs about 3 or 4 percent a year; secondly the — fairly high — cost of administration of money which even in very efficient big banks is at least 2 percent a year; third, the risk of not getting repaid, which is a genuine risk of loss — and, of course, much higher for some users than for others; and finally the risk that money itself will lose value, that is, the risk of inflation. Any user of money, whatever his sources for it, and irrespective of the legal form in which he obtains money, whether from a bank as a short-term loan, as a long-term mortgage or against long-term bonds such as those of the Federal Government, or by selling common shares, always has to pay all four kinds of "cost money" — and all four are genuine costs.

We know that all businesses have to pay these costs. We also know that very few businesses actually earn enough to cover these costs. The costs of capital in the period after World War II rarely fell below 10 percent and in inflationary years they were much higher, of course. But very few companies earn consistently as much as 7 percent after taxes on the money employed in the business. So far, however, only a handful of businesses seem to know that there is such a cost. Fewer still seem to know whether they cover it or not. And even these few never talk about it and never in their published accounts subject their own performance to the test. Yet not to earn the cost of capital is as much a failure to cover costs as not to earn the costs of wages or of raw materials.

Risk and Uncertainty as Genuine Cost

Economic activity is the commitment of existing resources to future expectations. It is a commitment, therefore, to risk and uncertainty — in respect to obsolescence of products, processes, and equipment; in respect to changes in markets, distributive channels, and consumer values; and in respect to changes in the economy, technology, and society. The odds in any commitment to the future are always adverse; it is not given to human beings to know the future. The odds, therefore, are always in favor of loss rather than gain. And in a period of rapid change such as ours the risks and uncertainties are surely not getting smaller.

These risks and uncertainties are not capable of precise determination. But the minimum of risk in these commitments to the future is capable of being determined, and indeed quantified, with a fair degree of probability. Where this has been attempted in any business — and in both Xerox and IBM, for instance, it is known to have been done for years in respect to products and technologies — the risks have proven to be much higher than even conservative "business plans" assumed.

The risks of natural events — fire, for instance — have long been treated as normal business costs. A business that fails to set aside the appropriate insurance premiums for such risks would rightly be considered to be endangering the wealth-producing assets in its keeping. Economic, technological and social risks and uncertainties are no less real. They too require an adequate "insurance premium" — and to supply it is the function of profit and profitability.

The proper question for any management therefore is not: "What is the *maximum* profit this business can yield?" It is: "What is the *minimum* profitability needed to cover the future risks of this business?" And if the profitability falls short of this minimum — as it does in most companies I know — the business fails to cover genuine costs, endangers itself and impoverishes the economy.

Cost of Future Jobs and Pensions

Profit is also tomorrow's jobs and tomorrow's pensions. Both are costs of a business and equally costs of the economy. Business earnings, whether retained in the business or paid out (returned to the capital market), are the largest single source of capital formation for tomorrow's jobs and, at least in the United States, the largest single source of capital formation for tomorrow's pensions.

The most satisfactory definition of "economic progress" is a steady rise in the ability of an economy to invest more capital for each new job and thereby to produce jobs that yield a better living as well as a better quality of work and life. By 1965, before inflation made meaningful figures increasingly difficult to obtain, investment per job in the American economy had risen from $35,000 to $50,000. The requirement will go up fairly sharply, for the greatest investment needs and opportunities are in industries: energy, the environment, transportation, health care and, above all, increased food production, in which capital investment per job is far higher than the average in the consumer goods industries which have dominated the economy these last 25 years.

At the same time, the number of jobs required is going up sharply — the aftermath of the "baby boom" between 1948 and 1960. We will have to increase the number of people at work by 1 percent, or almost a million people, each year these next few years to stay even with the demographics. And at the same time, the number of people on pensions will also increase, if only because workers reaching retirement age live longer, and so will the expectations of the pensioners. Any company which does not produce enough capital, i.e., enough earnings, to provide for this expansion in jobs and pensions fails both to cover its own predictable and quantifiable costs and the costs of the economy.

Three Conclusions

These three kinds of costs — the costs of capital, the risk premium of economic activity and the capital needs of the future — overlap to a considerable extent. But any company should be expected to cover adequately whichever of these three costs is the largest one in its own business. Otherwise it operates at a genuine, certain, and provable loss.

There are three conclusions from these elementary premises:

1. "Profit" is not peculiar to capitalism. It is a prerequisite for any economic system. Indeed, the Communist economies require a much higher rate of profit. Their costs of capital are higher, both because costs of administration are very high in a centralized economy, and because risks are high in the absence of the automatic (or semi-automatic) controls of a market system. And central planning adds an additional and major economic uncertainty. In fact, the Communist economies do operate at a substantially higher rate of profit than any market economy, no matter that for ideological reasons it is called "turnover tax" rather than "profit." And the only economies that can be considered as being based on "profit planning" are precisely Communist economies in which the producer (state planner) imposes the needed profitability in advance rather than let market forces determine it.

2. The costs of the future, the costs of risk and uncertainty, which are paid for out of the difference between current revenues and current expenses of production and distribution are fully as much "economic reality" as wages or payments for supplies. Since a company's accounts are supposed to reflect "economic reality," these costs should be shown. They are, to be sure, not as precisely known or knowable as the accountants' "costs of doing business" supposedly are. But they are known and knowable within limits that are probably no wider or fuzzier than those of most cost accounting or depreciation figures — and they may be more important both for managing a business or for analyzing its performance.

3. Finally, people in business owe it to themselves and owe it to society to hammer home that there is no such thing as "profit." There are only "costs": costs of doing business and costs of staying in business; costs of labor and raw materials, and costs of capital; costs of today's jobs and costs of tomorrow's job and tomorrow's pensions.

There is no conflict between "profit" and "social responsibility." To earn enough to cover the genuine costs which only the so-called "profit" can cover, is economic and social responsibility, indeed it is the specific social and economic responsibility of business. It is not the business that earns a profit adequate to its genuine costs of capital, to the risks of tomorrow and to the needs of tomorrow's worker and pensioner, that "rips off" society. It is the business that fails to do so.

Managing Capital Productivity

Chapter 15

*Productivity of Capital Has Been Increasing almost from the Time
    Marx Predicted It Wouldn't*
*Know Where the Capital Is in a Business and What It Does for the
    Business*
*To Increase the Productivity of Capital: Make Capital Work Harder or
    Smarter*
Working Capital and Fixed Capital Require Different Approaches
Fixed Capital: Look for Time-Not-Worked and Product-Mix
Working Capital Supports, It Doesn't Produce
Time Must Be Managed as if It Were Fixed Capital

A hundred years ago, Karl Marx based his prediction of the inevitable and imminent collapse of what we now call "capitalism" or the "free enterprise system" (both terms were not coined until long after Marx's death) on the "law" of the diminishing return on capital.

What happened instead is that for a century the productivity of capital in the developed countries with a market economy — has been going up except during the most severe depression years. This is one of the major achievements of modern business and the one on which the other achievements perhaps ultimately rest. In part, this achievement was entrepreneurial: The steady shifting of capital from old and rapidly less productive areas of investment into new and more highly productive areas — that is, into areas of technical or social innovation.

But the steady increase in the productivity of capital is equally the result of managerial action, of continuing effort to improve the amount of productive work a given unit of capital performs in the business. One example is commercial banking, where one unit of capital today finances five times as large a volume of transactions as it did in Marx's time.

The Easiest Way to Improve Profitability

The evidence of the last 100 years is quite clear: productivity of capital can be maintained and even increased, provided only that the people in business work at it constantly and purposefully.

In fact, working on the productivity of capital is the easiest and usually the quickest way to improve the profitability of a business and the one with the greatest impact. The total profit of a business is profit margin multiplied by turnover of capital, that is, by productivity of capital. If a product costs 94 cents to produce and sells for one dollar, the profit margin is 6 percent. If the producer turns over his capital once a year, then there is a 6 percent return on the total capital. If capital turnover can be raised to 1.2 times a year, total return on capital will go up to 7.2 percent.

To raise profit margins by 20 percent is usually extremely difficult and may be impossible in a competitive market. But to raise capital turnover from once a year to 1.2 times a year often requires only consistent but routine hard work. Indeed, on the basis of quite a few years experience in this field, I am willing to predict that an improvement of this magnitude — that is, an improvement of 20 percent in the productivity of capital over perhaps four or five years — should be available to anyone who seriously tackles the job.

Know Where the Capital Is and What It Does

Yet, despite its importance and payoff, not many business managers pay much attention to the productivity of capital, let alone work systematically at raising it. This, by the way, is just as true of managers of such public service enterprises as hospitals (where productivity of capital has fallen a good deal more sharply these last few years than in private business) as it is of managers in business.

One reason, perhaps the single most important one, is that managers, as a rule, get little information on the productivity of capital in their business. Most businesses know, of course, how many times a year they turn over their entire capital. But the annual turnover of the company's entire capital in a business, say a papermill or a department store, is an aggregate. One always has to manage — and therefore to measure first — major components separately. Yet few managements know what the meaningful components of capital are in their business, let alone what the productivity of capital for each of them is, could be or should be.

The first step toward managing the productivity of capital is therefore to determine the main areas in one's own company in which capital is actually invested. There rarely are more than a handful. In a typical manufacturing business, for instance: machinery and equipment; inventories of materials, supplies and finished goods; and receivables — together these usually account for three-quarters of money invested. In a typical department store there are shelf space (or selling space), receivables and inventories (inventories in retailing usually have to be subdivided, e.g., into wearing apparel, home furnishings and furniture, appliances, etc., to be meaningful and manageable). How much productive work does the capital employed in each of these areas do? How often does it turn over? How much does it return or contribute? Then one can ask: How much could it and how much should it produce, and what do we have to do to bring this about?

Make Capital Work Harder or Smarter

Managements also need to learn a few elementary rules about managing the productivity of capital.

One can increase the productivity of capital in two ways. One can make capital work harder. And one can make it work smarter. This is one of the main reasons, by the way, why the productivity of capital is more easily managed than that of the other two main resources — physical resources and human resources. The productivity of human resources can usually be raised only by making them work smarter; that of physical resources only by making them work harder.

Locating one's inventory in strategically placed regional warehouses, so that the same amount of inventory can support a larger volume of sales, is making capital work harder. Controlling the product mix to sell a larger proportion of high-contributing products, or a smaller proportion of low-contributing ones, is making capital work smarter. Often one can do both simultaneously. But it is difficult to predict in advance which approach is likely to be appropriate in a given situation, more productive and less risky. Both need to be thought through for each major area of investment in each individual business.

Fixed Capital and Working Capital Require Different Approaches

In every business there is "fixed capital" — that is, money invested permanently in buildings, in machinery, in equipment. And there is "working capital," money in inventories, for instance, or in credit given to customers (called commonly "receivables"). Fixed capital and working capital, while both capital, require different approaches in managing their productivity. Many businesses use sophisticated methods for making capital investment decisions. But once the capital investment decision has been made, there is often amazingly little information about the productivity of the capital asset obtained by spending the money.

Most business people know that nothing is more wasteful in a fixed asset than time not worked. Yet few seem to realize that the standard-cost accounting model assumes — and has to assume — continuous production at a pre-set "standard" for a given fixed asset, whether a rolling mill in a steel plant, a unit of selling space in a store, or a clinical-care hospital bed. The standard-cost accounting model, in other words, neither measures nor controls the single largest cost on a fixed asset: the cost of capital non-productivity.

Similarly, cost accounting has to assume a "standard" product mix, even though both costs and revenues vary tremendously with different mixes (perhaps most for the hospital bed among all major pieces of fixed-capital investment). Managing time-not-worked and product-mix are the most effective ways to improve the productivity of capital for most fixed investments. For this, however, one has to *know* first how much time is not being worked and why. One has to know the economics of various product mixes. One has to have, in other words, economic information on productivity of capital in addition to the analytical data of the accounting model. Then one usually can improve greatly the utilization of time and, with it, the productivity of fixed capital.

But working capital needs to be measured differently and to be managed differently. Unlike fixed assets, it is not "producing capital" but "supporting capital." It does not "create" wealth, that is, goods or services. It brings goods and services to market, or finances the time between their production and the time the buyer pays. The question, therefore, must be asked: "What does it, and what should it, support?"

Receivables — that is credit extended by a business to its customers — are the obvious example. Companies typically measure their credit management by the proportion of the outstanding loans they collect. "We do a first-rate credit job since our credit losses are less than 1 percent," is a frequently heard comment. But manufacturers are not in the banking business nor, considering their cost of capital, could they compete with banks. They give credit to make profitable sales. What then should the objective of a credit policy be in respect to market creation, product introduction, sales, and profits — with low-loss experience as a restraint rather than a goal or measurement? Every business that has asked this question has found (a) that it puts the bulk of its credit where it gets the least back; and (b) that it gives the least credit where it gets the most back. Over a three to four year period, a business that systematically works on the productivity of the capital employed in receivables can expect that with two-thirds of the money now tied up in credit it can finance a larger and more profitable volume of sales.

The Phantom Fixed Capital: Time

Finally, few managements seem to know that there are important areas in a business which are not normally considered "capital investment" — and surely do not appear as such in the balance sheet — but which behave economically very much like fixed capital and have to be managed, above all, for "productivity of capital." These are the areas in which *time* is the major cost element while, over any given period, other costs are relatively fixed and inflexible. Main among them is the sales force, but also the nursing staff in a hospital. This is "fixed human capital." And economically it has to be managed very much as if it were "fixed capital," without any qualifications.

There are great differences in selling ability between sales people which no amount of training seems to be able to overcome, or even significantly to narrow. But the ablest sales person — or the most dedicated nurse — has only one resource: time. There is a fairly constant relationship between the time a sales person has for sales calls and the number of sales actually closed. Time not available for work is the major, though usually totally hidden, cost element in these "fixed human assets." And this means that, as in the case of all fixed assets, management first needs to know the productivity of time, and especially how much time that should be available for work is actually time not worked and not available for work, and why (e.g., because the sales person spends two-thirds of his or her time on paperwork rather than selling). Sometimes it takes then very little change to bring about substantial productivity increases. To put a floor clerk in to take over paperwork has, in some hospitals, for instance, almost doubled the time the nurses have available for what they are trained for, are paid for, and want to do — patient care.

Balance among the Three Factors of Production

Productivity is the combined result of the productivities of all three "factors of production": capital, natural resources, and human resources. And it is just as dangerous to increase productivity of capital at the expense of lowering the productivity of the other two factors as it is to increase, say, the productivity of the human resource at the expense of downgrading the productivity of capital (as was done only too often these last 25 years).

Business managers must learn and accept that they are paid for managing productivity, especially the productivity of capital, on which, in the last analysis, all other productivities depend; that the productivity of capital can be managed; and that the productivity of capital *must* be managed.

Managing the Public Service Institution

Chapter 16

Half the U.S. Personal Income Is Spent on Public Service
Public Service Institutions Do Not Perform Because They Are Not
   Managed for Performance
The Three Copouts: Managers Aren't Businesslike, Need "Better
   People," Objectives Are Intangible
Budget Allocation: The Basic Difference and a Main Problem
Successful Examples: The Bell Telephone System, The American
   University
Managing the Hospital through Its Objectives and Priorities
The Six Requirements for Success

*S*ervice institutions are an increasingly important part of our society. Schools and universities; research laboratories; public utilities; hospitals and other health-care institutions; professional, industry, and trade associations; and many others — all these are as much "institutions" as is the business firm, and, therefore, are equally in need of management. They all have people who are designated to exercise the management function and who are paid to do the management job — even though they may not be called "managers," but "administrators," "directors," "executives," or some other such title.

These "public service" institutions — to give them a generic name — are the real growth sector of a modern society. Indeed, what we have now is a "multi-institutional" society rather than a "business" society.

All public service institutions are being paid for out of the economic surplus produced by economic activity. The growth of the service institutions in this century is thus the best testimonial to the success of business in discharging its economic task. Yet unlike, say, the early 19th-century university, the service institutions are not mere "luxury" or "ornament." They are, so to speak, main pillars of a modern society, load-bearing members of the main structure. They *have* to perform if society and economy are to function. It is not only that these service institutions are a major expense of a modern society; half of the personal income of the United States (and of most of the other developed countries) is spent on public service institutions (including those operated by the government). Compared to these "public service" institutions, both the "private sector" (i.e., the economy of goods) and the traditional government functions of law, defense, and public order, account for a smaller share of the total income flow of today's developed societies than they did around 1900 — despite the enormous growth of military spending.

Every citizen in the developed, industrialized, urbanized societies depends on the performance of the public service institutions. For it is in the form of education and health care, knowledge and mobility — rather than primarily in the form of more "food, clothing, and shelter" — that our society obtains the fruits of its increased economic capacities and productivity.

Yet the evidence for performance in the service institutions is not impressive. Schools, hospitals, universities have grown today beyond the imagination of an earlier generation. They all dispose of astronomical budgets. Yet everywhere they are "in crisis." A generation or two ago, their performance was taken for granted. Today, they are being attacked for lack of performance. Services which the 19th century managed with aplomb and apparently with little effort — the postal service, for instance — are deeply in the red, require enormous and ever-growing subsidies, and yet give poorer service everywhere. In every country citizens complain ever more loudly of "bureaucracy" and mismanagement in the institutions that are supposed to serve them.

Are Service Institutions Manageable?

The response of the service institutions to this criticism has been to become "management conscious." They increasingly turn to business to learn "management." In all service institutions, "manager development," " management by objectives," and many other concepts and tools of business management are becoming increasingly popular. This is a healthy sign — but no more than that. It does not mean that the service institutions understand the problems of managing themselves. It only means that they have begun to realize that, at present, they are not being managed. Yet, though "performance" in the public service institutions is the exception rather than the rule, the exceptions do prove that service institutions can perform.

What is it that the few successful service institutions do that makes them capable of performance? This is the question to ask. And it is a *management* question — of a special kind. In most respects, the service institution is not very different from a business enterprise. It faces similar — if not precisely the same — challenges in seeking to make work productive. It does not differ significantly from a business in its "social responsibility."

Nor does the service institution differ very much from business enterprise in respect to the manager's work and job, in respect to organizational design and structure, or even in respect to the job and structure of top management. *Internally,* the differences tend to be differences in terminology rather than in substance.

But the service institution is in a fundamentally different "business" from business. It is different in its purpose. It has different values. It needs different objectives. And it makes a different contribution to society. "Performance and results" are quite different in a service institution from what they are in a business. "Managing for performance" is the one area in which the service institution differs significantly from a business.

Why Service Institutions Do Not Perform

There are three popular explanations for the common failure of service institutions to perform:

1. Their managers aren't "businesslike";
2. They need "better people";
3. Their objectives and results are "intangible."

The popular view is that the service institution will perform if only it is managed in a "businesslike" manner. Chambers of commerce, presidential and royal commissions, ministers in the Communist countries, and so on, all say: if only their administrators were to behave in a "businesslike" way, service institutions would perform. And of course, this belief also underlies, in large measure, today's "management boom" in the service institutions.

But it is the wrong diagnosis; and being "businesslike" is the wrong prescription for the ills of the service institution. The service institution has performance trouble precisely because it is *not* a business. What being "businesslike" usually means in a service institution is little more than control of cost. What characterizes a business, however, is focus on results – return on capital, share of market, and so on.

To be sure, there is a need for efficiency in all institutions. Because there is usually no competition in the service field, there is no outward and imposed cost control on service institutions as there is on business in a competitive market. But the basic problem of service institutions is not high cost but lack of effectiveness. They may be very efficient some are. But they then tend not to do the right things.

The belief that the public service institution will perform if only it is put on a "businesslike" basis underlies the numerous attempts to set up many government services as separate "public corporations." There may be beneficial side effects, such as freedom from petty civil service regulation. But the intended main effect, performance, is seldom achieved. Costs may go down. But services essential to the fulfillment of the institution's purpose may be slighted or lopped off in the name of "efficiency."

The best and worst example of the "businesslike" approach in the public service institution may well be the Port of New York Authority, set up in the 1920's to manage automobile and truck traffic throughout the two-state area (New York and New Jersey) of the Port of New York. The Port Authority has, from the beginning, been "businesslike" with a vengeance. The engineering of its bridges, tunnels, docks, silos, and airports has been outstanding. Its construction costs have been low and under control. Its financial standing has been extremely high, so that it could always borrow at most advantageous rates of interest. It made being "businesslike" — as measured, above all, by its standing with the banks — its goal and purpose. As a result, it did not concern itself with transportation policy in the New York metropolitan area, even though its bridges, tunnels, and airports generate much of the traffic in New York's streets. It did not ask: "Who are our constituents?" Instead it resisted any such question as "political" and "unbusinesslike." Consequently, it has come to be seen as the villain of the New York traffic and transportation problem. And when it needed support, it found itself without a single backer, except the bankers. As a result the Port Authority may well become "politicized"; that is, denuded of its efficiency without gaining anything in effectiveness.

Better People Are Not Needed for Better Performance

Service institutions cannot, any more than businesses, depend on superstars to staff their managerial and executive positions. There are far too many institutions to be staffed. If service institutions cannot be run and managed by people of normal — or even fairly low — endowment, if, in other words, we cannot organize the task so that it will be done on a satisfactory level by people who only try hard, it cannot be done at all. Moreover, there is no reason to believe that the people who staff the managerial and professional positions in our "service" institutions are any less qualified, any less competent or honest, or any less hard-working than those who manage businesses. By the same token, there is no reason to believe that business managers, put in control of service institutions, would do better than the "bureaucrats." Indeed, we know that they immediately become "bureaucrats" themselves.

One example of this was the American experience during World War II, when large numbers of business executives who had performed very well in their own companies moved into government positions. Many rapidly became "bureaucrats." These executives did not change. But whereas in business they had been capable of obtaining performance and results, in government they found themselves producing primarily procedures and red tape — and deeply frustrated by the experience.

Similarly, effective business people who are promoted to head a "service staff" within a business (e.g., the hard-hitting sales manager who gets to be "Vice President — marketing services") tend to become "bureaucrats" almost overnight. Indeed, the "service institutions" within business — research and development departments, personnel staffs, marketing or manufacturing service staffs, and the like — apparently find it just as hard to perform as the public service institutions of society at large, which business people themselves often criticize as being "unbusinesslike" and run by "bureaucrats."

Intangible Objectives Can Yield Measurable Goals

The most sophisticated and, at first glance, the most plausible explanation for the non-performance of service institutions is the last one: The objectives of service institutions are "intangible," and so are their results. This is at best a half-truth.

The definition of "what our business is" is always "intangible," in a business as well as in a service institution. Surely, to say, as Sears Roebuck does, "Our business is to be the informed buyer for the American family," is "intangible." And to say, as Bell Telephone does, "Our business is service to the customers," may sound like a pious and empty platitude. At first glance, these statements would seem to defy any attempt at translation into operational, let alone quantitative, terms. To say, "Our business is electronic entertainment," as Sony of Japan does, is equally "intangible," as is IBM's definition of its business as "data processing." Yet, as these businesses have clearly demonstrated, it is not exceedingly difficult to derive concrete and measurable goals and targets from "intangible" definitions like those cited above.

"Saving souls," as the definition of the objectives of a church is, indeed, "intangible." At least the bookkeeping is not of this world. But church attendance is measurable. And so is "getting the young people back into the church."

"The development of the whole personality" as the objective of the school is, indeed, "intangible." But "teaching a child to read upon completing the third grade" is by no means intangible; it can be measured easily and with considerable precision.

"Abolishing racial discrimination" is equally unamenable to clear operational definition, let alone measurement. But to increase the number of black apprentices in the building trades is a quantifiable goal, the attainment of which can be measured.

Achievement is never possible except against specific, limited, clearly defined targets, in business as well as in a service institution. Only if targets are defined can resources be allocated to their attainment, priorities and deadlines be set, and somebody be held accountable for results. But the starting point for effective work is a definition of the purpose and mission of the institution — which is almost always "intangible," but nevertheless need not be vacuous.

It is often said that service institutions differ from businesses in that they have a plurality of constituencies. And it is indeed the case that service institutions have a great many "constituents." The school is of vital concern not only to children and their parents, but also to teachers, to taxpayers, and to the community at large. Similarly, the hospital has to satisfy the patient, but also the doctors, the nurses, the technicians, the patient's family — as well as taxpayers or, as in the United States, employers and labor unions who through their insurance contributions provide the bulk of the support of most hospitals. But business also has a plurality of constituencies. Every business has at least two different customers, and often a good many more. And employees, investors, and the community at large — and even management itself — are also "constituencies."

Misdirection by Budget

The one basic difference between a service institution and a business is the way the service institution is paid. Businesses (other than monopolies) are paid for satisfying the customer. They are only paid when they produce what the customer wants and is willing to purchase. Satisfaction of the customer is, therefore, the basis for performance and results in a business.

Service institutions, by contrast, are typically paid out of a budget allocation. Their revenues are allocated from a general revenue stream that is not tied to what they are doing, but is obtained by tax, levy, or tribute. Furthermore, the typical service institution is endowed with monopoly powers; the intended beneficiary usually has no choice.

Being paid out of a budget allocation changes what is meant by "performance" or "results." *"Results" in the budget-based institution means a larger budget. "Performance" is the ability to maintain or to increase one's budget.* The first test of a budget-based institution and the first requirement for its survival is to obtain the budget. And the budget is, by definition, related not to the achievement of any goals, but to the *intention* of achieving those goals.

This means, first, that efficiency and cost control, however much they are being preached, are not really considered virtues in the budget-based institution. The importance of a budget-based institution is measured essentially by the size of its budget and the size of its staff. To achieve results with a smaller budget or a smaller staff is, therefore, not "performance." It might actually endanger the institution. Not to spend the budget to the hilt will only convince the budget-maker — whether a legislature or a budget committee — that the budget for the next fiscal period can safely be cut.

Thirty or 40 years ago, it was considered characteristic of Russian planning, and one of its major weaknesses, that Soviet managers, towards the end of the plan period, engaged in a frantic effort to spend all the money allocated to them, which usually resulted in total waste. Today, the disease has become universal, as budget-based institutions have become dominant everywhere. And "buying-in" — that is, getting approval for a new program or project by grossly underestimating its total cost — is also built into the budget-based institution.

It is obviously not compatible with *efficiency* that the acid test of performance should be to obtain the budget. But *effectiveness* is even more endangered by reliance on the budget allocation. It makes it risky to raise the question of what the "business" of the institution should be. That question is always "controversial"; such controversy is likely to alienate support and will therefore be shunned by the budget-based institution. As a result, it is likely to wind up deceiving both the public and itself.

Take an instance from government: The U.S. Department of Agriculture has never been willing to ask whether its goal should be "farm productivity" or "support of the small family farm." It has known for decades that these two objectives are not identical as had originally been assumed, and that they are, indeed, becoming increasingly incompatible. To admit this, however, would have created controversy that might have endangered the Department's budget. As a result, American farm policy has frittered away an enormous amount of money and human resources on what can only (and charitably) be called a public relations campaign, that is, on a show of support for the small family farmer. The effective activities, however — and they have been very effective indeed — have been directed toward eliminating the small family farmer and replacing him by the far more productive "agribusinesses," that is, highly capitalized and highly mechanized farms, run as a business and not as a "way of life." This may well have been the right thing to do. But it certainly was not what the Department was founded to do, nor what the Congress, in approving the Department's budget, expected it to do.

Take a non-governmental example, the American community hospital, which is "private" though "non-profit." Everywhere it suffers from a growing confusion of missions and objectives, and the resulting impairment of its effectiveness and performance. Should a hospital be, in effect, a "physician's facility" — as most older American physicians still maintain? Should it focus on the major health needs of a community? Or should it try to do everything and be "abreast of every medical advance," no matter what the cost and no matter how rarely certain facilities will be used? Should it devote resources to preventive medicine and health education? Or should it, like the hospital under the British health service, confine itself strictly to repair of major health damage after it has occurred?

Every one of these definitions of the "business" of the hospital can be defended. Every one deserves a hearing. The effective American hospital will be a multi-purpose institution and strike a balance between various objectives. What most hospitals do, however, is pretend that there are no basic questions to be decided. The result, predictably, is confusion and impairment of the hospital's capacity to serve any function and to carry out any mission.

Pleasing Everyone and Achieving Nothing

Dependence on a budget allocation militates against setting priorities and concentrating efforts. Yet nothing is ever accomplished unless scarce resources are concentrated on a small number of priorities. John Doakes, a shoe manufacturer who has 22 percent of the market for work shoes, may have a profitable business. If he succeeds in raising his market share to 30 percent, especially if the market for his kind of footwear is expanding, he is doing very well indeed. He need not concern himself too much with the 78 percent of the users of work shoes who buy from somebody else. And the customers for ladies' fashion shoes are of no concern to him at all.

Contrast this with the situation of an institution on a budget. To obtain its budget, it needs the approval, or at least the acquiescence, of practically everybody who remotely could be considered a "constituent." Where a market share of 22 percent might be perfectly satisfactory to a business, a "rejection" by 78 percent of its "constituents" — or even by a much smaller proportion — would be fatal to a budget-based institution. And this means that the service institution finds it difficult to set priorities; it must instead try to placate everyone by doing a little bit of everything — which, in effect, means achieving nothing.

Finally, being budget-based makes it even more difficult to abandon the wrong things, the old, the obsolete. As a result, service institutions are even more encrusted than businesses with the barnacles of inherently unproductive efforts.

No institution likes to abandon anything it does. Business is no exception. But in an institution that is being paid for its performance and results, the unproductive, the obsolete, will sooner or later be killed off by the customers. In a budget-based institution no such discipline is being enforced. The temptation is great, therefore, to respond to lack of results by redoubling efforts. The temptation is great to double the budget, precisely *because* there is no performance.

Human beings will behave as they are rewarded for behaving — whether the reward be money and promotion, an autographed picture of the boss, or a pat on the back. This is one lesson the behavioral psychologist has taught us during the last 50 years. A business, or any institution that is paid for its results and performance in such a way that the dissatisfied or disinterested customer need not pay, has to "earn" its income. An institution that is financed by a budget — or that enjoys a monopoly which the customer cannot escape — is rewarded for what it "deserves" rather than for what it "earns." It is paid for good intentions and for "programs." It is paid for not alienating important constituents rather than for satisfying any one group. It is misdirected, by the way it is paid, into defining "performance" and "results" as what will maintain or increase its budget.

What Works: Set Priorities and Allocate Resources

The exception, the comparatively rare service institution that achieves effectiveness, is more instructive than the great majority that achieves only "programs." It shows that effectiveness in the service institution is achievable — though by no means easy. It shows what different kinds of service institutions can do and need to do. It shows limitations and pitfalls. But it also shows that the service institution manager can do unpopular and highly "controversial" things if only he or she makes the risk-taking decision to set priorities and allocate resources.

The first and perhaps simplest example is that of the Bell Telephone System. A telephone system is a "natural" monopoly. Within a given area, one supplier of telephone service must have exclusive rights. It lies therefore in the nature of the service to have a monopoly. The one thing any subscriber to a public telephone service requires is access to all other subscribers, which means territorial exclusivity for one monopolistic service. And as a whole country or continent becomes, in effect, one telephone system, this monopoly has to be extended over larger and larger areas.

An individual may be able to do without a telephone — though in today's society only at prohibitive inconvenience. But a professional person, anyone in a trade, an office, or a business *must* have a telephone. Residential phone service may still be an "option." Business phone service is compulsory. Theodore Vail, the first head of the Bell System, saw this in the early years of this century. He also saw clearly that the American telephone system, like the telephone systems in all other industrially developed nations, could easily be taken over by government. To prevent this, Vail thought through what the telephone company's business was and should be, and came up with his famous definition: "Our business is service."[1] This totally "intangible" statement of the telephone company's "business" then enabled Vail to set specific goals and objectives and to de-

---

[1] This was so heretical that the directors of the telephone company fired Vail when he first propounded his thesis in 1897 — only to rehire him 10 years later when the absence of clear performance objectives had created widespread public demand for telephone nationalization even among such non-radicals as the Progressive wing of the Republican Party.

velop measurements of performance and results. His "customer satisfaction" standards and "service satisfaction" standards created nationwide competition between telephone managers in various areas, and became the criteria by which the managers were judged and rewarded. These standards measured performance as defined by the customer, e.g., waiting time before an operator came on the line, or time between application for telephone service and its installation. They were meant to direct managers' attention to results.

Vail also thought through who his "constituents" were. This led to his conclusion that it was the telephone company's task to make the public utility commissions of the individual states capable of effective state regulation. This was even more shocking to the conventional wisdom of 1900 than Vail's "service" objective. But Vail argued that a national monopoly in a crucial area could expect to escape nationalization only by being regulated. Helping to convert the wretchedly ineffectual, corrupt, and bumbling public utility commissions of late 19th-century populism into effective, respected, and informed adversaries was in the telephone company's own survival interest.

Finally, Vail realized that a telephone system depends on its ability to obtain capital. Each dollar of telephone revenue requires a prior investment of three to four dollars. Therefore, the investor too had to be considered a "constituent," and the telephone company had to design financial instruments and a financial policy that focused on the needs and expectations of the investor, and that made telephone company securities, whether bonds or shares, a distinct and preferred financial "product."

The American University

The building of the American university from 1860 to World War I also illustrates how service institutions can be made to perform. The American university as it emerged during that era was primarily the work of a small number of men: Andrew D. White (President of Cornell, 1868–1885); Charles W. Eliot (President of Harvard, 1869–1909); Daniel Coit Gilman (President of Johns Hopkins, 1876–1901); David Starr Jordan (President of Stanford, 1891–1913); William Rainey Harper (President of Chicago, 1892–1904); and Nicholas Murray Butler (President of Columbia, 1902–1945).

These men all had in common one basic insight: The traditional "college" – essentially an 18th-century seminary to train preachers – had become totally obsolete, sterile, and unproductive. Indeed, it was dying fast; America in 1860 had far fewer college students than it had had 40 years earlier with a much smaller population. The men who built the new universities shared a common objective: to create a new institution, a true "university." And they all realized that while European examples, especially Oxford and Cambridge and the German university, had much to offer, these new universities had to be distinctively American institutions.

Beyond these shared beliefs, however, they differed sharply on what a university should be and what its purpose and mission were. Eliot, at Harvard, saw the purpose of the university as that of educating a leadership group with a distinct "style." His Harvard was to be a "national" institution rather than the parochial preserve of the "proper Bostonian" that Harvard College had been. But it also was to restore to Boston – and to

New England generally — the dominant position of a moral elite, such as in earlier times had been held by the "Elect," the Puritan divines, and their successors, the Federalist leaders in the early days of the Republic. Butler, at Columbia — and, to a lesser degree, Harper at Chicago — saw the function of the university as the systematic application of rational thought and analysis to the basic problems of a modern society, from education to economics, and from domestic government to foreign affairs. Gilman, at Johns Hopkins, saw the university as the producer of advanced knowledge; indeed, originally Johns Hopkins was to confine itself to advanced research and was to give no undergraduate instruction. White, at Cornell, aimed at producing an "educated public."

Each of these men knew that he had to make compromises. Each knew he had to satisfy a number of "constituencies" and "publics," each of whom looked at the university quite differently. Both Eliot and Butler, for instance, had to build their new university on an old foundation (the others could build from the ground up) and had to satisfy — or at least to placate — existing alumni and faculty. They all had to be exceedingly conscious of the need to attract and hold financial support. It was Eliot, for instance, with all his insistence on "moral leadership," who invented the first "placement office" and set out to find well-paying jobs for Harvard graduates, especially in business. It was Butler, conscious that Columbia was a late-comer and that the millionaire philanthropists of his day had already been snared by his competitors (e.g., Rockefeller by Chicago), who invented the first "public relations" office in a university, designed — and most successfully — to reach the merely well-to-do and get their money.

These founders' definitions did not outlive them. Even during the lifetime of Eliot and Butler, for instance, their institutions escaped their control, began to diffuse objectives and to confuse priorities. In the course of this century, all these universities — and many others, like the University of California and other major state universities — have converged towards a common type. Today, it is hard to tell one "multiversity" from another. Yet the imprint of the founders has still not been totally erased. For while each of the founders of the modern American university made compromises and adapted to a multitude of constituencies, each had an objective and a definition of the university to which he gave priority and against which he measured performance. Clearly, the job the founders did almost a century ago will have to be done again for today's "multiversity," if it is not to choke on its own services.

Hospitals: An Emerging Solution

The solution to the problem of the hospital, as is becoming increasingly clear, will lie in thinking through objectives and priorities. The most promising approach may well be one worked out by the Hospital Consulting Group at Westinghouse Electric Corporation, which recognizes that the American hospital has a multiplicity of functions, but organizes each as an autonomous "decentralized" division with its own facilities, its own staff, and its own objectives. There would thus be a traditional care hospital for the fairly small number of truly sick people who require what today's "full-time" hospital offers; an "ambulatory" medical hospital for diagnosis and out-patient work; an "ambulatory" surgical hospital for the large number of surgical patients — actually the majority — who, like patients after cataract surgery, a tonsilectomy, or most orthopedic surgery, are not "sick" and need no medical and little nursing care, but need a bed (and a bedpan) till the stitches are firm or the cast dries; a psychiatric unit — mostly for out-patient or overnight care; and a convalescent unit that would hardly differ from a good motel (e.g., for the healthy mother of a healthy baby). All these would have common services. But each would be a separate health care facility with different objectives, different priorities, and different standards of performance.

The Requirements for Success

Service institutions are a most diverse lot. The one and only thing they all have in common is that, for one reason or another, they cannot be made subject to the performance test of market competition. But however diverse the various kinds of "service institutions" may be, all of them need first to impose on themselves the discipline practiced by the managers and leaders of the institutions in the preceding examples.

1. They need to answer the question, *"What is our "business" and what should it be?"* They need to bring out into the open alternative definitions and to think them through carefully, perhaps even to work out (as did the presidents of the emerging American universities) the balance of different and sometimes conflicting definitions. What service institutions need is not to be more "business-like." They need to be more "hospital-like," "university-like," "government-like," and so on. They need to be subjected to a performance test as much as possible. In other words, they need to think through their own specific function, purpose, and mission.

2. Service institutions need to derive *clear objectives and goals* from their definition of function and mission. What they need is not "better people," but people who do the management job systematically and who focus themselves and their institutions purposefully on performance and results. They do need efficiency — that is, control of costs. But, above all, they need effectiveness — that is, emphasis on the right results.

3. They then have to think through *priorities* of concentration which enable them to select targets; to set standards of accomplishment and performance (that is, to define the minimum acceptable results); to set deadlines; to go to work on results; and to make someone accountable for results.

4. They need to define *measurements of performance* — the "customer satisfaction" measurements of the telephone company.

5. They need to use these measurements to *"feed back"* on their efforts — that is, *they must build self-control from results into their system.*

6. Finally, they need an organized audit of *objectives and results,* so as to identify those objectives that no longer serve a useful purpose or have proven unattainable. They need to identify unsatisfactory performance, and activities which are obsolete, unproductive, or both. And they need a mechanism for *sloughing off* such activities rather than wasting their money and their energies where the results are not.

   This last requirement may be the most important one. The absence of a market test removes from the service institution the discipline that forces a business eventually to abandon yesterday's products — or else go bankrupt. Yet this requirement is the least understood.

No success lasts "forever." Yet it is even more difficult to abandon yesterday's success than it is to reappraise failure. Success breeds its own *hubris* (the Greek word for the arrogance of success that destroys the successful). It creates emotional attachments, habits of thought and action, and, above all, false self-confidence. A success that has outlived its usefulness may, in the end, be more damaging than failure. Especially in a service institution, yesterday's success becomes "policy," "virtue," "conviction," if not indeed "Holy Writ," unless the institution imposes on itself the discipline of thinking through its mission, its objectives, and its priorities, and of building in feedback control from results over policies, priorities, and action. We are in such a "welfare-mess" today in the United States largely because the welfare program of the New Deal had been such a success in the 1930's that we could not abandon it, and instead misapplied it to the radically different problem of the migrants to the cities in the 1950's and 1960's.

To make service institutions perform does not require "great people." It requires instead a system. The essentials of this system may not be too different from the essentials of performance in a business enterprise, as the present "management boom" in the service institutions assumes. But the application will be quite different. For the service institutions are not businesses; "performance" means something quite different for them.

Few service institutions today suffer from having too few administrators; most of them are over-administered, and suffer from a surplus of procedures, organization charts, and "management techniques." What now has to be learned, is to manage service institutions for performance. This may well be the biggest and most important management task for the remainder of this century.

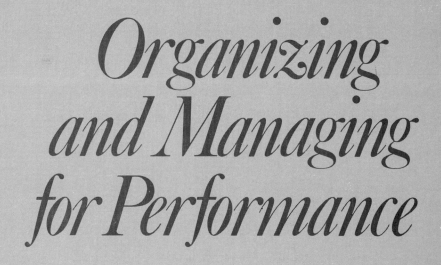

Organizing and Managing for Performance

Part Four

The Innovative
Organization

Chapter 17

Innovation an Economic or Social Term
Innovation Characteristics
The Dynamics of Innovation
Innovation Strategy and Its Basic Assumption
The Need for Planned Abandonment of the Old
The Need to Aim High
The Batting Average
The Progress of an Innovation
Measurements and Budgets
The Risk of Failures or of "Near Success"
Innovative Attitudes and Practices
Management's Different Role
Focus on Responsibility
Continuous Learning
The Structure for Innovation
The Du Pont Example
Innovation a "Business" Rather than a "Function"
The Team
The Innovating Unit as an Entrepreneur
The Challenge of the Innovative Organization

*T*he need to innovate is mentioned — indeed emphasized — in every book on management. But beyond this the books, as a rule, pay little attention to what management and organization need to be and need to do to stimulate, to direct, and to make effective innovation. Most discussions stress, almost exclusively, the administrative function of management, that is, the task of keeping going and of improving what is already known and what is already largely being done. Little thought or space is normally devoted to the entrepreneurial function of creating effectively and purposefully the new and the different.

In this neglect of the management of innovation, the books only mirror business reality. Every management stresses the need to innovate. But few, in the large as well as the small businesses, organize innovation as a distinct and major task. To be sure, during the past thirty years, that is, since the end of World War II, "research" has become fashionable. Large sums of money are being spent on it. But in many companies the outcome has been improvement rather than innovation.

This is even more true of the public-service institutions.

There were good reasons in the past for the focus on the administrative function to the neglect of innovation. When management first became a concern, in the early years of this century, the great and new need was to learn how to organize, structure, and direct the large-scale human organization which was suddenly coming into being. Innovation was largely not seen at all as a task for the manager. It was considered the job of the "inventor" working in his own workshop, maybe with a helper or two. And even when the "inventor" was succeeded by the organized research lab — the first of which came up in the years around 1900 — "innovation" still remained the job of a "specialist," that is scientific and technical and a matter for "Research."

Moreover, there was not too much scope for innovation in the years from 1920 to 1950 when most of the basic work on management was being done. For contrary to common belief, these were not years of rapid change, either in technology or in society. They were years in which, by and large, technology built on foundations that had been laid before World War I, that is before 1914, and largely before 1900. And while they were years of tremendous political turbulence, social and economic institutions were stagnant. Indeed, the same can be said for social and economic ideas. The great revolutionary ideas which have been at work in the last fifty years are those of thinkers living, or at least rooted, in the nineteenth century.

Now, however, we may be entering a period of rapid change more comparable in its basic features to the closing decades of the nineteenth century than to the immediate past with which we are familiar. In the late nineteenth century, a new major invention, leading almost immediately to the emergence of a new major industry, surfaced every few months on average. This period began in 1856, the year that saw both Siemens' dynamo and Perkins' aniline dye. It ended with the development of the modern electronic tube in 1911. In between came typewriter and automobile, electric light bulb, man-made fibers, tractors, streetcars, synthetic drugs, telephone, radio, and airplane — to mention only a few. In between, in other words, came the modern world.

By contrast, no truly new major industry was started after 1914 until the late 1950s, when computers first became operational.

Between 1870 and 1914 the industrial geography of the world was in rapid change.

A new major industrial area emerged on average every decade or so: the U.S. and Germany between 1860 and 1870, western Russia and Japan during the next twenty years, Central Europe (that is, the western part of the old Austria-Hungary and northern Italy) by 1900. Between World War I and World War II, however, no major new industrial area joined the "industrial club."

Now, however, there are signs of rapid change, with Brazil and China, for instance, approaching "the takeoff point" — Brazil may well have reached it. Now, in other words, there are signs that fundamental economic relationships will be in rapid change and flux. The abandonment of the dollar as the "key currency" in 1971 ended the period in which yesterday was the norm and ushered in a period of great and rapid change and of major innovation in international economy, international currency, and international credit.

But the need for innovation will be equally great in the social field. And the public-service institutions too will have to learn how to manage innovation.

Just as the late nineteenth century was a period of tremendous innovative activity in technology, so also was it in social and economic institutions. And just as the fifty years after World War I were years of technological continuity rather than of rapid change and innovation, so also were they years of continuity in social and economic institutions. Government as we know it today had largely been created by the time of World War I. The Local Government reform in Great Britain which began in the middle of the nineteenth century started the work on re-defining one of man's oldest institutions, government, created new institutions, new relationships, and, above all, established new tasks for government. And by 1860 the British had, in effect, created the modern government agency. Building the modern welfare state began shortly thereafter in Bismarck's Germany. At about the same time — the 1880s — the United States made a major contribution to the arts and practice of government: the regulatory commission. Every one of the New Deal reforms of the 1930s had been discussed, worked out, and in many cases put in practice on the local or state level twenty years earlier, that is, in the Progressive Era just before World War I.

The great American university was the innovative creation of half a dozen brilliant university presidents between 1860 and 1900. The modern hospital was essentially designed between 1900 and 1920. Armed services took their present shape in the two major conflicts of the mid-nineteenth century, the American Civil War and the Franco-Prussian War of 1870. Since then, the development has been linear — larger armies, more firepower, more armor, but fundamentally the same strategies and tactics and indeed even the same stress on "hardware technology." Even such radical technical innovations as the tank and the airplane were largely integrated into traditional command structures and traditional military doctrines.

Now the need for social and political innovation is becoming urgent again. The modern metropolis needs new governmental forms. The relationship between people and their environment has to be thought through and restructured. No modern government governs effectively anymore. The crisis of the world is, above all, an institutional crisis demanding institutional innovation.

The business enterprise, its structure and organization, the way in which it integrates knowledge into work and work into performance — and the way in which it integrates enterprise with society and government — are also areas of major innovative need and innovative opportunity. Surely there is need in the social and economic sphere for another period of innovative activity such as we last lived through in the second half of the nineteenth century.

In sharp contrast to the nineteenth century, however, innovation from now on will have to be built into existing organizations. Large businesses — and equally large public-service institutions — will have to become increasingly capable of organizing themselves for innovation as well as for administration.

In the first place, they command access to human resources and capital to a degree undreamed of a hundred years ago. But also the ratio between invention or research and the efforts needed to convert the results of research or invention into new businesses, new products, or new institutions has changed significantly. It is by now accepted, if only as a rule of thumb, that for every dollar spent on generating an idea, ten dollars have to be spent on "research" to convert it into a new discovery or a new invention. For every ten dollars spent on "research," at least a hundred dollars need to be spent on development, and for every hundred dollars spent on development, something between a thousand and ten thousand dollars are needed to introduce and establish a new product or a new business on the market. And only after a new product or a new business has been established in the market is there an "innovation."

Innovation is not a technical term. It is an economic and social term. Its criterion is not science or technology, but a change in the economic or social environment, a change in the behavior of people as consumers or producers, as citizens, as students or as teachers, and so on. Innovation creates new wealth or new potential of action rather than new knowledge. This means that the bulk of innovative efforts will have to come from the places that control the human resources and the money needed for development and marketing, that is, from the existing large aggregation of trained people and disposable money — existing businesses and existing public-service institutions.

This may be particularly true with respect to the public-service institution. A hundred years ago there were few of them and they were small. The task then was largely to create new institutions where none existed. Today these institutions are massive and dominate the social, political, and economic landscape. They represent existing bureaucracies, existing concentrations of expertise, existing assignments, and ongoing programs. If they cannot become innovative, the new we need has little chance of becoming effective innovation. It is likely to be smothered by muscle-bound giants of big government and big armed service, big university and big hospital, and many others.

This does not mean that the small business, or even the lone entrepreneur, will not continue to play an important role. Nothing is further from the truth than the hoary myth of the Populists that the small individual is being squeezed out of the marketplace by the giants. The innovative growth companies of the last twenty-five years all started as small businesses. And by and large the small businesses have done far better than the giants.

In every single industry, except those where monopoly is protected by government (e.g., in railroading), small upstarts which a few short years ago were unknown have acquired major market positions and have proven themselves more than capable of competition with the giants. This is particularly true, as has been said before, where the giants, through natural growth or deliberate policy, grew into conglomerates. In the chemical industry, in the electrical apparatus industry, and in many others, the traditional giant, a GE, has lost market position and market share in many markets — and largely to small or medium-sized newcomers with an innovative bent.

An established company which in an age demanding innovation is not capable of innovation is doomed to decline and extinction. And a management which in such a period does not know how to manage innovation is incompetent and unequal to its task. Managing innovation will increasingly become a challenge to management, and especially to top management, and a touchstone of its competence.

Innovative Examples

While in a minority, especially among big businesses, innovative companies do exist. One might mention Renault in France and Fiat in Italy, Marks & Spencer in England, ASEA in Sweden (The Swedish General Electric Company), Sony in Japan — or, between the two World Wars, the publishing house of Ullstein in Germany. In the United States 3M (Minnesota Mining and Manufacturing, St. Paul, Minnesota), the Bell Laboratories of the Telephone Company, or the Bank of America come to mind. These firms apparently have no difficulty innovating and no difficulty getting change accepted in their organizations. Their managements, one would expect, rarely have occasion to ask, "How can we keep our organization flexible and willing to accept the new?" These managements are much too busy finding the right people and the money to run with the innovations their own organizations force on them.

Innovative organizations are not confined to business. Both the Manhattan Project in the United States, which developed the atomic bomb during World War II, and the joint European organization for nuclear research and for peaceful application of atomic power, CERN (*Conseil Européen pour la Rechrche Nucleaire*), in Geneva under its first Director-General, Victor Weisskopf, furnish examples of innovative organizations. Both innovated scientifically and technically. But both also innovated in social terms; the forms of organization now popular as "team" or "matrix" organizations, e.g., were invented essentially by the Manhattan Project. This is all the more remarkable, as these two institutions were heavily staffed with university professors who, in their natural habitat, are remarkably resistant to change and notoriously slow to innovate.

These examples indicate that an organization's ability to innovate is a function of management rather than of industry, size, or age of the organization, let alone to be explained with that common excuse of poor managers, a country's "culture and traditions."

Nor can the explanation be found in research. Bell Laboratories — perhaps the most productive industrial research laboratory — has indeed been stressing for many years fundamental inquiries into the laws of nature. But Renault and Fiat are not particularly distinguished for their research; what makes them innovative organizations is ability to get new designs and new models rapidly into production and on the market. The Bank of America, finally, innovated mainly in its customers' businesses, and in terms of financial structure and credit, inventory and marketing policies.

These examples imply that the innovative organization institutionalizes the innovative spirit and creates a habit of innovation. At the beginning of these organizations there might well have been an individual, a great innovator. He might have succeeded in building around him an organization to convert into successful business reality his new ideas and inventions — as did Werner von Siemens in Germany a hundred years ago, A.P. Giannini in building the Bank of America seventy years ago, and as Edwin H. Land of Polaroid has been doing since World War II. But no such founding genius presided over Bell Laboratories, over 3M, or over Renault. The innovative organization manages to innovate as an organization, that is, as a human group organized for continual and productive innovation. It is organized to make change into norm.

These various innovative organizations are very different indeed in their structures, their businesses, their characteristics, and even their organization and management philosophies. But they do have certain characteristics in common.

1. Innovating organizations know what "innovation" means.
2. Innovative organizations understand the dynamics of innovation.
3. They have an innovative strategy.
4. They know that innovation requires objectives and goals that are different from management objectives and goals, and measurements appropriate to the dynamics of innovation.
5. Management, especially top management, plays a different role and has a different attitude in an innovative organization.
6. The innovative organization is structured differently and set up differently from managerial work and managerial organization.

The Meaning of Innovation

Innovation organizations first know what "innovation" means. They know that innovation is not science or technology, but value. They know that it is not something that takes place within an organization but a change outside. The measure of innovation is the impact on the environment. Innovation in a business enterprise must therefore always be market-focused. Innovation that is product-focused is likely to produce "miracles of technology" but disappointing rewards. Technically the IBM computer was for long years, at best "almost as good" as the products of the competitors — and the competitors developed most of the new technology until well into the 'sixties. But the competitors found out what the product could do — and then looked around for applications. IBM started out with the needs of the users and adapted technology to it — and acquired market dominance in a few short years.

The outstanding innovators among the world's pharmaceutical companies define their goal as new drugs that will make a significant difference to medical practice and to patient health. They do not define innovation in terms of research, but in terms of the practice of medicine. Similarly, Bell Laboratories always starts out with the question "What will make a difference to telephone *service*?"

Not surprisingly, however, it is precisely the most market-focused innovator who has come up with some of the most important technical or scientific advances. Bell Labs, for instance, created the transistor, produced the basic mathematics of information theory, and is responsible for some of the fundamental discoveries underlying the computer.

To start out with the consumer's or client's need for a significant change is often the most direct way to define new science, new knowledge, and new technology, and to organize purposeful and systematical work on fundamental discovery.

The Dynamics of Innovation

Innovating businesses are aware of the dynamics of innovation. They do not believe that innovation is determined — or at least they know that there are so many factors in whatever causal patterns may exist that no one can possibly unravel them. Neither, however, do they share the common belief that innovation is haphazard and incapable of being predicted or foreseen.

They know that innovation follows a probability distribution. They know that it is possible to say what kind of innovation, if successfully brought about, is likely to become a major product or process, a major new business, a major market. They know how to look systematically for the areas where innovative activity, if it produces results, is likely to enjoy success and to be rewarding.

One such guide to finding what one could call "the innovation-prone" is basic *economic* vulnerability of a process, a technology, or an industry. Wherever an industry enjoys growing market demand without being able to turn the demand into profitability, one can say, with high probability, that a major innovation which changes process, product, distributive channel, or customer expectations will produce high rewards.

Examples abound. One is the paper industry, which, all the world over, has enjoyed rapidly expanding consumer demand — on the order of 5 to 10 percent a year, year in and year out — without being able apparently to earn a decent return on its capital. There is the steel industry, which is in a very similar position. But there is also life insurance, which is one of the few "products" a customer is ready to buy — one of the few products, by the way, in which producer and consumer have an identical interest in the policy holder's surviving beyond a normal life-span, — and which yet has to be sold through "hardsell" methods and against apparently very high buyer resistance.

Similarly, innovative opportunity exists where there is glaring disparity between various levels of an economy or of a market.

The major growth industry in Latin America in the 1960s, for instance, was not manufacturing. It was retail distribution. Huge masses of people flocked into the cities and from a subsistence economy into a money economy. Individually they were, of course, mostly very poor. But collectively they represented large new purchasing power. Yet the distribution system in most Latin American countries remained in the pre-urban mold — small shops, undercapitalized, undermanaged, poorly stocked, and yet with very slow turnover. Wherever an entrepreneur moved in to offer modern distribution — Sears, Roebuck was the first to recognize the opportunity — success was instantaneous.

Another area of innovative opportunity is the exploitation of the consequences of events that have already happened but have not yet had their economic impacts. Demographic developments, i.e., changes in population, are among the most important. They are also the most nearly certain. Changes in knowledge are less certain — the lead time is difficult to predict. But they too offer opportunities. And then, most important, but least certain, are changes in awareness, changes in vision, changes in people's expectations.

The pharmaceutical industry, for instance, earned its success largely because it anticipated the impact of fundamental changes in awareness. After World War II health care every place became a "good buy." And drugs are the only way to health care easily accessible to poor and poorly educated rural countries. Where physicians and hospitals are scarce, drugs can still be dispensed and will be effective for a great many health problems. The pharmaceutical company which understood this and went into the developing countries found that, with respect to drug purchases, they are "fully developed."

Finally, of course, there are the innovations which are not part of the pattern, the innovations that are unexpected and that change the world rather than exploit it. They are the innovations in which an entrepreneur sets out to make something happen. They are the truly important innovations. They are the innovations of a Henry Ford, who envisioned something that did not exist at the time, namely a mass market, and then set about to make it happen.

These innovations lie outside of the probability distribution — or, at least, they place so far toward the extreme as to be grossly improbable. They are also clearly the most risky ones. For every one such innovation that succeeds, there must be ninety-nine that fail, ninety-nine of which nothing is ever heard.

It is important for the innovating business to realize that these atypical innovations exist and that they are of supreme importance. It is important to keep watching for them. But, by their very nature, they cannot be the object of systematic, purposeful organized activity within the business enterprise. They cannot be managed.

And they are sufficiently rare to be treated as exceptions, despite their overreaching importance. The business that focuses on the probability pattern and organizes its innovation strategy to take advantage of it will innovate. And it will in the process become sensitive to the exceptional, the great, the truly historic innovation, and equipped to recognize it early and to take advantage of it.

To manage innovation, a manager need not be a technologist. Indeed, first-rate technologists are rarely good at managing innovation. They are so deeply engrossed in their specialities that they rarely see development outside of it. It is not a metallurgist who is likely to recognize the importance of basic new knowledge in plastics even though it may, within a reasonably short time, obsolete a good many of his or her proudest products. Similarly, the innovative manager need not be an economist. The economist, by definition, becomes concerned with the impact of innovations only after they have become massive. The innovating manager needs to anticipate vulnerabilities and opportunities — and this is not the economist's bent. The innovative manager needs to study innovation as such and to learn its dynamics, its pattern, its predictability. To manage innovation, a manager has to be at least literate with respect to the dynamics of innovation.

Innovative Strategy

Like all business strategies, an innovative strategy starts out with the question "What is our business and what should it be?" But its assumptions regarding the future are different from the assumptions made with respect to the ongoing business. There the assumption is that present product lines and services, present markets and present distribution channels, present technologies and processes will continue. The first objective of a strategy for the ongoing business is to optimize what already exists or is being established.

The ruling assumption of an innovative strategy is that whatever exists is aging. The assumption must be that existing product lines and services, existing markets and distribution channels, existing technologies and processes will sooner or later — and usually sooner — go down rather than up.

The governing device of a strategy for the ongoing business might therefore be said to be: "Better and More." For the innovative strategy the device has to be: "New and Different."

The foundation of innovative strategy is planned and systematic sloughing off of the old, the dying, the obsolete. Innovating organizations spend neither time nor resources on defending yesterday. Systematic abandonment of yesterday alone can free the resources, and especially the scarcest resource of them all, capable people, for work on the new.

Unwillingness to do this may be the greatest obstacle to innovation in the existing large business. That the General Electric Company did not succeed in establishing itself as a computer producer is, within the company itself, explained in large part as the result of unwillingness or inability to make available managers and professionals of the high quality and proven performance capacity needed. To be sure, GE assigned a great many good people to its computer group. But few of them were allowed to stay there long. No sooner were they gone from their original post in a research lab or a large division, than the cry went up "we cannot do without them, " and back they went to their old assignments of improving what was already known and what was already done.

The new and especially the as-yet unborn, that is, the future innovation, always looks insignificant compared to the large volume, the large revenue, and the manifold problems of the ongoing business. It is all the more important, therefore, for an existing business to commit itself to the systematic abandonment of yesterday if it wants to be able to create tomorrow.

Second in a strategy of innovation is the clear recognition that innovation efforts must aim high. It is just as difficult, as a rule, to make a minor modification to an existing product as it is to innovate a new one.

Michael J. Kami, who served successfully as head of long-range planning for IBM and Xerox, states as a rule of thumb that the projected results of innovative efforts should be at least three times as large as the results needed to attain company objectives. This is probably an underestimate. In improvement work — adding a new product, upgrading a product line, broadening the market, and so on — one can assume a success rate of 50 percent. No more than half the projects should be total failures.

This is not the way innovation works. Here the assumption must be that the majority of innovative efforts will not succeed. Nine out of every ten "brilliant ideas" turn out to be nonsense. And nine out of every ten ideas which, after thorough analysis, seem to be worthwhile and feasible turn out to be failures or, at best, puny weaklings. The mortality rate of innovations is — and should be — high.

Innovative strategy therefore aims at creating a new business rather than a new product within an already established line. It aims at creating new performance capacity rather than improvement. It aims at creating new concepts of what is value rather than satisfying existing value expectations a little better. The aim of innovating efforts is to make a significant difference. What is significantly different is not a technical decision. It is not the quality of science that makes the difference. It is not how expensive an undertaking it is or how hard it is to bring it about. The significant difference lies in the impact on the environment.

"Success" in innovating efforts is a batting average of one out of ten. This is, of course, the reason for aiming high in innovative efforts. The one winner has to make up for nine losers and has to produce its own results.

Bernard Baruch is mostly remembered today as the head of the U.S. war economy in World War I and the friend, confidant, and advisor of presidents from Woodrow Wilson to Harry Truman. But before Baruch became America's elder statesman, he had amassed a very sizable fortune as a venture capitalist. While other financiers of his era, the thirty years before World War I, speculated in real estate and railroad bonds, Baruch looked for new and innovative businesses. He knew apparently little about technology — or at least affected ignorance. He invested in the person rather than in the idea. And he invested at the very early stage at which the budding business, as a rule, did not need much money beyond a few years' support for someone with an idea. He invested on the principle that eight out of every ten investments would turn out failures and would have to be written off. But he maintained — and his own record proved him right — that if only two out of ten turned out to be successful, he would reap a far larger harvest than the shrewdest investor in already existing businesses could possibly attain.

An innovation does not proceed in a nice linear progression. For a good long time, sometimes for years, there is only effort and no results. The first results are then usually meager. Indeed, the first products are rarely what the customer will eventually buy. The first markets are rarely the major markets. The first applications are rarely the applications that, in the end, will turn out to be the really important ones.

The social impacts of new technology are very difficult, and sometimes impossible, to predict. But this difficulty extends to everything connected with the truly new — as demonstrated by the example of the gross underestimation of the size of the computer market in the thorough market-research study conducted around 1950. But even more difficult to predict than the eventual success of the genuinely new is the speed with which it will establish itself. "Timing is of the essence" — above all in innovation. Yet timing is totally incapable of being predicted. There are the computer, the antibiotics, the Xerox machine — all innovations that swept the market. But for every successful innovation that has results faster than anyone anticipates, there are five or six others — in the end perhaps, equally successful ones — which for long years seem to make only frustratingly slow headway. The outstanding example may be the steam-driven ship. By 1835 its superiority was clearly established; but it did not replace the sailing ship until fifty years later. Indeed, the "golden age of sail" in which the great clippers reached perfection began only after the steamship had been fully developed. For almost half a century, in other words, the steamship continued to be "tomorrow" and never seemed to become "today."

But then, after a long, frustrating period of gestation, the successful innovation rises meteorically. It becomes within a few short years a new major industry or a new major product line and market. But until it has reached that point it cannot be predicted when it will take off, nor indeed whether it ever will.

Measurements and Budgets

Innovation strategy requires different measurements and different use of budgets and budgetary controls from those appropriate to an ongoing business.

To impose on innovating efforts the measurements, and especially the accounting conventions, that fit ongoing businesses, is misdirection. It cripples the innovative effort the way carrying a one-hundred-pound pack would cripple a six-year-old going on a hike. And it also fails to give true control. Finally, it may become a threat when the innovation becomes successful. For then it needs controls that are appropriate to rapid growth, that is, controls which show what efforts and investments are needed to exploit success and prevent overextension.

The successfully innovating businesses learned this long ago.

The oldest, best-known, and most successful managerial control system is probably that of the Du Pont Company, which, as early as the 1920s, developed a model for all its businesses focused on return on investment. But innovations were not included in that famous model. As long as a business, a product line, or a process was in the innovating stage, its capital allocation was not included in the capital base on which the individual Du Pont division in charge of the project had to earn a return. Nor were the expenses included in its expense budget. Both were kept separate. Only after the new product line had been introduced in the market and had been sold in commercial quantities for two years or more were its measurements and controls merged into the budget of the division responsible for the development.

This made sure that division general managers did not resist innovation as a threat to their earnings record and performance. It also made sure that expenditures on, and investments in, innovative efforts could be tightly controlled. It made it possible to ask at every step, "What do we expect at the end, and what is the risk factor, that is, the likelihood of nonsuccess?" "Can we justify continuing this particular innovative effort or not?"

Budgets for ongoing businesses and budgets for innovative efforts should not only be kept separate, they should be treated differently. In the ongoing business, the question is always "Is this effort necessary? Or can we do without it?" And if the answer is "We need it," one asks, "What is the minimum level of support that is needed?"

In the innovative effort the first and most serious question is "Is it the right opportunity?" And if the answer is yes, one asks, "What is the maximum of good people and key resources which can productively be put to work *at this stage?*"

A separate measurement system for innovative effort makes it possible to appraise the three factors that determine innovative strategy: the ultimate opportunity, the risk of failure, and the effort and expenditure needed. Otherwise, efforts will be continued or will even be stepped up where the opportunity is quite limited while the risk of nonsuccess is great.

Examples are the many broad-spectrum antibiotics produced with great scientific ingenuity by pharmaceutical companies in the late sixties. By then the probability of synthesizing a new broad-spectrum antibiotic with properties significantly better than those already on the market had become fairly small. The risk of nonsuccess was high, in other words. At the same time the opportunity had become much more limited than ten years earlier. Even an antibiotic with significantly better performance than the existing ones would have to compete against perfectly good products with which the physicians were familiar and which they had learned to use. Even a scientific breakthrough would in all likelihood have produced a "me-too" product. At the same time, the expenditure and effort needed to find anything really new in a field that had been worked over so thoroughly were rising fast. Traditional market thinking, that is, thinking that looks at the size of the market and deduces therefrom great success for a new product that is "better," would have been totally misleading — as indeed it misled a substantial number of companies.

Nothing is therefore as inimical to successful innovation as a goal of "5 percent growth in profits" every year. Innovations for the first three or five years — some for longer — show no growth in profits. They do not show any profits at all. And then their growth rate for five to ten years should be closer to 40 percent a year than to 5 percent a year. It is only after they have reached relative maturity that they can be expected to grow year by year by a small percentage. But then they are no longer innovations.

Innovative strategy, therefore, requires a high degree of discipline on the part of the innovator. He has to operate without the crutch of the conventional budget and accounting measures which feed back fairly fast and reasonably reliable information from current results to efforts and investments. The temptation is to keep on pouring people and money into innovative efforts without any results. It is therefore important in managing innovation to think through what one expects, and when. Inevitably, these expectations are changed by events. But unless there are intermediate results, specific progress, "fallouts" to actual operation along the way, the innovation is not being managed.

When Du Pont engaged, in the late twenties, in the polymer research that eventually led to nylon more than ten years later, no one was willing or able to predict whether mastery of polymer technology would lead to synthetic rubber, to textile fibers, to synthetic leathers, or to new lubricants. (In the end, of course, it led to all of them.) It was not until fairly close to the end of the work that it became clear that synthetic fibers would be the first major commercial product. But from the beginning Du Pont, together with Dr. Carrothers, the research scientist in charge, systematically laid out a road map of what kind of findings and results could be expected and when. This map was changed every two or three years as results came in. but it was always redrawn again for the next stages along the road. And only when he came up with polymer fibers, which then made large-scale development work possible, did Du Pont commit itself to massive investment. Until then, the total cost was essentially the cost of supporting Carrothers and a few assistants.

The Risk of Failure

A strategy for innovation has to be based on clear acceptance of the risk of failure — and of the perhaps more dangerous risk of "near-success."

It is as important to decide when to abandon an innovative effort as it is to know which one to start. In fact, it may be more important. Successful laboratory directors know when to abandon a line of research which does not yield the expected results. The less successful ones keep hoping against hope, are dazzled by the "scientific challenge" of a project, or are fooled by the scientists' repeated promise of a "breakthrough next year." And the unsuccessful ones cannot abandon a project and cannot admit that what seemed like a good idea has turned into a waste of people, time, and money.

But a fair number of innovative efforts end up in near-success rather than in success or failure. And near-success can be more dangerous than failure. There is, again and again, the product or the process that was innovated with the expectation that it would "revolutionize" the industry only to become a fairly minor addition to the product line, neither enough of a failure to be abandoned nor enough of a success to make a difference. There is the innovation which looks so "exciting" when work on it is begun, only to be overtaken, during its gestation period, by a more innovative process, product or service. There is the innovation which was meant to become a "household word" that ends up as another "specialty" which a few customers are willing to buy but not willing to pay for.

It is therefore particularly important in managing innovation to think through and to write out one's expectations. And then, once the innovation has become a product, a process, or a business, one compares one's expectations to reality. If reality is significantly below expectations, one does not pour in more people or more money. One rather asks, "Should we not go out of this, and how?"

Bernard Baruch knew this seventy years ago. When asked whether there were not investments in innovations that were neither great successes nor great failures, he is reported to have answered, "Of course — but those I sell as early as possible and for whatever I can get." He then added, "In my early days those were the ventures on which I spent all my time. I always thought I could turn them around and make them the success we had originally expected. It never worked. But I found that I missed the real opportunities and that I misallocated my money by putting it into 'sound investments,' rather than into the big opportunities of the future."

The Innovative Attitude

Resistance to change, by executives and workers alike, has for many years been considered a central problem of management. Countless books and articles have been written on the subject. Countless seminars, discussions, and courses have been devoted to it. Yet it is questionable that much progress has been made in resolving the problem.

Indeed, it is incapable of being resolved as long as we talk of "resistance to change." Not that there is no such resistance, or that it is not a major obstacle. But to focus on resistance to change is to misdefine the problem in a way that makes it less, rather than more, tractable. The right way to define the problem so as to make it capable of resolution is as a challenge to create, build, and maintain the innovative organization, the organization for which change is norm rather than exception, and opportunity rather than threat. Innovation is, therefore, attitude and practices. It is, above all, top-management attitude and practices. The innovative organization casts top management into a different role and embodies a different concept of top management's relationship to the organization.

In the traditional managerial organization such as management texts discuss, top management is *final judge.* This means, in effect, that management's most important power is the veto power, and its most important role is to say no to proposals and ideas that are not completely thought through and worked out. This concept is caricatured in that well-known jingle composed many years ago by a senior executive of Unilever, the British-Dutch-American food and soap giant:

> Along this tree
> From root to crown
> Ideas flow up
> And vetoes down.

In the innovative organization, the first and most important job of management is the opposite: it is to convert impractical, half-baked, and wild ideas into concrete reality. In the innovative organization, top management sees it as its job to listen to ideas and to take them seriously. Top management, in the innovative organization, knows that new ideas are always "impractical." It also knows that it takes a great many silly ideas to spawn one viable one, and that in the early stages there is no way of telling the silly idea from the stroke of genius. Both look equally impossible or equally brilliant.

Top management in the innovative organization, therefore, not only "encourages" ideas, as all managements are told to do. It asks continuously, "What would this idea have to be like to be practical, realistic, effective?" It organizes itself to think through rapidly even the wildest and apparently silliest idea for something new to the point where its feasibility can be appraised.

Top management in the innovative organization is the major "drive" for innovation. It uses the ideas of the organization as stimuli to its own vision. And then it works to make ideas a concern of the entire organization. Top management in the innovative organization fashions thought and work on the new into both organizational energy and entrepreneurial discipline.

This, however, presupposes restructuring relations between top management and the human group within the enterprise. The traditional organization, of course, remains. Indeed, on the organization chart there may be little to distinguish the innovative organization from the most rigidly bureaucratic one. And an innovative organization need not be "permissive" or "democratic" at all. But the innovative organization builds, so to speak, a nervous system next to the bony skeleton of the formal organization. Where traditional organization is focused on the logic of the work, there is also an additional relationship focused on the logic of ideas.

In innovative companies senior executives typically make it their business to meet with the younger people throughout the organization in scheduled (though not necessarily regular) sessions in which there is no "agenda" for top management. Rather, the seniors sit down with the younger group and ask, "What opportunities do *you* see?"

In the period of its greatest growth and development, the 3M Company was anything but a permissive company. It was tightly run by two or three executives at the top who made all the decisions. But even the most junior engineer was encouraged, indeed practically commanded, to come to the top-management people with any idea, no matter how wild. And again and again he would be told, "The idea makes no sense to me; but are you willing to work on it?" If the reply was yes, the engineer would then be asked to write up the idea, together with a budget request — and more often than not he would be freed from all other responsibilities, given a modest sum of money for a year or two, and told to go ahead. As a result, the company grew from a small and obscure producer of abrasives into one of America's largest businesses.

Yet the young engineers at 3M were held strictly accountable. Not all of them succeeded, of course. Indeed, only one or two out of every ten did. And failure of an idea was not held against them — at least, not the first time. But failure to take responsibility, to organize the task, to work at it, and to appraise progress realistically — let alone to keep top management fully informed of the progress of the project — was not tolerated.

The innovative organization requires a learning atmosphere throughout the entire business. It creates and maintains continuous learning. No one is allowed to consider himself or herself "finished" at any time. Learning is a continuing process for all members of the organization.

Resistance to change is grounded in ignorance and in fear of the unknown. Change has to be seen as opportunity by people — and then there will be no fear. It is seen as opportunity by the Japanese because they are guaranteed their jobs and are not afraid of putting themselves or their colleagues out of work by proposing something new. And even in Japan, if workers know that the organization is overstaffed and that their jobs are really redundant — the grossly overstaffed Japanese National Railways are an example — there is dogged resistance to all change despite a legal guarantee of absolute job security. But fear and ignorance are also overcome in Japan by making continuing change the opportunity for personal achievement, for recognition, for satisfaction. The person who in a Japanese training session comes up with a new idea receives no monetary reward, even if the idea is a big and profitable one. But even it it is a very small improvement, the proponent derives stature, recognition, and public praise.

We need not go to Japan to learn this. Every one of the "suggestion systems" that are so widely used in American business teaches the same lesson. The suggestion system in which the reward is recognition, achievement, participation, is the successful system. And in those departments in a plant where the suggestion system is being run this way, there is very little resistance to change, despite fears for job security and union restrictions. Where this does not prevail — as in the great majority — the suggestion system is not a success, no matter how well it pays for successful suggestions. It also has none of the effect on worker behavior and attitude which the proponents of the suggestion system promise.

Structure for Innovation

The search for innovation needs to be organized separately and outside of the ongoing managerial business. Innovative organizations realize that one cannot simultaneously create the new and take care of what one already has. They realize that maintenance of the present business is far too big a task for the people in it to have much time for creating the new, the different business of tomorrow. They also realize that taking care of tomorrow is far too big and difficult a task to be diluted with concern for today. Both tasks have to be done. But they are different.

Innovative organizations, therefore, put the new into separate organizational components concerned with the creation of the new.

The oldest example is probably the Development Department at E.I. du Pont de Nemours in Wilmington, Delaware, founded in the early twenties. This unit is concerned exclusively with the making of tomorrow. It is not a research department — Du Pont has a separate, big research lab. The job of the Development Department is to develop new businesses; production, finance, and marketing are as much its concern as technology, products, and processes. 3M, too, has set up a business development lab in parallel with, but separate from, its research labs.

This was not understood in 1952 when the General Electric Company embarked on its massive reorganization which then became the prototype for major organization changes in large businesses around the world. Under the GE plan the general manager of every "product business" was to have responsibility for both the ongoing business and the innovative efforts for tomorrow's new and different business. This seemed plausible enough. Indeed it seemed an inescapable conclusion from the idea that the general manager of a product business should, as much as possible, behave like the chief executive of an independent business. But it did not work — the general managers did not innovate.

One reason was the press of ongoing business. General managers had neither the time nor the motivation to work on obsoleting what they were managing. Another, equally important reason was that true innovation is rarely an extension of the already existing business. It rarely fits into the scope, objectives, goals, technologies or processes of today. But, of course, one can define only the scope, products, technologies, processes — even the markets — of today. The most important innovative opportunities always fall outside existing definitions — and thereby outside the "assigned scope" of an existing decentralized product business. After ten years or so GE began to draw the proper conclusions from its frustrations and began to organize major innovation separately and outside of existing product departments and product divisions — and very similar to the way innovative efforts had been organized at Du Pont for many years, that is, in a separate organizational "business development" unit.

Experience in public-service institutions also indicates that innovative efforts best be organized separately and outside of existing managerial organization.

The greater innovative capacity of the American university as compared to the universities of continental Europe has often been remarked upon. The main reason is clearly not that American academicians are less resistant to change. It is the ease with which the American university can set up a new department, a new faculty, or even an entirely new school to do new things. The European university, by contrast, tends to be compelled by law and tradition to set up a new activity within an already existing department or faculty. This not only creates immediately a "war of ancients against the moderns" in which the new is fought as a threat by the established disciplines. It also deprives the new, as a rule, of the resources needed to innovate successfully. The ablest of the young scholars, for instance, will be under great pressure to stick to the "safe" traditional fields which still control the opportunities for promotion. For a significant innovation to move fast in the European academic setting usually requires "break-away institutions." The great age of English physics and chemistry in the late seventeenth century was ushered in by setting up the Royal Academy outside the established university system. More than two hundred years later, a similar break-away institution, the London School of Economics, created the opportunity for genuine innovation in teaching — and learning — in the economic and social fields. In France Napoleon systematically set up the *grandes écoles* such as the École Polytechnique and the École Normale outside the university system as a vehicle for innovation in learning and research, e.g., to make effective the then brand-new idea that engineers and teachers needed training and could be trained. One of the main reasons why the Germans, in the decade before World War I, set up the separate scientific research institutes of the Kaiser-Wilhelm Gesellschaft (now Max-Planck Gesellschaft) was to gain freedom to develop new disciplines and new approaches in old disciplines, that is, to gain freedom for innovation.

Similarly the Manhattan Project, which developed the atomic bomb, as well as CERN, the European nuclear-research facility, were set up outside the existing academic and governmental structures precisely because their purpose was to be innovation.

Innovation as a "Business"

At the same time, the innovative organizations realize that innovation needs from the beginning to be organized as a "business" rather than as a "function." In concrete terms, this means setting aside the traditional time sequence in which "research" comes first, followed by "development," followed by "manufacturing," with "marketing" at the very end. The innovative organizations consider these functional skills as part of one and the same process, the process of developing a new business. When and how each of these tools is to be put into play is decided by the logic of the situation rather than by any preconceived time sequence.

A project manager or business manager is therefore put in charge of anything new as soon as it is decided to pay attention to it. This manager may come from any — or from no — function at all, and usually he or she can draw on all the functions right from the beginning; use marketing, for instance, before there is any research; or work out the financial requirements of a future business even before knowing whether there will be any products.

The traditional functions organize work from where we are today to where we are going. The innovative function organizes work from where we want to be, back to what we now have to do in order to get there.

The design principle for innovation is the team, set up outside of existing structures, that is, as an "autonomous unit." It is not a "decentralized business" in the traditional sense of the word, but it has to be autonomous and separate from operating organizations.

One way to organize innovative units within a large business might well be to group them together into an innovative group, which reports to one member of top management who has no other function but to guide, help, advise, review, and direct the innovating team at work. This is, in effect, what the Du Pont Development Department is. Innovation has its own logic, which is different from the logic of an ongoing business. No matter how much the innovative units may themselves differ in their technologies, their markets, their products, or their services, they all have in common that they are innovative.

Even such autonomous team organization may be too restricted for the kind of innovation that will increasingly be needed, innovation in fields that are quite different from anything that business has done so far. We may need to set up the innovating unit as a genuine entrepreneur.

Several large companies in the United States, e.g., GE and Westinghouse — and also several large companies in Europe — have set up innovative efforts in the form of partnerships with the "entrepreneurs" in charge. The innovative effort is organized as a separate company, in which the parent company has majority control and usually the right to buy out the minority stockholders at some prearranged price. But the entrepreneurs, that is, the people who are responsible directly for developing the innovation, are substantial shareholders in their own right.

One advantage of such a relationship is that it eases the compensation problem. Innovative people can command substantial salaries in the managerial organization, as senior research scientists or as senior marketing people. Yet it is highly undesirable to saddle an innovative venture with high salary costs — it cannot afford them. At the same time, it is highly desirable to compensate the entrepreneurs for results. But results in the innovative effort are unlikely to be known for a good many years. A method of compensation which induces these entrepreneurs to work for modest salaries until results are achieved, while promising substantial rewards in case of success — whether through stock ownership or through a special bonus — is therefore appropriate. A "partnership" between the company and "entrepreneurs" makes this possible. It also — and this is no small advantage — lessens (although it never completely eliminates) the friction which setting up separate innovative organizations within the company structure otherwise creates.

The same results, however, can also be achieved without a partnership — provided the tax laws permit it (which, in many countries, they no longer do). 3M, for instance, never organized a partnership with its young engineers heading a project team. It never set up a separate corporation in which the entrepreneurs became shareholders. Still, the salaries of the entrepreneurs were kept low until the innovation had proven itself and had become successful. And then the entrepreneurs not only had the opportunity to stay on and manage what they had created, at salaries commensurate to the size and performance of the business they had built they also received handsome bonuses.

Whether these "confederations" in which the entrepreneurs become partners and shareholders will become general will depend as much on the tax laws as on economics or organization structure. The principle, however, is important: compensation of the innovators should be appropriate to the economic reality of the innovating process. This is a process in which the risks are high, the lead time long, and the rewards, in case of success, very great.

Whether the innovating team is a separate company or simply a separate unit, an innovating company is likely to apply some of the design principles of systems management. There will be managerial units engaged in managing what is already known and what is already being done. And there will be innovative units, separate from them, working with them but also working on their own, and charged with their own responsibility. Both will have to report independently of each other to the top-management group and work with top-management people. To innovate within existing organizations will require acceptance of a hybrid and rather complex organization design. It is neither centralized nor decentralized. Within such a company, functional organization, federal decentralization, simulated decentralization, and teams may all be found next to each other and working together.

The innovative organization, the organization that resists stagnation rather than change, is a major challenge to management, private and public. That such organizations are possible, we can assert with confidence; there are enough of them around. But how to make such organizations general, how to make them productive for society, economy, and individual alike, is still largely an unsolved task. There is every indication that the period ahead will be an innovative one, one of rapid change in technology, society, economy, and institutions. There is every indication, therefore, that the innovative organization will have to be developed into a central institution for the last quarter of the twentieth century.

New Templates for Today's Organizations

Chapter 18

The Organization Crisis: Changes in the Objective Task
The Early GM Model versus Present Realities
Today's Realities: Non-manufacturing, Diversity, Multinational,
    Information Flow, Knowledge Work, Innovation
Three New Design Principles
Design Logics: Work and Task, Results and Performance, Relationships,
    and perhaps also, Decisions
Integral Parts of the Structure
Building the New Structure

*O*rganization structures are becoming increasingly short-lived and unstable.

The "classical" organization structures of the 1920s and 1930s, which still serve as textbook examples, stood for decades without needing more than an occasional touching up. American Telephone & Telegraph, General Motors, Du Pont, Unilever, and Sears Roebuck maintained their organizational concepts, structures, and basic components through several management generations and major changes in the size and scope of the business. Today, however, a company no sooner finishes a major job of reorganizing itself than it starts all over again.

General Electric, for instance, finished a tremendous organization overhaul around 1960, after almost a decade of hard work; since then it has revamped both its structure and its overall strategies at least twice. Similarly, Imperial Chemicals in Great Britain is restructuring an organization design that is barely 10 years old. And the same restlessness and instability afflict organization structures and concepts in the large U.S. commercial banks, in IBM, and in U.S. government agencies. For instance, the Health, Education and Welfare Deparment has been subjected to a "final" reorganization almost every year in its 20-year history.

To some extent this instability is a result of gross overorganizing. Companies are resorting to reorganization as a kind of miracle drug in lieu of diagnosing their ailments. Every business observer can see dozens of cases where substantial, even massive organization surgery is being misapplied to take care of a fairly minor procedural problem, or — even more often — to avoid facing up to personnel decisions. Equally common is the misuse of reorganization as a substitute for hard thinking on objectives, strategies, and priorities. Few managers seem to recognize that the right organization structure is not performance itself, but rather a prerequisite of performance. The wrong structure is indeed a guarantee of nonperformance; it produces friction and frustration, puts the spotlight on the wrong issues, and makes mountains out of trivia. But "perfect organization" is like "perfect health": the test is the ills it does not have and therefore does not have to cure.

Even if unnecessary organization surgery were not as rampant in our institutions as unnecessary appendectomies, hysterectomies, and tonsillectomies are said to be in our hospitals, there would still be an organization crisis. Twenty years ago many managers had yet to learn that organization design and organization structure deserve attention, thinking, and hard work. Almost everyone accepts this today; indeed, organization studies have been one of the true "growth industries" of the past twenty years. But while a few years ago organization theory had "the answers," today all is confusion.

The crisis is simultaneously a crisis of organization theory and of organization practice. Ironically, what is happening is not at all what organization theorists like Chris Argyris, Warren Bennis, Douglas McGregor (and I myself) have been predicting for at least 10 years: pressures for a more free-form and humanistic organization that provides greater scope for personal fulfillment play almost no part in the present organization crisis. Instead the main causes of instability are *changes in the objective task,* in the kind of business and institution to be organized. This is at the root of the crisis of organization practice.

The organization theorists' traditional answer to "organization crisis" — more organization development — is largely irrelevant to this new problem. Sometimes they seem to be pushing old remedies to cure a disease that no one has heard of before, and that inhabits a totally unfamiliar type of body. The kind of business and institution to be organized today is an enormously different beast from that of 20 years ago.

These changes in the objective task have generated new design principles for organization that do not fit traditional organization concepts. And therein lies the crisis of theory. On the other hand, the past 20 years have also seen the emergence of new understandings of which organization needs require the most attention and of how to go about the job of analyzing organization needs and designing organization structures. Only when we have an idea of what the new "body" looks like can we begin to treat its ills.

In what follows I compare old models of organization with new organizational realities and describe the new design principles. These principles can be matched to the tasks of modern management as well as to the formal needs of all organizations, independent of their purpose. In exploring these relationships, we can discern a way to avoid the organization crisis that affects so many businesses and institutions.

The Early Models

Twice in the short history of management we have had the "final answer" to organization problems.

The first time was around 1910 when Henri Fayol, the French industialist, thought through what were, to him, the universally valid functions of a manufacturing company. Fayol's structure was based on related work: engineering, manufacturing, selling and so on. Of course, at that time the manufacturing business presented the one truly important organization problem.

Then in the early 1920s Alfred P. Sloan, Jr., in organizing General Motors, took the next step. He found "the answer" for organizing a large, multidivisional manufacturing company. The Sloan approach built the individual divisions on the functional structure that Fayol had specified for a manufacturing business, that is, on engineering, manufacturing, selling, and so on; but it organized the business itself by the concept of federal decentralization, that is, on the basis of decentralized authority and centralized control. The individual divisions of GM, the various automotive or accessory divisions such as Pontiac or AC Spark Plug, were set up as "autonomous businesses," each with its own complete management and with full profit-and-loss responsibility. But a small but strong top management kept central control. It made key personnel decisions with respect to management appointments in the division. It alone made major capital-allocation decisions. It set policy for all divisions. It set, or at least approved, the goals and standards of performance. And it controlled executive compensation. By the mid-1940s GM's structure had become the model for larger organizations around the world.

Where they fit the realities that confront organization designers and implementers today, the Fayol and Sloan models are still unsurpassed. Fayol's functional organization is still the best way to structure a small business, especially a small manufacturing business. Sloan's federal decentralization is still the best structure for the big, single-product, single-market company like GM. But more and more of the institutional reality that has to be structured and organized does not "fit." Indeed the very assumptions that underlay Sloan's work — and that of Fayol — are not applicable to today's organization challenges.

GM Model vs. Present Realities

There are at least six ways in which the GM structure no longer serves as a model for present organization needs.

1. General Motors is a manufacturing business. Today we face the challenge of organizing the large nonmanufacturing institution. There are not only the large financial businesses and the large retailers, but also, equally, there are worldwide transportation, communications, and customer service companies. The latter, while they

may manufacture a product, have their greatest emphasis on outside services (as most computer businesses do). Then there are, of course, all the nonbusiness service institutions, e.g., hospitals, universities, and government agencies. These "nonmanufacturing" institutions are, increasingly, the true center of gravity of any developed economy. They employ the most people, and they both contribute to and take the largest share of the gross national product. They present the fundamental organization problems today.

2. General Motors is essentially a single-product, single-technology, single-market business. Even accounting for the revenues of its large financial and insurance subsidiaries, four fifths of its total revenue are still produced by the automobile. Although Frigidaire and Electromotive are large, important businesses and leaders in the consumer appliance and locomotive markets, respectively, they are but minor parts of GM. Indeed, GM is unique among large companies in being far less diversified today than it was 30 or 40 years ago. Then, in the late 1930s and early 1940s, General Motors had major investments in the chemical industry (Ethyl), in the aircraft industry (North American Aviation), and in earth-moving equipment (Euclid). All three are gone now and have not been replaced by new diversification activities outside the automotive field.

The cars that General Motors produces differ in details, such as size, horsepower, and price, but they are essentially one and the same product. No one who came up the line in, say, the Pontiac Division, will find Chevrolet — or even Opel, GM's German subsidiary — totally alien or surprisingly different.

By contrast, the typical businesses today are multiproduct, multitechnology, and multimarket. They may not be conglomerates, but they are diversified. And their central problem is a problem General Motors did not have: the organization of complexity and diversity.

There is, moreover, an even more difficult situation to which the GM pattern cannot be applied: the large single-product, single-technology business that, unlike GM, cannot be subdivided into distinct and yet comparable parts. Typical are the "materials" businesses such as steel and aluminum companies. Here belong, also, the larger transportation businesses, such as railroads, airlines, and the large commercial banks. These businesses are too big for a functional structure; it ceases to be a skeleton and becomes a straitjacket. They are also incapable of being genuinely decentralized; no one part on its own is a genuine "business." Yet as we are shifting from mechanical to process technologies, and from making goods to producing knowledge and services, these large, complex, but integrated businesses are becoming more important than the multidivisional businesses of the 1920s and 1930s.

3. General Motors still sees its international operations as organizationally separate and outside. For 50 years it has been manufacturing and selling overseas, and something like one quarter of its sales are now outside North America. But in its organization structure, in its reporting relationships, and above all in its career ladders, GM is a U.S. company with foreign subsidiaries. Rather than leaning toward an international, let alone a multinational operation, GM's top management is primarily

concerned with the U.S. market, the U.S. economy, the U.S. labor movement, the U.S. government, and so on. This traditional structure and viewpoint of GM's top management may, in large part, explain the substantial failure of GM to take advantage of the rapid expansion and growth of such major non-U.S. automobile markets as Europe, where GM's share has actually been dropping, or Brazil, where GM failed to anticipate a rapidly emerging automobile market.

In contrast, during the last 20 years many other companies have become multinational. For these companies, a great many cultures, countries, markets, and governments are of equal, or at least of major, importance.

4. Because GM is a one-product, one-country company, information handling is not a major organization problem and thus not a major concern. At GM everyone speaks the same language, whether by that we mean the language of the automotive industry or American English. Everyone fully understands what the other one is doing or should be doing, if only because, in all likelihood, he has done a similar job before. GM can, therefore, be organized according to the logic of the marketplace, and the logic of authority and decision. It need not, in its organization, concern itself a great deal with the logic and flow of information.

By contrast, multiproduct, multitechnology, and multinational companies have to design their organization structure to handle a large flow of information. At the very least they have to make sure that their organization structure does not violate the logic of information. And for this task, GM offers no guidance — GM did not have to tackle the problem.

5. Four out of every five GM employees are either manual production workers or clerks on routine tasks. In other words, GM employs yesterday's rather than today's labor force.

But the basic organization problem today concerns knowledge work and knowledge workers. They are the fastest growing element in every business; in service institutions, they are the core employees.

6. Finally, General Motors has been a "managerial" rather than an "entrepreneurial" business. The strength of the Sloan approach lay in its ability to manage, and manage superbly, what was already there and known.

Today's organizer is challenged by an increasing demand to organize entrepreneurship and innovation. But for this undertaking, the General Motors model offers no guidance.

Three New Design Principles

We do not know how to handle these new organization realities or how to satisfy their structural demands. Nevertheless, the organizing task has not waited. To tackle the new realities, we have in the past 13 years improvised ad hoc design solutions to supplement the Fayol and Sloan models. As a result, the organization architect now has available five so-called design principles, i.e., five distinct organization structures. The two traditional ones already mentioned have been known as principles of organization design for many years:

- Henri Fayol's functional structure;

- Alfred P. Sloan's federal decentralization.

Three are new; indeed they are so new that they are not generally known, let alone recognized, as design principles:

- Team organization;
- Simulated decentralization;
- Systems structure.

In team organization, a group — usually a fairly small one — is set up for a specific task rather than for a specific skill or stage in the work process. A team, for instance with members drawn from research, from the medical department, from manufacturing, marketing and finance, may be jointly responsible in the pharmaceutical company for introducing new prescription drugs in the market. In the past 30 years we have learned that whereas team design was traditionally considered applicable only to short-lived, transitory, exceptional task-force assignments, it is equally applicable to some permanent needs, especially to the top-management and innovating tasks.

In an organization that is both too big to remain functionally organized and too integrated to be genuinely decentralized, simulated decentralization is often the organization answer. It sets up one function, one stage in the process, or one segment as if it were a distinct business with genuine profit and loss responsibility. This "simulates" decentraliation, for the units, a group of manufacturing plants in a steel company, for instance, are not truly "autonomous businesses." In simulated decentralization therefore, internal accounting decisions, e.g., the prices at which goods are being transferred from one unit of the company to another, are treated as if they were realities of the marketplace. For all its difficulties and frictions, simulated decentralization is probably the fastest growing organization design around these days. It is the only one that fits, albeit poorly, the materials, computer, chemical, and pharmaceutical companies, as well as the big banks; it is also the only design principle suited for the large university, hospital, or government agency.

Finally, in systems structure, team organization and simulated decentralization are combined. The prototype for this design principle was NASA's space program, in which a large number of autonomous units — large government bodies, individual research scientists, profit-seeking businesses, and large universities — worked together, organized and informed by the needs of the situation rather than by logic, and held together by a common goal and a joint top management. The large transnational company, which is a mix of many cultures, governments, businesses, and markets, is the present embodiment of an organization based on the systems concept.

None of the new design principles is easy or trouble-free. Compared to the traditional designs of functionalism and federal decentralization, they are indeed so difficult, complex, and vulnerable that many organization theorists maintain that they are not principles at all, but abominations. And there is no question that wherever the traditional principles can be used, they should be; they are infinitely easier. The traditional principles are, however, far more limited in their scope than the new ones, and when misapplied they can cause even greater problems.

Design Logics

Each of the five design principles expresses or embodies a logic that makes that principle the appropriate one to apply when one or another task of management requires a structure. In this discussion we can identify three, or maybe four, logics upon which the five principles are based. For instance, although they do it differently, the functional and team design principles both embody *work* and *task* and are thus appropriate designs to consider when faced with work- or task-oriented management problems.

Historically these two design principles have been viewed as opposing each other, but actually they are complementary. In the functionally organized structure, the work skills — manufacturing, accounting, and so on — are designed to be static; the work moves from one stage to others. In team structure, the work is conceived as static, with skills moving to meet the requirements of the task. Because of their complementary nature, these two design principles are the only possible choices for dealing with, say, the structure of knowledge. For if you need a specific task performed and a team effort would do it best, then you need static functions as bases from which persons, and their expertise, can be moved to form a team.

Two other design logics, corresponding to those involving work and task, can also be defined. Simulated decentralization and Sloan's federal decentralization both deal with *results* and *performance*. They are result-focused designs. Unlike functional and team structures, however, they are not complementary, they are not even alternatives. Federal decentralization is an "optimum"; the results it shows, for a GM division for instance, are very close to the results which the division would report were it actually a separate, independent business and wholly on its own. Simulated decentralization is a "lesser evil" to be resorted to only when the stringent requirements of federal decentralization cannot be met. "Results" under simulated decentralization are at best an approximation, can always be argued with, and usually are.

The last of the available design principles, systems design, is focused on *relationships*, another dimension of management. Because relations are inevitably both more numerous and less clearly definable than either work and task or results, a structure focused on relations will present greater difficulties than either a work-focused or a result-focused design. There are, however, organization problems, as in the true multinational business, in which the very complexity of relationships makes systems design the only appropriate design principle.

This rough classification indicates that at least one additional design principle might yet be developed. *Decision* is as much a dimension of management as are work and task, results and performance, and relations. Yet, so far, we know of no decision-focused design principle of organization structure, but should one ever be developed, it might have wide applicability.

Ideally, an organization should be multiaxial, that is, structured around work and task, *and* results and performance, *and* relationships, *and* decisions. It would function as if it were a biological organism, like the human body with its skeleton and muscles, a number of nervous systems, and with circulatory, digestive, immunological, and respiratory systems, all autonomous yet interdependent. But in social structures we are still limited to designs that express only one primary dimension.

So, in designing organizations, we have to choose among different structures, each stressing a different dimension and each, therefore, with distinct costs, specific and fairly stringent requirements, and real limitations. There is no risk-free organization structure. And a design that is the best solution for one task may be only one of a number of equally poor alternatives for another task, and just plain wrong for yet a third kind of work.

The Integral Parts of the Structure

A somewhat different way of viewing the relationships between the design logics and principles is to identify the principal tasks of management that the principles can structure. We have learned that, in a very general analysis, organization design should simultaneously structure and integrate three different kinds of work:

1. The operating task, which is responsible for producing the results of today's business;
2. The innovative task, which creates the organization's tomorrow; and
3. the top-management task, which directs, gives vision, and sets the course for the business of both today and tomorrow.

No one organization design is adequate to all three kinds of work; every business will need to use several design principles side-by-side.

In addition, each organization structure has certain formal specifications that have nothing to do with the purpose of the structure but are integral parts of the structure itself. Just as a human body can be described as having certain characteristics, regardless of the occupation of its inhabitant, so can an organization structure. Bodies have arms and legs, hands and feet, all related to each other; similarly, organizations are structured to satisfy the need for:

- *Clarity,* as opposed to simplicity. (The Gothic cathedral is not a simple design, but your position inside it is clear; you know where to stand and where to go. A modern office building is exceedingly simple in design, but it is very easy to get lost in one; it is not clear.)
- *Economy* of effort to maintain control and minimize friction. (If the people in top-management have to spend all their time on internal problems of organizational and human relationships within the business and have no time for the business itself, the design is truly uneconomical. It abuses energy — using resources as lubricants.)
- *Direction of vision* toward the product rather than the process, the result rather than the effort. The people who do quality control need to be concerned with the reasons for quality control, e.g., the values and needs of the customer rather than worry only about quality control techniques.
- *Understanding* by each individual of his own task as well as that of the organization as a whole. The quality control people need to know specifically what they have to do to provide effective quality control.
- *Decision making* that focuses on the right issues, is action-oriented, and is carried out at the lowest possible level of management.

- *Stability,* as opposed to rigidity, to survive turmoil, and *adaptability* to learn from it.
- *Perpetuation and self-renewal,* which require that an organization be able to produce tomorrow's leaders from within, helping each person develop continuously; the structure must also be open to new ideas.

Surveying the Structures

Even though every institution, and especially every business, is structured in some way around all the dimensions of management, no one design principle is adequate to all these demands and needs. Nor does any one of the five available design principles adequately satisfy all of the formal specifications. The functional principle, for instance, has great clarity and high economy, and it makes it easy to understand one's own task. But even in the small business it tends to direct vision away from results and toward efforts, to obscure the organization's goals, and to sub-optimize decisions. It has high stability but little adaptability. It perpetuates and develops technical and functional skills, that is, middle managers, but it resists new ideas and inhibits top-management development and vision. And every one of the other four principles is similarly both a "good fit" against some formal organization specifications and a "misfit" against others.

One conclusion from this discussion is that organization structures can either be "pure" or they can be effective and do the job. They are unlikely to be both. Indeed, even the purest structure we know of, Alfred Sloan's GM, was actually mixed. It was not composed just of decentralized divisions, with functional organization within the divisions. It also contained, from the beginning, some sizable simulated decentralization. For instance, Fisher Body had responsibility for all body work but not for any final product. And top management was clearly structured as a team, or rather as a number of interlocking teams.

This does not mean that an organization structure must by necessity be unwieldy or a confused mixture. The tremendous vitality of some older structures — Sears Roebuck and GM, for instance — shows that a dynamic balance can be achieved. One implication is clear, however, and that is that pure structure *is* likely to end up badly botched. (This tendency may explain the difficulties that both GE and Imperial Chemicals — each trying for pure decentralization — have been experiencing.) Above all, our observations lead us to conclude that organization design is a series of risk-taking decisions rather than a search for the "one best way." And by and large, organization theorists and practitioners have yet to learn this.

Building the New Structure

There are a number of important lessons to be learned from the previous discussion and from the experiences of the past 30 years. Some concern new ideas or conclusions we have not recognized before, while others involve rethinking old concepts and relationships that we thought were settled years ago.

The first thing we can conclude is that Fayol and Sloan were right: good organization structures will not just evolve. The only things that evolve by themselves in an organization are disorder, friction, and malperformance. Nor is the right structure — or even the livable one — intuitive, any more than Greek temples or Gothic cathedrals were. Traditions may indicate where the problems and malfunctions are, but they are of little help in finding solutions. Organization design and structure require thinking, analysis, and a systematic approach.

Second, we have learned that designing an organization structure is not the first step, but the last. The first step is to identify and organize the building blocks of organization, that is, the key tasks that have to be encompassed in the final structure and that, in turn, carry the structural load of the final edifice. This is, of course, what Fayol did with his functions of a manufacturing company, when he designed them according to the work to be done.

We now know that building blocks are determined by the kind of contribution they make. And we know that the traditional classification of the contributions, e.g., the traditional distinction in U.S. organization theory between "line functions" which "operate" (manufacturing, for instance) and "staff functions" which "develop concepts" and "advise" but do not "operate" (personnel, for instance), is more of a hindrance to understanding than a help.

Designing the building blocks or tasks is, so to speak, the "engineering phase" of organization design. It provides the basic materials. And like all meterials, these building blocks have their specific characteristics. They belong in different places and fit together in different ways.

We have also learned that "structure follows strategy." Organization is not mechanical. It is not done by assembly, nor can it be prefabricated. Organization is organic and unique to each individual business or institution. We realize now that structure is a means for attaining the objectives and goals of an institution. And if a structure is to be effective and sound, we must start with objectives and strategy.

This is perhaps the most fruitful new insight we have in the field of organization. It may sound obvious, and it is. But some of the worst mistakes in organization building have been made by imposing on a living business a mechanistic model of an ideal organization.

Strategy — that is, the answer to the question: "What is our business? What should it be? What will it be?" — determines the purpose of structure. It thereby determines the key tasks or activities in a given business or service institution. Effective structure is the design that makes these key activities function and produce results. In turn the key activities are the load-bearing elements of a functioning structure. Organization design is, or should be, primarily concerned with the key acitivities; other purposes are secondary.

Some of the new insights into organization design require us to unlearn old ideas. A few of the noisiest and most time-consuming battles in organization theory and practice are pure sham. They pose an either/or dichotomy when the correct answer is "both — in varying proportions."

The first of these sham battles that had better be forgotten is between task-focus and person-focus in job design and organization structure. Structure and job design have to be task-focused. But assignments have to fit both the person and the needs of the situation. There is not point in confusing the two, as the old and tiresome discussion of the nonproblem insists on doing. Work is always objective and impersonal; the job itself is always done by a person.

Somewhat connected with this old controversy is the discussion of hierarchical versus free-form organization.

Traditional organization theory knows only one kind of structure, applicable alike to building blocks and whole buildings. It is the so-called scalar organization, that is, the hierarchical pyramid of superior and subordinates.

Today another — equally doctrinaire — organization theory is becoming fashionable. It maintains that shape and structure are what we want them to be — they are, or should be, free form. Everything — shape, size, and apparently tasks — derive from interpersonal relations. Indeed, it is argued, the purpose of the structure is to make it possible for each person "to do his thing or her thing." It is simply not true, however, that one of these forms represents total regimentation and the other total freedom. The amount of discipline required in both is the same; they only distribute it differently.

Hierarchy does not, as the critics allege, make the person at the top of the pyramid more powerful. On the contrary, the first effect of hierarchical organization is to protect the subordinate against arbitrary authority from above. A scalar or hierarchical organization does this by defining a sphere within which the subordinate has authority, a sphere within which the superior cannot interfere. It protects subordinates by making it possible for each one to say, "This is *my* assigned job." Protection of the subordinate also underlies the scalar principle's insistence that a worker have only one superior. Otherwise, the subordinate is likely to be caught between conflicting demands, commands, interests, and loyalties. There is a lot of truth in the old proverb, "Better one bad master than two good ones."

At the same time, the hierarchical organization gives the most individual freedom. As long as each incumbent does whatever are the assigned duties of his or her position, each has done his or her job. There is no responsibility beyond the job.

We hear a lot of talk these days about the individual's right to "do your own thing." But the only organization structure in which this is remotely possible is a hierarchical one. It makes the least demands on individuals to subordinate themselves to the goals of the organization or to gear their activities into the needs and demands of each other.

Teams, by contrast, demand, above all, very great self-discipline from each member. Everybody has to do the team's "thing." Everybody has to take responsibility for the work of the entire team and for its performance. The one thing one cannot do on a team is one's own "thing."

Organization builders (and even organization theorists) will have to learn that sound organization structure needs both (a) a hierarchical structure of authority, and (b) a capacity to organize task forces, teams, and individuals for work on both a permanent and a temporary basis.

The One Final Answer: It Doesn't Exist

Organization theory and organization practice still assume that there is "one final answer," at least for a particular business or institution. In itself, this belief is a large part of today's organization crisis. It leads to doctrinaire structures that impose one template on everybody and everything — e.g., operating and innovating components; manufacturing and service units; single-product and multimarket businesses. And if any person or process, no matter how insignificant, seems out of place, a total root-and-branch reorganization has to be done to accommodate it.

Maybe there is one right answer — but if so, we do not yet have it. Indeed for certain businesses and institutions, such as a large airline or government agency, we do not even have one poor answer — all we have are a multitude of equally unsatisfactory approaches. But, as remarked before, the organizing task will not wait; it will by necessity continue to be a central preoccupation of managers. Therefore, they had better learn to understand the design principles we already have. They must also learn the formal specifications of organization, and the relationships between the tasks of a business and the structures available to it.

The true lesson of the organization crisis is, however, quite different. It is that the traditional quest for the one right answer — a quest pursued as wholeheartedly by the new "heretics" of free-form organization as by the most orthodox classicists — pursues the wrong quarry. It misconceives an organization as something in itself rather than as a means to an end. But now we can see that liberation and mobilization of human energies — rather than symmetry, harmony, or consistency — are the purpose of organization. Human performance is both its goal and its test.

The Building Blocks of Organizations...

Chapter 19

The Four Tasks of the Organizer
Finding the Key Activities
Key Vulnerabilities
Values
When Key Activities Have to Be Reanalyzed
The Contributions Analysis
Revenue-Producing Activities
Result-Producing Work
Support Work
The "Conscience" Areas
Making Service Staffs Effective
The Two Faces of Information
Information: An Unanswered Organization Problem
Hygiene and Housekeeping
Contribution Determines Function

*I*n designing the building blocks of organization four questions face the organizer.

1. What should the units of organization be?
2. What components should join together, and what components should be kept apart?
3. What size and shape pertain to different components?
4. What is the appropriate placement and relationship of different units?

From the earliest beginnings of work on organization, well over a century ago, these were the tasks the organizer had to confront before designing a structure.

We therefore now have a considerable amount of experience. There are no prescriptions for the design of the building blocks or for the design of the structure itself. But one can clearly indicate what the right approaches are and what approaches are unlikely to work.

The traditional approach to the identification of the basic units of organization has been to analyze *all* the activities needed for performance in the enterprise. This then results in a list of typical functions of a manufacturing business or of a retail business.

This approach to the typical functions sees organization as mechanical, as an assemblage of functions. But organization has to be "organic." Organizations will indeed use typical activities — though not necessarily all of them. But how the structure is to be built depends on what results are needed. Organizing has to start out with the desired results.

The Key Activities

What we need to know are not all the activities that might conceivably have to be housed in the organization structure. What we need to know are the load-bearing parts of the structure, the *key activities*.

Organization design, therefore, starts with these questions:

In what area is excellence required to obtain the company's objectives?

In what areas would lack of performance endanger the results, if not the survival, of the enterprise?

Here are some examples of the kind of conclusions these questions lead to.

Sears, Roebuck in the United States and Marks & Spencer in England are in many ways remarkably similar, if only because the founders and builders of Marks & Spencer consciously modeled their company on Sears, Roebuck. But there is a pronounced difference in the organizational placement and organizational role of the "laboratory" in these two companies. Sears, which defines its business as being "the *buyer* of the right goods for the American family," uses its laboratory to test the merchandise it buys. Accordingly, the laboratory, while large, competent, and respected, is organizationally quite subordinate; for what goods Sears will buy has already been decided by the marketplace. The buyer in Sears makes the decision; the laboratory determines only standards and checks up on the goods the manufacturer delivers. Marks & Spencer, on the other hand, defined its business as "creating and developing upper-class goods for the working-class family." The goods Marks & Spencer sells did not, as a rule, exist until Marks & Spencer took an expensive "upper-class" article and completely redesigned it so that it retained or improved its quality but could be made at a fraction of its former price. And this has largely been the task of the laboratory. As a result, the laboratory is central to Marks & Spencer's organization structure. The laboratory rather than the buyer decides what new products are desirable, develops the new merchandise, designs it, tests it, and then gets it produced. Only then does the buyer take over. As a result, the head of the Marks & Spencer laboratory is a senior member of management and, in many ways, the chief business planner.

Any company that shows outstanding success will be found to have made the key activities — and especially those in which excellence is needed to attain business performance and business objectives — the central, load-carrying elements in its organization structure.

But equally important are the questions "In what areas could malfunction seriously damage us? In what areas do we have major vulnerability?" They are questions, however, that are much less often asked.

The New York brokerage community, by and large, did not ask it. If it had, it would have realized that malfunction of the "back office," where customer orders, customer accounts and securities are handled, could seriously endanger the business. Failure to organize the back office as a key activity was the single most important cause for the severe crisis that overtook Wall Street in 1969 and 1970 and destroyed a good many of the best-known and apparently most successful firms. The one Wall Street firm, however, that had asked those questions, Merrill Lynch, and had organized the back office as a load-bearing key activity in its structure, emerged from the crisis as the giant of the brokerage business.

Finally, the question should be asked "What are the *values* that are truly important to *us* in this company?" It might be product or process safety. It might be product quality. It might be the ability of the company dealers to give proper service to the customer and so on. Whatever the values are, they have to be organizationally anchored. There has to be an organizational component responsible for them — and it has to be a key component.

These three questions will identify the key activities. And they in turn will be the load-bearing, the structural elements of organization. The rest, no matter how important, no matter how much money they represent, no matter how many people they employ, are secondary. Obviously, they will have to be analyzed, organized, and placed within the structure. But the first concern must be those activities that are essential to the success of a business strategy and to the attainment of business objectives. They have to be identified, defined, organized, and centrally placed.

An analysis of key activities is needed in the business that has been going for some time, and especially in the business that has been going well. In such a business the analysis will invariably reveal that important activities are either not provided for or are left hanging in midair to be performed in a haphazard fashion. It will almost invariably bring out activities that, once important, have lost most of their meaning but continue to be organized as major activities. It will demonstrate that historically meaningful groupings no longer make sense but have, instead, become obstacles to proper performance. And it will certainly lead to the discovery of unnecessary activities that should be eliminated.

The new business needs such thinking. But the greatest need for key-activity analysis is found in the business that has been growing fast. Rapid growth is both a disorganized and a disorganizing process. The enterprise that starts out, so to speak, in a lowly but functional two-room cottage, puts in, as it grows, a new wing here, an attic there, a partition elsewhere, until it is housed in a twenty-six-room monstrosity in which all but the oldest inhabitants need a St. Bernard to bring them back from the water cooler. To reorganize mechanically in such a situation — the usual approach — will make things worse. To copy the "GM organization" in such a situation will put on a tremendous superstructure of "staff" and "coordinators," without remedying the basic structural defects. Only a key-activities analysis starting out from objectives and strategy can provide the organization structure the business really needs.

A business should always analyze its organization structure when its strategy changes. Whatever the reason — a change in market or in technology, diversification or new objectives — a change in strategy requires a new analysis of the key activities and an adaptation of the structure to them. Conversely, reorganization that is undertaken without change in strategy is either superfluous or indicates poor organization to begin with.

The Contributions Analysis

From the earliest days of concern with organization, a hundred years ago, the most controversial question has been "What activities belong together and what activities belong apart?" A number of answers have been given over the years.

Perhaps the earliest one was the German division of a business into two major areas: the "technical," embracing research, engineering, and production, and the "commercial," embracing sales and finance. Somewhat later came "line" and "staff," which tried to distinguish "operating" and nonoperating "advisory" activities. Finally there was Henri Fayol's analysis of functions, defined (too narrowly) as "bundles of related skills," which still underlies the typical organization of most businesses.

All of these have merit. But a more searching analysis is needed which groups activities by the *kind of contribution* they make.

There are, by and large, four major groups of activities, if distinguished by their contribution.

There are, first, *result-producing activities* — that is, activities which produce measurable results which can be related, directly or indirectly, to the results and performance of the entire enterprise. Some of these activities are directly revenue-producing. Others contribute measurable results.

There are, second, *support activities* which, while needed, and even essential, do not by themselves produce results but have results only through the use made of their "output" by other components within the business.

There are, third, activities which have no direct or indirect relationship to the results of the business, activities which are truly ancillary. They are *hygiene and housekeeping activities.*

Finally, and different in character from any of these, is the *top-management activity.*

Among the result-producing activities, there are some that directly bring in revenues (or, in service institutions, directly produce "patient care" or "learning"). Here belong innovating activities, selling and all the work needed to do a systematic and organized selling job, such as forecasting, market research, sales training, and sales management. Here also belongs the treasury function, that is, the supply and management of money in the business.

In a commercial bank, all lending operations, the fiduciary activities of managing other people's money, and, of course, the money-making operation of the bank itself, that is, the management of its own liquid funds, are revenue-producing activities. In a department store buying and selling are always revenue-producing operations (and at Marks & Spencer innovation has also been a revenue-producing activity). In a life insurance company selling is obviously revenue-producing. But so is the actuarial activity insofar as it develops new types of policy; and finally, investment is an important — in many insurance companies the most important — revenue-producing activity.

The second group of result-producing activities are those which do not generate revenue but can still be directly related to the results of the entire business, or of a major revenue-producing segment. I call them *result-contributing* rather than result-producing.

Manufacturing is typical of these activities. But training of people belongs here too, as does their original recruitment and employment, that is, the activities concerned with the supply of qualified and trained people to the enterprise. Purchasing and physical distribution are result-contributing but not revenue-producing activities. "Engineering," as the term is normally understood in most manufacturing businesses, is a result-contributing but not a revenue-producing activity. In a commercial bank "operations," that is, the handling of data and papers, belong here; in a life insurance company, claims settlement. Labor negotiations and many other similar "relations" activities are result-contributing though not revenue-producing.

The third group of result-producing activities are information activities. They do produce a "finished product" that is needed by everyone in the system. Information performance can also be defined and measured, or at least appraised. Yet information, by itself, does not produce any revenue. It is "supply" to revenue and cost centers alike.

First among the "support" activities which do not by themselves produce a "product" but are "input" to others stand the "conscience" activities. These activities set standards, create vision, and demand excellence in *all* the key areas where a business needs to strive for excellence.

Conscience activities tend to be slighted in most organizations. But every company — and every service institution — needs to provide itself and its managers with vision, with values, with standards, and with some provision for auditing performance against these standards.

There are indeed in all larger businesses people who are supposed to do this job, usually the executives who head up major "service staffs." But their first duty is not to be the organization's conscience but to be servant of, and advisor to, operating managers. As a result they rarely get around to doing the conscience job systematically. Instead they run departments.

Another support function is advice and teaching, i.e., the traditional service staffs. The contribution is not in what the activity itself does or can do, but the impact it has on the ability of others to perform and to do. The "product" is an increased performance capacity of the rest of the organization.

A good many of the "relations" activities are also "support" — as is the legal staff, or the patent department.

The last group of activities defined by their contribution are the hygiene and house-keeping activities, ranging from the medical department to the people who clean the floor, from the plant cafeteria to the management of pension and retirement funds, from finding a plant site to taking care of all the manifold record-keeping requirements imposed on business by government. These functions contribute nothing directly to the results and performance of the business. Their malfunction, however, can damage the business. They serve legal requirements, the morale of the work force, or public responsibilities. Of all activities they are the most diverse. And of all activities they tend to get the shortest shrift in most organizations.

This is a very rough classification, and far from scientific. Some activities may be put into one category in one business, into another one in another, and in a third company will be left fuzzy and without clear classification at all.

In some manufacturing companies, manufacturing is a cost center. It contributes results but does not generate revenue. But there are some true manufacturing businesses, i.e., businesses whose revenue is generated by manufacturing sans research, sans engineering, sans selling. There are businesses where licensing, selling, and buying of patents are major revenue producers.

Purchasing, while normally a support activity, can also be defined as part of a result-contributory activity: "materials management," which includes manufacturing and physical distribution, all three managed together to minimize costs of goods and money needs, and maximize quality, delivery, and customer satisfaction.

Why classify then? The answer is that activities that differ in contribution have to be treated differently. Contribution determines ranking and placement.

Key activities should never be subordinated to nonkey activities.

Revenue-producing activities should never be subordinated to nonrevenue-producing activities.

And support activities should never be mixed with revenue-producing and result-contributory activities. They should be kept apart.

The "Conscience" Activities

Activities that are the conscience of an organization must never be subordinated to anything else. They also should never be placed with any other activity; they should be clearly separate.

The conscience function of giving vision, of setting standards, and of auditing performance against these standards is basically a top-management function. But it has to work with the entire management group. Every business, even a small business, needs this function. In a small business, it need not be set up as a separate function but can be discharged as part of the top-management job. In any business of more than medium size, however, the function has usually to be set up and staffed separately.

However, there should be very few people actually doing the conscience job. It is a job for a single individual rather than a staff. It is a job for someone whose performance has earned the respect of the management group. It is not a job for a "specialist." It is best discharged by a senior member of the management group with proven performance record who has manifested concern, perception, and interest in the area for which that senior member is supposed to act as the conscience.

Only those few areas that are vital and central to a company's success and survival should become areas of conscience. Objectives and strategy determine what conscience activities are needed. Managing people is always a conscience area, and so is marketing. The impact of a business on its environment, its social responsibilities and basic relations with the outside community, are also basic conscience areas. Innovation (whether technological or social innovation) is likely to be a conscience area for any large business.

Beyond these, however, there is no formula.

Conscience work is incompatible with operating and with giving advice.

The only activity that should "report" to a person in charge of a conscience activity is auditing and the actual performance of managers. For it is not enough to have vision and to set standards. Performance of the organization against these standards needs to be appraised regularly.

"Conscience," many people will argue, is a very strong, in addition to being a rather strange, term. But it is the right term. The task of the conscience activities is not to help the organization do better what it is already doing. The task is to remind the organization all the time of what it should be doing and isn't doing. The task is to be uncomfortable, to hold up the ideal against the everyday reality, to defend the unpopular and to fight the expedient.

This requires, however, self-discipline on the part of the conscience executive and the organization must accept the conscience executive's competence and integrity.

The tenure of the few conscience executives should be limited as a rule. No matter how greatly they may be respected, and no matter how successful they have been, most conscience executives will eventually wear out either their integrity or their welcome. This is a good place for a senior person to end a distinguished career. A younger person in the job should be moved out after a few years — preferably back into a "doing" job.

Making Service Staffs Effective

There are similarly stringent rules with respect to advisory and teaching activities, that is, with respect to service staffs.

There should be very few of them. They should be set up only in key activity areas. It is counterproductive to have a service staff in every function. The secret of effective service work is concentration rather than busyness.

Advisory and teaching staffs should never try to do a little bit of everything. They should zero in on a very small number of crucial areas. Rather than serve everybody they should select "targets of opportunity," i.e., areas within the organization where the managers are receptive and do not have to be "sold," and where achievement will lead to widespread imitation throughout the company.

The staffs and their activities should be kept lean.

The supply of people of the right temperament for this kind of work is not very large. To do a decent job in an advisory and teaching capacity requires someone who genuinely wants others to get the credit. It requires someone who starts out with the aim of enabling others to do what *they* want to do, provided only that it is neither immoral nor insane. It requires further a person who has the patience to let others learn rather than go and do the work himself or herself. And finally, it requires the kinds of people who will not abuse the position in headquarters close to the seat of power to politick, to manipulate, and to play favorites. People who possess these personality traits are rare. Yet people without them in services work can do only mischief.

One basic rule for advisory and teaching staffs is that they abandon an old activity before they take on a new one. Otherwise they will soon start to "build empires" or to produce "canned goods," that is, programs and memoranda, rather than develop the knowledge and performance capacity of the operating staff whose job it is to produce. They will also otherwise be forced to use second-raters rather than people of outstanding competence. Only if they are being required to abandon an old activity before taking on a new one will they be able to put on the job the really first-rate people in the group.

Advisory and teaching activities should never "operate." A common weakness of personnel staffs is that they operate. They run the labor negotiations, they do a lot of housekeeping chores such as managing the cafeteria, or they train. As a result the advisory and teaching work does not get done. The "daily crisis" in "operations" takes precedence over the work of advice and teaching which can always be postponed. Mixing advice and operations means building large staffs rather than building performance.

Other service staffs are just as guilty of mixing "doing" work in with advice and teaching — and thereby shifting either the one or the other.

A company may have need for acoustics engineering while no division, however, has enough work in the area to justify its own acoustics engineers. It seems logical therefore to put a few good acoustics engineers into "manufacturing services" or "engineering services." The acoustics people, however, are not service staff but result-producers who go to work wherever, in a given division, an acoustics job is to be done. They are not expected to give advice or to teach, but to do. If placed into a services component the unit will rarely produce. The good people in it will become frustrated and are unlikely to stay long. Acoustics engineering is "operating" work, no matter where it is done. And if no division needs enough of it to support a full effort, it has to be set up as "joint operating" work by a number of divisions, either within the division that needs it the most but serving the other divisions as well, or as a separate group that has a number of "customers," that is, a number of divisions for whom it does acoustics work.

If "joint-operating work" is needed — and it often is — there might be a separate central operating pool under one manager for all such work, regardless of technical area. The management problems in all joint operating work are the same: relations, assignments, priorities, and standards.

Advisory and teaching activities are service institutions. They should be required to impose on themselves the self-discipline of setting objectives, of setting targets, of determining priorities and measuring their results against them. They should not have a monopoly. If consulting or teaching work has to be done other than in their areas of concentration somebody from the outside should be brought in to do it. And insofar as possible, their "customers," the managers of the various units, should have the choice between using the internal advisory and teaching staff, going on the outside, or not using any staff at all.

Advisory and teaching work should not be a career. It is work to which managers or career professionals should be exposed in the course of their growth. But it is not work which someone should, normally, do for long. As a career it corrupts. It breeds contempt for "those dumb operating people," that is, for honest work. It puts a premium on being "bright," rather than on being right. It is also frustrating work because one does not have results of one's own but results only at secondhand.

But it is excellent training, excellent development, and a severe test of a person's character and ability to be effective without having the authority of command. It is an experience everyone should have had who rises to the top of an organization. But it is an exposure no one should suffer for more than a limited period of time.

There is constant discussion these days whether this kind of work requires a high degree of specialized knowledge or whether a good "generalist" can rapidly acquire enough of a "smattering of ignorance" to be effective in advisory and teaching work. The debate rages forever in any consulting practice. There is no answer to the question — indeed, it is probably the wrong question. In some areas, clearly, professional and highly specialized competence is a requirement. If a company, for instance, needs advice and teaching in advanced areas of polymer chemistry or in structuring highly complex and risky international capital transactions, somebody with a background in marketing or in purchasing need not apply, no matter how good and perceptive a teacher he or she is. But in many areas of advice and teaching the generalist who is willing to learn, who will think through the relationship with the "client," and who takes responsibility for his or her contribution, is likely to do a better job than the highly specialized expert who refuses to try to be understood and is contemptuous of the "laity." Indeed, in most successful advisory and teaching activities, the expert is the "inside" man or woman who furnishes the tools for the consultants, but who is not active, let alone effective, in advising and teaching work.

The Two Faces of Information

Information activities present a special organizational problem. In the terms the chemist uses, they are "bi-valent"; they have two faces, two dimensions, and require two different "bonds." Unlike most other result-producing activities, they are not concerned with the entire process itself. This means that they have to be both centralized and decentralized.

Information-producing activities, whether accounting work or operations research, resemble the nervous system of a biological organism which is also both centralized and decentralized down to the smallest and most remote cell in the body.

Information activities therefore have two organizational homes rather than one.

The traditional organization chart expresses this in the two different lines that connect an information activity to "bosses": a solid line to the head of the unit for which it is the information provider, and a dotted line to the central information group, for instance, the company controller. One conclusion from this is that information work should be kept separate from other kinds of work.

American business has typically violated this rule by putting accounting, i.e., a traditional information activity, into one component with the treasurer, i.e., the result-producing operating work of supplying capital and managing money in the business. The justification has been that both "deal with money." But, of course, accounting does not deal with money; it deals with figures. The consequence of the traditional approach has been the slighting of financial management. As long as money was — or seemed — cheap this could be excused; to neglect money management did not cost very much. But the era of cheap money came to an end around 1970; since then too slight financial management has become an expensive mistake.

The tough question with respect to information activities is which of them belong together and which should be kept apart. There is much talk today about "integrated total information systems." This of course implies that all — or at least most — information activities should be in one component. Insofar as this means that new and different information activities, e.g., operations research or a computer system, should not be subordinated to traditional accounting, the point is well taken. But should they be coordinated? Or should they be separate?

There is, so far, no clear answer and no satisfactory way to organize information work — though it is clearly a key activity. Nobody has yet seen a total information system. No one may ever see one. But as we develop information capacity we will have to grapple with the organizational problem and will have to find answers, or at least approaches.

Hygiene and Housekeeping

The last group of activities according to their contribution are hygiene and housekeeping activities. They should be kept separate from other work, or else they will not get done. The problem is not that these activities are particularly difficult. Some are. Many others are not. The problem is that they are not even indirectly related to results. Therefore, they tend to be looked down upon by the rest of the organization. They are "donkey work" because they are neither result-producing nor professional work.

One reason for the tremendous increase in health-care costs in the U.S. is managerial neglect of the "hotel services" by the people who dominate the hospital, such as doctors and nurses. They all know that the hotel services are essential and that patients do not get well unless they are reasonably comfortable, are being fed, have their beds changed and their rooms cleaned. But these are not professional activities for a doctor, for a nurse, or an X-ray technician. They are not willing to yield an inch to make it possible for the people in charge of the hotel services to do their jobs. They are not willing to have these activities represented on the upper levels of hospital management. As a result, no "respectable" manager in a hospital wants to have anything to do with these activities. They are left unmanaged. And this means they are done badly and expensively.

There rarely is such a problem with the medical department within a company – if only because our value system respects and places the doctor high in our social hierarchy. But even so important a function as the selection of a plant site, or the construction of a plant are often considered "extraneous" by the people within a business. Activities where less seems to be at stake, whether the parking lot, the cafeteria, or maintenance in general, tend to be slighted and neglected.

This extends even to activities in which a great amount of money is at stake. Very few companies in the United States for instance have done even an adequate job of managing the pension funds of their employees, despite the enormous amount of money involved and the serious impact on the company's future. It is an activity which does not, it seems, have any relationship to results and therefore it is an activity which tends to be relegated to somebody else.

One way out is to turn hygiene and housekeeping activities over to the work community to run. They are activities "for" the employees and they are therefore best managed *by* the employees. Or, such activities may be farmed out to somebody whose business it is to run a pension fund or to manage a cafeteria.

But insofar as a company's management has to do these things itself – and picking a plant site and building a factory is something a company has to do for itself, or at least has to participate in actively – hygiene and housekeeping activities ought to be kept separate from all others. They require different people, different values, different measurements – and should require little supervision by business management itself.

One example are the autonomous real estate management companies which large businesses have created to handle everything concerned with the procurement of real estate, the construction of a building or a factory, and the management and maintenance of buildings. Another example is the General Services Administration of the U.S. Government, which handles all housekeeping tasks for all government agencies. For the senior members of the departments of government, managing the automotive fleets for their units is a chore for which they have neither interest nor respect. Yet there obviously is a good deal of money at stake – and cars need organized, systematic purchasing and organized, systematic maintenance. For the General Services Administration the administration of the government automotive fleet is its business and can be organized as such.

There is one overall rule. Activities that make the same kind of contribution can be joined together in one component and under one management, whatever their technical specialization. Activities that do not make the same kind of contribution do not, as a rule, belong together.

It is entirely feasible – indeed, it often is the best way – to put all advising and teaching activities, in personnel, in manufacturing, in marketing, or in purchasing, in one "services" group under one manager. Similarly, in any but large companies, one person might well be the company's conscience in major conscience areas. Contribution rather than skill determines function.

...And How They Join Together

Chapter 20

Decision Analysis
Where Does Certain Work Belong?
Relations Analysis
Where Does a Particular Unit Belong?
Keeping Relationships to a Minimum
But Making Each Count
Malorganization, Its Symptoms and Its Causes
Too Many Levels
Recurrent Organization Problems
Meetings
Overconcern with "Feelings"
Reliance on Nonjobs
"Organizitis" as a Chronic Affliction

*I*dentifying key activities and analyzing their contributions defines the building blocks of organization. But to place the structural units which make up the organization requires two additional pieces of work: an analysis of decisions and an analysis of relations.

Decision Analysis

What decisions are needed to obtain the performance necessary to attain objectives?

What kinds of decisions are they? On what level of the organization should they be made? What activities are involved in, or affected by, them? Which managers must therefore participate in the decisions — at least to the extent of being consulted beforehand? Which managers must be informed after they have been made? The answers to these questions very largely determine where certain work belongs.

It will be argued that it is impossible to anticipate what kinds of decisions will arise in the future. But while their content cannot be predicted their kind and subject matter have a high degree of predictability.

In one large company well over 90 percent of the decisions that managers had to make over a five-year period were found to be "typical," and fell within a small number of categories. In only a few cases would it have been necessary to ask, "Where does this decision belong?" had the problem been thought through in advance. Yet, because there was no decision analysis, almost three-quarters of the decisions had to "go looking for a home," as the graphic phrase within the company put it, and most of them went to a much higher level of management than was needed. The company's components had been placed according to the size of their payroll rather than according to their decision responsibility so that the activities that should have made key decisions were placed so low as to be without authority and also without adequate information.

To place authority and responsibility for various kinds of decisions requires first that they be classified according to kind and character. Such standard classification as "policy decisions" and "operating decisions" are practically meaningless, however, and give rise to endless debates of a highly abstruse nature. Not much more helpful is classification according to the amount of money involved.

There are four basic characteristics which determine the nature of any business decision.

First, there is the degree of *futurity* in the decision. For how long into the future does it commit the company? And how fast can it be reversed?

The buyers at Sears, Roebuck have practically no limit as to the amount to which they can commit the company. But no buyer or buying supervisor can either abandon an existing product or add a new one without the approval of the head of the entire buying operation who, traditionally, is the number two or number three executive in the entire Sears, Roebuck organization.

The second criterion is the *impact* a decision has on other functions, on other areas, or on the business as a whole. If it affects only one function, it is of the lowest order. Otherwise it will have to be made on a higher level, where the impact on all affected functions can be considered; or it must be made in close consultation with the managers of the other affected functions. To use technical language, "Optimization" of process and performance of one function or area must not be at the expense of other functions or areas; this is undesirable "suboptimization."

One example of a decision which looks like a purely "technical" one affecting one area only, but which actually has impact on many areas, is a change in the methods of keeping the parts inventory in a mass-production plant. This affects all manufacturing operations. It makes necessary major changes in assembly. It affects delivery to customers — it might even lead to radical changes in marketing and pricing, such as the abandonment of certain designs and models and of certain premium prices. And it may require substantial changes in engineering design. The technical problems in inventory-keeping — though quite considerable — pale into insignificance compared to the problems in other areas which any change in inventory-keeping will produce. To "optimize" inventory-keeping at the expense of these other areas cannot be allowed. It can be avoided only if the decision is recognized as belonging to a fairly high order and handled as one affecting the entire process: either it has to be reserved for management higher than the plant; or it requires close consultation among all functional managers.

The consideration of the impact of a decision and the need to prevent "suboptimization" may shift the focus of a decision decisively, as the following example shows.

In the early days of the Du Pont Company, when it was still solely an explosives manufacturer, the company was by far the world's largest buyer of nitrate, without, however, owning any nitrate fields. Yet the purchasing department was given a completely free hand in buying nitrate. It did so, indeed, most successfully — from the point of view of purchasing. It bought nitrate when the market prices were low and succeeded in obtaining the vital raw material for the company at prices far below what the competitors usually had to pay. Yet this was suboptimization. For the low prices for nitrate and the resulting competitive cost advantage were paid for by tying up large sums of money in inventory. This, in the first place, meant that a good deal of the cost advantage of low nitrate prices was illusory and offset by high interest payments. More serious, it also meant that the company, in the event of a downturn in business, might find itself in a liquidity crisis. The decision to balance cheap raw material prices against the cost of money and the danger of illiquidity was therefore properly made as a top-management decision. But after the new limits for inventory had been established, the buying decisions again became exclusively the task of the purchasing people.

The character of a decision is also determined by the number of *qualitative factors* that enter into it: basic principles of conduct, ethical values, social and political beliefs, etc. The moment value considerations have to be taken into account, the decision moves into a higher order and requires either determination or review at a higher level. And the most important as well as the most common of qualitative factors are human beings.

Finally, decisions can be classified according to whether they are periodically *recurrent* or *rare,* if not unique, decisions. The recurrent decision requires the establishment of a general rule, that is, of a decision in principle. Since suspending an employee deals with a person, the rule has to be decided at a fairly high level in the organization. But the application of the rule to the specific case, while also a decision, can then be placed on a much lower level.

The rare decision, however, has to be treated as a distinct event. Whenever it occurs, it has to be thought through.

A decision should always be made at the lowest possible level and as close to the scene of action as possible. However, a decision should always be made at a level insuring that all activities and objectives affected are fully considered. The first rule tells us how far down a decision *should* be made. The second how far down it *can* be made, as well as which managers must share in the decision and which must be informed of it. The two together tell us where certain activities should be placed. Managers should be high enough to have the authority needed to make the typical decisions pertaining to their work, and low enough to have the detailed knowledge and the first-hand experience, "where the action is."

Relations Analysis

The final step in designing the building blocks of organization is an analysis of relations. It tells us where a specific component belongs.

With whom will a manager in charge of an activity have to work, what contribution does that manager have to make to managers in charge of other activities, and what contribution do these other managers have to make in return?

The basic rule in placing an activity within the organization structure is to impose on it the *smallest possible number of relationships.* At the same time, it should be so placed that the crucial relations, that is, the relationship on which depend its success and the effectiveness of its contribution, should be easy, accessible, and central to the unit. The rule is to keep relationships to a minimum but make each count.

This rule explains why functions are not, as traditional organization theory would have them be, "bundles of related skills." If we followed that logic, we would, for instance, put production planning into a planning component in which all kinds of planners would work together. The skills needed in production planning are closely related to all other operational planning skills. Instead we put the production planner into manufacturing and as close as possible both to the plant manager and to the first-line supervisors.

There is often a conflict between placement according to decision analysis and placement according to relations analysis. By and large, one should try to follow the logic of relations as far as possible.

If organization design has to follow the logic of decisions in order to avoid suboptimization (as is usually the case with respect to the accounting function) the work itself should be planned according to relations analysis, that is, as close as possible to the scene of action. The direction of the work, the setting of rules, of standards, but also the appraisal and evaluation of the work should be placed according to decision analysis in a central component which can see the entire business and think through the impacts.

The four analyses — of key activities, of contributions, of decisions, of relations — should always be kept as simple and as brief as possible. In a small enterprise they can often be done in a matter of hours and on a few pieces of paper. In a very large and complex enterprise, though, such as General Electric, the First National City Bank, or Unilever (not to mention the Department of Defense) the job may well require months of study and the application of highly advanced tools of analysis and synthesis. But these analyses should never be slighted or skimped. They should be considered a necessary task and one that has to be done well in every business.

Symptoms of Malorganization

There is no perfect organization. At its best an organization structure will not cause trouble. But what are the most common mistakes in designing the building blocks of organization and joining them together?   And what are the most common and the most serious flaws in organization?

The most common and the most serious symptom of malorganization is multiplication of the number of management levels.   A basic rule of organization is to build the *least possible* number of management levels and forge the shortest possible chain of command.

Every additional level makes more difficult the attainment of common direction and mutual understanding.   Every additional level distorts objectives and misdirects attention.   Mathematical "information theory" has a law that any additional relay in a communications system halves the "message" and doubles the "noise."   Any "level" in an organization is a "relay."   Every link in the chain sets up additional stresses and creates one more source of inertia, friction, and slack.

Every additional level, especially in the big business, adds to the difficulty of developing tomorrow's managers, both by adding to the time it takes to come up from the bottom and by making specialists rather than managers out of the people moving up through the chain.

In some large companies there are today twelve or even fifteen levels between first-line supervisor and company president.   Assuming that someone gets appointed first-line supervisor at age twenty-five, and then spends only five years on each intervening level — both optimistic assumptions — that person could not be considered for the company's presidency until age eighty or ninety.   And the usual "cure" — a special promotion ladder for hand-picked young "geniuses" or "crown princes" — is as bad as the disease.

How few levels are really needed is shown by the example of the oldest, largest, and most successful organization of the West, the Catholic Church.   There is only one level of authority and responsibility between the Pope and the lowliest parish priest: the bishop.

The second most common symptom of malorganization is recurrence of organizational problems.   No sooner has a problem supposedly been "solved" than it comes back again in a new guise.

A typical example in a manufacturing company is product development.   The marketing people think it belongs to them, the research and development people are equally convinced that it belongs to them.   But placing it in either component simply creates a recurring problem.   Actually both placements are wrong.   In a business that wants innovation, product development is a key activity and a revenue-producing activity. It should not be subordinated to any other activity.   It deserves to be organized as a separate innovative component.

The recurrent organization problem indicates unthinking application of traditional "organization principles" such as that of the "typical function" or that of "staff and line."   The answer lies in making the right analyses — the key activities analysis, the contributions analysis, the decisions analysis, and the relations analysis.   An organization problem that comes back more than a couple of times should not be treated mechanically by shuffling little boxes on a piece of paper.   It indicates lack of thinking, lack of clarity, and lack of understanding.

Equally common and equally dangerous is an organization structure that puts the attention of key people on the wrong, the irrelevant, the secondary problems.   Organization should put the attention of people on major business decisions, on key activities, and on performance and results. If, instead, it puts attention on proper behavior, on etiquette, on procedure, let alone on jurisdictional conflict, organization misdirects. Then organization becomes a bar to performance.

Again, this is the result of mechanical rather than organic organization building. It is the result of slapping on so-called principles, instead of thinking through what organization the strategy of the business demands. It is the result of focusing organization on symmetry rather than on performance.

No organization chart is likely ever to be displayed in a major art museum. What matters is not the chart but the organization. A chart is nothing but an oversimplification which enables people to make sure that they talk about the same things in discussing organization. One never makes organizational changes for the sake of the chart. This always results in malorganization.

There are a number of common symptoms of poor organization which, usually, require no further diagnosis. There is, first, the symptom of *too many meetings* attended by too many people.

There are, especially in large organizations, managerial organs which do their work in and by meetings. The top committees in General Motors are examples. And so are the boards of directors composed of the top officers which govern both Standard Oil of New Jersey and Du Pont. But these are exceptions — deliberative organs which do not have operating functions and, as a rule, do not have decision-making functions either. They are organs to guide, to reflect, to review — and perhaps their most important function is to compel the operating top managers who sit down with the committee to think through their own direction, their own needs, and their own opportunities.

But apart from such deliberative bodies, which discharge their functions in meetings, meetings should be considered as a concession to organizational imperfection. The ideal is the organization which can operate without meetings — in the same sense in which the ideal of the machine designer is to have only one moving part in his contraption. In every human organization there is far too much need for cooperation, coordination, and human relations to have to provide for additional meetings. And the human dynamics of meetings are so complex as to make them very poor tools for getting any work done.

Whenever executives, except at the very top level, spend more than a fairly small fraction of their time — maybe a quarter or less — in meetings, there is evidence of a case of malorganization. An excess of meetings indicates that jobs have not been defined clearly, have not been structured big enough, have not been made truly responsible. Also the need for meetings indicates that the decisions and relations analyses have not been made at all or have not been applied. The rule should be to minimize the need for people to get together to accomplish anything.

An organization in which people are all the time concerned about feelings and about what other people will like is not an organization that has good human relations. On the contrary, it is an organization that has very poor human relations. Good human relations, like good manners, are taken for granted. Constant anxiety over other people's feelings is the worst kind of human relations.

An organization that suffers from this — and a great many do — can be said unequivocally to suffer from overstaffing. It might be overstaffed in terms of activities. Instead of focusing on key activities, it tries to do a little bit of everything — especially in advice and teaching activities. Or the individual activities are overstaffed. It is in crowded rooms that people get on each other's nerves, poke their elbows into each other's eyes, and step on each other's toes. Where there is enough distance they do not collide. Overstaffed organizations create work rather than performance. They also create friction, sensitivity, irritation, and concern with feelings.

It is a symptom of malorganization to rely on "coordinators," "assistants," and other such *whose job it is not to have a job.* This indicates that activities and jobs have been designed too narrowly, or that activities and jobs, rather than being designed for one defined result, are expected to do a great many parts of different tasks. It usually indicates also that organizational components have been organized according to skill rather than according to their place in the process or according to their contribution. For skill always contributes only a part rather than a result. And then one needs a coordinator or some other such nonjob to put pieces together that should never have been separated in the first place.

"Organizitis" as a Chronic Affliction

Some, indeed a good many, businesses, especially large and complex ones, suffer from the disease of "organizitis." Everybody is concerned with organization. Reorganization is going on all the time. At the first sign of any trouble, be it only a spat over a specification between a purchasing agent and the people in engineering, the cry goes up for the "organization doctors," whether outside consultants or inside staff. And no organizational solution ever lasts long, indeed few organizational arrangements are even given enough time to be tested and worked out in practice, before another organization study is put in train.

In some cases this does indeed suggest malorganization. "Organizitis" will set in if organization structure fails to come to grips with fundamentals. It is, especially, the result of not rethinking and restructuring the organization when there is a fundamental change in the size and complexity of a business or in its objectives and strategy.

But just as often "organizitis" is self-inflicted and a form of hypochondria. It therefore should be emphasized that organizational changes should not be undertaken often and should not be undertaken lightly. Reorganization is a form of surgery; and even minor surgery has risks.

The demands for organization studies or for reorganization as a response to minor ailments should be resisted. No organization will ever be perfect. A certain amount of friction, of incongruity, of organizational confusion is inevitable.

The Multinational Corporation

Chapter 21

The Major Social Innovation Since World War II
What Explains the Multinational?
Not an American Development
Not Confined to Big Business
Not Confined to Manufacturing
Not the Response to Protectionism
The Emerging Common World Market
From "Multinational" to "Transnational" Company
The Internal Forces
The Need for Business Strategy and Strategies
The Need to Concentrate
The Top-Management Teams
The Need for Systems Management
The Individual Manager
A Manager Needs a Home
How to Pay?
The Multinational and Its Environment
Its Position in Its Host Country
Its Position in Its Home Country
Not an Economic but a Political Problem
The Multinational in the Developing Countries
The Problems of Success
The Petroleum Concession
The Multinational Tomorrow

*T*he multinational corporation raises diversity and complexity to new levels and makes new and unprecedented demands on top management with respect to business strategy as well as structure and behavior.

The multinational corporation is the outstanding social innovation of the period since World War II — a period otherwise lacking in social innovation and in social imagination. It has become the foremost non-nationalist institution in a world torn asunder by paroxysms of nationalist fever and an organ of integration in a world of political fission. This makes the multinational corporation important beyond its service as a business institution. But this also makes the multinational corporation a difficult and problematical institution. Indeed, the testing period is still ahead for the multinational corporation. If it cannot resolve the contradictions it has created, both internally and externally, as a result of being multinational in a nationalistic world, it is unlikely to prosper. For the multinational corporation is both cause and result — but also symbol — of a most profound event of the post-World War II period — the split between economy and sovereignty.

Multinational public-service institutions are absent so far. There are "international agencies," but they are, for the most part, coordinating, rule-making, or research organizations rather than actors and performers. The only truly multinational public-service agencies capable of action in their own right rather than as agents of governments are the World Bank and the International Monetary Fund.

This chapter discusses *businesses* and uses only business examples and business illustrations — it is all we have so far. But everything said in it should be applicable to the multinational public-service institution if and when it emerges.

Some Common Myths . . .

If multinationalism is the most dramatic economic development since World War II, it is also the least understood. Myths abound regarding the multinational corporation. It is commonly believed to be something radically new and indeed unprecedented. But it is also the revival of an old trend. There were multinationals galore in the nineteenth century. And the fear of the multinationals is nothing new either. The most articulate outcry against being "taken over by the Americans" can be found in English books and magazine articles of 1900.

Both in the United States and in Europe, major scientific and technical inventions of the nineteenth century led almost immediately to the emergence of multinational corporations; that is, of companies that were making and selling goods in many countries. This was the case with Siemens in the 1850s; the English subsidiary was founded almost immediately after the German parent company, as was a subsidiary in Russia; for long years these subsidiaries almost overshadowed the German parent. McCormick's harvester and the reaper-thresher of his English rival, Fowler, also went multinational in the nineteenth century. So did Singer's sewing machine and the Remington typewriter within a few years after the original patents had been issued. The trend accelerated in the early twentieth century when, for instance, the Swiss chemical and pharmaceutical companies became multinational. Fiat and Ford both established subsidiaries abroad within a few years of their founding. In the 1920s such prototypes of the multinational businesses of today as Unilever and Royal Dutch/Shell were established.

The surge of the multinationals in the fifties and sixties represented in large measure a resumption of the pre-World War I trend rather than a totally new development. It expressed a return of the economic vitality and capacity to grow which World War I had paralyzed. Even in form, the multinationals of the present closely resemble the pre-World War I development: a parent company with wholly-owned subsidiaries and affiliates in other countries. Unilever and Royal Dutch/Shell — the Anglo-Dutch companies with two parent companies in two countries and with top management and headquarters in two countries — are far more truly multinational in their structure than the new multinationals of the recent past.

Another myth about the multinational corporation is that it is entirely or primarily an American development. To be sure, when the development got going in the fifties, it did so under the leadership of American companies. The reason for this was in part American economic and financial strength during this period. More important, however, were the economic policies of European governments. Despite the Common Market, the governments of Europe for a long time were unwilling to let their businesses become European businesses. Mergers or even "communities of interest" across the national boundaries of Europe were discouraged and frowned upon by most European governments (the British being the exception). It was therefore left to the Americans to avail themselves of the opportunities which the Common Market created. It is not too much exaggeration to say that it is largely the American initiative which converted the Common Market from good intentions into economic reality.

But the phase in which the leadership in the development of multinational corporations was in American hands came to an end in the mid-sixties. Since then, non-American businesses have taken the lead. By the early 1970s a little more than half of the business done by the multinationals was still done by companies headquartered in the United States. The other half was done by companies headquartered in many other places and managed as Dutch, Swiss, German, Swedish, French, English, Japanese — and, in a few cases, Latin American — companies.

By the mid-1960s the movement toward multinationalism had become general. The growth of the non-American multinationals since has been far faster than that of the American-based ones. And it promises to be faster still. The Pan-European company, in particular, is likely to emerge as a major factor in the world economy.

Another prevailing myth is that multinational business development is confined to big business. A prediction widely quoted in the early seventies asserted that by the mid-eighties of this century the entire manufacturing of the world would be in the hands of three hundred large multinational world companies, each doing business worldwide, and each doing many billion dollars in sales.

Actually multinational companies come in as many sizes as national companies do. The concentration of economic power is not necessarily greater in the multinational sector than it is within any national economy. Small multinational businesses may even have proportionately grown faster all along and may have done better. They just do not make the headlines.

Such small to medium-sized companies are building a multinational business on excellence and leadership in one small niche. Here is one example:

A Swiss-based company doing precision mechanics employs 1,800 people all over the world for a total sales volume of less than $50 million. It operates in almost fifty countries and manufactures in almost a dozen countries. It has grown from fifty employees in 1960; that is, it has grown more than thirtyfold in fifteen years.

Yet it is still small business and likely to remain so — even though it has become as fully multinational as the big companies.

The idea that it is manufacturing that has gone multinational is a misunderstanding. The fastest growth has been in finance, where the large American commercial banks went multinational before their clients did.

The most dramatic development on the multinational front are the new "consortium" banks in which large and medium-sized commercial banks pool their resources in a joint venture to become multinational "universal banks." One example is CCB, the group formed by the German Commerz Bank, the French Crédit Lyonnais, and the Italian Banco di Roma. Other consortium banks have British, American, Canadian, Brazilian, Belgian, Dutch, Japanese, Australian, Austrian, and Scandinavian partners.

The management consultants, the auditors, and the advertising agencies have also moved well ahead of the American-based manufacturing companies. And Sears, Roebuck started to go multinational in the late 1940s when it moved simultaneously into Canada and into Latin America, and later on, in the 1960s, into a number of European countries. In fact, the Sears, Roebuck store may have had greater impact on economy and society of Latin America, in Peru, in Colombia, and in Brazil, than any of the manufacturing companies that established subsidiaries in Latin American countries. And when Britain decided in 1972 to join the Common Market, retailers such as Lyons and Marks & Spencer moved much faster to become "European" than did manufacturers.

. . . and all an Invalid Explanation

Even less valid than the common beliefs about the nature of multinationalism are the popular explanations of its causes. One sees in it a response to protectionism. Companies build factories abroad, it is being argued, because they can no longer export. But this explanation, while plausible, simply does not fit the facts.

The period of most rapid growth of multinationals — the fifties and sixties — was the period of the most rapid growth of international trade. Indeed, during this period the world trading economy grew faster — at an annual rate of 15 percent or so in most years — than even the fastest growing domestic economy, i.e., that of Japan. And the Japanese clearly could not have grown at the rate they did if protectionism had made impossible economic expansion based on exports abroad. It is not in the most heavily protected industries where multinationalism has forged ahead the fastest. It came late, for instance, in the chemical industry, which is very heavily protected. But pharmaceuticals, where protection plays a minor role, was a leader from the start. And there has been almost no multinationalism in the heavily protected steel industry.

But the best proof that protectionism is not at the bottom of the multinational trend is the European development. The rise of the multinationals began when continental Europe abolished protection and joined in a common market.

The common belief that the growth of the multinational companies has to do with trade restrictions will not hold up. The multinationals create export markets for their country's products. The multinational's subsidiary abroad is the best market for its home country's machinery, its chemical intermediates, and so on.

This shows clearly in American trade figures. Neither the export markets which America has been losing nor the markets in which imports have become important in the U.S. are those in which American multinationals are active. The American textile companies are still almost completely domestic. So are the American producers of chinaware, of flat glass, and of shoes. The foreign automobiles which have taken an increasing share of the American market are not those the overseas subsidiaries of the American automobile companies make. They are Volkswagens and Toyotas. But of the American exports, an increasing share, perhaps amounting to as much as one-third of the exports of manufactured goods in the late sixties and early seventies, were exports by the same companies that vigorously expanded multinationally, and were, above all, exports to the subsidiaries of such companies abroad. Very much the same thing applies to the Dutch, Swiss, Swedish, German, and Italian balances of trade.

Multinationalism and expanding world trade are two sides of the same coin. And far from being a cause of multinationalism, protectionism is incompatible with it. Indeed, an emergence of protectionism would be the greatest threat to the multinational corporation.

The Common World Market

The true explanation of the explosive upsurge of the multinational corporation is something far more important than either American economic strength or protectionism. It is the emergence of a genuine world market, that is, a market which is not limited or defined by national, cultural, or even ideological boundaries, but transcends them. The market is no longer even international but increasingly "non-national," and based on common worldwide demands and expectations.

Any market is defined by demand. It is demand which creates the supply. It is demand which determines, indeed, what is "supply." And it is demand that determines the opportunities, the needs, the characteristics which make the market.

The great and unprecedented event of the post-World War II period is the fact that country after country, as its income and, above all, its information, increased, developed the same or similar demand patterns. This was unexpected. When World War II came to an end, it was "known" that the European countries and Japan, should they ever regain economic health, would develop different demand patterns. No one then doubted that an economically recovered France would surely have appetites and demands totally different from the United States, but also from Japan, from the Soviet Union, from Germany, or probably even from neighboring Belgium. This certainty — a certainty grounded in the reality of nineteenth- and early-twentieth-century experience — explains why such different people as De Gaulle and Krushchev considered the emergence of a common demand, that is, of a genuine worldwide market, as "abnormal" and proof of some sort of "conspiracy."

By now we know that all the talk in the 1950s about the "Coca-Colanization" of Europe was nonsense. It was not that Europe became "Americanized." It was simply that the mass market, the "post-industrial" market to use a slogan of the sociologists, had first become visible and overt in the United States. But when conditions appeared that were similar to those in the United States — not so much, however, higher incomes as greater mobility and a wider horizon of information — the demand pattern all over the world proved to be the same.

The demand pattern that has emerged in the world economy is not the demand pattern the economists expected. The customers proved again that they knew better than the experts what they wanted.

The great demand has been for a little mobility — and a little power — that is, for such satisfactions as the automobile gives; earlier they had been inaccessible to any but a few very rich and very powerful. Another common demand is for a little health care so that a child has a fair chance to live to adulthood in a reasonable state of physical health and unscarred by disease or crippling deformation. It is demand for a little education. It is demand for access to a big world, which is what the news media, the movie, the radio, the television set offer to the masses who for millennia were limited in their knowledge, their horizon, and their vision, to the confining valley around them and to the small town in which everybody knew everybody else and in which everybody lived exactly the same life. And then there is the desire for the "small luxuries," for the things that are, in effect, assertions of personality over the confinement of poverty — the lipstick, the candy bar, the soft drink, and the high-fashion sandal.

These have emerged as the universal demands. They are not based on affluence. They are based on something far more potent: information. The world has become a "global shopping center."

The World Market as Integrator

A market integrates. It converts "resources" into "factors of production." The national markets — the great achievement of the "commercial revolution" of the seventeenth and eighteenth centuries — integrated "factors of production" within a national economy. The common world market, as it is emerging now, integrates the same factors of production within a world economy.

The traditional theory of the international economy still sees countries having "comparative advantages" with respect to their "factorial costs." And insofar as they produce those things in which they have the greatest advantage, everybody's resources will be optimized. The guiding example is still Adam Smith's exchange of English wool against Portuguese wine. In this theory the individual country is the market that integrates the factors of production. And what is being traded are finished goods. Goods are mobile. The factors of production stay put.

But with a common world economy as the integrator, it is no longer a country that is the unit of production. The goods are the same everywhere — or pretty much so. The mobility is in the factors of production. Whereas international trade meant trade in goods or services, it now increasingly means trade in the factors of production.

To be specific, the most advanced multinational of the nineteenth century was probably Singer Sewing Machines with big, ultramodern plants in Scotland, France, Russia,

Japan, and many other places, in addition to the original plant in Bridgeport, Connecticut. The Scottish plant at Clydeside near Glasgow was probably a more efficient plant with lower costs than the Bridgeport plant; it was also the bigger plant. It produced the same machines Bridgeport produced; and it produced the full range of Singer machines. But even though tariff walls were minimal in those days, Clydeside produced only for the British market; at the same time it produced everything Singer sold in Britain.

Compare this to the multinational of today. A major pharmaceutical company sells drugs in more than eighty countries of the world. In each of these countries it sells its entire product line. It has manufacturing plants in eleven countries: the U.S., Canada, Mexico, and Brazil in the Americas; in Britain, France, Germany, and Italy in Europe; in South Africa, Japan, and Australia. Only a few of the main drug products in the company's line are made by all eleven plants. Most of the company's drugs are made in only one plant, a few in two or three. Even the U.S. plants do not turn out the full product line. As a result, each of the plants sells some drugs to every one of the eighty-odd sales companies; and every one of these sales companies buys some drugs from each of the eleven manufacturing plants. Pharmaceutical drugs are made from chemical intermediates, e.g., from citric acid, which is the chemical base for many antibiotics. The company manufactures intermediates in seven countries: U.S., Mexico, Ireland, Great Britain, France, Australia, and Japan. Again, no country makes all the intermediates – each specializes. Each therefore supplies all eleven manufacturing plants. But each also sells a good part of its output – in some cases, more than half – directly on the outside to other competing pharmaceutical companies and to a wide range of chemical manufacturers. Research, finally, is being carried on in four countries – the U.S., Britain, France, and Japan, with a fifth research lab, in Brazil, to open in the late seventies. Again, each lab is specialized. The French lab, for instance, does all the company's research on central-nervous-system drugs but also all the work to convert drugs originally designed for the treatment of human diseases into drugs suitable for the veterinarian. And a drug developed by any one of these four research labs may be put into chemical testing and market introduction first in any one of the eighty countries in which the company operates.

But it is not only the – admittedly complex – pharmaceutical industry that integrates factors of production rather than trade in goods.

The most successful Detroit-designed "small" car, Ford's Pinto, gets its engine from Ford's German company, its transmission from Ford's British company, and much of its electrical system from Ford's Canadian company – but is sold exclusively in the U.S. and by Ford's American company. Similarly, major components for the Volkswagen sold in the U.S. are being made by Volkswagen do Brazil in São Paulo.

When it was announced in the spring of 1972 that all British government agencies would henceforth buy their computers from the one British computer company, ICL, the British subsidiary of the American Honeywell company pointed out in protest that its computers, though made by an American-owned company, contained a larger proportion of British-made components than the computers of British-owned ICL which buys its components largely from American manufacturers.

In the services areas, this integration of the factors of production within a common world market has gone even further.

A major U.S. bank arranged a $15 million, five-year loan for a Japanese manufacturing company in early 1974. The deal was initiated in Tokyo and by the bank's Japanese representative. The deal was worked out by the bank's offices in London and Frankfurt. The syndicate that advanced the money contained eight banks, one each from the U.S., Japan, Great Britain, Holland, Sweden, France, Switzerland, and Latin America. Most of the money was raised in Germany, where interest rates at the time were favorable. And the purpose of the loan was to finance a manufacturing subsidiary of the Japanese company in Latin America. Yet this was a routine transaction such as each of the participating banks engages in every week.

The Multinational Reality: Transnational

So far, most multinationals are still cast in the nineteenth-century, Singer-Sewing-Machine mold — that is, each subsidiary makes products or furnishes services for its own discrete national market. But the trend is toward the integration of the factors of production for a common worldwide market. It is the trend that follows from the logic of the market itself.

The term multinational is of very recent coinage: it was unknown even twenty years ago. It fits the nineteenth-century structure — Singer Sewing Machine — much better than it fits the development to which it is being applied. Singer Sewing Machine was truly "multinational." But the pharmaceutical company that integrates eleven drug-manufacturing plants, seven intermediate plants, and four research labs into sales of many drug products in eighty countries is not multinational. It is "transnational." And so is the automobile company that integrates plants in Germany, Britain, Mexico, and Canada for a sale in the U.S., or the commercial bank that integrates banking resources in eight countries to raise money in a ninth country to finance a development in a tenth country. National boundaries are no longer determinants. They are restraints, obstacles, complications. What determines is the reality of a non-national common market. The opportunities — but also the problems — of the so-called multinational lie not in its being multinational, that is, in its doing business in many countries. They lie in its being *transnational,* that is, based on the reality of a common world market — common in its demands, in its vision, and in its values.

This means that it is not factors of production that explain the new multinational, inform its strategy, and explain its behavior. It is factors of demand. It is demand that exerts the pull. The multinational business is in every case a marketing business.

The Problems of Strategy

What distinguishes the multinational corporation from any other business is that it faces both internal and external diversity. It has to create unity within its own managerial organization and yet do justice to the diversity of peoples, nationalities, and loyalties within it. And it has to create a unified business that can optimize factorial costs and factorial advantages within a common world market and yet live in peace — or at least without constant conflict — with a multitude of separate political sovereignties.

The pharmaceutical company mentioned earlier needs a strategy for the company as a whole. But each of the eighty-odd national companies needs one as well. So do the manufacturing units, the units making intermediates, and the research laboratories. Each has to be managed as an autonomous business with its own objectives, its own priorities and plans, its own profit and loss responsibility.

But at the same time, none of these units is truly autonomous. All are interdependent. It may, for instance, seem to be purely a concern of the subsidiary in a given Latin American country whether to accept an offer from the country's national health service of a contract that guarantees a sizable market for a drug for five years but at a 25 percent reduction in price. Yet such a price concession may set off demands for lower prices from the health services of other Latin American countries — and without any five-year purchase guarantee. It may appear purely a matter for one of the intermediate plants within the system whether it decides to expand its facilities because outside customers, that is, other pharmaceutical manufacturers, are increasing their uses of a substance it makes. But this immediately raises the question whether the company's own plants for finished products are to be considered preferred customers whose orders will be given priority, or whether the new outside customers are to be considered as preferred customers, or at least as equals. If the first line is taken, the company decides in effect to optimize its own manufacturing unit's results at the expense of suboptimizing the results of the intermediate unit. If the second alternative is taken, the company decides, in effect, that being an intermediate manufacturer is more advantageous than being a drug manufacturer.

These are strategic decisions. They have long-term — and often irreversible — impact. They cannot be made by "the top" alone. They require local knowledge. But they cannot be made locally either. They affect the whole company and must be made at the top. A multinational strategy which takes into account only the overall company is condemned to futility. Unless it can be translated into specific strategy for individual markets, it cannot succeed. But the multinational strategy which is decentralized, that is, a strategy which considers each unit and each market as an autonomous business, is equally condemned to futility.

The large-scale commercial banks have a similar problem. It is their very strength — it is indeed the reason for their existence as multinationals — that they can give financial service anyplace in the world. Equally it is their strength that they can offer one-stop banking — that is, that they can satisfy the major financial needs of a customer, whether for short-term money or for long-term loans, and even for equity capital, whether in dollars, in German marks, or in Japanese yen. This, however, requires one strategy which focuses on the needs of a major customer, such as, for instance, one of the big international companies, wherever they might arise. Whoever is in charge of this particular area, e.g., the major airlines, therefore has to look upon the entire bank as one business, as one resource, as one pool of capital, and as one pool of services. But at the same time, the bank's manager in any one particular market needs a business strategy. The manager needs to think through which companies in, for instance, Japan, are potential customers and for what services of the bank. The manager needs to be able to mobilize the resources of the bank worldwide for their needs. But the manager also needs to build up a purely local business. For the multinational customers of today are, as a rule, yesterday's satisfied local customers. Again, neither one global, bank-wide strategy nor local strategies can suffice. The bank needs both — and can never say in advance which of the two should come first, or which of the two actually govern a particular business relationship.

Few multinationals have thought through business strategy so far. One exception might be Unilever, which, for many years, has systematically planned both for the entire Unilever group, for major product lines within, such as edible oils and fats (margarine), soaps and detergents or fish, and for each major country. A more recent and so far not yet truly tried case is Philips in Holland, with business strategies both for major product groups — of which Philips has sixteen — and for each of the countries in which Philips does business. No American company, to my knowledge, has so far done anything comparable.

But every multinational company faces the complexity of business strategy, precisely because it has to be both unified for the entire company and specific for each major product category as well as for each major market. This means that the multinational has complexity built into its very structure. It is multicultural, it is multinational, it is multimarket, and also multimanagement.

Adding to this a diversity of businesses makes the company unmanageable.

The successful multinationals are in effect single-market or single-technology companies. There is IBM, which has only one product. There are the pharmaceutical companies which have only one customer, the physician. There are the multinational commercial banks which have only one technology: financing business. There is Sony, which is the most multinational of all Japanese companies with almost half of its sales and profits coming from outside of Japan — yet concentrated on consumer electronics, and on a fairly small range at that.

Without such fundamental business unity, the multinational company splinters into fragments. Management people lose the ability to understand each other, even with the help of an interpreter. The company then rapidly degenerates into a bureaucracy which adds more layers the less it truly directs and controls. The temptation to diversify, no matter how great in any given case, should be firmly resisted in a multinational corporation. The multinational conglomerate is an abomination.

The Top-Management Teams

Of necessity, the multinational has not one but many top-management teams. It has as many top-management teams as it has business strategies. Corporate top management is one such team. But for each country, region, or product line there is another team. Insofar as members of the corporate top management also sit on a top-management team for a country or a market they are members thereof, rather than the team leader.

No one so far has found a satisfactory answer to the problem of top-management structure in the large multinational corporation. One thing, however, is clear. The traditional pattern is not the answer.

The traditional pattern constructs towering hierarchies in which levels are heaped on levels. The head of a national company typically reports to a regional executive who reports to another regional level — such as a European or a Latin American executive — who in turn reports to an international vice-president who in turn then reports to corporate top management. This not only denigrates the manager who has to make the actual decisions, that is, the head of a business in a given country, it also creates a cumbersome bureaucracy, the main achievement of which is to delay decisions.

Some alternatives to this pattern can already be seen, and they do offer advantages.

The most satisfactory structure is perhaps that which Unilever has been developing. There each company in any country reports to one of the two head offices of the parent company, that is, either to London or to Rotterdam. But for each of the major product groups, e.g., soaps or fish or retail trade, there is a coordinating committee at headquarters, usually composed of people who have successfully operated businesses in the particular area. And within each major country, such as Germany, where Unilever has a number of companies, there is a "national board" composed of former senior executives of the companies in the country and chaired, as a rule, by a distinguished citizen of the country. This is cumbersome enough. But at least someone like Berthold Freyberg, who in the mid-seventies, headed Nordsee-Fischerei, a German Unilever affiliate which is the world's largest fishing company outside of Soviet Russia, had direct access to top-management people who can make a decision. Normally he did not use the right of access. He rather worked with his national board or with the committee in his product area. But organizationally he reported directly to top management. And this status within the company gave him status outside, within the industry in his country, with the country's government, with labor unions, and so on.

But even within Unilever the balance between the need to look upon each company as an autonomous business, the need to look upon each major product area as a unified business in its own right, and the need to look upon the whole company as a unit, in terms of capital appropriation or of key personnel, for instance, is difficult, precarious, and easily upset. At the very least, far too much time is spent on working out organizational relationships and on keeping the system going.

There are other alternatives.

One of the leading American multinationals, CPC (formerly Corn Products), has organized itself into five distinct companies: two American ones (consumer goods and industrial products), a European one, a Latin-American one, and a Far Eastern one. Each is headed by its own president whose headquarters are within his territory. The company's top-management team of three or four executives constitutes the board of each of these companies. It spends equal time working with the presidents of each of these companies and their senior managers at *their* locations, acting as the presidents' advisors, review organ, and resource.

Only one organizational conclusion has emerged clearly. In the multinational, the top-management team of the overall company must not, at the same time, be the top-management team of any of the operating companies, and least of all of the operating company where the headquarters are located. As soon as more than a very small fraction of a company's business is multinational, top management has to divorce itself from running any one national or regional component on any product area. Otherwise, it will spend all its time on its own immediate management job and will neglect the other businesses.

This, in other words, means that the traditional organization in which top manage-

.ment is both the top management of the overall company and that of its largest single — and usually the domestic — company, while all the rest of the business is under an international division, is the wrong structure. Wherever it persists — and it is still fairly common — it does damage or weakens the company's performance.

A multinational organization needs a headquarters, it cannot be ambulatory.

A fixed place of business is a necessity for managing. Work requires time, continuity and rhythm and schedule. One needs the organized, systematic support which one can build up only over long years in one place. Executive vice-presidents can perhaps travel all the time. Market research men, accountants, personnel people, that is, people paid to think — not to mention secretaries or computer experts — have to stay put if they are to produce.

But at the same time, local decisions have to be made at the scene of action. The local decision has to be made within the framework of corporate strategy. But it has to be a local rather than a corporate decision if it is to be effective. The headquarters for the local business — and this may be European or it may be Swedish — has to be where the decision is to be effective. It has to be made with full knowledge of local conditions. It has to be made in cooperation with people on the spot and in relationships with local institutions. It has to fit local laws, local expectations, local habits. It has to be, above all, comprehensible to the people who have to carry it out, that is, to local people whose knowledge of the overall company is of necessity limited. The factory manager in Spain or the manager of the branch bank in Hong Kong achieve their results through local knowledge, local contacts, local action.

Yet the pharmaceutical company manager in a Latin American country, the manufacturing manager in Ford's engine plant in Germany, or the Chase Bank branch manager in Frankfurt must know enough about the objectives, strategies, and needs of the entire company not to make the wrong decisions. The manager must know enough not to make decisions that optimize his or her own business but suboptimize the whole company.

There is another important problem in top-management structure for the multi-national. Top-management structures are not mechanical; they are, above all, cultural. The top-management structure which an American management group accepts as right and proper may appear decidedly odd and uncomfortable to a French, a Japanese, or a German management group. Yet these French, Japanese, or German managers have to understand their own local top-management group, have to feel comfortable with it, have to work with it. To be successful, the top-management teams in a multinational have therefore to be different in their structure in different countries, or else they will not make local sense. Yet thay have to be compatible at least throughout the company, or else various top-management teams cannot work together.

Top-management structure in the multinational, therefore, has to be built on the most complex and most difficult of all design principles: systems management.

The Individual Manager

Even more perplexing than top-management structure in the multinational is the design of the individual manager's job and function.

The head of the subsidiary of a major pharmaceutical company — whether the company be American, Swiss, Dutch, British, or German — in, say, a medium-sized Latin American country, e.g., Colombia, has to be a big person in the country. With health care a major political and governmental matter in such countries — as it should be — the subsidiary head better have considerable standing. Among the heads of pharmaceutical subsidiaries in such Latin American countries are, for instance, several who were deans of the leading medical schools in their countries before they went into industry, and several who had served as ministers of health.

Drugs are the one part of modern medicine which a developing country can use effectively. It is easier and cheaper to obtain modern drugs than to educate and pay physicians, build hospitals, or develop health services in poor rural areas and in urban slums. Drugs, therefore, are likely to play a far more important part in the health-care system of such a country.

Yet in terms of sales, the country does not account for much more than a fair-sized sales district in one of the major developed countries, such as Kansas City in the United States or Manchester in England. How then should the executive be positioned within the overall organization?

This is a problem which conventional organization theory cannot solve. The Unilever structure described earlier comes closest to solving it. But again, the only solution is to say that the head of the Colombian subsidiary is *both* manager of a fair-sized sales district and a member of company top management. Which of the two he or she is depends on the situation. In fact, it must largely be left to the head to decide which role the situation demands. The subsidiary head should always have immediate access to the company's very top but should rarely use it. Also the subsidiary head should be the kind of person whom corporate top management looks to for leadership, guidance, advice, and counsel on major policy matters, e.g., on relationships with governments throughout Latin America, on long-range strategy in Latin America, and so on. He or she surely should not report to a Latin American vice-president in Basel or New York.

Again, only systems-management concepts, nebulous though they are, are truly pertinent. Ordinary organization charts are likely to confuse rather than to clarify.

A Manager Needs a Home

Equally difficult are the problems of management personnel policy, of opportunities, status, pay.

The ablest manager, by common consent, in the entire management group of one of the major American-based multinationals was the head of the Italian company, Dr. Manzoni. Manzoni had first become known to the company as the lawyer representing the Italian owners of a medium-sized business the American company acquired. The American president was so impressed by him that he asked Manzoni to take over when the Italian subsidiary ran into trouble a few years later. Manzoni restored the Italian subsidiary to health and rapidly built it into the leading Italian business in its industry. When the Common Market came into being, Manzoni planned and spearheaded the company's expansion throughout Western Europe, found the right acquisitions and partners, found management people for the new companies, trained and developed them, and, to all intents and purposes, ran the European companies of the group from his Italian headquarters. When finally replacement for the company's aging chief executive in the United States had to be found, everybody at once thought of Manzoni. But Manzoni turned the job down flat. "My sons are in high school, and I do not want them to become expatriates. My wife has old parents whom she cannot leave behind. And frankly, I myself see little that would make me feel at home in a small Midwestern town, and few attractions there that could compare with those of Rome. I know that I could do the job you want me to do — and the job is a fascinating one and far more than I would ever have dared aspire to in my wildest dreams. But, still, it is the wrong job for me."

People need roots. They need a home. They have a right to be concerned with the education of their children. They have a duty to aging parents. And they are probably more realistic than the company's personnel vice-president when they argue that they are unlikely to "transplant" well. If (as this company did, by the way) it concludes that someone who acts like Manzoni, is no longer "promotable" and relegates them to second-class citizenship, it cuts off its nose to spite its face. These people will leave — as Manzoni did within a year or two. A way has to be found to accommodate someone like Manzoni and yet keep him working with contentment and enthusiasm. But should a company go so far — one large U.S. company did it — as to move its entire headquarters staff — fifteen people — to Brussels in Belgium when the ablest person with the group, a German, said that he would leave unless given the top job, but would also not live except in Europe?

One needs a management structure which recognizes and indeed respects the roots of a person and yet builds a truly multinational team.

It is clear that one requirement is equal opportunity regardless of passport. A Manzoni must have the opportunity to get to the top according to abilities. To deny the opportunity and to reserve senior management positions to people of a given nationality is to deprive the multinational corporation of its ability to attract capable people in every country in which it works.

Companies domiciled in small countries, such as Holland, Switzerland, and Sweden, confine, by and large, senior management positions in all their subsidiaries and affiliates to nationals of the parent company who have been trained and who have started their careers in the parent company. (The only exception to this rule is the United States, where the major Dutch and Swiss companies have, for many years, promoted Americans into their top management. But the American subsidiary of these companies is usually the largest unit within the entire group and has to be managed as a truly separate entity.) There are advantages to this — communications obviously are much easier. And some of the disadvantages which companies domiciled in large countries, such as the United States or Great Britain, would suffer if they followed this practice are not incurred by companies headquartered in smaller, neutral countries. No one worries much about Swiss imperialism.

But even in these cases, the policy is clearly not in the company's best interest. With competition for first-rate management people intense, good young people will not come to work in a company — or will not stay — unless they have equal opportunities. A company which, no matter what its professions, promotes only nationals of the mother country into senior positions, in its subsidiaries and affiliates or at home, is unlikely to obtain or to hold the managerial resources it requires.

The multinational corporation needs to offer the able young people in any country in which it operates *more* opportunities than a purely domestic one does. It needs, in other words, to make a virtue out of its being transcultural. Otherwise it will be less attractive than a well-managed purely domestic company. Yet a person's national roots, national loyalties, national culture, and need for a "home" must be respected.

How to Pay?

There are also serious compensation problems of the multinational executive. Should executives around the world be paid the same salary in line with their position? Or should salaries fit the widely varying local standards? Should the American or Dutchman who is sent from a parent company into the management of a subsidiary be paid on the local scale — which, for instance, in Japan would mean a salary far too low for an expensive place like Tokyo — but also receive substantial "benefits," e.g., in the form of housing or an unlimited expense account? And what about the manager who heads what is in effect a small business within the corporate structure — for example, a person who is president of a pharmaceutical subsidiary in Colombia who in terms of the size of the business is a middle-level executive, but who in terms of position in the country is a top executive?

Again, the requirements are not easily compatible. It is highly desirable to make it possible for people to move and not to be penalized by a promotion. Yet if people are being paid according to the prevailing standards in the country in which they work, being promoted very often will mean that they are being asked to take a cut in pay.

The most extreme cases of this are the Japanese executives who are sent to work in the United States or in Europe. Even though what Japanese executives in New York and Düsseldorf receive is low by American or German standards, it is unheard of by Japanese standards. When after five years or so, successful Japanese executives are transferred back to a much bigger job at home, they often have to take a cut of 50 percent of income or more.

But, to have one member of a management group, and especially a member from abroad who is also a foreigner, paid quite differently from the rest of the group is disruptive.

By far the most serious compensation problem arises out of the fundamental business strategy of the multinational. For the multinational manager needs to be both a member of the top-management team of the whole company and of the top-management team of the unit for which he or she works. Traditional compensation plans, especially plans with big bonuses geared to the results of the unit which the manager manages directly are therefore likely to be both unfair and destructive. They penalize teamwork, just where teamwork is needed the most.

This can be seen in its most acute form in the multinational commercial bank. In the earlier example, the New York bank's representative in Japan, who initiated the business and produced a new and major client for the bank, had nothing to show for it in the profit and loss statement of the Japanese branch. The London branch, which did all the work, showed in its books only a liability. The Frankfurt branch, simply because it had a German mark surplus available, showed all the income from the deal. The typical bonus policy would highly reward Frankfurt, penalize London, and leave Tokyo out altogether.

To tie managers' compensation to the results of their own branch or territory will therefore make them slight the very opportunities that might produce the greatest results — in this example of the bank's representative, opportunities where the actual transaction might be done by another branch or by headquarters. To pay on any other basis, however, or to rely on personal and subjective judgment rather than on impersonal and objective yardsticks, is equally undesirable. But what *is* desirable is by no means clear yet — let alone how it can be achieved.

In almost every area throughout this book examples of successful approaches could be given. But I have not been able to find yet a successful and working compensation policy for managers in multinational business. American companies profess the same frustration and confusion as European or Japanese ones. And every compensation policy in multinational corporations I know of is forever being restudied, reorganized, revised. The most successful policy may well be that of a major Swiss pharmaceutical company which frankly says, "We know that whatever we do will at best take care of symptoms for a few months; but at least we try to make our management people understand that there is no solution and that day-to-day accommodations to the worst problems of the moment is the best they — and we — can expect."

A true multinational which completely transcends in its management structure, in its managerial jobs, and in its personnel policies, national and cultural boundaries is neither likely nor perhaps desirable. What is needed is a floating balance between conflicting needs and conflicting demands. A multinational must be able to use a Dr. Manzoni as a member of the top management of an American-based company and yet respect his legitimate desire to remain a resident in his own country and a member of his own culture. It must be able to have both an overall company strategy and local strategies for a given unit. It must be able to pay for performance and yet encourage teamwork. It must be able to be both centralized and decentralized, and to know when to be one or the other.

This requires a great deal of formal structure and policy. But it requires, even more, a great deal of mutual knowledge, mutual trust, and shared experience. Above all, it requires tremendous self-discipline throughout the entire managerial group.

The Multinational and Its Environment

Practically every argument against the multinational corporation advanced in any country is by itself a fallacy. It can be disproven easily. And yet the disproof is not going to convince the critics and enemies of multinationalism. They may be using the wrong arguments. But their hostility is directed toward a reality. They are formulating the problem wrongly. But there is a real problem.

In its host countries, even highly developed ones with substantial economic strength of their own, the multinational is attacked as being impervious to the country's economic, social, and financial policies, and as undermining the country's sovereignty and its government. It is attacked as having a power of decision over what will be produced, over jobs, over industrial and economic policy, which is illegitimate and beyond proper control. Decisions, rather than rest in the country's legitimate authority, such as its parliament or government, are exercised in a shadowy and indefinable way, someplace far away, by faceless people who neither know the country nor care for it.

But in the multinational's home country it is also attacked — and in strong countries, including the United States, as well as in weak ones. Here too, the multinational is seen as a means to evade, if not to subvert, political authority and of creating a superpower, not accountable to anyone and yet in control of economic policy, of jobs, and even, to a large extent, of policies in noneconomic areas. The American-based multinational is accused in the United States of "exporting jobs" but also of using its subsidiaries abroad to evade U.S. policies such as the former ban on trading with Red China. And it has been attacked with equal bitterness in host countries abroad because the subsidiaries in these countries, by not being willing to trade with Red China, defied and subverted the host country's, e.g., Canada's or Sweden's, own policies in international affairs.

The counterargument of the multinational companies is a perfectly valid one. No business, no matter how rich and big it may be, has any power against a national government. In any clash between economic and political power, at least in this century, economic power has come out a very poor second. The multinational exists, like any business, at the sufferance of national government.

But this argument does not go to the heart of the matter. The real problem is that the multinational by its very nature must look upon the economy in non-national terms. It must look upon resources, such as manufacturing plants, as part of a transnational economic system rather than as national assets. It must try to optimize in accordance with the market rather than in accordance with national boundaries.

This is the true difference between the twentieth-century multinational and its predecessors before World War I.

It is the function of the multinational in a common world market to allocate production and markets according to economic logic; that is, to optimize production and distribution across very large areas, if not the entire world. But "production and distribution" is simply another term for jobs, for imports and exports, that is, for balances of trade and balances of payment, for wage levels — and altogether for economic conditions and economic policies.

It is simply not true that the economic optimization of the multinational "exports jobs." Every study has shown that it creates jobs. The goods its subsidiaries abroad produce and market would not otherwise have been made in, and bought from, the multinational's home country. But the subsidiary buys equipment and supplies from the multinational's home country. Indeed the multinational, by moving production to people, may be a major force in preventing dislocation and turbulence. The alternative — large-scale migration of low-skill and low-income peoples — whether Blacks into Harlem, Algerians into France, Turks into Germany, sharecroppers from Brazil's Northeast into Sao Paulo, or Sicilians into Torino — creates, we now know, unbearable tensions. The economist — almost any economist — would therefore conclude that all the criticism of, and resistance to, the multinational, is misinformed.

But this misses the point. The multinational is a problem precisely because its decisions are based on economic rationality and divorced from political sovereignty.

There is no solution. The multinational is a political problem not because of anything it does or does not do. It is a problem because political sovereignty and economic reality no longer coincide. It does the multinational no good to protest that it and each of its subsidiaries are "good corporate citizens" of the country in which each operates. Of course, it and each of its subsidiaries observe the laws — at least to the same extent to which the country's nationals observe it. But if the phrase is meant to imply — as it usually does — that the multinational in every country in which it operates thinks and acts in terms of that country's national economy and market, it is nonsense. To do so would deny the whole logic of the multinational corporation, which is to optimize resources within the world market reality.

But to reassert against the multinational the reality of national sovereignty is also futile. This is what De Gaulle tried to do. The only result was a rapid decline in the competitive position of the French economy in the world. It is no accident that the French have become the strongest advocates of the proposed law for a "European transnational company."

There is indeed a real need for new international law to come to grips with this tension. Such law will not only have to define under what conditions countries accept multinationals and what limitations they may impose on ownership, on remittance of profits and repayments of capital, and on freedom of movement of goods, people, and capital from one subsidiary of a multinational to another.

It will, above all, have to "depoliticize" the multinational. Insofar as this means that the multinational will be forbidden to try to use the political strength of its home government for its own ends, beyond what it is entitled to under the new international law, this should present relatively little problem. As far as relations between developed countries are involved, such use of political power for corporate ends has long ceased to be feasible. And as far as relations between the developed and economically strong home country of a multinational and an economically weak developing country are concerned, it is by now abundantly clear that "multinational imperialism" is futile.

After the electoral victory of the Left in Chile in 1970, an officer of ITT suggested to the Nixon Administration that it foment economic and political chaos in Chile to prevent the inauguration of a Marxist president and to save ITT's Chilean telephone company from expropriation. The officer only ensured that the Nixon Administration — despite its hostility to the new Chilean government — would do nothing and remain scrupulously uninvolved. Still the Chileans seized upon this to attack all foreign business, and business altogether.

Any future international law regarding the multinational must outlaw any action of this kind. In whatever country it operates, the subsidiary or affiliate of a multinational is clearly entitled to no more political support from its home government than a private citizen.

Far more difficult will be the legal resolution of the question of preference given by governments to their own national businesses. To what extent should it be permitted? To what extent, for instance, should the universal practice of giving limited or absolute preferences to national producers in public works or government purchases be legalized? And who is a national producer in the age of the multinationals?

In the example cited earlier of the British government ruling to have British government departments give preference in buying computers to British-owned ICL, "national" was defined by ownership. British Honeywell's protest against the ruling, in effect, asked that nationality be defined by the number and location of jobs. Both companies are, of course, British in terms of their incorporation and location. And with respect to many other products even the British government accepts the logic of the Honeywell argument.

The thorniest issue is that of the reach of the home country's jurisdiction. It is also the one which the U.S. will find the most difficult.

Traditional U.S. legal — or at least governmental — doctrine has held that any subsidiary or affiliate of an American company abroad is subject to American jurisdiction, with respect to antitrust, for instance, but also with respect to restrictions on trade with certain countries. But American antitrust ideas are by no means universally accepted as sound or even as moral. Compulsory cartels, for instance, are in most continental countries (and in Japan) considered normal instruments of economic policy. And competition is seen as more of a vice than a virtue. Making gifts to government officials or contributions to political parties is not considered "bribery" but a civic duty.

Resolving these problems by a common code of behavior is the only way to make the multinational what it should and could be: a powerful instrument for economic strength and political harmony. The problems are largely political and legal. But they are problems which it is the duty — and the opportunity — of top management in the multinationals to think through. Otherwise, it is safe to predict, political solutions will be imposed on the multinationals which can only damage them and the world economy.

Few of the multinationals even seem to be aware of the task. They seem to assume that the problems will go away if only no one talks about them — which is neither intelligent nor responsible.

The Multinationals and the Developing Countries

Some 80 percent of multinational investment and business — after taking out as not truly multinational the plantation and extractive industries (such as crude oil production or iron-ore mining) — is in developed countries. And so is some 80 percent of world trade, again subtracting agricultural products and raw materials.

But both the greatest contributions and the greatest problems of multinationalism lie in the developing countries.

On the one hand, there are few things a developing country needs as much as the multinational corporation. There are few contributions from which it can benefit so much as from those only the multinational corporation can make. A developing country needs capital. It needs access to technology even more. It needs access to markets for whatever goods its one surplus resource — labor — can produce.

The greatest contribution the American multinationals have made to countries like Taiwan, Hong Kong, and Singapore, has been neither capital nor technology. It has not even been entrepreneurial and managerial skill — these countries, being ethnically Chinese, have adequate supplies of both. It was a guaranteed market in the U.S. for the textiles, the Christmas ornaments, and the radio sets which these countries manufacture.

Most of all, a developing country needs a way to acquire skills — industrial skills, managerial skills, entrepreneurial skills. And no other institution has so far proven capable of providing the transfer of skills, on which rest all hopes for the economic and social development of a developing country.

But at the same time, a developing country, almost by definition, has a balance of payments problem. The more capital it imports, the more foreign exchange will it have to produce to service the capital it has brought in — payments interest and principal on bank loans or bonds borrowed abroad, dividends on equity capital and — perhaps the most onerous burden of all — orders for goods from abroad to show one's gratitude for "foreign aid" which always creates dependence regardless of who does the giving. Even more important, a developing country, almost by definition, has a severe problem of national identity. It may be — and usually is — "nationalist." But it rarely has a tradition of nationhood. And the multinational company in which a country's ablest, or at least its most affluent, people are subordinate to "bosses" elsewhere — in London or New York, Rotterdam or Tokyo — creates a problem of national loyalty and allegiance, at least in the minds of people who are desperately struggling to define their own national identity. It also creates a "brain drain" — the ablest people go to work for a foreign employer. This creates a feeling of dependence, if not of helpless impotence, in the face of concentrations of economic power compared to which a poor country looks puny indeed.

It is not just paranoia that makes a Peruvian or, for that matter, an Indian minister feel that a big multinational, domiciled elsewhere in a developed country, is a threat. They know perfectly well that no matter how important the company's subsidiary may be to their own national economy, it matters little to the treasurer of the multinational at headquarters. For Peru or India, a given subsidiary of a multinational — the pharmaceutical subsidiary of an American company in Peru or Hindustani Lever in India — may be a giant on which the national economy heavily depends. But it produces at best a small percent of the total revenue of the pharmaceutical multinational or of Unilever. In its decisions, the central management of the multinational cannot possibly subordinate the interest of the total company to the interests of Peru or India. It may not willfully do damage — indeed there is no reason why it should. But it must treat as trivial the very concerns which are central and essential to the Peruvian or to the Indian cabinet minister or politician.

And then the very qualities which make it an economic asset to the developing country also make it a powerful competitor to the local entrepreneur, the local business establishment. Both in Brazil and in India, the local businesspeople, while themselves deeply engaged in joint ventures with multinationals based in Europe and in the United States, have also been most vocal in their demand for "protection" from the multinational, for majority ownership, or at least controlling ownership to be in the hands of local investors, or for closing whole sectors of the economy to the multinationals.

The ambivalence of the developing countries was shown dramatically by the very different reaction of the countries along the north and west coasts of South America to the so-called Andean Pact which proposes, in effect, that multinationals be strictly limited, and confined to narrow sectors of the economy and to minority holdings.

Chile and Peru demanded even more stringent provisions which, in effect, would have banished the multinationals within ten or fifteen years. Colombia signed the pact —

but with severe reservations and indeed with the clear and declared intention of not carrying it out. Venezuela long refused to sign at all.

The reason for these differences in attitude is not ideology — the Venezuelan government was more leftist than was the Chilean at the time (around 1968) the pact was drafted. The reason is that each country has different multinationals. In Chile and Peru the foreign company was still nineteenth century, as a rule: extractive industries such as copper mining and petroleum, and "infrastructure" utilities such as power and light, and telephone companies. In both countries foreigners largely managed these businesses, and local people were kept out of both management and ownership. In Columbia, the multinational did not make its appearance until after World War II. It is active mostly in manufacturing, both for the home market and for export. The Colombia subsidiaries of the multinationals are, almost without exception, managed by Colombians. And many are partnerships with Colombian entrepreneurs. Venezuela, finally, eagerly wants multinational manufacturing companies to offset its industrial oligarchy — the few families who, as local representatives and confidants of the big international petroleum companies, have come to dominate whatever industry there is in the country. Venezuela — in part because of its oil revenues — has a large number of highly trained young people who find opportunities seriously limited in the family-run companies of the country and who, highly nationalist though they are, would welcome the coming of the foreign multinationals with their career opportunities for the able manager or professional regardless of family background.

These examples show that it is up to the multinational and its top management to structure the right relationship with a developing country. The tension cannot be eliminated. But it can be reduced.

An intelligent multinational management will, for instance, refrain from going into businesses that will, inevitably, become a burden on the slender foreign-exchange resources of a developing country or into businesses that cannot exist unless so heavily protected as to become a burden on the country's consuming masses.

It is clearly undesirable to build a manufacturing facility where the costs — of raw materials, of labor, or of capital — are so high as to make economic operations highly problematical. It is foolish to depend on promises of governmental protection in such a case.

Any investment made anywhere should be capable of survival in a competitive market. If there is little reason to hope that within a few years a new plant or a new business will gain competitive strength, at least adequate to survival without protection, it should not be started in the first place.

This, of course, has been known since the first protectionist theory was developed — in the early decades of the nineteenth century, by Henry Clay in the United States, and by his disciple, Friedrich List, in Germany. "Infant industries" may need protection, may indeed deserve it. But the purpose of such protection is to enable them to grow into "adults" who can stand on their own feet. If that is not accomplished, the industry will sooner or later be in trouble, no matter how great the protectionist subsidy.

It can also be said that the traditional nineteenth-century pattern of the wholly-owned subsidiary does not fit the developing countries. It discourages rather than encourages what the country needs the most: native investment and capital formation, and native managers and entrepreneurs. Yet the local subsidiary must be capable of being part of an integrated worldwide economic and business strategy. It must be capable, for example, of specializing in making one major component for the multinational's plants and markets everywhere but of importing, from the other plants of the multinational, whatever components it is not suited to make.

Ford's Mexican subsidiary, as mentioned before, specializes in making electrical assemblies for the Pinto. But it probably should not make engines at all but get them from Ford's Canadian, German, or English plants.

But this then raises the very difficult problem of harmonizing the interests of the local partners — let alone those of the local governments — and those of the multinational system. Who makes the optimization decisions?

In many developing countries the traditional congruence of capital investment and management control needs to be re-examined. Some developing countries can — and should — generate their own capital. Brazil is one example. But so are, to a large extent, the Chinese territories of Taiwan, Hong Kong, and Singapore. What they need is technology, management, and access to markets. Here management contracts rather than ownership of subsidiaries may be needed.

Other developing countries need the capital as well but need also either provision for eventual participation in ownership by nationals or, from the beginning, financing other than investment by the multinational. Otherwise the relationship will become unbearable when the country develops.

The key case is, of course, Canada. That Canadian industry is so heavily owned by foreign, and especially by U.S. companies, is the result of *Canadian* decisions and actions, and especially of the deliberate policy of the Liberal governments of Canada in the thirty years after the Great Depression of the thirties, to channel Canadian capital into "infrastructure" investments such as public works and leave industrial investment to the foreigner. The result, in economic terms, has been a brilliant success. Canada which, in 1930, was a poor and largely pre-industrial economy is by now one of the world's most highly developed and wealthiest economies. Politically the result has, however, been undesirable. A major economic power, which is what Canada has become, cannot be "owned" abroad.

The only large company that has understood this is the American Telephone Company. At the end of World War II it owned practically all of the two telephone companies in Canada's most populous provinces, Ontario and Quebec. Then it began systematically to divest itself of share ownership to the point where these companies are now entirely Canadian-owned. Yet, technically and in terms of operations, they have remained members of the Bell System.

Finally, the multinational needs to think ahead and solve the problems which its own success will create in a developing country. As a result of such success the country will no longer be a developing country but, like Canada, become a developed one. At the least it will change to the point where the old relationship becomes untenable.

The petroleum concession becomes untenable as it succeeds. For this first means that a formerly dirt-poor country becomes oil-rich. It means also that nomadic Bedouins become skilled mechanics, geologists, and chemical engineers. The concession made sense in the beginning, if only because of the enormous costs and high risks of exploration. The petroleum-producing country still needs the international oil company — perhaps more than ever. For it needs a complex and highly expensive transportation and marketing system worldwide. But the concession as a relationship has outlived its usefulness and becomes a millstone around the neck of both producing country and oil company.

That not one international petroleum company, at least to public knowledge, faced up to the problem and thought through a new relationship is a severe indictment of top management.

The Multinational Tomorrow

One thing is clear: the multinational tomorrow will be different from the multinational of today.

We still, substantially, have the nineteenth-century multinational but use it to do the twentieth-century task of the transnational. We are, in other words, in a transition period.

About the relationship between the multinational and its political environment, it is easier to say what will not work than what will.

1. What will not work is clearly what might be called the Canadian pattern. Somehow the multinationals must be built into the political reality of their host countries so that political sovereignty becomes a support of multinationalism.

2. Also untenable is the nineteenth-century pattern of foreign domination and control of the infrastructure businesses, such as electric power, transportation, and telephone. One reason is that the foreigner cannot afford these investments in an inflation-prone world. These are capital-intensive businesses. Yet they are also politically very sensitive businesses, the prices of which are everywhere under government control. In an inflation, a foreign company will not be allowed to raise telephone rates — only a government can get away with this. And in an inflation a foreign company cannot raise the capital to maintain, let alone expand, service — only a government with the power of taxation can do this.

3. A position such as IBM has in the world's computer industry is not a tenable one and goes beyond the limits that will be allowed to any one multinational company. IBM has a near-monopoly on the vital new social function of information technology. The IBM dominance may be overcome gradually as other businesses in the computer and information industry grow more rapidly than IBM. This would be the most desirable solution. Or governments in other areas, such as Western Europe and Japan, may succeed in their attempts to organize their own effective competitors to IBM. Finally, IBM may be deprived of its dominant position by governmental fiat.

   There might even be a totally new way to resolve the IBM problem. IBM might become the first truly transnational public utility. It might continue as a company enjoying worldwide leadership, if not near-monopoly position, and yet be anchored in the economic and even political structure of the host countries, through partnership with local governments, local part ownership, and local regulation.

But one way or another the IBM dominance on a key necessity of modern society will be curbed.

4. Finally, multinationals will not be permitted to operate in developing countries without thinking through the consequences of their success as developers of the local economy and without planning ahead for the change in the relationship that is mutually desirable.

But as to what will be, one can only say that top management has the responsibility to develop the relationships that will work — and especially the relationships with developing countries.

Tomorrow's Management Structures

Tomorrow's management structure of the multinational will also be different from today's.

Even within the developed countries the multinational will have to be able to harmonize, in one structure, the need for "polycentric" management with the need for a common business strategy. One reason for this is the need to have the necessary corporate flexibility to exploit whatever capital markets are most advantageous in the form preferred by each capital market.

The American-based multinational is already heavily owned by Europeans — perhaps up to a full fifth of total capital. But little of this is in the form of common shares, which to an American means "ownership." But the European investor has long preferred a convertible debenture to common share investment. A convertible debenture is a bond earning fixed interest and without any right of ownership — until and unless it is "converted," that is, exchanged at the owner's demand into common shares at a pre-set price. And this is the form in which Europeans have chosen to finance the American multinationals, often in European currencies and owned mainly by European institutions and investors.

But this might mean also the creation of European subsidiaries and affiliated companies with direct European stock ownership, of a similar Brazilian subsidiary and affiliated companies with shares in the hands of Brazilians, of joint ventures and similar partly owned partnerships in Japan and other places, and so on. Organizationally what is required — and evolving — is systems management.

The multinational cannot hope to solve its internal problems or the problems of its relationship to its political environment unless it organizes itself as a highly disciplined, centrally directed, but flexible, federation of equals. This is the only way in which the president of the Colombian subsidiary of the worldwide pharmaceutical company can be both top management and a regional sales manager. It is the only way in which the president can operate in two different roles according to the logic and the needs of different situations. It is the only way in which the multinational can adopt and turn to its own advantage very different forms of relationships with different hosts and environments:

joint ventures here; partnerships there; ownership of substantial minorities in regional or local subsidiaries by local investors; partnership with governments in the many countries where government enterprises are important and indeed central factors in the economy; management contracts rather than ownership in certain developing countries, and many others.

At the same time, it is equally clear that the multinational company needs to be structured so as to be able to manage common resources for one world common market. One such resource is capital. Another one is knowledge. The most important and most difficult one is managers and professionals. Unless managers and professionals can be both "full citizens" within the overall company and important leading members of their own communities, the multinational companies will not be able to attract and hold the kind of people they need. They will fail to capitalize on what is their greatest asset: the desire of the young to be part of a bigger world, to travel and to live in different cultures, and to have a wide range of choices. The multinational company offers this in a way yesterday's domestic company could never do. At the same time, it must be able to offer to the same young people in the developing countries, the opportunity to make a contribution to their own country, their own society, their own economy.

It is also reasonably clear that tomorrow's multinational company will have to be able to embrace within one and the same corporate framework, and within one and the same management group, different managerial traditions. In Japan it will have to be able to make productive the Japanese traditions of structure, of promotion, of management. But in Germany it will have to be a German company. It will not only have to build its top management the way Germans expect their top management to be built — that is, as a team under a presiding officer — it will also have to satisfy German notions of the proper qualifications for management, for instance, the German valuation of an engineering career as a preeminent preparation for top management (a valuation which no other country shares, at least not to anything like the same extent). In France, whether it approves of it or not, it will have to be able to accept the French emphasis on the graduate of the Grandes Écoles, such as the École Polytechnique, as an elite corps, and even the French tradition under which a *polytechnicien* starts his career in government service — in which he usually does not use his technical education at all but works mainly in finance — then around age forty-five or fifty, when at the top of the government ladder, switches directly into the top management of major business enterprise. And in America — as most multinational Europeans operating in this country learned long ago — top management will have to bear the American top-management stamp.

But at the same time the multinational company will have to be unified. Its management people, even in middle management, will have to be able to understand these differences, will have to be willing to accept them, will have to learn to respect them. Where today the tendency in most multinationals is to say, "This is how we do it in Chicago (or Munich, or Osaka, or Eindhoven)," they will have to learn tomorrow to say, "This is what we want to achieve; how does one get it done in Peoria (or Munich, or Osaka, or Amsterdam)?"

The multinational of tomorrow will inevitably have to have more than one management team. Its corporate top management will be such a team. But at the same time, it will be a member of a great many other top-management teams. And in the other top managements, somebody who is not necessarily corporate top management will have to be the team leader.

CPC, the American-based company already mentioned, is a first example. Corporate top management is a team of about four or five people. But it is also a member of top management of each of its five companies. The president of each of these companies is the presiding officer for the top-management team of his company, of which the corporate top management are members. They can, of course, replace the president. But with respect to his own area each "sits at the head of the table." Each president, and especially the presidents of the European, Latin American, and Far Eastern companies which preside over a large number of autonomous companies in different countries, is in turn a member of the top-management team of each of these companies, with the head of that company "in the chair."

This is a complex and difficult structure. It requires not only that corporate top management free itself from all operating responsibility. It requires that management think through clearly what its business — or businesses — are and should be. It requires management by objectives and self-control. It requires that conscience functions are organized and made effective. It requires the highest degree of self-discipline on the part of managers and willingness to take upward responsibility to keep higher management, and especially the corporate top management, informed, knowledgeable, and educated.

And there is need for highly effective boards of directors, both for the overall company and for major parts, and functioning both as review and control boards and as public and community-relations boards.

But multinational management, like all systems management, also demands personal contact, vigorous efforts on the top to create and to maintain communications, and willingness both to learn and to teach. It cannot be run by "systems," though it requires a high degree of it. People in New York or in Basel must have enough time to sit down with their associates in Sao Paulo or Sydney — not with a problem, not with their own concerns, but as learners, as listeners, as resource. Similarly the top-management people, the members of the corporate top-management team as well as the members of all other top-management teams down to the smallest local company need time for direct personal relationships with important groups in their environment: the government people, the political leadership, the opinion-makers, whether in the communications media or in the universities. They cannot hope to reconcile the cleavage between the reality of a world economy and the reality of national sovereign states. But it is their job to make it bearable.

The multinational company is surely the most important economic instrument in today's world. It is important precisely because it reflects the new reality of a world market and of a world economy. It is important because it is an effective tool for optimizing the economic resources available. But precisely because it reflects a new reality rather than the extension of yesterday's business, it also requires new structures, new methods of integration, and new relationships. The multinational company is still new enough to be crippled. If so, the world would be the poorer. And the greatest sufferers would be precisely those developing countries which are, at the same time, most afraid of the multinational company, most conscious of the disparity between its strength and their own weakness, most in need of psychological, but also of economic, security and identity. But to make the multinational corporation live up to its promise requires innovative work of high quality from its top managements.

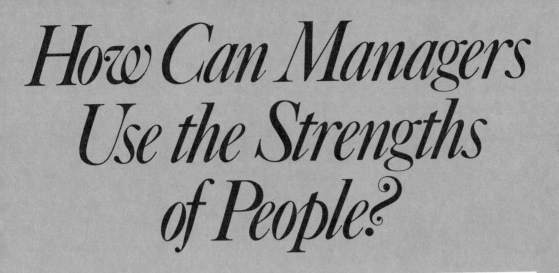

How Can Managers Use the Strengths of People?

Part Five

Is Personnel Management Bankrupt?

Chapter 22

Personnel Administration and Human Relations
A Survey of Personnel Administration
Its Three Basic Misconceptions
The Insight of Human Relations
And Its Limitations
"Scientific Management," Our Most Widely Practiced Personnel-
*   Management Concept*
Its Basic Concepts
Its World-Wide Impact
Its Stagnation Since the Early Twenties
Its Two Blind Spots
The Confusion of Analysis with Action
The "Divorce of Planning from Doing"
Scientific Management and the New Technology
Is Personnel Management Bankrupt?

A few years ago I received the following letter from the president of a company:

> I employ 2,300 people mostly women doing unskilled assembly work. Please send me at your earliest convenience a suitable personnel policy and enclose a statement of your fee.

For a long time I thought this letter a good, though unintentional, joke. But lately it has dawned on me that the laugh was really on me. My correspondent, I have come to suspect, is much like the child in Andersen's story of "The Emperor's New Clothes" who had the innocence to say out loud that the emperor was naked when everybody else was trying to pretend that he could see the ruler's garments.

A good deal of what passes today for management of the human organization is mechanical in nature and might indeed be dispensed by mail. The two generally accepted concepts of managing the worker — Personnel Administration and Human Relations — see the task to be done as something one tacks onto a business. Personnel Administration concerns itself with activities and procedures: hiring people, paying them, training them. Human Relations, as the term is commonly used, concerns itself with employee satisfaction, with communication and with attitudes. Yet both approaches seem to agree that to manage worker and work does not seem to require any change in the way the business is being conducted. And the tools and concepts needed seem to apply equally to any business.

An indication that this may not be the right approach is the lack of progress, of new thinking and of new contributions in either Personnel Administration or Human Relations. There is no field in the entire area of management where so many people are so hard at work. Personnel departments are growing like Jack's beanstalk; and every one contains some research men equipped with computers and Ph.D. degrees. In every university hundreds of people lecture, research and gather data in the field. Indeed, a raft of new disciplines has been created — industrial psychology, industrial sociology, industrial anthropology, industrial relations, personnel management and so forth. They all produce supposedly original dissertations. They produce books and hold meetings. There are dozens of magazines devoted to the field. And no self-respecting business organization, whether the Seedgrowers of America or the Sioux City Chamber of Commerce, would consider a convention complete without at least one talk on the management of people at work.

And what has been the result of all this activity, what has all this work by so many good, devoted, intelligent people produced?

Personnel Administration and Human Relations

Personnel Administration, as the term is commonly understood, began with World War I. It grew out of the recruiting, training and payment of vast masses of new workers in the war-production effort. World War I has been over for sixty years. Yet everything we know today about Personnel Administration was known by the early twenties, everything we practice now was practiced then. There have been refinements, but little else. Everything to be found in one of the big textbooks of today (save only the chapter on union relations) can be found, for instance, in the articles and papers Thomas Spates (one of the founding fathers of Personnel Administration) published in the early twenties. We have only poured on a heavy dressing of humanitarian rhetoric — the way a poor cook pours a brown starchy sauce on overcooked brussels sprouts.

There has been the same intellectual aridity in the field of Human Relations — though there is perhaps even more activity there. Human Relations, too, grew out of World War I; but it took a little longer to mature. It reached its bloom in the famous experiments conducted by Elton Mayo of Harvard and his associates around 1928 — a half century ago — in the Hawthorne, Illinois, plant of the Western Electric Company (the manufacturing subsidiary of the Bell Telephone System). These experiments showed that social and psychological factors, the amount of attention workers receive, for instance, may have more to do with productivity than objective working conditions, e.g., lighting at the workplace, or pay. And the reports of the Harvard group on the work at Hawthorne are still the best, the most advanced and the most complete works on the subject. Indeed, it is debatable whether the many refinements added since by the labor of countless people in industry, labor unions and academic life have clarified or obscured the original insight.

Novelty is, of course, no argument for soundness. Still, it is most unlikely for any new discipline to emerge fully formed and perfected at its birth like Venus from the waves. It takes decades to build the edifice on the foundations laid by the first thinkers in the field. That two new disciplines should have been blessed with full maturity at their birth is altogether improbable. Perhaps the reason that there has been so little building on the foundations of Personnel Administration and Human Relations is that the foundations themselves were inadequate.

A Survey of Recent Personnel Administration

The limitations of Personnel Administration are not hard to perceive. They are indeed admitted by most of the people in the field — at least by implication. The constant worry of all personnel administrators is their inability to prove that they are making a contribution to the enterprise. Their preoccupation is with the search for a "gimmick" that will impress their management associates. Their persistent complaint is that they lack status. For personnel administration — using the term in its common usage — is largely a collection of incidental techniques without much internal cohesion. Some wit once said maliciously that it puts together and calls "personnel management" all those things that do not deal with the work of people and that are not management.

There is, unfortunately, some justice to the gibe. As personnel administration conceives the job of managing worker and work, it is partly a file clerk's job, partly a housekeeping job, partly a social worker's job and partly "fire-fighting" to head off union trouble or to settle it. The things the personnel administrator is typically responsible for — safety and pension plans, the suggestion system, the employment office and union grievances — are necessary chores. They are mostly unpleasant chores. I doubt, though, that they should be put together in one department; for they are a hodgepodge, as one look at the organization chart of the typical personnel department, or at the table of contents of the typical textbook on personnel management, will show. They are neither one function by kinship of skills required to carry the activities, nor are they one function by being linked together in the work process, by forming a distinct stage in the work of the manager or in the process of the business.

None of these activities is in itself of such a nature as to call for more than moderate capacity in its management. None by itself has a major impact upon the business. Putting a great many of these activities together in one function does not produce a major function entitled to representation in top management or requiring the services of a top executive. For it is quality (that is, the kind of work and its impact upon the business) that alone makes a major function or defines the orbit of a senior executive.

Even if these things were best assembled into one department, they would not add up to managing people. They have indeed little to do with the job to be done in this area. Not only does the personnel department as a rule stay away from the management of the enterprise's most important human resource, managers, it also generally avoids the two most important areas in the management of workers: the organization of the work, and the organization of people to do the work. It accepts both as it finds them.

Three Misconceptions

The reason for the sterility of Personnel Administration is its three basic misconceptions. First it assumes that people do not want to work. Personnel Administration views "work as a kind of punishment that people must undergo in order to get satisfaction elsewhere." It tends therefore to put emphasis on satisfactions outside and beyond the work. Secondly, Personnel Administration looks upon the management of worker and work as the job of a specialist rather than as part of the manager's job. To be sure, there is constant talk in all personnel departments of the need to educate operating managers in managing people. But 90 percent of the budget, manpower and effort is devoted to personnel programs, thought up, established and operated by the personnel deparment. The typical textbook of Personnel Administration starts out by saying that the two first jobs of the personnel administrator are to advise operating management and to diagnose the stability or morale of the organization as an effective team. But then it spends 95 percent of its pages on the programs that the department itself organizes and manages.

This means, in effect, either that personnel administration has to usurp the functions and responsibility of the operating manager (since whoever manages the people under the operating manager is the "boss," whatever his or her title); or else it means that operating managers, in self-defense, have to confine personnel administration to the handling of incidental chores, that is, to those things that are not essential to the management of worker and work. It is not surprising that the latter has been the all but universal trend.

Finally, Personnel Administration tends to be "fire-fighting," to see "personnel" as concerned with "problems" and "headaches" that threaten the otherwise smooth and unruffled course of production. It was born with this tendency. But the unionization drives of the thirties have made it dominant. It is not too much to say that many personnel administrators, though mostly subconsciously, have a stake in trouble. Indeed, there was some truth in the joking remark made by a union leader about the personnel department of a big company: "Those fellows ought to kick back 10 percent of their salaries into the union treasury; but for the union they'd still be hundred-dollars-a-week clerks." But worker and work simply cannot be managed if trouble is the focus. It is not even enough to make "fire prevention" rather than "fire-fighting" the focus; managing worker and work must focus on the positive and must build on underlying strength and harmony.

The Insight of Human Relations — and Its Limitations

Human Relations, the second prevailing theory of the management of worker and work, starts out with the right basic concepts: people want to work; and managing people is the manager's job, not that of a specialist. It is therefore not just a collection of unrelated activities. It also rests on a profound insight — the insight summarized when we say that "one cannot hire a hand; the whole person always comes with it."

Human Relations recognizes that the human resource is a specific resource. It emphasizes this against mechanistic concepts of the human being, against the belief in the "slot-machine people" who respond only and automatically to monetary stimulus. It has made American management aware of the fact that the human resource requires definite attitudes and methods, which is a tremendous contribution. Human Relations, when first developed, was one of the great liberating forces, knocking off blinkers that management had been wearing for a century.

Yet Human Relations is, at least in the form in which it exists thus far, primarily a negative contribution. It freed management from the domination of viciously wrong ideas; but it did not succeed in substituting new concepts.

One reason is the belief in "spontaneous motivation." "Remove fear," the Human Relations people seem to say, "and people will work." This was a tremendous contribution at a time when management still felt that people could be motivated only through fear. Even more important was the implied attack on the assumption that people do not want to work. Yet, absence of wrong motivation, we have learned, is not enough. And on positive motivations Human Relations offers little but generalities.

Human Relations also lacks an adequate focus on work. Positive motivations must have their center in work and job, yet, Human Relations puts all the stress on inter-personal relations and on the "informal group." Its starting point was in individual psychology rather than in an analysis of worker and work. As a result, it assumes that it is immaterial what kind of work a person does since it is a worker's relationship to co-workers that determines his or her attitude, behavior and effectiveness.

Its favorite saying, that "the happy worker is an efficient and a productive worker," though a neat epigram, is at best a half truth. It is not the business of the enterprise to create happiness but to sell and make shoes. Nor can the worker be happy in the abstract.

Despite its emphasis on the social nature of people, Human Relations refuses to accept the fact that organized groups are not just the extension of individuals but have their own relationships, involving a real and healthy problem of power, and conflicts which are not conflicts of personalities but objective conflicts of vision and interests; that, in other words, there is a political sphere. This shows in the almost panicky fear of the labor union that runs through the entire work of the original Human Relations school at Harvard University.

Finally, Human Relations lacks any awareness of the economic dimension of the problem.

As a result, there is a tendency for Human Relations to degenerate into mere slogans which become an alibi for having no management policy in respect to the human organization. Worse still, because Human Relations started out from the attempt to adjust the "maladjusted" individual to the "reality" (which is always assumed to be rational and real), there is a strong manipulative tendency in the whole concept. With it there is the serious danger that Human Relations will degenerate into a new Freudian paternalism, a mere tool jor justifying management's action, a device to "sell" whatever management is doing. It is no accident that there is so much talk in Human Relations about "giving workers a sense of responsibility" and so little about their responsibility, so much emphasis on their "feeling of importance" and so little on making them and their work important. Whenever we start out with the assumption that individuals have to be adjusted, we search for ways of controlling, manipulating, selling them — and we deny by implication that there may be anything in our own actions that needs adjustment. In fact, the popularity of Human Relations in this country today may reflect, above all, the ease with which it can be mistaken for a soothing syrup for irritable children, and misused to explain away as irrational and emotional resistance to management and to its policies.

This does not mean that we have to discard Human Relations. On the contrary, its insights are a major foundation in managing the human organization. But it is not the building. Indeed, it is only one of the foundations. The remainder of the edifice has still to be built. It will rest on more than Human Relations. It will also have to rise well above it.

"Scientific Management" — Our Most Widely Practiced Personnel-Management Concept

Personnel Administration and Human Relations are the things talked about and written about whenever the management of worker and work is being discussed. They are the things the Personnel Department concerns itself with. But they are not the concepts that underlie the actual management of worker and work in American industry. This concept is Scientific Management. Scientific Management focuses on the work. Its core is the organized study of work, the analysis of work into its simplest elements and the systematic improvement of the worker's performance of each of these elements. Scientific Management has both basic concepts and easily applicable tools and techniques. And it has no difficulty proving the contribution it makes; its results in the form of higher output are visible and readily measurable.

Indeed, Scientific Management is all but a systematic philosophy of worker and work. Altogether it may well be one of the most powerful and lasting contributions America has made to Western thought. As long as industrial society endures, we shall never lose again the insight that human work can be studied systematically, can be analyzed, can be improved by work on its elementary parts.

Like all great insights, it was simplicity itself. People had worked for thousands of years. They had talked about improving work all that time. But few people had ever looked at human work systematically until Frederick W. Taylor started to do so around 1885. Work was taken for granted; and it is an axiom that one never sees what one takes for granted. Scientific Management was thus one of the great liberating, pioneering insights. Without it a real study of human beings at work would be impossible. Without it we could never, in managing worker and work, go beyond good intentions, exhortations or the "speed up." Although its conclusions have proved dubious, its basic insight is a necessary foundation for thought and work in the field.

Scientific Management has been stagnant for a long time. It is the oldest of our three approaches to the management of worker and work; it rose together with the new profession of engineering in the last decades of the nineteenth century. It also ran dry first. From 1890 to 1920 Scientific Management produced one brilliant new insight after the other and one creative new thinker after the other — Taylor, Fayol, Gantt, the Gilbreths. During the last fifty or sixty years, it has given us little but pedestrian and wearisome tomes on the techniques, if not on the gadgets, of narrower and narrower specialties. There are, of course, exceptions — especially Mrs. Lillian Gilbreth and the late Harry Hopf. But on the whole there have been oceans of paper but few, if any, new insights. There has been a great deal of refinement; yet the most mature and most cogent statement on Scientific Management is still the testimony Taylor gave before a Special Committee of the House of Representatives in 1912.

The reason for this is that Scientific Management, despite all its worldly success, has not succeeded in solving the problem of managing worker and work. As so often happens in the history of ideas, its insight is only half an insight. It has two blind spots, one engineering and one philosophical. What it does not see is as important as what it does see; indeed, if we do not learn to see where Scientific Management has been blind, we may lose even the benefit of its genuine vision.

Confusing Analysis with Action: A Blind Spot

The first of these blind spots is the belief that because we must analyze work into its simplest constituent motions we must also organize it as a series of individual motions, each if possible carried out by an individual worker. It is possible that Taylor himself saw the need to integrate; Harry Hopf certainly did. But practically all other writers — and all practitioners — see in the individual motion the essence of good work organization.

This is false logic. It confuses a principle of analysis with a principle of action. To take apart and to put together are different things. To confuse the two is grossly unscientific. For the beginning of science is the realization that classification, while absolutely necessary, does not tell us any important fact about the nature of the thing classified.

The belief that work is best performed as it is analyzed is also wretched engineering.

The best proof of this is in the greatest achievement resulting from the application of the concepts that underlie Scientific Management: the alphabet. Its inventor, an anonymous clerk in a long-forgotten Semitic trading town, 3,500 years ago, will never be awarded the Gold Medal of the International Management Congress. But his analysis of the basic, simple and standardized elements that underlay the thousands of pictograms, ideograms, logograms, syllable signs and phonetic marks of the writing of his day, and their replacement by two dozen signs capable of expressing all sounds and of conveying all words and thoughts, was straight Scientific Management — of the highest order. Yet, the alphabet would not only be totally useless — it would be a complete barrier to communication — were we expected to say "Cee-Ay-Tee," when we wanted to say "cat," just because we spell the word with these three letters.

The job of integrating letters into words is not a simple one. Even retarded children can usually learn the letters, but even a bright one has difficulty making the jump from Cee-Ay-Tee to cat. Indeed, practically all reading difficulties of children (the biggest problem of elementary education) are problems of integrating letters into words; many people, we know, never learn to do that but learn instead to recognize common words and syllables — they learn pictograms and ideograms rather than letters. And yet the alphabet not only triumphed despite the difficulty of integration. It is the integration that is its triumph and its real achievement.

Finally, the confusion between analysis of work and action in work is a misunderstanding of the properties of the human resource. Scientific Management purports to organize human work. But it assumes — without any attempt to test or to verify the assumption — that the human being is a machine tool (though a poorly designed one.)

It is perfectly true that we have to analyze the work into its constituent motions. It is true that we can best improve work by improving the way the individual operations are performed. But it is simply not true that the closer the work comes to confining itself to the individual motion or operation, the better the human being will perform it. This is not even true of a machine tool; to assert it of human beings is nonsense. The human being does individual motions poorly; viewed as a machine tool, a human is badly designed. Let us leave aside all such considerations as a person's will, personality, emotions, appetites and soul. Let us look at people only as a productive resource and only from the point of view of engineers concerned with input and output. We have no choice but to accept the fact that the specific contribution of people is always to perform many motions to integrate, to balance, to control, to measure, to judge. The individual operations must indeed be analyzed, studied and improved. But the human resource will be utilized productively only if *a job* is being formed out of the operations, a job that puts to work the specific qualities of people.

Planning Divorced from Doing: The Other Blind Spot

The second blind spot of Scientific Management is the "divorce of planning from doing" one of its cardinal tenets. Again a sound analytical principle is being mistaken for a principle of action. But in addition the divorce of planning from doing reflects a dubious and dangerous philosophical concept of an elite which has a monopoly on esoteric knowledge entitling it to manipulate the unwashed peasantry.

To have discovered that planning is different from doing was one of Taylor's most valuable insights. To emphasize that the work will become the easier, more effective, more productive, the more we plan before we do, was a greater contribution to America's industrial rise than stopwatch or time-and-motion study. On it rests the entire structure of modern management. That we are able today to speak seriously and with meaning of management by objectives is a direct result of Taylor's discovery of planning as a separate part of the job, and of his emphasis on its importance.

But it does not follow from the separation of planning and doing in the analysis of work that the planner and the doer should be two different people. It does not follow that the industrial world should be divided into two classes of people; a few who decide what is to be done, design the job, set the pace, rhythm and motions, and order others about; and the many who do what and as they are being told.

Planning and doing are separate parts of the same job; they are not separate jobs. There is no work that can be performed effectively unless it contains elements of both. One cannot plan exclusively all the time. There must be at least a trace of doing in one's job. Otherwise one dreams rather than performs. One cannot, above all do only; without a trace of planning his or her job, the worker does not have the control needed even for the most mechanical and repetitive routine chore. Advocating the divorce of the two is like demanding that swallowing food and digesting it be carried on in separate bodies. To be understood, the two processes have to be studied separately. They require different organs, are subject to different ailments and are carried out in different parts of the body. But to be nourished at all, the same body needs both, just as a job must contain planning as well as doing.

> Taylor's divorce of planning from doing was both specifically American and specifically late nineteenth century. It is a descendant of our oldest tradition: the New England theocracy of the early Puritans. It puts the priestly-elite concept of Increase and Cotton Mather into modern dress, but leaves it otherwise almost unchanged; and like the Puritan divines Taylor deduced a God-given right of the planning elite to rule. It is no accident that we hear this right to rule described today as the "prerogative of management" — the term has always been applied to right by divine or priestly anointment.
>
> But the divorce of planning and doing was also part of the elite philosophy that swept the Western World in the generation between Nietzsche and World War I — the philosophy that has produced such monster offspring in our time. Taylor belongs with Sorel, Lenin and Pareto. This movement is usually considered to have been anti-democratic. It was — in intent and direction — fully as much anti-aristocratic. For the assertion that power is grounded in technical competence — be it for revolutionary conspiracy or for management — is as hostile to aristocracy as to democracy. Both oppose to it the same absolute principle: power must be grounded in moral responsibility; anything else is tyranny and usurpation.

The divorce of planning from doing deprives us of the full benefit of the insights of Scientific Management. It sharply cuts down the yield to be obtained from the analysis of work, and especially the yield to be obtained from planning. We have seen cases where productivity greatly increased when the workers were given responsibility for planning their work. The same increase in productivity (not to mention the improvement in worker attitude and pride) has been obtained wherever we have combined the divorce of planning from doing with the marriage of the planner to doer.

The Blind Spots Explain Resistance to Change

The two blind spots of traditional Scientific Management explain why its application always increases workers' resistance to change. Because they are being taught individual motions rather than given a job, their ability to unlearn is stifled rather than developed. They acquire experience and habit rather than knowledge and understanding. Because workers are supposed to do rather than to know — let alone to plan — every change represents the challenge of the incomprehensible and therefore threatens their psychological security.

It is an old criticism of Scientific Management that it can set up a job so as to get the most output per hour but not so as to get the most output over five hundred hours. It may be a much more serious and better-founded criticism that it knows how to organize the present job for maximum output but only by seriously impairing output in the worker's next job. Of course, if the job were considered unchangeable, this would not matter. Henry Ford (one of the most thorough practitioners of Scientific Management, though he had never heard Taylor's name) believed that once the putting on of a fender had been properly engineered, the job would remain unchanged in all eternity.

But *we know* that change is inevitable; it is, indeed, a major function of the enterprise to bring it about. We also know that the next few decades will bring tremendous changes — and nowhere more than in the worker's job.

Scientific Management and the New Technology

The coming of the new technology converts what may have been considered limitations on the full effectiveness of Scientific Management into crippling diseases. Indeed the major problems of managing worker and work under the new technology will be to enable the worker to do a complete and integrated job and to do responsible planning.

Workers under Automation will no longer do the repetitive routine chores of machine feeding and materials handling. Instead, they will build, maintain and control machines that do the repetitive routine work. To do this they must be able to do many operations, must have the largest rather than the smallest content to their jobs, must be able to co-ordinate. This does not mean that they must be again manually skilled workers as the workers of yore. On the contrary, every one of the operations should be analyzed by means of Scientific Management to the point where they can be done by unskilled people. But the operations must be integrated again into a job — otherwise the work needed under Automation cannot be done. In the new technology we have no choice, but to say "cat." We must learn how to put together — now that Scientific Management has taught us how to pull apart.

Similarly, we will not be able to organize worker and work in the new technology on the basis of the divorce of planning from doing. On the contrary, the new technology demands that the least production worker be capable of a good deal of planning. The more planning a worker can do and the more responsibility a worker can take for what he or she does, the more productive that worker will be. A worker who does only as instructed can do only harm. To maintain the equipment, to program it, to set it and to control it, all demand of the worker in the new technology knowledge, responsibility and decision-making – that is, planning. Our problem will not be that planning and doing are not divorced enough; it will be that many workers of tomorrow may have to be able to do more planning than a good many people who call themselves managers today are capable of.

We must preserve the fundamental insights of Scientific Management – just as we must preserve those of Human Relations. But we must go beyond the traditional application of Scientific Management, must learn to see where it has been blind. And the coming of the new technology makes this task doubly urgent.

Is Personnel Management Bankrupt?

Is Personnel Management bankrupt? asks the title of this chapter. We can now give the answer: "No, it is not bankrupt. Its liabilities do not exceed its assets. But it is certainly insolvent, certainly unable to honor, with the ready cash of performance, the promises of managing worker and work it so liberally makes. Its assets are great – the fundamental insights of Human Relations, the equally fundamental insights of Scientific Management. But these assets are frozen. There is also a lot of small stuff lying around in the form of Personnel Administration techniques and gadgets. But it does not help us too much in the big job of unfreezing the frozen assets, though it may produce enough saleable merchandise to pay the petty bills. Perhaps the biggest working capital is the things we have learned not to do; but what banker ever lent on such collateral?"

The facts permit, however, of a more optimistic interpretation. The last fifty years were years of minor refinements rather than of vigorous growth, of intellectual stagnation rather than of basic thinking. But everything points to a different picture for the years ahead. Technological change is forcing new thinking, new experimentation, new methods. The process has already begun. The relationship between workers and the kind of work they do, which traditional Human-Relations thinking pushed aside as almost irrelevant, is now being studied by the Human-Relations school. The problem of the organization of the job according to the properties of the human resource, rather than on the assumption of a person as a badly designed machine tool, is being given serious attention in the school of Scientific Management. And the practitioners are well ahead of the writers and theoreticians, and are already moving across the frontiers of the traditional concepts. At the very least we already know what we do know, what we don't know and what we need to know about work, working, and workers.

What We Know About Work, Working, and Worker

Chapter 23

The Primitive State of Our Knowledge
The Three Requirements of Productive Work
Analysis, Synthesis and Control of Work
The Five Dimensions of Working: Physiology; Psychology;
        Community; Economics; Power
Machine Design and "Human Design"
Work as Curse and Blessing
Work as Social and Community Bond
"Wage Fund" and "Capital Fund"
Work as Living and Work as Cost
The Mirage of Worker Ownership
The Power Dimension of Working
Organization Is Alienation
The Sixth Dimension: Power in the Economic Sphere
Organization as a Redistributive System
The Fallacy of the Dominant Dimension
Wants as Hierarchy and as Configuration
Wants Change in the Process of Being Satisfied
What Can the Manager Do?

*W*ork has been central to human consciousness for untold ages. Man is not truly defined as the toolmaker, but making tools, the systematic, purposeful, and organized approach to work, is specific and unique in human activity. Work has, therefore, been a profound concern for millennia.

What was always a profound concern became central with the industrial revolution. The economic and social theories of the last two hundred years center on work.

However central work has been all along, organized study of work did not begin until the closing decades of the nineteenth century. Frederick W. Taylor was the first person in recorded history who deemed work deserving of systematic observation and study. On Taylor's "scientific management" rests, above all, the tremendous surge of affluence in the last seventy-five years which has lifted the working masses in the developed countries well above any level recorded before, even for the well-to-do. Taylor, though the Isaac Newton (or perhaps the Archimedes) of the science of work, laid only first foundations, however. Not much has been added to them since.

The worker has been given even less attention — and the knowledge worker has received so far almost none. Rhetoric there is aplenty, but serious, systematic study has been confined to only a few aspects of working.

There is *industrial physiology*, dealing with the relationship of such things as lighting, tool and machine speeds, design of the work place, and so on, to the human being who is the worker; the fundamental work here was done in the early years of this century, e.g., in the fatigue and vision studies of the German-born Harvard psychologist Hugo Muensterberg. Cyril Burt, an Englishman, might be called the father of *industrial psychology*. During World War I he studied aptitudes, that is, the relationship between the demands of specific manual work and the physical skill, motor coordination, and reactions of individual workers. Finally, in the early nineteenth century, Australian-born Elton Mayo, working primarily at Harvard, developed *human relations*, that is, the study of the relationship between people working together — though in human relations work itself, that is, the task to be done, received almost no attention.

The totality of "worker" and "working," the totality of task and job, perception and personality, work community, rewards and power relations, has received practically no attention. It may be far too complex ever to be truly understood.

The manager cannot wait till the scientists and scholars have done their work. Nor can the worker. The manager has to manage today and to put to work the little we know. The manager has to try to make work productive and the worker achieving. It might, therefore, be appropriate to put down what we know about work and working.

Analysis, Synthesis, and Control

The most important thing we know is that work and working are fundamentally different phenomena. The worker does, indeed, do work; and work is always done by a worker who is working. But what is needed to make work productive is quite different from what is needed to make the worker achieving. The worker must, therefore, be managed according to both the logic of the work and the dynamics of working. Personal satisfaction of the worker without productive work is failure; but so is productive work that destroys the worker's achievement. Neither is, in effect, tenable for very long.

Work is impersonal and objective. Work is a task. It is a "something." To work, therefore, applies the rule that applies to objects. Work has a logic. It requires analysis, synthesis, and control.

As with every phenomenon of the objective universe, the first step toward understanding work is to *analyze it*. This, as Taylor realized a century ago, means identifying the basic operations, analyzing each of them, and arranging them in logical, balanced, and rational sequence.

Taylor worked, of course, on manual operations. But Taylor's analysis applies just as well to mental and even to totally intangible work. The "outline" which the budding writer is being told to work out, before starting to write, is in effect scientific management. And the most advanced, most perfect example of scientific management was not developed by industrial engineers during the last hundred years. It is the alphabet, which enables all words in a language to be written with a very small number of repetitive and simple symbols.

But then — and Taylor did not realize this — work has to be synthesized again. It has to be put together into a process. This is true for the individual job. It is, above all, true for the work of a group, that is for a work process. We need *principles of production* which enable us to know how to put together individual operations into individual jobs, and individual jobs into "production."

Some of Taylor's fellow pioneers, especially Gantt, saw this clearly. The Gantt Chart, in which the steps necessary to obtain a final work result are worked out by projecting backward, step by step from end result to actions, their timing and their sequence, though developed during World War I, is still the one tool we have to identify the process needed to accomplish a task, whether making a pair of shoes, landing a man on the moon, or producing an opera. Such recent innovations as PERT chart, critical path analysis, and network analysis are elaborations and extensions of Gantt's work.

But the Gantt Chart tells us very little about the logic that is appropriate to given kinds of processes. It is, so to speak, the multiplication table of work design. It does not even tell us when to multiply, let alone what the purpose of the calculation is.

Finally, work, precisely because it is a process rather than an individual operation, needs a built-in control. It needs a feedback mechanism which both senses unexpected deviations and with them the need to change the process, and maintains the process at the level needed to obtain the desired results.

Those three elements, analysis, synthesis into a process of production, and feedback control are particularly important in knowledge work. For knowledge work by definition does not result in a product. It results in a contribution of knowledge to somebody else. The output of the knowledge worker always becomes somebody else's input. It is, therefore, not self-evident in knowledge work, as it is in making a pair of shoes, whether the work has results or not. This can be seen only by projecting backward from the needed end results. At the same time, knowledge work, being intangible, is not controlled by its own progress. We do not know the sequence of knowledge work in the way we know — at least since Taylor and Gantt — the sequence of manual operations. Knowledge work, therefore, needs far better design, precisely because it cannot be designed *for* the worker. It can be designed only *by* the worker.

The Five Dimensions of Working

Working is the activity of the worker; it is a human being's activity and an essential part of humanity. It does not have a logic. It has dynamics and dimensions.

Working has at least *five dimensions*. In all of them the worker has to be achieving in order to be productive.

Machine Design and Human Design

There is, first, a *physiological* dimension. The human being is not a machine and does not work like a machine.

Machines work best if they do only one task, if they do it repetitively, and if they do the simplest possible task. Complex tasks are done best as a step-by-step series of simple tasks in which the work shifts from machine to machine, either by moving the work itself physically, as on the assembly line, or, as in modern computer-controlled machine tools, by bringing machines and tools in prearranged sequence to the work, with the tool changing with each step of the process. Machines work best if run at the same speed, the same rhythm, and with a minimum of moving parts.

The human being is engineered quite differently. For any one task and any one operation human beings are ill-suited. They lack strength. They lack stamina. The get fatigued. Altogether the human being is a very poorly designed machine tool. The human being excels, however, in coordination. A human excels in relating perception to action and works best if the entire person, muscles, senses, and mind, is engaged by the work.

If confined to an individual motion or operation, the human being tires fast. This fatigue is not just boredom, which is psychological; it is genuine physiological fatigue as well. Lactic acid builds up in the muscles, visual acuity goes down, reaction time slows and becomes erratic.

The human being works best at a configuration of operations rather than at a single operation. But also — and this may be even more important — the human being is singularly ill-equipped to work at an unvarying speed and a standard rhythm. People work best if capable of varying both speed and rhythm fairly frequently.

There is no "one right" speed and no "one right" rhythm for human beings. Speed, rhythm, and attention span vary greatly among individuals. Studies of infants strongly indicate that patterns of speed, rhythm, and attention span are as individual as are fingerprints and vary fully as much. Each individual, in other words, has his or her own pattern of speeds and his or her own need to vary speeds. Each individual has his or her own pattern of rhythms, and has his or her own pattern of attention spans. Nothing, we now know, creates as much fatigue, as much resistance, as much anger, and as much resentment, as the imposition of an alien speed, an alien rhythm, and an alien attention span, and above all, the imposition of one unvarying and uniform pattern of speed, rhythm, and attention span. That is alien and physiologically offensive to every human being. It results speedily in a buildup of toxic wastes in muscle, brain, and bloodstream, in the release of stress hormones, and in changes in electrical tension throughout the nervous system. To be productive the individual has to have control, to a substantial extent, over the speed, rhythm, and attention spans with which he is working — just as an infant, learning to speak or to walk, has to have substantial control over learning speed, learning rhythm, and learning attention span.

While *work* is, therefore, best laid out as uniform, *working* is best organized with a considerable degree of diversity. Working requires latitude to change speed, rhythm, and attention span fairly often. It requires fairly frequent changes in operating routines as well. What is good industrial engineering for work is exceedingly poor human engineering for the worker.

Work as Curse and Blessing

The next dimension of people at work is *psychological*. Work, we know, is both a burden and a need, both a curse and a blessing. Whether this is genetic or culturally conditioned, we do not know — and it does not greatly matter. By the time human beings have reached the age of four or five, they have been conditioned to work. To be sure, child labor is outlawed in most countries, but learning the fundamentals of being a person, especially learning to talk, is work and creates the habit of work. Unemployment we long ago learned creates severe psychological disturbances, not because of economic deprivation, but primarily because it undermines self-respect. Work is an extension of personality. It is achievement. It is one of the ways in which a person defines himself or herself, measures his or her worth and humanity.

"Loafing" is easy, but "leisure" is difficult. For younger people especially, it is likely to mean frantic activity — or the hard work of bucking traffic on overcrowded highways — rather than philosophical repose. "To be an aristocrat one has to start learning dignified idleness in early childhood," was a common saying in that most snobbish of all Western societies, the Whig society of late eighteenth- and early nineteenth-century England. And, "The devil finds work for idle hands," says an even older proverb.

The peculiar characteristic of the work ethic of the West — which goes back all the way to Saint Benedict of Nursia in the sixth century rather than to Calvin in the sixteenth — is not that it glorified and sanctified work. That was neither new nor particularly Western. It sanctified the "calling"; it preached that *all* work was service and contribution and equally deserving of respect. The Benedictine monks made *manual* work in field and workshop equal to the work of praying and teaching. This was a deliberate break with the earlier beliefs of antiquity which held that the "gentleman" or the "free man" had to be freed from manual chores to have time for higher work, for learning, for statecraft, for civic duties, and for military service. As a result, antiquity — but also most non-Western civilizations — ordered different kinds of work in a hierarchy of personalities, with manual work pertaining to the ignoble, whether slave, peasant, or artisan, and soldiers' and knowledge work pertaining to the full personality. Neither Socrates nor Cicero believed in idleness; on the contrary, their full personality was working harder than the ignoble or obscure — and did more demanding, more responsible work. When the Chinese Mandarin retired to his ancestral estate after a successful government career, he was not supposed to lead a life of leisure. He was supposed instead to take up other but even more productive work, calligraphy and painting, music and writing. And the justification of these activities was above all their social contribution; in the Confucian social ethic, these pursuits are necessary to maintain the social harmony on which all else depends.

There is little doubt, however, that the commercial and industrial revolutions of the eighteenth and nineteenth centuries brought a sharp stepup in the hours worked by farmers, machine tenders, merchants, and industrialists alike.

In large measure this reflected a sizable improvement in living conditions and, above all, in nutrition, which greatly increased the physical energy available for work (just as the eighteenth-century English draft animal, whether horse or ox, could do far more work in the course of a year than its grandsire a hundred years earlier had been able to do, because the invention of the silo provided adequate food during the winter months). No matter how horrible living conditions were in the nineteenth-century slums of the industrial towns — or today in the slums and shanty towns that ring Latin America's cities — they were better with respect to food than the living conditions under which the landless laborer or the weavers and spinners in the cottage industries had subsisted. If anyone doubts this he need only note the food on which seamen in the sailing vessels were supposed to live and work; there are abundant records in such literary classics as Dana's *Two Years Before the Mast*, Melville's *Typee* and *Moby Dick*, or in the once widely popular naval stories of Captain Marryat. Yet sailors, by all reports, were the best-fed workers, both because the work was hard and made great physical demands and because of the ever-present danger of mutiny.

The great increase in working in these centuries also represented a shift in values. Economic rewards became more meaningful — mostly, perhaps, because economic satisfactions became more generally available. The "proletarians" in the nineteenth-century slums of Liverpool or Manchester could not buy much even if they had a job and received a wage; they lacked purchasing power. But purchasing power would not have helped their grandfathers, the landless laborers; there wasn't anything much around to buy in 1750 or so.

The rejection of the work ethic — if there is such a phenomenon outside of the headlines — therefore does not represent hedonism. In part it represents a reaction against long decades of overworking, and a righting of the balance. In larger part it may, however, represent a return to earlier elitist work concepts which relate certain kinds of work to nobility or to baseness of the person. What lends support to this hypothesis is the strong, positive value which the educated young people who supposedly repudiate the work ethic give to the work of teacher and artist. Teaching and art, however, are far more demanding taskmasters than tending machines or selling soap.

The workless society of the futurist utopia may, indeed, be ahead. Should it come, it would, however, produce a major personality crisis for most people. It is perhaps fortunate that so far there is not the slightest fact to support the prediction of the imminent demise of work. So far the task is still to make work serve the psychological need of humanity.

Work as Social and Community Bond

Work is *social bond* and *community bond*. In the employee society it becomes primary access to society and community. It largely determines status. For someone to say, "I am a doctor" or "I am a plumber" is a meaningful statement. It tells us something about that person's position in society and role in the community.

Perhaps more important, work, since time immemorial, has been the means to satisfy our need for belonging to a group and for a meaningful relationship to others. When Aristotle said that man is a *zoon politikon*, i.e., a social animal, he said in effect that we need work to satisfy our need for community.

To be sure, few people are determined in their social and community functions solely by and through the work group to which they belong. Most people have other societies and communities. It is by no means unusual to find someone who ranks low socially in a work group but who is a "big shot" elsewhere; the inconspicuous engineer who is a big man in the Boy Scouts or in his church, for instance. But even for this man, work will provide much of his companionship, group identification, and social bond.

Work is for most people the *one* bond outside of their own narrow family — and often more important than the family, especially for the young not-yet married and for older people whose children have grown up. This is exemplified strongly by the experience of companies who hire mature women. The work place becomes their community, their social club, their means of escaping loneliness, with their husbands at their own jobs and the children gone.

The Bell Telephone Company, for instance, has many women employees who leave the job to raise a family but a dozen years later become available for part-time work. They are hired to handle clerical peak loads, especially in such large-scale financial work as new stock or bond issues, mailing dividends or annual reports, and so on. The work, when available, is usually rushed and high-pressure, the hours long, and the pay far from exceptional. Yet the competition for a place on the roster is intense, and the morale of the group exceptionally high. When, for whatever reasons, a few months go by without such work, the women will start to call in and ask, "How soon can I come in again? I want to see my friends; I want to know what they are doing; I miss their company."

Similarly every company that has polled its retired employees has found the same reaction. "What we miss isn't the work; it's our colleagues and friends." "What we want to know isn't how the company is doing but what the people do with whom we worked, where they are, how they are coming along." "Don't, please, send me the annual report," a retired senior vice-president of a big company once said in a burst of candor, "I'm no longer interested in sales. Send me the gossip. I miss even the people I couldn't stand."

This last comment puts the finger on the greatest strength of the work bond and its singular advantage compared to all other bonds of community. It is not predicated on personal likes or dislikes. It can function without making emotional demands. People can work very well with somebody whom they never see away from the job, and for whom they feel neither friendship nor warmth nor liking. People can even function well in a work relationship with somebody whom they cordially dislike — if only they respect the other person's skills and ability to work. But the worker can also be a close friend with whom one spends as many hours away from work as possible, with whom one goes hunting or fishing, spends one's vacation, spends one's evenings, and shares much of one's life. The work relationship has an objective, outside focus, the work itself. It does make possible strong social and community bonds that are as personal or as impersonal as one desires.

This may explain why, throughout man's history, and above all, among primitive peoples, work groups have always been sexually differentiated. Men work together and women work together. But we rarely hear, either in history or in cultural anthropology, of work groups of mixed sex. Men hunt and women tend the village. Men build boats and women grow yams. In Europe women have traditionally milked the cows, in America men; but on neither side of the Atlantic has milking been done by sexually mixed groups. That in modern society men and women increasingly work side by side in the same work groups — a process that began around 1880 when typewriters and telephones first took women out of homes and small shops and into large-scale organizations — thus represents a major social change. "Women's Lib" may thus be something far more important than a reaction to "sexual inequality." It may be a response to the increasing disappearance of the age-old separation of the sexes at work.

The Economic Dimension

Work is a "*living.*" It has an economic component the moment a society adopts even the most rudimentary division of labor. The moment people cease to be self-sufficient and begin to exchange the fruits of their labor, work creates an economic bond that connects them, but also an economic conflict.

There is no resolution to this conflict. One has to live with it.

Work is living for workers. It is the foundation of their economic existence. But work also produces the capital for the economy. It produces the means by which an economy perpetuates itself, provides for the risks of economic activity and the resources of tomorrow, especially the resources needed to create tomorrow's jobs and with them the livelihood for tomorrow's workers. There is need in any economy for a wage fund and for a capital fund.

But the capital fund is in direct competition with the workers' need for a livelihood here and now. Marx tried to deny the need for a capital fund. The great appeal of Marxism to the workers was precisely that it presented capital accumulation as exploitation and as unnecessary. The great appeal of Marxism was its prophesy that the capital fund would disappear once the workers owned the means of production. This very soon was seen as a total misunderstanding. No matter how bitterly Lenin attacked the German "revisionist socialists" who pointed out in the early years of this century that the capital fund was an objective necessity and not founded in social or power structure, every communist regime, most of all the Soviet Union, has put the capital fund into the center of its economic planning. In other words, they all have realized that profit is not a result of power, let alone exploitation, but objective necessity.

Still, it does little good to argue, as the classical economists did, that there is no conflict between the demands of the capital fund, that is, the demands for a surplus, and the demands of the wage fund. The classical economists argued that, in the long run, these two harmonize. The worker needs the capital fund fully as much as the wage fund. The worker needs more than anyone else, to be protected against the risks of uncertainty. The worker, more than anyone else, needs the jobs of tomorrow.

The rapid improvement in wages and living standards of the American worker has in large measure been the result of steadily increasing capital investment, that is, the capital fund. The researches of Simon Kuznets (first at the University of Pennsylvania and later at Harvard) into capital formation in the United States, have demonstrated this. But "the worker" is an abstraction. The beneficiary of the capital fund is rarely the same worker who has made the contribution to the fund. The capital accumulated in one industry, e.g., the American textile industry in the 1890s, went to finance a new industry such as the chemical industry, rather than to create new jobs in the textile industry. Also, the capital fund creates jobs and incomes tomorrow, whereas the contribution to it has to be made today.

There is, in addition, the tremendous problem of comparative gains and sacrifices among different kinds of workers. It is probably true, as labor economists have argued (e.g. Paul Douglas [1892–1976], originally an economist at Chicago, and later for many years a prominent U.S. senator), in their studies of real wages, that trade-union activities do not — and cannot — much influence the total level of real wages in an economy. It is still true, however, that one group of workers, e.g., workers in the building trades, can and do obtain sizable wage advantages at the cost of other groups of workers.

In other words, it is true that there is no ultimate conflict between wage fund and capital fund but this is largely irrelevant for the individual. For him there is a real and immediate conflict.

Work as Living and Work as Wage

There is an even more fundamental conflict between wage as living and wage as cost. As "living," wage needs to be predictable, continuous, and adequate to the expenditures of a family, its aspirations, and its position in society and community. As "cost," wage needs to be appropriate to the productivity of a given employment or industry. It needs to be flexible and to adjust easily to even minor changes in supply and demand in the market. It needs to make a product or service competitive. It is determined, in the last result, by the consumer, that is, without regard to the needs or expectations of the worker. Again, here is a conflict which cannot easily be resolved and can at best be assuaged.

No society, no matter how designed, has been able to eliminate these conflicts. Expropriating the capitalist, the traditional Marxist formula, does not change the situation. All it might do is to make possible a larger capital fund because the state has absolute control. But even this Russia could achieve only by outlawing labor unions. Japan has traditionally been able to minimize the conflict between wage as living and wage as cost but rising living standards threaten the Japanese accommodation. The conflict between wage fund and capital fund rages as fiercely in Japan as any place else. The Yugoslavs, by vesting ownership of a plant in the worker's plant community, rather than in the state, hoped to abolish the conflict. Under the Yugoslav system, the needs of the capital fund should be more clearly apparent to the plant community than under any other system known so far, but they are being resisted just as much. The Yugoslav experiment is in danger of collapsing because of the inflationary pressures generated by workers' demands for more wages than the enterprise can afford to pay either under the aspect of wage as cost or in consideration of its own and the economy's need for the capital fund.

Worker ownership has been the alternative to both capitalism, that is ownership by the providers of capital, and nationalization, that is ownership by the government. It has a long — though not a very distinguished — history.

It may be highly desirable that workers have a financial stake in the business. But wherever tried — and we have been trying worker ownership for well over a century — it has worked only as long as the enterprise is doing well. It works only in highly profitable businesses. And so do all the variants of workers' participation in profits. As soon as business profits drop, worker ownership no longer resolves the conflict between wage as living and wage as cost, or that between the wage fund and the capital fund.

A financial stake in the business must always remain a secondary interest to the worker compared to his or her job. Even in the most prosperous business, profit, that is, the contribution to the capital fund, is never more than a small fraction of wages. In manufacturing industries, wage costs typically are 40 percent or so of gross sales. Profits after taxes are rarely more than 5 or 6 percent, that is, one-eighth of wage costs. In the total economy the wage and salary bill runs around 70 percent of gross national product, profits fluctuate from zero to 7 percent or so — they are at most one-tenth of the wage bill.

Profits, at their lushest, can, therefore, rarely contribute more than a very small additional bonus — welcome but not fundamental.

It is also highly debatable whether worker ownership is in the worker's own *financial* interest. No enterprise will be profitable forever. And if the workers then, as in the typical worker-ownership plan, are dependent for their future, e.g., for their retirement benefits, on investment in the company they work for, they are exceedingly vulnerable. Workers should no more than any other investor have all their financial eggs in one basket. In that respect, the approach to pensions adopted in the United States in the last twenty-five years — development of a pension fund which invests broadly, and typically does not invest at all in the business that employs the future beneficiaries — is financially far sounder and far more in the workers' own financial interest than worker ownership in the enterprise that employs the workers.

From a theoretical point of view, the developments in the United States during the last twenty or thirty years would seem to represent the optimal approach to the resolution of these conflicts. The employees of American business are gradually becoming the true "owners" through their pension funds and mutual funds, which have become the dominant investors in the American economy. By now these institutional investors, i.e., the trustees for the employee's savings, control, in effect, the large publicly owned American corporations. America, in other words, has socialized ownership without nationalizing it. Yet this has by no means resolved — or even lessened — the conflict between wage fund and capital fund and between wage as living and wage as cost.

It would help if we learned to think and speak of the costs of capital and of the costs of the future rather than of profit. But it would only help; it would not make the conflicts go away. They are built into this situation, whether business operates in a market economy or in a government-run one, whether it is privately owned, government-owned, or plant community-owned.

The Power Dimension of Working

There is always a *power relationship* implicit in working within a group, and especially in working within an organization.

The farmer of old who tilled his own stony acres had to impose on himself a very strict discipline. What he *wanted* to do was not very relevant, if haying had to be done. But the forces to which he was subordinated were impersonal. They were wind and weather, season and frost, or the impersonal forces of a market. But in any organization, no matter how small, there has to be a personal authority. The organization member's will is subordinated to an alien will.

The imposition of the clock on the lives of people which forces them to come to work at a given hour might appear a trivial exercise of power, and one that affects everybody equally. But it came as a tremendous shock to pre-industrial people, whether peasants in developing countries, the former craftsmen in the mills of England in the early years of the industrial revolution, or Blacks from the ghettos of the American city today. In an organization jobs have to be designed, structured, and assigned. Work has to be done on schedule and in a prearranged sequence. People are promoted or not promoted. In short, authority has to be exercised by someone.

Anarchists are right in their assertion that "organization is alienation." Modern organization theorists such as Howard University's Chris Argyris who hope for organization without alienation are romantics (though many of their concrete proposals for "participation" are highly constructive, and needed). Modern society is an employee society and will remain one. This means power relationships that affect everybody directly and in his or her capacity as a worker. Authority is an essential dimension of work. It has little or nothing to do with ownership of the means of production, democracy at the work place, worker representation at the board of directors, or any other way of structuring the "system." It is inherent in the fact of organization.

The Sixth Dimension: The Power Dimension of Economics

In all modern organization there is what might be called a sixth dimension of working: a need for authority with respect to *economic shares.*

Power and economics are inextricably tied together in the modern organization, whether business enterprise, government agency, university, or hospital. Apportioning the economic rewards of the members of the institution demands a central organ of authority with power of decision. The reason is not capitalism or any other "ism." It is the fundamental fact that the modern institution is an organ of society, existing to provide satisfactions outside of itself. It, therefore, must obtain its revenue from the outside — either from a customer in the marketplace, from the taxpayers through a budget-making authority, or from preset fees paid by users such as patients in a hospital, patrons of the post office, or students in a college. At the same time, the contribution of the individual member of the institution cannot be directly related to the revenue. It is impossible to say, even approximately, how much of the sales of a business an individual employee contributes, whether chief executive or lowliest sweeper. The same is true of hospital or university. Does the great scholar in ancient Chinese who has six graduate students contribute more or less than the graduate assistant teaching English composition to a freshman class of 150? And what about the dean? All one can say is that everybody's contribution is, in theory, indispensable, although not everybody's contribution enters into every single product or performance, nor is everybody's contribution in any way equal in importance, skill, or difficulty.

An authority is, therefore, needed which divides the revenue available among the members. The institution itself, whether business enterprise or hospital, is necessarily a *redistributive system.*

Where the contributions are simple, similar, and few in number, redistribution on the basis of complete equality is possible. This is, for instance, the case in the Israeli kibbutz, where everybody works on the farm, producing a very few products, most of them for internal comsumption, that is, for basic self-sufficiency. But the moment the kibbutz went into industrial production, as a good many did, it had to abandon the principle of primitive socialism on which it had been founded and under which everybody receives exactly the same. It had to become an employer.

The simple fact that the results of a modern institution always lie outside of itself and that, therefore, the economic rewards for its members always come from the outside and are not determined internally, inescapably leads to power and authority. In fact, it creates two power relationships. There is a power relationship between management and labor. But the various groups within the work force, while in a common power relationship to management, also stand in sharp and intense competition to each other with respect to their relative shares in the total "product" available for internal distribution.

If the last hundred years have taught us anything, however, it is that the distribution problem is generic rather than historical. It cannot be manipulated away. There has to be a decision how to divide the revenue available from the outside among the members inside the enterprise. The moment the institution, business, hospital, or other, produces more than a very few simple commodities, meant mostly for consumption within the group, the relationship between the individual input and the institution's output can no longer be determined "impersonally" or "scientifically." At this moment also, equality of reward becomes at once impossible — as Russians learned in the thirties, and as all other socialist experimenters, e.g., the Yugoslavs and the Chinese, have learned since.

There has then to be a redistribution and an authority to make the redistribution decisions. Redistribution, however, is in effect a political rather than an economic decision. It is influenced and restrained by a great number of forces: supply and demand, social convention, traditions, and so on. But in the last analysis, a decision by authority and a decision based on power structure and power relationships has to be made somehow by somebody. And this decision, no modern institution — and least of all, the business enterprise — can escape.

The Fallacy of the Dominant Dimension

These dimensions of working — the physiological, the psychological, the social, the economic, and the power dimension — are separate. Each can — and, indeed, should — be analyzed separately and independently. But they always exist together in the worker's relationship to work and job, fellow workers and management. They have to be managed together. Yet they do not pull in the same direction. The demands of one dimension are quite different from those of another.

The basic fallacy of our traditional approaches to working has been to proclaim one of these dimensions to be *the* dimension.

Marx — and most other economists — saw the economic dimension as dominating everything else. If only economic relationships could be changed, there would be no more alienation. Marxism became bankrupt when it became apparent that the "expropriation" of the "exploiters" did not fundamentally change the workers' situation and their alienation because it did no change in any way any of the other dimensions (and did not indeed even change the economic problem).

Elton Mayo, to give another and radically different example, saw the dominant dimension as the interpersonal relations within the work group, that is, in psychological and social aspects. And yet it is not only true that one cannot "hire a hand; the whole person always comes with it"; the work itself matters and affects group relations. And neither the economic nor the power dimension were seen by Mayo and his associates.

These dimensions stand in highly complex relationship to each other. They are a true "configuration" but one that changes rapidly as the worker's circumstances change.

The late Abraham H. Maslow, the father of humanist psychology, showed that human wants form a hierarchy. As a want of a lower order is being satisfied, it becomes less and less important, with a want of the next-highest order becoming more and more important. Maslow applied to human wants what might be called "marginal utility" — and his was a profound and lasting insight. Maslow put economic want at the bottom and the need for self-fulfillment at the top. But the order is not of first importance. What matters is the insight that wants are not absolute: the more one want is being satisfied, the less its satisfaction matters.

But what Maslow did not see is that a want changes in the act of being satisfied. As the economic want becomes satisfied, that is, as people no longer have to subordinate every other human need and human value to getting the next meal, it becomes less and less satisfying to obtain more economic rewards. This does not mean that economic rewards become less important. On the contrary, while the ability of the economic reward to provide a positive incentive diminishes, its capacity to create dissatisfaction, if disappointed, rapidly increases. In Herzberg's words, economic rewards cease to be "incentives" and become "hygiene factors." If not properly taken care of — that is, if there is dissatisfaction with the economic rewards — they become deterrents.

This, we now know, to be true of every one of Maslow's wants. As a want approaches satiety, its capacity to reward and with it its power as an incentive diminishes fast. But its capacity to deter, to create dissatisfaction, and to act as a disincentive rapidly increases.

Two vice-presidents in the same company whose salaries are only a few hundred dollars apart are equals economically. At that salary level, the income tax is so high as to make the pay differential meaningless. Yet the vice-president with the lower salary, no matter how good it is, may be eaten up by frustration and envy. The same applies all the way down the organization. Every trade-union leader knows that his biggest problem today is not absolute pay scales. It is the pay differentials among various kinds of workers within the union. There is no way of satisfying either the skilled worker who insists on receiving 20 percent more than the semiskilled worker, or the semiskilled worker. They are equally dissatisfied. If the pay differential is being narrowed, the skilled worker will feel deprived. And if the differential is not being narrowed, the semiskilled worker will feel deprived.

But also, contrary to what Maslow seemed to imply, the various dimensions of people at work change their character as they approach being satisfied. Pay, as we have just seen, becomes part of the social or psychological dimension rather than the economic one.

The opposite can also happen; power and status can become the basis for economic demands. In Yugoslav industry, for instance, the worker representatives on the workers' council, who hold positions of great social prestige and considerable power, almost immediately want more money as well. At the least, they want perquisites — housing, an office, a secretary, preferential prices at the company store, and so on — which are, as they see it, economic rewards befitting their new rank.

We need to know much more than we now know about the dimensions of working and about their relationships. We are dealing with a configuration likely to defy analysis.

Nevertheless, managers have to manage now. They have to find solutions — or at least accommodations — which will enable them to make work productive and the worker achieving. They have to understand what the demands are. They cannot expect to succeed by continuing the practices of the last two hundred years. They will have to develop new approaches, new principles, and new methods — and fast.

Worker and Working: Theories and Reality

Chapter 24

McGregor's Theory X and Theory Y
The Evidence for "Theory Y"
And Its Weaknesses
Maslow's Criticism
What Is the Manager's Reality?
Why "the Stick" No Longer Works
"Big Fear" and "Little Fears"
The Overly Potent "Carrot"
The Myth of Antimaterialism
The Demand for "Much More"
And Its Toxic Side Effects
From Master to Manager
Can We Replace Carrot and Stick?
Enlightened Psychological Despotism
Why It Will Not Work
What Then Can Work?

*S*ince the writings of the human-relations school first came to the notice of managers around World War II, there has been a proliferation of books, papers, and studies on motivation and achievement, on industrial psychology and industrial sociology, on interpersonal relations at work and on worker satisfaction. Indeed, the literature on managing worker and working, in quantity at least, exceeds the literature in any other management field, including even the management sciences and the computer.

The most widely read and most often quoted of these books is probably Douglas McGregor's *The Human Side of Enterprise,* with its Theory X and Theory Y. McGregor conducted no original research. He acknowledged freely in his book that he had developed no new ideas but had formulated the ideas of others. But his book fully deserves the wide attention it has received. McGregor powerfully presented fundamental choices for managing worker and working. His Theory X — the traditional approach to worker and working — assumes that people are lazy, dislike and shun work, have to be driven and need both carrot and stick. It assumes that most people are incapable of taking responsibility for themselves and have to be looked after. By contrast, Theory Y assumes that people have a psychological need to work and want achievement and responsibility. Theory X assumes immaturity. Theory Y assumes fundamentally that people want to be adults.

McGregor presented these two theories as alternatives and pretended to impartiality. Yet no reader ever doubted — or was meant to doubt — that McGregor himself believed wholeheartedly in Theory Y.

There is impressive evidence for Theory Y. On most jobs most workers, even those hostile to boss and organization, want to like their work and look for achievement. In most jobs even the most alienated workers manage to find something that gives them satisfaction.

This was first brought out in the late 1940s, when General Motors conducted a large-scale contest on "My Job and Why I Like It." Almost 190,000 workers wrote in and discussed their jobs — by far the larges sample of worker attitudes we have ever obtained. Indeed the response was so overwhelming that the material could never be fully exploited; very few results have ever been published. Very few of the GM workers were uncritical. But even fewer did not find something that made them like the job, did not mention some challenge in it, some achievement and satisfaction, some true motivation.

Equally convincing are the extensive studies of Frederick Herzberg on knowledge workers. Herzberg produced example after example that knowledge workers want achievement and will indeed *work* only if there is achievement in their job. Otherwise they will at best go through the motions.

Yet things are far less simple than McGregor's followers would make us — and themselves — believe. In the first place, we have learned that Theory Y is not by itself adequate. When I first propounded what McGregor later formulated and popularized as Theory Y, I laid great stress on the fact that this was not "permissive." On the contrary, I said that to manage worker and working by putting responsibility on the worker and by aiming at achievement made exceedingly high demands on both worker and manager. McGregor also saw this, though he did not stress it. (An oversight repaired in his posthumous *The Professional Manager*; McGraw-Hill, 1967.)

Maslow's Criticism

An ardent enthusiast for Theory Y, the late Abraham H. Maslow, pointed out that the demands are actually much higher than even I had seen. Maslow spent one year working closely with a small company in Southern California which at the time tried to practice Theory Y. Maslow pointed out that the demand for responsibility and achievement may well go far beyond what any but the strong and healthy can take. He sharply criticized me and McGregor for "inhumanity" to the weak, the vulnerable, the damaged, who are unable to take on the responsibility and self-discipline which Theory Y demands. Even the strong and healthy, Maslow concluded, need the security of order and direction; and the weak need protection against the burden of responsibility. The world is not, Maslow concluded, peopled by adults. It has its full share of the permanently immature.

Maslow, although always a strong advocate of Theory Y, concluded that it is not enough to remove restraints. One has to *replace* the security of Theory X and the certainty it gives by another but different structure of security and certainty. There is need to provide by different means what commands and penalties do under Theory X. Theory Y, in other words, has to go far beyond Theory X. It cannot simply be substituted for it.

This is an important insight. And it is clearly proven by all our experience with Theory Y.

In fact, one of McGregor's closest friends and disciples proved Maslow's point. Warren Bennis, himself a distinguished industrial psychologist (and the editor of McGregor's posthumous book, *The Professional Manager*) attempted in the late sixties to convert the University of Buffalo, in upstate New York, from an old, tired, and rundown school into a major, first-rate university. His approach and that of his colleagues was clearly based on Theory Y — but without giving structure, direction, and security. The result was tremendous excitement but also total failure. Instead of achievement, there was lack of direction, lack of objectives, lack of controls, and frustration — as Bennis (who later became president of the University of Cincinnati) himself recounts.

One conclusion from Maslow's work is that Theory Y is not permissive, as so many of its advocates believe. It is not freedom from restraint. It is not, as its critics contend, indulging or coddling the worker. It is a stern taskmaster, sterner in many ways than the Theory X which it replaces. It has to achieve what Theory X achieved, and then do a good deal more — or else it will prove too great a burden and will make demands human beings cannot meet.

It has now become clear that Theory X and Theory Y are not, as McGregor maintained, *theories about human nature* (a position never shared by me, by the way). Whether we will ever know enough about human nature to have any theories about it remains to be seen. But so far, the evidence is not at all conclusive.

Everybody knows that there are undoubtedly lazy people as there are undoubtedly energetic ones. Far more important, however, is that ordinary, everyday experience teaches us that the same people react quite differently to different circumstances. They may be lazy and resist work to the point of sabotaging it in one situation. They may be motivated to achievement in another one. It is clearly not human nature nor personality structure that is at issue. Or at the very least, there are different human natures which behave differently under different conditions.

Modern American slang talks of being "turned on" or "turned off" by an assignment, a teacher, a job, or a boss. These terms have been criticized as dehumanizing. They refer to people, it is being said, as if they were electrical appliances. But everyday experience shows that this is exactly how a great many people behave. They react rather than act. The motivation, the drive, the impulse lie outside of them.

But this is not compatible with either Theory X or Theory Y. It implies that it is not human nature but the structure of job and work that, in effect, determines how people will act and what management they will require.

We also now know that individuals can acquire the habit of achievement but can also acquire the habit of defeat. This again is not compatible with either the Theory X or the Theory Y of human nature.

The best-known work in this area has been done by David C. McClelland at Harvard. McClelland has taken the position that the desire to achieve is conditioned largely by culture and by experiences, both of which can be changed even in a nonachieving culture such as that of the Indian caste system. The most extensive study of actual worker behavior in large-scale industry, the work which the Canadian-English psychiatrist Elliott Jacques conducted for many years at the Glacier Metal Company in London (together with the company's chief executive, Wilfred Brown), supports the same conclusion.

What Is the Manager's Reality?

The debate over the scientific validity of Theory X versus Theory Y is, therefore, largely a sham battle. The question the manager needs to ask is not "which theory of human nature is right?" The question is "What is the reality of *my* situation and how can I discharge *my* task of managing worker and working in today's situation?"

The basic fact — unpalatable but inescapable — is that the traditional Theory X approach to managing, that is, the carrot-and-stick way, no longer works. In developed countries, it does not even work for manual workers, and nowhere can it work for knowledge workers. The stick is no longer available to the manager, and the carrot is today becoming less and less of an incentive.

The stick of the traditional approach to managing worker and working was hunger and fear. Traditionally, all but a handful of people in every society lived at the very margin of subsistence and in imminent threat of starvation. One bad harvest was enough to force an Indian or Chinese peasant to sell his daughters into prostitution. One bad harvest was enough for him to lose the tiny plot of land which was all that stood between him and beggary. Now, even in only moderately affluent countries, there is an economic floor well above subsistence level, even for the very poor. Workers know today, in every developed country, that losing a job doesn't mean starvation. Workers who suddenly become unemployed may have to do without a lot of things they would like to have, but they can survive.

Marx's *Lumpenproletariat*, that is, the unemployables, still exist even in some very rich countries. But Marx's proletariat has disappeared — and with it the stick of Theory X.

Even where fear exists, it has largely ceased to motivate. Instead of motivation, fear is becoming a demotivator. One reason for this is the spread of education, the other reason is the emergence of the society of organization. The spread of education makes people employable. It gives them a wider horizon. Even poorly educated people in today's society now know of opportunities. In a society of organizations it is possible to gain access to a new job. In a society of organizations there is lateral mobility. Losing one's job is still unpleasant. But it is no longer catastrophe.

The English tenant farmer, no matter how accomplished or industrious, who was evicted by his landlord became a "sturdy beggar." There was no other employment for him, except an occasional day of work as a casual laborer helping out with the harvest. Losing one's job was more than a life sentence; it usually condemned one's children and grandchildren. It made an unemployed person an outcast. Now anyone who loses a job registers with the employment exchange for another one. Even at the depth of a serious depression today, – e.g., the American recession of 1974–1976 – long term unemployment, that is, unemployment beyond the term of unemployment insurance payments, was quite rare for adult male heads of households.

In addition there is rising employment security which protects people in their jobs. It takes many forms. In Sweden a three-partite board guarantees another job and provides for training and support between jobs for anyone who loses a job. In most European (and Latin American) countries, there are legal restrictions on firing. There are seniority provisions which make job security into a right. In the United States, increasingly, income, if not employment, is maintained for long periods through such contractual provisions as supplemental employment compensation.

All developed countries are moving toward the system of the modern university, where a faculty member after a few years of service acquires tenure, which all but completely commits the university to a job for the teacher. At the same time, the faculty member has unlimited mobility and can freely move from one university position to another.

Japan has lifetime employment, which binds both employer and worker. Fear of being fired, therefore, does not exist in Japan, at least not in the "modern" sector. This is a major factor in Japan's economic achievement.

The Japanese example also shows that the more fear disappears as a stick, the more counterproductive remnants of fear become. The Japanese worker knows that he is tied to an employer and is unlikely to find other employment if he loses his present job. This makes him dedicated to the welfare of the organization that employs him. But it also makes him resent bitterly any stuctural change in the economy that might threaten the industry or occupation that employs him – the reason, for instance, for the extremely bad labor relations on the Japanese Railroads. The Japanese worker's inability to move also makes him defenseless against the pressure to conform exerted by the organization. This is increasingly unacceptable to the young educated people. Indeed, while still expecting the security of lifetime employment, they increasingly demand for themselves the right to move to another employer. Rousseau pointed out two hundred years ago that the "right to emigrate" is the ultimate safeguard of personal liberty.

Japan, it is reasonable to predict, will move toward a system under which the worker has guarantees of income and job, but also mobility.

Modern behavioral psychology has demonstrated that great fear coerces, while remnants of fear cause only resentment and resistance. Fear in all developed countries has lost its coercive power. The lesser fears that still remain do not motivate. They destroy motivation — precisely because they lack full power and full credibility.

"Big Fear" and "Little Fears"

The "big fear" still motivates where it is truly credible, as is shown by the quite unexpected success which a new approach to "curing" alcoholism has had. Everybody has "known" that the true alcoholics cannot stop drinking until they are completely down and out, if then. But a good many employers are now finding that a very large percentage of alcoholic workers do indeed stop drinking — permanently — if told in unequivocal language that they will otherwise be fired and that potential new employers will be told of their problem, so that they are unlikely to find another job.

But, save in such exceptional cases as the alcoholics who know that they are rapidly becoming unemployable, the big stick, the horrible fear which drove workers yesterday, is no longer available to today's manager in the developed countries, whether the manager likes it or not. It is extremely foolish to try to depend on "little sticks," that is, whatever remnants of fear are still available. To be sure, any organization needs disciplinary devices, but their role and purpose is to take care of marginal friction. They cannot provide the drive. If misused to drive, disciplinary devices can cause only resentment and resistance. They can only demotivate.

The Overly Potent Carrot

The carrot of material rewards has not, like the stick of fear, lost its potency. On the contrary, it has become so potent that it must be used with great caution. It has become too potent to be a dependable tool.

The Sunday issue of every newspaper these days contains an article by a learned sociologist or philosopher reporting that people are turning away from material satisfactions. On the front page of the same paper, Sundays *and* weekdays, there is then always a story that this or that group of workers — teachers or electricians, newspaper reporters or firefighters, salesclerks or stevedores — have presented the biggest wage demand ever or have obtained the biggest wage raise ever.

When the youthful rebels against material civilization half a century ago went back to nature, all they needed was a tent or a sleeping bag. These days, turning one's back on material civilization seems to require an $8,000 camper-truck. The youthful rebels of the 1920s played their back-to-nature songs on a ukulele; today we need an electronic guitar to express our rejection of technology. The same European intellectuals who so vocally inveigh against American materialism use the fees they get for their lectures and articles for such nonmaterial satisfactions as a sports car, an airplane trip to a plush resort, or the purchase of a villa on a Mediterranean beach.

There is not one shred of evidence for the alleged turning away from material rewards. On the contrary, affluence means that everybody believes that material rewards are and should be within easy reach. Samuel Gompers, the long-time head of the American labor movement, used to define the aims of a labor union in one word: "more." He would surely have to change this today to "much more." Antimaterialism is a myth, no matter how much it is extolled. So far, at least, the reality is tremendous and steadily rising material expectations, i.e., expectations for more goods and services.

This is not confined to the capitalist world. It has become the massive reality of communist societies as well. In the thirties Stalin did not hesitate to cut back drastically on the people's diet when Russia had a bad harvest. His successors, in 1972, faced by a much less poor harvest, instead dipped deeply into Russia's strategic gold reserves to buy grain from the archenemy, the United States. Mao, in the years of the Great Cultural Revolution in the sixties, thundered against "economism," i.e., against material incentives and rewards. By the early seventies the emphasis in China had shifted to heavy stress on such "capitalist" incentives as bicycles and sewing machines as rewards for performance.

The demand for much more is obviously going to run ultimately into the finite limitations of the earth's resources and the need to preserve the environment. What we experience today may therefore indeed be the final frenzied agony of the "material civilization." But, at least for the foreseeable future, this will mean above all an even faster shift from goods to services as carriers of satisfaction, and with it, from material-intensive to labor-intensive (and especially knowledge-labor-intensive) wants and purchases. It is most unlikely, for the foreseeable future, to alter the basic characteristics. On the contrary; that rising raw-material prices and ecology costs will push up the cost of goods is almost certain to add fuel to the fire of demands for more, much more, monetary rewards.

It is precisely the rising level of material expectations that makes the carrot of material rewards less and less effective as a motivating force and as a managerial tool.

The increment of material rewards capable of motivating people to work has to become larger. As people get more they do not become more satisfied with a little more, let alone with less. They expect much more. This is, of course, one of the major causes of the relentless inflationary pressures that besiege every major economy today. Whereas a 5 percent wage boost was, a short few years ago, a major satisfaction, the teamsters — or the teachers or the physicians — now demand 40 percent and expect 20 percent.

This may be a manifestation of Maslow's rule that the closer a need comes to being satisfied, the larger an increment of additional gratification will be required to produce the same satisfaction. But the demand for more and much more of material satisfaction has also been accompanied by a change in values that does not fit Maslow's scheme at all. Economic incentives are becoming rights rather than rewards. Merit raises are always introduced as rewards for exceptional performance. In no time at all they become a right. To deny a merit raise or to grant only a small one becomes punishment. The same is true of Japan's semiannual bonus.

But whatever the explanation, the result of the increasing demand for material rewards is rapidly destroying their usefulness as incentives and managerial tools. The manager must try to deemphasize the role of material rewards rather than use them as a carrot. If only very large — and steadily larger — increments have an incentive effect, then using material incentives becomes self-defeating. The expected result in terms of motivation will be obtained, but the cost will be so high as to exceed the benefits. The cost will eat up the additional productivity. This is, of course, what has been happening with respect to material incentives for managers (e.g., stock options or extra compensation plans) as well as with respect to material incentives for all other classes of workers.

That inflation has become the central problem of the developed economies is, in terms of traditional or Keynesian economic theory, pure paradox. Inflation should not occur under conditions of high productive capacity and high productivity. Instead it is the norm. The reason is the totally unexpected size of economic appetites, the totally unexpected potency of material rewards. The result, however, is that to enable the economy, society, and enterprise to survive, managers must try to curb and to contain economic incentives rather than rely on them. The economic incentive that has a true carrot effect is "too much." Only economic rewards that fall well below the threshold of motivational effectiveness are likely to be defensible economically and in terms of productivity and contribution.

This also means that the social side effects of the carrot are reaching toxic proportions. A potent medicine always has side effects; and the larger the dosage, the greater the side effects. Material incentives and rewards is a very strong medicine indeed, and becoming more potent. It therefore is bound to have potent side effects, which become more pronounced and more dangerous as the dosage required for effectiveness increases. In particular the more total income goes up, the more powerful does dissatisfaction over relative compensation become. As all our studies show — beginning with the GM contest "My Job" in the late forties — there is no more powerful disincentive, no more effective bar to motivation, than dissatisfaction over one's own pay compared to that of one's peers. Once people's incomes rise above the subsistence level, dissatisfaction with relative incomes is a far more powerful sentiment than dissatisfaction with one's absolute income. The "sense of injustice," as Edmond Cahn, the American legal philosopher, convincingly argued, is deeply ingrained in people. Nothing is as likely to offend the sense of injustice as dissatisfaction with relative economic rewards in an organization. An organization is a redistributive economy; relative economic rewards are therefore power and status decisions on the *worth* of a person or a group.

Reliance on the carrot of economic rewards therefore runs the risk of alienating both the recipient and all others. It runs the risk of dividing the group against itself while uniting it against the system, i.e., against the employing institution and its management.

Clearly no deemphasis of material rewards is likely. Managers face instead the tremendous challenge of finding some means to relate the growing emphasis on "much more" to economic reality, i.e., to productivity and profitability. Material rewards are too potent to be relied on as the main positive motivator. This can only mean growing inflationary pressures — and growing dissatisfaction.

This applies to managers as well as to blue-collar workers. There is little doubt that managerial carrots have grown into seven-course Victorian meals, e.g., from small bonuses to massive stock option plans. With respect to managerial incentives, we are moving from more to much more. At the same time there is growing evidence that inequalities in managerial incentives — real or fancied — are more demotivating than the rewards themselves satisfy and motivate.

The limitations of the effectiveness of carrot and stick apply with particular force to two groups in the work force: the new breed of manual workers, and knowledge workers.

In managing manual workers, the manager in the developed country more and more has to deal with men (and to a lesser extent with women) who start out as "losers," feel rejected, feel already defeated. These are people who have been driven all their lives and yet have not achieved. But losers always learn one thing, and that to perfection: resistance against being driven. They may not be able to achieve, but they know how to sabotage.

The best text on this is not a learned study by a professor of psychology but a best-selling humorous novel of the twenties, *The Good Soldier Schweik,* by the Czech writer Jaroslav Hasek. Schweik, one of the world's defeated, the archetypal dropout, single-handedly stultifies and frustrates the whole Theory X apparatus of the mighty army of a great power, pre-World War I Austria-Hungary. He does nothing overt. He knows how to sabotage.

To drive the new breed of manual workers therefore will not be successful. Hunger and fear no longer dominate them as they did their grandparents. But their very failure has made them impervious to pressures.

The knowledge worker will not produce if managed under Theory X. Knowledge has to be self-directed and has to take responsibility.

Fear is altogether incompatible with the production of knowledge. It may produce efforts and anxieties. It will not produce results. And fear inhibits learning, a basic finding of modern behavioral psychology. Rewards and reaffirmation will produce learning. In anything that has to do with knowledge, fear will produce only resistance.

Theory X assumes a "master." But in a society of organizations there are no masters. The manager is not a master. The manager is at the same time a superior, and a fellow employee. For the first time in history there is a society which lacks masters.

This is not the case in communist societies, which have assiduously worked at replacing the old masters with new masters. The role of the Communist party in a communist state is to be a master. It is in crisis precisely because even under communism a modern society becomes a society of organizations and as such requires managers and cannot tolerate masters.

The manager, not being a master, lacks both the master's authority and the master's credibility. The master's power is independent of the support he receives, either from his servants or from society around him. One can kill a master, but one cannot oust him. But, as the sixties amply showed, e.g., in the case of countless university presidents, even the chief executive of an organization can be ousted, precisely because he is a fellow employee. The authority he exercises is not his own, and cannot survive a challenge. Even in communist societies where managers have much more power and much more income as a rule, they are no longer "masters." That role is being played by the Communist party, its functionaries, secretaries, and commissars.

In terms of the ancient law of master and servant, the chief executive officer of the largest corporation is a fellow servant. Others may be subordinate in rank, but they are equal in law. They are not the chief executive's servants, they are his fellow workers.

This is much more than a semantic shift. It means that neither stick nor carrot will actually work if used by a manager, no matter how well they used to work for the master of old.

Can We Replace Carrot and Stick?

Can we replace the carrot of monetary rewards and the stick of fear with a new carrot and a new stick appropriate to the new managerial reality?

After all, carrot and stick have worked for an amazingly long time. One does not lightly toss out the tradition of the ages. Over the millennia during which worker and working have been managed, society has changed fundamentally. Yet managing worker and working has shown amazing continuity. The Theory X principles that were applied to managing worker and working in the building of the great pyramids of Egypt still inform the organization of worker and working in the modern mass-production plant.

Henry Ford's best-known epigram is "History is bunk." Ford was a bold innovator in organizing work, in marketing, and in economics, but when it came to managing worker and working he was completely the prisoner of history and a traditionalist.

The traditional way of managing working and worker cuts across all of man's cultures. There is no great difference between West and East, between pagan antiquity and Christendom, between China and the Occident, between Inca Peru and Mogul India. Nor does the organization of society itself seem to make much difference.

In that respect the Marxist analysis has altogether failed. The factory and office in Soviet Russia or in the Soviet satellites in Europe are organized no differently from the wicked capitalist West. Nor, all evidence clearly shows, is the worker any more achieving or the bosses any less the bosses. The same applies to the far more imaginative Yugoslav experiment of direct worker control of individual businesses, to direct worker ownership, to ownership by a cooperative, and so on.

We therefore know Theory X management. What to put in its place is — or so it seems — largely guesswork and speculation. Surely it would be the better part of wisdom to try to maintain the essence of Theory X by substituting "modern" drives for the old driving force of fear and money. What we need, one might argue, is to find the organizational equivalent to the gasoline engine which replaced the horse — but to keep the wheeled vehicle.

Not only managers ask this question. The labor unions are perhaps even more eager to keep the Theory X structure. The unions, after all, have a stake in the coercive relationship between master and servant of Theory X; if there were no master, what, indeed, would the union's role be? Also labor leaders derive their pride and sense of mission from opposition to Theory X, know how to behave under it, and have its rhetoric down pat.

When the younger workers in some General Motors plants began to talk about humanizing the assembly line, the greatest resistance did not come from General Motors management. It came from the United Automobile Workers' leadership, which insisted on talking about money, pensions, hours off, coffee breaks — and so on. The UAW leaders, in other words, insisted, against their own members, on maintaining and even strengthening a Theory X management on the part of the company.

To look for a new set of drives to take the place of the old carrot and stick seems not only rational but tempting. Such replacement drives are indeed being offered managers in the form of a new "enlightened psychological despotism."

Most, if not all, of the recent writers on industrial psychology profess allegiance to

Theory Y. They use terms like "self-fulfillment," "creativity," and "the whole person." But what they talk and write about is control through psychological manipulation. They are led to this by their basic assumptions, which are precisely the Theory X assumptions: people are weak, sick and incapable of looking after themselves. They are full of fears anxieties, neuroses, inhibitions. Essentially people do not want to achieve but want to fail. They therefore want to be controlled — not by fear of hunger and incentive of material rewards but through their fear of psychological alienation and the incentive of "psychological security."

I know that I am oversimplifying. I know that I am lumping under one heading half a dozen different approaches. But they all share the same basic assumptions, those of Theory X, and they all lead to the same conclusions. Psychological control by the superior, the manager, is "unselfish" and in the worker's own interest. By becoming the workers' psychological servant, however, the manager retains control as their "boss."

This is "enlightened" whereas the old carrot-and-stick approach may be condemned as crassly coercive (and is condemned as such by the psychologists). But it is despotism nonetheless. Under this new psychological dispensation, persuasion replaces command. Those unconvinced by persuasion would presumably be deemed sick, immature, or in need of psychotherapy to become adjusted. Psychological manipulation replaces the carrot of financial rewards; and empathy, i.e., the exploitation of individual fears, anxieties, and personality needs, replaces the old fear of being punished or of losing one's job. This is strikingly similar to the eighteenth-century philosopher's theory of the enlightened despot. As in modern organization today, affluence and education — in this case, the affluence and rising education of the middle class — threatened to deprive the sovereign of his carrot and stick. The philosopher's enlightened despot was going to maintain absolutism by replacing the old means with persuasion, reason, and enlightenment — all in the interest of the subjects, of course.

Psychological despotism, whether enlightened or not, is gross misuse of psychology. The main purpose of psychology is to acquire insight into, and mastery of, oneself. Not for nothing were what we now call the behavioral sciences originally called the moral sciences and "Know thyself" their main precept. To use psychology to control, dominate, and manipulate others is self-destructive abuse of knowledge. It is also a particularly repugnant form of tyranny. The master of old was content to control the slave's body.

We are concerned, however, here neither with the proper use of psychology nor with morality. But can the Theory X structure be maintained through psychological despotism? Can psychological despotism work?

Psychological despotism should have tremendous attraction for managers. It promises them that they can continue to behave as they have always done. All they need is to acquire a new vocabulary. It flatters them. And yet managers, while avidly reading the psychology books and attending psychological workshops, are shying away from trying the new psychological Theory X.

Managers show sound instincts in being leery. Psychological despotism cannot work any more than enlightened despotism worked in the political sphere two hundred years ago — and for the same reason. *It requires universal genius on the part of the ruler.*

Managers, if one listens to the psychologists, will have to have insight into all kinds of people. They will have to be in command of all kinds of psychological techniques. They will have to have empathy for all their subordinates. They will have to understand an infinity of individual personality structures, individual psychological needs, and individual psychological problems. They will, in other words, have to be omniscient. But most managers find it hard enough to know all they need to know about their own immediate area of expertise, be it heat-treating or cost accounting or scheduling.

And to expect any large number of people to have "charisma" — whatever the term might mean — is an absurdity. This particular quality is reserved for the very few.

Managers should indeed know more about human beings. They should at least know that human beings behave like human beings, and what that implies. Above all, like most of us, managers need to know much more about themselves than they do; for most managers are action-focused rather than introspective. And yet, any manager, no matter how many psychology seminars he or she has attended, who attempts to put psychological despotism into practice will very rapidly become its first casualty. This manager will immediately blunder. This manager will impair performance.

The work relationship has to be based on mutual respect. Psychological despotism is basically contemptuous — far more contemptuous than the traditional Theory X. It does not assume that people are lazy and resist work, but it assumes that the manager is healthy while everybody else is sick. It assumes that the manager is strong while everybody else is weak. It assumes that the manager knows while everybody else is ignorant. It assumes that the manager is right, whereas everybody else is stupid. These are the assumptions of foolish arrogance.

Above all, the manager-psychologists will undermine their own authority. There is, to be sure, need for psychological insight, help, counsel. There is need for the healer of souls and the comforter of the afflicted. But the relationship of healer and patient and that of superior to subordinate are different relationships and mutually exclusive. They both have their own integrity. The integrity of the healers is in their subordination to a patient's welfare. The integrity of the managers is in their subordination to the requirements of a common task. In both relationships there is need for authority; but each has a different ground of authority. A manager who pretends that the personal needs of the subordinate for, e.g., affection, rather than the objective needs of the task, determine what should be done, would not only be a poor manager; no one would — or should — believe that manager. All that managers like this do is destroy the integrity of the relationship and with it the respect for their person and their function.

Enlightened psychological despotism with its call for an unlimited supply of universal geniuses for managerial positions and its confusion between the healer's and the manager's authority and role is not going to deliver what it promises: to maintain Theory X while pretending to replace it.

But what then *can* work?

It is not simply McGregor's Theory X. The manager must indeed assume with Theory Y that there are at least a substantial number of people in the work force who want to achieve. Otherwise there is little hope. Fortunately the evidence strongly supports this assumption. Managers must further accept it as their job to make worker and working achieving. They must be willing, as a result, to accept high demands on themselves, their seriousness, and their competence. But managers cannot assume, as Theory Y does, that people will work to achieve if only they are given the opportunity to do so. More is needed — much more — to make even the strong and healthy accept the burden of responsibility. The structure we need cannot depend on driving the worker; neither carrot nor stick is dependable any more. But the structure must also provide substitutes to the weak — and not only to them — for Theory X's security of command and of being looked after.

How to Be an Employee

Chapter 25

*A Society of Employees Where There Is No Information on How to Be
   an Employee*
The Basic Skill: Communication
What Kind of Employee?
*Four Questions: Is Security for You? Start at Bottom or Top? Big
   Company or Small? Specialist or Generalist?*
The Importance of Being Fired
When to Quit
Who Gets Promoted
Your Life Off the Job

*M*ost workers today are employees and will be all their working lives, working for somebody else and for a pay check.

Ours has become a society of employees. A hundred years ago only one out of every five Americans at work was employed, that is, worked for somebody else. Today the ratio is reversed, only one out of five is self-employed. And where fifty years ago "being employed" meant working as a factory laborer or as a farmhand, the employee of today is increasingly a middle-class person with a substantial formal education, holding a professional or management job requiring intellectual and technical skills. Indeed, two things have characterized American society during these last fifty years: the middle and upper classes have become employees; and middle-class and upper-class employees have been the fastest-growing groups in our working population — growing so fast that the industrial worker, that oldest child of the Industrial Revolution, has been losing in numerical importance despite the expansion of industrial production.

This is one of the most profound social changes any country has ever undergone. It is, however, a perhaps even greater change for the young people about to start. Whatever they do, in all likelihood they will do it as employees; wherever they aim, they will have to try to reach it through being employees.

Yet you will find little if anything written on what it is to be an employee. You can find a great deal of very dubious advice on how to get a job or how to get a promotion. You can also find a good deal on work in a chosen field, whether it be metallurgy or salesmanship, the machinist's trade or bookkeeping. Every one of these trades requires different skills, sets different standards, and requires a different preparation. Yet they all have employeeship in common. And increasingly, especially in the large business or in government, employeeship is more important to success than the special professional knowledge or skill. Certainly more people fail because they do not know the requirements of being an employee than because they do not adequately possess the skills of their trade; the higher you climb the ladder, the more you get into administrative or executive work, the greater the emphasis on ability to work within the organization rather than on technical competence or professional knowledge.

Being an employee is thus the one common characteristic of most careers today. The special profession or skill is visible and clearly defined; and a well-laid-out sequence of courses, degrees, and jobs leads into it. But being an employee is the foundation. And it is much more difficult to prepare for it. Yet there is no recorded information on the art of being an employee.

The Basic Skill: Communication

The first question we might ask is: what can you learn that will help you in being an employee? The schools teach a great many things of value to the future accountant, the future doctor, or the future electrician. Do they also teach anything of value to the future employee? The answer is: "Yes — they teach the one thing that it is perhaps most valuable for the future employee to know. But very few students bother to learn it."

This one basic skill is the ability to organize and express ideas in writing and in speaking.

As an employee you work with and through other people. This means that your success as an employee — and I am talking of much more here than getting promoted — will depend on your ability to communicate with people and to present your own thoughts and ideas to them so they will both understand what you are driving at and be persuaded. The letter, the report or memorandum, the ten-minute spoken "presentation" to a committee are basic tools of the employee.

If you work as a hamburger clerk in a fast food chain you will, of course, not need much skill in expressing yourself to be effective. If you work on a machine your ability to express yourself will be of little importance. But as soon as you move one step up from the bottom, your effectiveness depends on your ability to reach others through the spoken or the written word. And the further away your job is from manual work, the larger the organization of which you are an employee, the more important it will be that you know how to convey your thoughts in writing or speaking. In the very large organization, whether it is the government, the large business corporation, or the Army, this ability to express yourself is perhaps the most important of all the skills you can possess.

Of course, skill in expression is not enough by itself. You must have something to say in the first place. The popular picture of the engineer, for instance, is someone who works with a calculator, drawing board, and compass. And engineering students reflect this picture in their attitude toward the written word as something quite irrelevant to their jobs. But the effectiveness of engineers — and with it their usefulness — depends as much on their ability to make other people understand their work as it does on the quality of the work itself.

Expressing one's thoughts is one skill that the school can really teach, especially to people born without natural writing or speaking talent. Many other skills can be learned later — in this country there are literally thousands of places that offer training to adult people at work. But the foundations for skill in expression have to be laid early: an interest in and an ear for language; experience in organizing ideas and data, in brushing aside the irrelevant, in wedding outward form and inner content into one structure; and above all, the habit of verbal expression. If you do not lay these foundations during your school years, you may never have an opportunity again.

You should take courses in the writing of poetry and the writing of short stories. Most of you won't become poets or short-story writers — far from it. But these two courses offer the easiest way to obtain some skill in expression. They force you to be economical with language. They force you to organize thought. They demand of you that you give meaning to every word. They train the ear for language, its meaning, its precision, its overtones — and its pitfalls. Above all they force you to write.

I know very well that the typical employer does not understand this and may look with suspicion on a young college graduate who has majored, let us say, in short-story writing. But the same employer will hire college graduates and complain — with good reason — that they do not know how to write a simple report, do not know how to tell a simple story, and are in fact virtually illiterate. And the employer will conclude — rightly — that the young graduates are not really effective, and certainly not employees who are likely to go very far.

What Kind of Employee?

The next question to ask is: what kind of employee should you be? Pay no attention to what other people tell you. This is one question only you can answer. It involves a choice in four areas — a choice you alone can make, and one you cannot easily duck. But to make the choice you must first have tested yourself in the world of jobs for some time.

Here are the four decisions — first in brief outline, then in more detail:

1. Do you belong in a job calling primarily for faithfulness in the performance of routine work and promising security? Or do you belong in a job that offers a challenge

to imagination and ingenuity — with the attendant penalty for failure?

2. Do you belong in a large organization or in a small organization? Do you work better through channels or through direct contacts? Do you enjoy more being a small cog in a big and powerful machine or a big wheel in a small machine?

3. Should you start at the bottom and try to work your way up, or should you try to start near the top? On the lowest rung of the promotional ladder, with its solid and safe footing but also with a very long climb ahead? Or on the aerial trapeze of "a management trainee," or some staff position close to management?

4. Finally, are you going to be more effective and happy as a specialist or as a "generalist," that is, in an administrative job?

Let me spell out what each of these four decisions involves.

Is "Security" for You?

The decision between secure routine work and insecure work challenging the imagination and ingenuity is the one decision most people find easiest to make. You know very soon what kind of person you are. Do you find real satisfaction in the precision, order, and system of a clearly laid-out job? Do you prefer the security not only of knowing what your work is today and what it is going to be tomorrow, but also security in your job, in your relationship to the people above, below, and next to you, and economic security? Or are you one of those people who tend to grow impatient with anything that looks like a "routine" job? These people are usually able to live in a confused situation in which their relations to the people around them are neither clear nor stable. They tend to pay less attention to economic security and find it not too upsetting to change jobs.

There is, of course, no such black-and-white distinction between people. The person who can do only painstaking detail work and has no imagination is not much good for anything. Neither is the self-styled "genius" who has nothing but grandiose ideas and no capacity for rigorous application to detail. But in practically everybody I have ever met there is a decided leaning one way or the other.

The difference is one of basic personality. It is not too much affected by a person's experiences; everyone is likely to be born with the one or the other. The need for economic security is often as not an outgrowth of a need for psychological security rather than a phenomenon of its own. But precisely because the difference is one of basic temperament, the analysis of what kind of temperament you possess is so vital. A man or woman might be happy in work for which they have little *aptitude*; they might be quite successful in it. But they can be neither happy nor successful in a job for which they are *temperamentally* unfitted.

In the large organization especially there are not enough job opportunities for young people who need challenge and risk. Jobs in which there is greater emphasis on conscientious performance of well-organized duties rather than on imagination — especially for the beginner — are to be found, for instance, in the inside jobs in banking or insurance, which normally offer great job security but not rapid promotion or large pay. The same is true of most government work, of the railroad industry, particularly in the clerical and engineering branches, and of most public utilities. The bookkeeping and accounting areas, especially in the larger companies, are generally of this type too — though a successful comptroller is an accountant with great management and business imagination.

At the other extreme are such areas as buying, selling, and advertising, in which the emphasis is on adaptability, on imagination, and on a desire to do new and different things. In those areas, by and large, there is little security, either personal or economic. The rewards, however, are high and come more rapidly. Major premium on imagination — though of a different kind and coupled with dogged persistance on details — prevails in most research and engineering work. Jobs in production, as supervisor or executive, also demand much adaptability and imagination.

Contrary to popular belief, very small business requires, above all, close attention to daily routine. Running a neighborhood drugstore or a small grocery, or being a toy jobber, is largely attention to details. But in very small business there is also room for quite a few people of the other personality type — the innovator or imaginer. If successful, a person of this type soon ceases to be in a very small business. For the real innovator there is, still, no more promisisng opportunity in this country than that of building a large out of a very small business.

Big Company or Small?

Almost as important is the decision between working for a large and for a small organization. The difference is perhaps not so great as that between the secure, routine job and the insecure, imaginative job; but the wrong decision can be equally serious.

There are two basic differences between the large and the small enterprise. In the small enterprise you operate primarily through personal contacts. In the large enterprise you have established "policies," "channels" of organization, and fairly rigid procedures. In the small enterprise you have, moreover, immediate effectiveness in a very small area. You can see the effect of your work and of your decisions right away, once you are a little bit above the ground floor. In the large enterprise even the person at the top is only a cog in a big machine. To be sure, his or her actions affect a much greater area than the actions and decisions of the person in the small organization, but his or her effectiveness is remote, indirect, and elusive. In a small and even in a middle-sized business you are normally exposed to all kinds of experiences, and expected to do a great many things without too much help and guidance. In the large organization you are normally taught one thing thoroughly. In the small one the danger is of becoming a jack-of-all-trades and master of none. In the large one it is of becoming the person who knows more and more about less and less.

There is one other important thing to consider: Do you derive a deep sense of satisfaction from being a member of a well-known organization — General Motors, the Bell Telephone System, the Government? Or is it more important to you to be a well-known and important figure within your own small pond? There is a basic difference between the satisfaction that comes from being a member of a large, powerful, and generally known organization, and the one that comes from being a member of a family; between impersonal grandeur and personal — often much too personal — intimacy; between life in a small cubicle on the top floor of a skyscraper and life in a crossroads gas station.

Start at the Bottom, or...?

You may well think it absurd to say that anyone has a choice between beginning at the bottom and beginning near the top. And indeed I do not mean that you have any choice between a beginner's job and, let us say, a vice presidency at General Electric. But you do have a choice between a position at the bottom of the hierarchy and a staff position that is outside the hierarchy but in view of the top. It is an important choice.

In every organization, even the smallest, there are positions that, while subordinate, modestly paid, and usually filled with young and beginning employees, nonetheless are not at the bottom. There are positions as assistant to one of the bosses; there are positions as private secretary; there are liaison positions for various departments; and there are positions in staff capacities, in industrial engineering, in cost accounting, in personnel, etc. Every one of these gives a view of the whole rather than of only one small area. Every one of them normally brings the holder into the deliberations and discussions of the people at the top, if only as a silent audience or perhaps only as an errand boy. Every one of these positions is a position "near the top," however humble and badly paid it may be.

On the other hand, the great majority of beginner's jobs are at the bottom, where you begin in a department or in a line of work in the lowest-paid and simplest function, and where you are expected to work your way up as you acquire more skill and more judgment.

Different people belong in these two kinds of jobs. In the first place, the job "near the top" is insecure. You are exposed to public view. Your position is ambiguous; by yourself you are a nobody — but you reflect the boss's status; in a relatively short time you may even speak for the boss. You may have real power and influence. In today's business and government organization the hand that writes the memo rules the committee; and the young staffer usually writes the memos, or at least the first draft. But for that very reason everybody is jealous of you. You are a youngster who has been admitted to the company of higher ups, and is therefore expected to show unusual ability and above all unusual discretion and judgment. Good performance in such a position is often the key to rapid advancement. But to fall down may mean the end of all hopes of ever getting anywhere within the organization.

At the bottom, on the other hand, there are very few opportunities for making serious mistakes. You are amply protected by the whole apparatus of authority. The job itself is normally simple, requiring little judgment, discretion, or initiative. Even excellent performance in such a job is unlikely to speed promotion. But one also has to fall down in a rather spectacular fashion for it to be noticed by anyone but one's immediate superior.

Specialist or Generalist

There are a great many careers in which the increasing emphasis is on specialization. You find these careers in engineering and in accounting, in production, in statistical work, and in teaching. But there is an increasing demand for people who are able to take in a great area at a glance, people who perhaps do not know too much about any one field — though one should always have one area of real competence. There is, in other words, a demand for people who are capable of seeing the forest rather than the trees, of making over-all judgments. And these "generalists" are particularly needed for administrative positions, where it is their job to see that other people do the work, where they have to plan for other people, to organize other people's work, to initiate it and appraise it.

The specialist understands one field. The main concern of specialists is with technique, tools, media. Specialists are "trained" and their educational background is properly technical or professional. The generalist — and especially the administrator — deals with people. The main concern of generalists is with leadership, with planning, with direction giving, and with coordination. Generalists are "educated" and the humanities are their strongest foundation. Very rarely is a specialist capable of being an administrator. And very rarely is a good generalist also a good specialist in a particular field. Any organization needs both kinds of people, though different organizations need them in different ratios. It is your job to find out, during your apprenticeship, into which of those two job categories you fit, and to plan your career accordingly.

Your first job may turn out to be the right job for you — but this is pure accident. Certainly you should not change jobs constantly or people will become suspicious — rightly — of your ability to hold any job. At the same time you must not look upon the first job as the final job; it is primarily a training job, an opportunity to analyze yourself and your fitness for being an employee.

The Importance of Being Fired

In fact there is a good deal to be said for being fired from the first job. One reason is that it is rarely an advantage to have started as an office clerk in the organization; far too many people will still consider you a "green kid" after you have been there for twenty-five years. But the major reason is that getting fired from the first job is the least painful and the least damaging way to learn how to take a setback. And whom the Lord loveth, the Lord teacheth early how to take a setback.

Nobody has ever lived, I daresay, who has not gone through a period when everything seemed to have collapsed and when years of work and life seemed to have gone up in smoke. No one can be spared this experience; but one can be prepared for it. Anyone who has been through earlier setbacks has learned that the world has not come to an end because he or she loses a job — not even in a depression. The lesson is that it's possible to survive. The lesson is that the way to behave in such a setback is not to collapse. But the person who comes up against it for the first time at the age of forty-five is likely to collapse for good. For the things that people are apt to do when they receive the first nasty blow may destroy a mature person, especially someone with a family, whereas a youth of twenty-five bounces right back.

Obviously you cannot contrive to get yourself fired. But you can always quit. And it is perhaps even more important to have quit once than to have been fired once. The person who walks out on his or her own volition acquires an inner independence that they will never quite lose.

When to Quit

To know when to quit is therefore one of the most important things — particularly for the beginner. For on the whole young people have a tendency to hang on to the first job long beyond the time when they should have quit for their own good.

One should quit when self-analysis shows that the job is the wrong job — that, say, it does not give the security and routine one requires, that it is a small-company rather than a big-organization job, that it is at the bottom rather than near the top, a specialist's rather than a generalist's job, etc. One should quit if the job demands behavior one considers morally indefensible, or if the whole atmosphere of the place is morally corrupting — if, for instance, only yes men and flatterers are tolerated.

One should also quit if the job does not offer the training one needs either in a specialty or in administration and the view of the whole. The beginner not only has the right to expect training from his first five or ten years in a job; he has an obligation to get as much training as possible. A job in which young people are not given real training — though, of course, the training need no be a formal "training program" — does not measure up to what they have a right and a duty to expect.

But the most common reason why one should quit is the absence of promotional opportunities in the organization. That is a compelling reason.

I do not believe that chance of promotion is the essence of a job. In fact there is no surer way to kill a job and one's own usefulness in it than to consider it as but one rung in the promotional ladder rather than as a job in itself that deserves serious effort and will return satisfaction, a sense of accomplishment, and pride. And one can be an important and respected member of an organization without ever having received a promotion; there are such people in practically every office. But the organization itself must offer fair promotional opportunities. Otherwise it stagnates, becomes corrupted, and in turn corrupts. The absence of promotional opportunity is demoralizing. And the sooner one gets out of a demoralizing situation, the better. There are three situations to watch out for:

The entire group may be so young that for years there will be no vacancies. That was a fairly common situation in business thirty years ago as a result of the depression. Middle and lower management ranks in many companies were solidly filled with men in their forties and early fifties — men who were far too young to be retired but who had grown too old, during the bleak days of the Thirties, to be promotable themselves. As a result the people under them were bottled up; for it is a rare organization that will promote a young person around an older superior. If you find yourself caught in such a situation, get out fast. If you wait it will defeat you.

Another situation without promotional opportunities is one in which the group ahead of you is uniformly old — so old that it will have to be replaced long before you will be considered ready to move up. Stay away from organizations that have a uniform age structure throughout their executive group — old or young. The only organization that offers fair promotional opportunities is one in which there is a balance of ages.

Who Gets Promoted?

And finally there is the situation in which all promotions go to members of a particular group — to which you do not belong. Some chemical companies, for instance, require a master's degree in chemistry for just about any job above sweeper. Some companies promote only engineering graduates, some government agencies only people who majored in economics, some railroads only male stenographers, some British insurance companies only members of the actuaries' association. Or all the good jobs may be reserved for members of the family. There may be adequate promotional opportunities in such an organization — but not for you.

On the whole there are proportionately more opportunities in the big organization than in the small one. But there is very real danger of getting lost in the big organization — whereas you are always visible in the small one. A young person should therefore stay in a large organization only if it has a definite promotional program which ensures that he or she will be considered and looked at. This may take several forms: it may be a formal appraisal and development program; it may be automatic promotion by seniority as in the prewar Army; it may be an organization structure that actually makes out of the one big enterprise a number of small organizations in which everybody is again clearly visible (the technical term for this is "decentralization").

But techniques do not concern us here. What matters is that there should be both adequate opportunites and fair assurance that you will be eligible and considered for promotion. Let me repeat: to be promoted is not essential, either to happiness or to usefulness. To be considered for promotion is.

Your Life off the Job

I have only one more thing to say: to be an employee it is not enough that the job be right and that you be right for the job. It is also necessary that you have a meaningful life outside the job.

I am talking of having a genuine interest in something in which you, on your own, can be, if not a master, at least an amateur expert. This something may be botany, or the history of your county, or chamber music, cabinetmaking, Christmastree growing, or a thousand other things. But it is important in this "employee society" of ours to have a genuine interest outside the job and to be serious about it.

I am not, as you might suspect, thinking of something that will keep you alive and interested during your retirement. I am speaking of keeping yourself alive, interested, and happy during your working life, and of a permanent source of self-respect and standing in the community outside and beyond your job. You will need such an interest when you hit the forties, that period in which most of us come to realize that we will never reach the goals we have set ourselves when younger — whether these are goals of achievement or of worldly success. You will need it because you should have one area in which you yourself impose standards of performance on your own work. Finally, you need it because you will find recognition and acceptance by other people working in the field, whether professional or amateur, as individuals rather than as members of an organization and as employees.

This is heretical philosophy these days when so many companies believe that the best employee is the man who lives, drinks, eats, and sleeps job and company. In actual experience those people who have no life outside their jobs are not the really successful people, not even from the viewpoint of the company. I have seen far too many of them shoot up like a rocket, because they had no interests except the job; but they also come down like the rocket's burned-out stick. The person who will make the greatest contribution to a company is the mature person — and you cannot have maturity if you have no life or interest outside the job. Our large companies are beginning to understand this. That so many of them encourage people to have "outside interests" or to develop "hobbies" as a preparation for retirement is the first sign of a change toward a more intelligent attitude. But quite apart from the self-interest of the employer, your own interest as an employee demands that you develop a major outside interest. It will make you happier, it will make you more effective, it will give you resistance against the setbacks and the blows that are the lot of everyone; and it will make you a more effective, a more successful and a more mature employee.

You have no doubt realized that I have not really talked about how to be an employee. I have talked about what to know before becoming an employee — which is something quite different. Perhaps "how to be an employee" can be learned only by being one. But one thing can be said. Being an employee means working with people; it means living and working in a society. Intelligence, in the last analysis, is therefore not the most important quality. What is decisive is character and integrity. If you work on your own, intelligence and ability may be sufficient. If you work with people you are going to fail unless you also have basic integrity. And integrity — character — is the one thing most, if not all, employers consider first.

There are many skills you might learn to be an employee, many abilities that are required. But fundamentally the one quality demanded of you will not be skill, knowledge, or talent, but character.

Managing the Knowledge Worker

Chapter 26

The Fastest Growing Group: Knowledge Workers
The Fastest Growing among Them: Managers
Improving Knowledge Workers' Productivity and Satisfaction
Direction toward Contribution
Let Knowledge Workers Do What They Are Paid to Do
Assignment Control: Matching Capability with Opportunity
Skills and Ability

*D*irect production workers — machinists, bricklayers, farmers — are a steadily declining portion of the work force in a developed economy. The fastest growing group consists of "knowledge workers" — accountants, engineers, social workers, nurses, computer experts of all kinds, teachers and researchers. And the fastest growing group among knowledge workers themselves are managers. People who are paid for putting knowledge to work rather than brawn or manual skill are today the largest single group in the American labor force — and the most expensive one.

The incomes of these people are not, as a rule, determined either by supply or demand or by their productivity. Their wages and fringe benefits go up in step with those of manual direct-production workers. When the machinists get a raise, the supervisor's salary goes up by the same percentage more or less automatically — and so does everybody else's in the company right up to the executive office.

But whether the productivity of the knowledge worker goes up is questionable. Is there reason to believe, for instance, that today's school teachers are more productive than the teachers of 1900 — or today's engineer, research scientist, accountant or even today's manager?

At the same time knowledge workers tend to be disgruntled, or at least not fully satisfied. They are being paid extremely well. They do interesting work and work that does not break the body as so much of yesterday's work did. And yet the "alienation" of which we hear so much today is not primarily to be found in the working class. It is above all a phenomenon of the educated middle class of employed knowledge workers.

Improving Productivity and Satisfaction

We do not know how to measure either the productivity or the satisfaction of the knowledge worker. But we do know quite a bit about improving both. Indeed the two needs, the need of business and the economy for productive knowledge workers and the need of the knowledge worker for achievement, while distinctly separate, are by and large satisfied by the same approaches to managing the knowledge worker.

Direction toward Contribution

We know first that the key to both the productivity of the knowledge workers and their achievements is to demand responsibility from them. All knowledge workers, from the lowliest and youngest to the company's chief executive officer, should be asked at least once a year: "What do you *contribute* that justifies your being on the payroll? What should this company, this hospital, this government agency, this university, hold you accountable for, by way of contributions and results? Do you know what your goals and objectives are? And what do you plan to do to attain them?"

Direction of the knowledge worker toward contribution — rather than toward effort alone — is the first job of anyone who manages knowledge workers. It is rarely even attempted. Often the engineering department only finds out, after it has finished the design, that the product on which it has been working so hard has no future in the marketplace.

Appraise the Contributions

But at the same time, knowledge workers must be able to appraise their contributions. It is commonly said that research is "intangible" and incapable even of being appraised. But this is simply untrue.

Wherever a research department truly performs (an exception, alas, rather than the rule), the members sit down with each other and with management once or twice a year and think through two questions: "What have we contributed in the last two or three years that really made a difference to this company?" and "What should we be trying to contribute the next two or three years so as to make a difference?"

The contributions may indeed not always be measurable. How to judge them may be controversial. What, for instance, is a greater "contribution": a new biochemical discovery that after five more years of very hard work may lead to the development of a new class of medicinal compounds with superior properties; or the development of a sugar-coated aspirin without great "scientific value" that will improve the effectiveness of pediatric medicine by making the aspirin more palatable for children, while also immediately increasing the company's sales and profits?

In fact, unless knowledge workers are made to review, appraise and judge, they will not direct themselves toward contribution. And they will also feel dissatisfied, nonachieving and altogether "alienated."

Let Knowledge Workers Do What They Are Paid For

Perhaps the most important rule — and the one to which few managements pay much attention — is to enable the knowledge workers to do what they are being paid for. Not to be able to do what one is being paid for infallibly quenches whatever motivation there is. Yet sales people, who are being paid for selling and know it, cannot sell because of the time demands of the paperwork imposed on them by management. And in research lab after research lab, highly paid and competent scientists are not allowed to do their work, but are instead forced to attend endless meetings to which they cannot contribute and from which they get nothing.

The manager may know the rule. But rarely does he know what he or the company does that impedes knowledge workers and gets in the way of their doing what they are being paid for. There is only one way to find out: Ask the individual knowledge worker (and the knowledge-work team he belongs to): "What do I, as your manager, and what do we in the company's management altogether, do that helps you in doing what you are being paid for?" "What do we do that hampers you?" "Specifically, do we give you the time to do what you are being paid for, the information you need to do it, the tools for the job?"

Assignment Control: Matching Capability with Opportunity

Knowledge is a high-grade resource. And knowledge workers are expensive. Their placement is therefore a key to their productivity. The first rule is that opportunities have to be staffed with people capable of running with them and of turning them into results. To make knowledge workers productive requires constant attention to what management consulting firms and law firms call "assignment control." One has to know where the people are who are capable of producing results in knowledge work — precisely because results are so very hard to measure.

Effective management of the knowledge worker requires a regular, periodic inventory and ranking of the major opportunities. And then one asks: "Who are the performing people available to us, whether they are researchers or accountants, salesmen or managers, manufacturing engineers or economic analysts? And what are these people assigned to? Are they where the results are? Or are their assignments such that they could not produce real results, no matter how well they perform?

Unless this is being done, people will be assigned by the demands of the organization — that is by the number of transactions rather than by their importance and their potential of contribution. In no time they will be mis-assigned. They will be where they cannot be productive, no matter how well-motivated, how highly qualified, how dedicated they are.

One also has to make sure that knowledge workers are placed where their strengths can be productive. There are no universal geniuses, least of all in knowledge work which tends to be highly specialized. What can this particular knowledge worker do? What is this knowledge worker doing well? And where, therefore, does this knowledge worker truly belong to get the greatest results from his or her strengths?

Most businesses and other organizations as well spend a great deal of time and money on the original employment of people who, it is hoped, will turn into knowledge workers. But at that stage one knows very little about the future employees — beyond the grades they got in school, which have little correlation with future performance capacity. The true personnel management job, in respect to knowledge workers, begins later, when one can place the worker where his or her strengths can be productive because one knows what he or she can do.

Skills and Ability

Manual strength is additive. Two oxen will pull almost twice the load one ox can pull. Skill is capable of subdivision. Three people, each of whom has learned one aspect of a skill, e.g., glueing the legs to a table, can turn out far more work of equal skill than one person skilled in all aspects of carpentry. But in knowledge work two mediocre people do not turn out more than one person capable of performance, let alone twice as much. They tend to get in each other's way, and to turn out much less than one capable person. In knowledge work, above all, one therefore has to staff from strength. And this means constant attention to placing the knowledge workers where what they can do will produce results and make a contribution.

Knowledge is perhaps the most expensive of all resources. Knowledge workers are far more expensive than even their salaries indicate. Each of them also represents a very sizable capital investment — in schooling and in the apprentice years during which the worker learns rather than contributes (such as the five years which every chief engineer knows will be needed before the young graduates can truly be expected to earn their salary). Every young engineer, every young accountant, every young market researcher represents a "social capital investment" of something like $100,000 to $150,000 before they start repaying society and their employer through their contributions. No other resource we have is equally "capital intensive" and "labor intensive." And only management can turn the knowledge worker into a productive resource.

But also, no one expects to achieve, to produce, to contribute quite as much as the knowledge worker does. No one, in other words, is more likely to be "alienated" if not allowed to achieve.

Not to manage a knowledge worker for productivity therefore creates both the economic stress of inflationary pressures and the highly contagious social disease of distemper. We can indeed measure neither the productivity nor the satisfaction of the knowledge worker. But we know how to enrich both.

What the Computer Will Be Telling You

Chapter 27

The Computer Doesn't Introduce New Capacity, It Multiplies It

Five Basic Computer Skills: A Mechanical Clerk; Handle Information at Dazzling Speeds; Design Physical Structures; Carry Out Orders (Control); and Make Decisions Based on Information and Assumptions

What the Computer Can't Digest

Freeing Middle Managers To Do Their Job

Developments Managers Must Learn about: Time-Sharing; Public Utility; Translating Graphics-Math; and Ordinary Language Programming

*T*here are still a good many business people around who have little use for, and less interest in, the computer. There are also still quite a few who believe that the computer somehow, someday will replace workers or become their master.

Others, however, realize by now that the computer, while powerful, is only a tool and is neither going to replace nor control anyone. Being a tool, it has limitations as well as capabilities.

The trick lies in knowing both what it can do and what it cannot do. Without such knowledge, the executive will be in real trouble in the computer age.

The computer is transforming the way businesses operate and is creating problems as well as opportunities. For example:

The mistakes you make are more likely to be whoppers.

You will have much more flexibility in how your business is set up.

You will need to have alternative courses of action planned in advance.

Eventually we will use computer centers as we now plug into public utilities.

We will be able to control manufacturing processes more through direct observation.

Someday we will have little need for computer programmers.

The Computer Multiplies Human Capacity

There are only two kinds of tools. Tools which do something people themselves cannot do, such as the saw. The saw, the wheel, the airplane all are tools that add to human resource a new dimension of capability.

The other kind of tool is one that does much better what people can do themselves. The hammer belongs here and the pliers. And so does the computer. These are the tools that multiply the capacity of human resource. They do not enable anyone to do something they could not do before, but to do it better, faster, and more reliably.

The computer is a logic machine. All it can do is add and subtract. This, however, it can do at very great speed. And since all operations of mathematics and logic are extensions of addition and subtraction, the computer can perform all mathematical and logical operations by just adding and subtracting very fast, very many times. And because it is inanimate, it does not get tired. It does not forget. It does not draw overtime. It can work 24 hours a day.

Finally, it can store information capable of being handled through addition and subtraction, theoretically without limits.

Five Basic Computer Skills

What, then, can the computer do for the business world? There are basically five major tasks it can perform.

1. The computer, as a mechanical clerk, can handle large masses of repetitive, but simple, paper work: Payroll, billing and so on. All this application really uses is the speed of the computer.
2. The computer can collect, process, store, analyze and present information at dazzling speeds.

So far, however, business has used only a small part of this capacity. There are, of course, exceptions. But most computer users, businesses, hospitals or government agencies, still do little with their computers except to collect, store, and present data. Very little use is yet made of the computer's capacity to analyze information. The computer can, if properly instructed, compare the data it receives against the data it had been told to expect — for instance, budget figures. It can immediately spot any difference between the two sets of data and alert management. It can do even more than that. It can analyze data against an expected pattern, and detect any significant deviation.

One business application, for instance, is the analysis of sales data to pinpoint a meaningful and important market segment.

Do physicians in the suburbs use the same prescription drugs as physicians in small towns, or are suburban physicians a distinct market segment? And do medical specialists — the pediatricians, for example, as against the internists — prescribe differently? Are they a specific market segment?

Or what about old doctors versus young ones?

Somebody has to think up the questions. But once the computer has been instructed, it can almost immediately analyze actual prescriptions written by physicians and come up with the answers.

Get the Right Facts

What this means is that managers must carefully think through what information it is that they need.

The first step towards using the computer properly is to ask this question: How do we use it to make available the minimum of data, but the right data? What data is relevant for the sales manager, the factory superintendent, the sales staff, the research director, the cost accountant or top management?

The computer's capacity to provide people with information they need, in the form they need it and at the time they need it is the great versatility of the tool. So far it is not used too well by most businesses.

Most companies, in deciding on capital investment, still look at only one kind of analysis: Expected return on the investment. The number of years it is likely to take before the investment repays itself. Or the present value of the anticipated future earnings, the co-called discounted cash flow.

Accountants argue hotly about the advantages of each of these methods. Actually they are all valid and all needed. Hitherto, management had to be content with one because it was simply too much work to get all three. This is no longer true. Management can now ask to have capital investments calculated in all three ways by the computer — then look at all three and see which tells the most.

In other words, management has to make the information capacity of the computer fully productive.

Design Physical Structures

3. The computer can also help design physical structures.

Program into the computer all the factors that go into building a highway, plus the basic features of the country across which it is to be built. The computer can then work out very rapidly where the highway should go to take full advantage of the physical and economic characteristics of the terrain.

Here the great capacity of the computer to handle large masses of variables quickly comes into play. Here also its ability to convert graphics into numbers and numbers into graphics is of great importance.

This ability to work out physical design will find its greatest application in the physical sciences where there are clear, known predictable occurrences — that is, natural events. Social events are at best probable, never certain. Therefore, this physical design capacity is a tool of engineering, of chemistry or physics, rather than of business.

Computer Control: Carrying Out Orders

4. The computer has the capacity to restore a process to preset conditions, to "control" a process, and this application is highly relevant to business operations.

For instance, if the computer has been programed for a desired level of inventory and for the factors that determine inventory levels (sales volume, volume of shipments, volume of stock, etc.), it can control inventory. It can tell you when your stock of certain items should be renewed. It can order goods to be assembled for shipping to a customer. It can even actuate machinery bins and put the goods together into one shipping order.

It can do the same for all processes for which we can set the desired level.

This is what people mean when they talk of the computer's making "operating decisions." But this is a gross misnomer. The computer does not make any decisions. It simply carries out orders. The decision has to be made first, and the computer told what to do.

What the computer can do is serve as a monitor and immediately notice any change between the expected and actual course of events. It can then report what it has noticed.

We can go one step further and tell the computer how to react to a given event. The computer can carry out our orders. It can shut down a machine or speed it up. It can close a valve or open it, thereby changing mixtures. It can print out a purchase order or a shipping order.

It can carry out whatever order we first put into it.

Decision-making Based on Assumptions

5. Finally, the computer can, and will, play an increasing role in strategic business desion-making — deciding what course of action to take. Here we no longer deal with restoring a process to a predetermined level. We are talking about decisions to change the process.

What the computer can do here is simulate. It can rapidly work out what would happen if certain things were done under certain assumed conditions. It cannot determine what things might be done. And it cannot determine the assumptions. Both have to be determined for it.

But it can tell you, for instance, that the introduction of a new product at a given price and given cost would be justified only if you could assume a certain volume of sales.

It can tell you that a new product at a certain price and with a certain volume of sales would have to cost no more than a certain amount to be economical.

It can tell you what market you have to assume for a new product to have a chance of success.

It can also tell executives what assumptions management has made, consciously or subconsciously, when it reaches a decision. If we build a new plant with a certain capacity, for instance, how much must it be able to sell, for how long and at what price to earn a given return on the investment?

Simulation has largely been used for events which are predictable and occur regularly.

This, however, means that the simulation of the truly important, the strategic, decision is still beyond our grasp. Such a decision involves future social, political and economic events for which there are no known predictabilities and laws. Thus, strategic business decisions will remain risk-taking decisions. But the computer can point out what we assume when we make this or that decision and what decision follows logically from this or that assumption. And there are by now quite a few businesses, including a fair number of small ones, which use the computer to define and test the assumptions underlying their decisions. This applies particularly for recurrent business decisions, such as introduction of new products, pricing decision and the simpler kinds of capital investment.

The use of the computer as a tool in strategic decision-making is perhaps our most exciting possibility. For it means that business managers will have to learn to think systematically about strategic decision, and learn how to find and analyze alternatives of strategy.

What the Computer Can't Digest

However, the computer can't handle all information. It can accept only information capable of being quantified and dealt with logically. This is only a part of the information necessary in the business world.

The information most important to business people is not capable of being quantified. It can only be perceived. This is information about something that is about to happen, information about a change in the trend.

This becomes particularly critical in events outside your business, events in the economy, the market, in society. Here what matters is the new, the unique, the event that signals a change.

The computer cannot bring outside events, by and large, to the attention of management. Therefore, management must realize this limitation of the computer. It is above all a tool for controlling events within the business.

However, it is only on the outside that a business has results. Inside a business there are only costs. Only a customer converts the efforts of a business into value, revenues and profits.

This all means, indeed, that the computer can become a terrific obstacle. If the tremendous amount of inside information the computer makes available causes management to neglect to look outside — or become contemptuous of the messy, imprecise, unreliable data outside — then management will end up on the scrap heap.

On the other hand, the computer can enable business people to devote a good deal more time looking at the outside and studying it than they can now.

As a result of the computer, there will be fewer and fewer small decisions and fewer and fewer small mistakes. The computer will make small decisions into big decisions. And if they are made wrongly, the mistakes will be pretty big ones.

It is simply not true that the computer will eliminate middle managers. On the contrary, the computer will force middle managers to learn to make decisions.

A regional sales manager today makes inventory and shipping decisions on an *ad hoc* basis. They are not really decisions, but adaptations. But the sales manager also does not run much of a risk. Each decision stands by itself and usually can be easily reversed.

But to enable the computer to control inventory, a decision has to be made and the decision has to be thought through. It is neither easy nor riskless.

On the contrary, it implies very major decisions with impact on the entire business, including customer service, production schedules and money tied up in inventory. You have to think through whether you can afford to give all customers 24-hour service on all products. This usually means an absolutely impossible inventory and a totally chaotic production schedule.

If you can't afford that, do you give this kind of service only to good customers? And how do you define a good customer?

And do you give this service to all your products, or only the major products?

And again, what is a major product?

These are not easy decisions. Until recently there was no need to tackle them. Each specific case was handled as a unique event. If a customer didn't like the way he or she was treated and squawked, one treated that customer differently the next time.

But as far as the computer is concerned, inventory and shipping instructions have to be based on a fundamental policy: They have to be decided on principle. And this goes for all other so-called operating decisions.

They all become true decisions. Otherwise, one cannot instruct the computer to execute them.

Making Better Middle Managers

The greatest weakness of business at present is the fact that middle managers, by and large, are not being trained and tested in risk-taking decisions. Hence, when moved into top management, middle managers suddenly find themselves up against decisions they have not been exposed to before. This is the major reason why so many fail when they reach the top.

The computer will force us to develop managers who are trained and tested in making the strategic decisions which determine business success or failure.

I doubt that the computer will much affect the number of middle management jobs. Instead the computer is restructuring these jobs, enabling us to organize work where it logically belongs and to free middle managers for more important duties.

For instance, by tradition a district sales manager had three jobs.

One job was to train and lead a sales force. This was the main job on paper. In reality a sales manager gave very little time to it.

The second job was to be an office manager, handling a lot of paper work — bills, credits, collections and payroll.   The third job, a big one, was running a warehouse and taking care of the physical movement of merchandise to customers in his or her district.

Now the computer makes it possible to centralize all paper work in the head office — bills, payroll, invoices, credits, shipping instructions. We can print out computer-handled paper work any place in the world from a central computer.

At the same time, the computer makes possible a sharp cut in the number of warehouses. For the computer can handle all inventory as one inventory, no matter where it is.

The computer, therefore, can supply customers from a much smaller number of warehouses and with a very much smaller inventory. There is no longer any reason why, in most businesses, a warehouse needs to be in the same place as the district sales office. We may have 50 district sales offices, but need only eight warehouses — and only one location for all paper work.

This frees district sales managers for the job that always should have been their main preoccupation — managing the sales effort.

In other words, the computing ability enables us to structure according to need. In the past, corporate structure was largely determined by geography and the limitations on information. This is no longer necessary. We can now decide how we want to set up the business.

We can build decision centers where the decisions are best made, rather than where geography and absence of information force us to locate.

More than likely, this will mean that more people will have decision making authority, simply because more people can get the information they require to make the decision.

At the same time, the computer will enable top management to insist that decisions be made as decisions and with proper thought and understanding. It will, above all, enable top management to insist that alternatives are thought through, including what to do if the decision does not work out.

With the computer and its ability to process information fast, there is no reason why alternatives should not be worked out in advance.

Advice to Managers — Get Smart

There are good reasons why managers better learn fast what the computer can do for them and what it cannot do. For the developments in computer use just ahead will make it a much more common, more usable and more widely used tool. It will also be a much cheaper tool.

The costs of storing as well as the costs of computation per unit will tomorrow be only a fraction of what they are today; and they are today only a fraction of what they were only a few years ago.

There are four developments in particular managers should be aware of.

Time Sharing

We now realize that we can design and build computers of such capacity that a great many users can use them at the same time, each for their own purpose. We can, in other words, make the computer a public utility into which almost any number of users can plug in simultaneously.

Public Resource and Public Utility

Information is going to become a public resource and a public utility. It is the oldest human resource in one way, but it is also the newest. Its becoming available to everyone for a very low cost will mean a virtual revolution in information.

Almost certainly within the next 10 years we will have on the market a small appliance that can be plugged in like the radio or the TV set – or into the telephone – which will enable any student from first grade through college to get all the information they need for their school work from a centrally located computer. Such universal access computers are even now being installed in quite a few colleges.

Closely connected with this is the rapid development of terminal and accessory equipment, equipment that enables the computer information to be used anyplace, and in turn, makes it possible to put data into the computer from any point.

In 10 or 15 years data transmission will be as common as voice transmission over the telephone. Data transmission long distance is already growing much faster than ordinary long-distance telephone calls. This means fast printers, two-way sets, for instance, that enable a branch office to get all the information it needs immediately from its central computer and, in turn, to feed into the computer everything that happens in the branch office.

Equally important is the rapid increase in our capacity to translate from geometry into arithmetic, that is, from graphics into binary codes. That any geometric figures can be expressed as an equation we have known since the 17th century. Now we can make this knowledge effective and turn figures into computer language, and computer language into figures and patterns.

There is a great deal of work to be done in this field. But it is not work on computer design. It is work on understanding graphic patterns.

We cannot yet analyze the millions of cloud photographs weather satellites take each day. But not because we cannot translate these cloud pictures into computer language. The reason is simply that we do not yet know enough about the weather to know what we are looking for in the pictures.

We cannot yet tell the computer what to do. But if we could, the computer could do it. Increasingly, we will learn to make use of this capacity to go from one kind of mathematics into another. Increasingly, we will be able to analyze visual material in terms of its logic and to present logic (for example, an equation) in visual form.

This will have tremendous impact on our ability to control manufacturing processes through direct observation. It will have tremendous impact on our ability to design physical structures of all kinds.

Doing Away with Programmers

Finally, we will become less and less dependent on the programmer. We will be more and more able to put information into the computer directly in something akin to ordinary language and to get out of the computer something akin to ordinary language.

Today the programmer has to translate from ordinary language into the computer code.

This is the greatest limitation of the present system. It cuts the computer's speed down to the speed of a human being — and this, in handling logic, means it cuts it down to a very slow speed. It also creates the need for employment of many essentially semi-skilled people. Yet on their skill and understanding the ability of the computer to perform depends altogether.

To the extent to which we can jump the programming stage and get closer to computers able to handle information directly, to that extent will the computer become more effective, more flexible and more universal.

The idea that it will master us is absurd — one can always pull the plug and cut it off anyhow. But it is a tool of tremendous potential, if used properly.

It cannot, and it will not, make decisions. But it will greatly multiply the ability, the effectiveness and the impact of those people of intelligence and judgment who take the trouble to find out what the computer is all about.

Management
in Society
and Culture

Part Six

Management
and the Quality
of Life

Chapter 28

The Changed Meaning of "Social Responsibility"
What Explains It?
The Price of Success
The Disenchantment with Government
The New Leadership Groups
Why Public Relations Are Inadequate
Three Cautionary Tales
Union Carbide and Vienna, West Virginia
Swift do Argentina and Deltec
Civil Rights and the Quaker Conscience
Social Responsibilities Have to Be Managed

*T*he "social responsibilities of business" have been discussed for a century. Indeed, a chapter or two on social responsibility — or some similar heading — can be found in almost any text on general management.

But since the early sixties the meaning of the words "social responsibility of business" has changed radically.

Earlier discussions of social responsibilities of business centered in three areas. One was the perennial question of the relationship between private ethics and public ethics. To what extent are you as a manager in charge of an organization beholden to the ethics of the individual and to what extent does your responsibility to the organization permit you — or perhaps even compel you — to resort to privately unethical behavior for the good of your organization? The text for this discussion, consciously or not, is an old epigram of the politicians: "What scoundrels we would be if we did in our private lives what we do in our public capacity for our countries."

The second major topic was the social responsibility which employers bear toward their employees by virtue of their power and wealth.

Finally, social responsibility was the term used to assert — or assign — leadership responsibility of business people with respect to the "culture" of the community; support of the arts, the museums, the opera, and the symphony orchestra; service as a trustee on the boards of educational and religious institutions, and also giving money to philanthropic and other community causes. And in the United States in particular, willingness to serve in governmental or quasi-governmental positions has become in this century an important social responsibility of the executive.

By and large the traditional approach was not concerned, as it claimed to be, with the social responsibility of business but with the social responsibility of business people. And the greatest emphasis was put on what they should or might contribute outside of business hours and outside their businesses.

After World War II there was increasing emphasis on the contribution of business. But this was a result of tax laws which, on the one hand, slowed down the accumulation of large fortunes by individuals, and on the other hand encouraged and made highly attractive charitable contributions on the part of a company. The emphasis otherwise remained unchanged. Where an earlier generation had looked to the "rich businessman" to endow a hospital, post-World War II big business was expected to support worthy causes. Emphasis was still on outside "causes" rather than on the behavior and actions of business itself.

When social responsibilities are being discussed these days, however, the emphasis is quite different. It is on what business should or might *do* to tackle and solve problems of society. The emphasis is on the contribution business can make to such social problems as racial discrimination and racial integration in the United States, or on the maintenance and restoration of the physical environment. One of the best examples of the new attitude comes from Sweden.

Several large Swedish companies, especially ASEA, the big electrical-apparatus company, were harshly attacked in the late sixties in the Swedish press for participating in a major electric-power project in Africa. The project was sponsored by the UN and financed by the World Bank; it also had been endorsed by the socialist government of Sweden. Its purpose was to raise the living standards of a desperately poor region of Black Africa. But it was located in a Portuguese colony. Hence, it was vehemently argued, the Swedish companies participating in it "supported colonialism" by helping to raise the standards of living of the native population. It was their duty, so the argument ran, to work for the "downfall of colonialism," which would best be achieved by keeping the natives desperately poor rather than have them prosper under an "imperialist exploiter."

The most extreme assertion of social responsibilities of business is perhaps a statement made during the sixties by the Mayor of New York City, John Lindsay.

The Mayor called on the big corporations of New York City to "adopt" a Black ghetto neighborhood and to make sure that the people in that neighborhood would have the necessities of life, would get education, and would get jobs. He then added that he hoped that these major corporations would also make sure that each Black family had a man in the house who would be husband to the wife and father to the children.

Only ten years earlier one could not have imagined anyone, not even the most extreme "leftist" or "progressive," berating business for its refusal to nullify the foreign policy of its own government (and a socialist one to boot) or for shunning paternalistic control over the sex life of citizens who were not even employees.

This new concept of social responsibility no longer asks what the limitations on business are, or what business should be doing for those under its immediate authority. It demands that business take responsibility for social problems, social issues, social and political goals, and that it become the keeper of society's conscience and the solver of society's problems.

But increasingly such social responsibility is also being demanded of nonbusiness institutions in society. Universities, hospitals, and government agencies, but also learned societies, whether of physicians, historians, or linguists, are all increasingly being confronted with similar demands and attacked for not assuming responsibility for society's ills and problems.

In the early sixties student riots against the university arose out of student grievances. But the student riots of 1968 that almost destroyed Columbia University in New York City were sparked by complaints that the university had failed to take full social responsibility for the neighboring Black community of Harlem and had failed to subordinate its own educational goals to the alleged needs of Harlem's hard-core unemployables.

What Explains It?

The most popular and most obvious explanation is the wrong one. It is not hostility to business that explains the surge of demands for social responsibility. On the contrary, it is the success of the business system which leads to new and, in many cases, exaggerated expectations. The demand for social responsibility is, in large measure, the price of success.

In developed countries we now take economic performance for granted. This has led to the belief that there is, or should be, universal capacity for economic performance. It has led us to believe that the same efforts which, within a century, lifted one-third of humanity from poverty into affluence can in much less time raise the remaining two-thirds into affluence, or can at least bring them into rapid economic development.

Less than two generations ago, in the years around World War I, poverty was still taken for granted as the universal condition. No one then assumed economic development to be the rule. It was considered an exception. What was considered surprising in 1900, or even in 1950, was not that India remained poor. Indeed anyone who would then have talked about the economic development of India would have been considered inane. What was exceptional, and truly surprising, was that Japan had managed to break out of the all but universal poverty of humanity and to start on the road to development. Today lack of development is considered the exception and the "problem." And no matter how rapid development is — e.g., in Brazil since World War II — it is considered inadequate because it does not transform an entire country, within one generation, from extreme misery to comfortable affluence.

No one, only two generations ago, expected poverty to disappear, even in the developed and wealthy countries at that time. Few people today would believe the descriptions and illustrations in the first systematic survey of the poor in what was then the world's richest city, London, which Charles Booth published just before the turn of the century. Only the horror stories that come out of Calcutta equal them today. Yet, to contemporaries, the London poor of the 1890s seemed so affluent by comparison with the conditions described and illustrated twenty years earlier, that Marx's partner, Friedrich Engels, in reissuing in 1896 his earlier *The Conditions of the Working Classes in England,* was forced to admit that his and Marx's earlier prophecy of the increasing "pauperism" of the "proletariat" could no longer be maintained.

In particular, the poverty that is most offensive to us today, that is, poverty in the midst of affluence, was then taken for granted. No one in the nineteenth or early twentieth centuries expected pre-industrial immigrants into the industrial cities to be other than poor, destitute, incompetent, and wretched. No one expected a rapid transformation of the slums of industrial Lancashire or of the industrializing Vienna in Austria around 1900. All anyone expected was a little humanity to assuage the worst of the suffering, and a little charity. At best there were attempts to help a few of unusual endowment and personal ambition to raise themselves out of abject destitution. To the orthodox Marxist even this was sentimental romanticism. Following his master he considered these people *Lumpenproletariat* and incapable of improving themselves either individually or collectively.

Nothing in earlier social and economic history equals the recent economic and social development of the American Negro. Within twenty years, from 1950 to 1970, two-thirds of one of the least prepared and most disadvantaged of pre-industrial immigrants into modern civilization have risen from extreme poverty into middle-class status. They have acquired competence and jobs. A larger proportion of their children acquire higher education than of the children of older immigrant groups in the city, such as Italians or Poles who encounter no "racial" barrier.

Admittedly the American Negro is a very special problem. But still, the difference between what was considered success only a half century ago and what is now considered grim failure illustrates the extent to which success has changed expectations. Even rather well-to-do "middle-class" people yesterday had only little of the qualities of life we now expect routinely.

The apartment buildings of the late nineteenth century still stand in most European cities. They are hardly "good housing" — airless and dark, with mean little flats, five floors high without elevator, heating — a coal or wood stove — only in the "parlor," and with one tiny, grimy bathroom for a family of seven. Yet they were built for the new middle classes. Health care was almost nonexistent, education beyond the elementary level a privilege of the few, the newspaper a luxury. And no matter how serious an environmental problem the automobile poses in today's big city, the horse was dirtier, smelled worse, killed and maimed more people, and congested the streets just as much.

And life on the farm, that is, life for the great majority, was, if anything, poorer, dirtier, more dangerous to life and limb, and more brutish.

As late as 1900 or 1914 quality of life was a concern only of the few rich. To all the others it was "escapism" that could be permitted in the syrupy romances that sold by the millions. Reality, however, was the numbing daily struggle for a little food, a dreary job and enough money to pay the premium on burial insurance.

That we can worry about the qualities of life is thus very great success. And it is only right and natural that the same leadership groups which were responsible for the success in providing the quantities of life are expected to assume the responsibility now for providing the quality of life.

The same reason explains the demand for social responsibility on the part of the university. For the university too is a success story of the twentieth century.

"If science can tell us how to put an astronaut on the moon," the student activists of the sixties said again and again, "it surely can tell us how to create a decent environment, save our cities from drugs, make marriages happy and children enjoy school. If it doesn't, the only explanation must be 'wrong value priorities' or malicious conspiracy."

To be sure, these arguments are naive. But they are not irrational. The clamor for social responsibility expects too much. But it expects the right things. Its root is not hostility to authority, but overconfidence in managers and management.

The Disenchantment with Government

On top of this comes the growing disenchantment with government, the growing disbelief in government's ability to solve major social problems.

Only a generation ago the people who now demand social responsibility from business (or the university) expected government to be able to take care of every problem of society, if not of every problem of the individual as well. There is still, in all countries, pressure for more and more government programs — though there is also growing resistance to more and more expenditures and taxes. But even the most fervent advocate of an activist government no longer truly expects results, even in countries where respect for and belief in government are still high, such as in Japan, Sweden, and Germany. Even the most fervent advocate of a strong government no longer believes that a problem has been solved the moment it has been turned over to government. As a result, the people most concerned with these problems, the liberals and progressives who, a generation ago, rallied under the banner of "more government," now increasingly look to other leadership groups, other institutions, and, above all, to business, to take on the problems which government should but is not able to solve.

Robert Kennedy, rather than the National Association of Manufacturers, proposed that the rehabilitation of the slums in the big American cities be taken on by business. And one of the staunchest and most respected advocates of government activism, and America's leading labor union theoretician, the late Frank Tannenbaum of Columbia University, at the very end of his life, in the spring of 1968, proclaimed that the multinational corporation was "the last best hope" and the only foundation of a peaceful world.

The New Leadership Groups

Altogether it is the succession of management to the leadership position in society that underlies the demands for social responsibility.

In this century the managers of our major institutions have become the leaders in every developed country, and in most developing countries as well. The old leadership groups, whether the aristocracy or the priesthood, have either disappeared entirely or have become insignificant. Even the scientists, the priesthood of the post-World War II period, have lost much of their prestige. The only new leadership groups to emerge are managers, managers of business enterprise and of universities, of government agencies and of hospitals. They command the resources of society. But they also command the competence. It is, therefore, only logical that they are expected to take the leadership role and take responsibility for major social problems and major social issues.

As a result of these shifts — the emergence of managers as the major leadership group; the growing disenchantment with government, and the shift in focus from the quantities of life to the quality of life — the demand has arisen that managers, and especially business managers, make concern for society central to the conduct of business itself. It is a demand that the quality of life become the business of business. The traditional approach asks, "How can we arrange the making of cars (or of shoes) so as not to impinge on social values and beliefs, on individuals and their freedom, and on the good society altogether?" The new demand is for business to *make* social values and beliefs, create freedom for the individual, and produce the good society.

This demand requires new thinking and new action on the part of the managers. It cannot be handled in the traditional manner. It cannot be handled by public relations.

Public relations asks whether a business or an industry is "liked" or "understood." Public relations would therefore be worried that Black Power advocates blame the profit motive for the ghetto, and that they presumably like business just as little as they like any other part of the white establishment. But what really matters is that the Black Power leaders expect business to perform miracles with respect to ghetto employment, ghetto education, ghetto housing; and they expect these miracles virtually overnight. The relevant questions are: "Can business tackle these huge problems? How? Should business tackle them?" These are not questions which public relations is equipped to handle.

Three Cautionary Tales

Books and magazines these days are full of horror stories of "business irresponsibility," of "greed," and "incompetence." There is no doubt that there are irresponsible, greedy, and incompetent managers and businesses. Managers, after all, are members of the human race. But the real problems of social responsibility are not irresponsibility, greed, and incompetence. If they were the problem would be easy. One could then set forth standards of conduct and hold business to them. Unfortunately the basic problems of social responsibility are different. They are problems of good intentions, honorable conduct, and high responsibility — gone wrong.

This can be illustrated by three "cautionary tales."

Union Carbide and Vienna, West Virginia

West Virginia, never one of the more prosperous areas of the United States, went into rapid economic decline in the late twenties as the coal industry, long the state's mainstay, began to shrink. The decline of the coal industry was hastened by rising concern with mine accidents and miners' diseases. For many of the coal mines of West Virginia were small and marginal and could not afford modern safety precautions or adequate health protection.

By the late 1940s the leading industrial company in the state became alarmed over the steady economic shrinkage of the region. Union Carbide, one of America's major chemical companies, had its headquarters in New York. But the original plants of the company had been based on West Virginia coal, and the company was still the largest employer in the state, other than a few large coal mines. Accordingly, the company's top management asked a few young engineers and economists in its employ to prepare a plan for the creation of employment opportunities in West Virginia, and especially for the location of the company's new plant facilities in areas of major unemployment in the state. For the worst afflicted area, however, the westernmost corner of the state on the border of Ohio, the planners could not come up with an attractive project. Yet this area needed jobs the most. In and around the little town of Vienna, West Virginia, there was total unemployment, and no prospects for new industries. The only plant that could possibly be put in the Vienna area was a ferroalloy plant using a process that had already become obsolete and had heavy cost disadvantages compared to more modern processes such as Union Carbide's competitors were already using.

Even for the old process, Vienna was basically an uneconomical location. The process required very large amounts of coal of fair quality. But the only coal available within the area was coal of such high sulfur content that it could not be used without expensive treatment and scrubbing. Even then — that is, after heavy capital investment — the process was inherently noisy and dirty, releasing large amounts of fly ash and of noxious gases.

In addition, the only transportation facilities, both rail and road, were not in West Virginia but across the river, on the Ohio side. Putting the plant there, however, meant that the prevailing westerly winds would blow the soot from the smokestacks and the sulfur released by the power plants directly into the town of Vienna, on the other bank of the river.

Yet the Vienna plant would provide 1,500 jobs in Vienna itself and another 500 to 1,000 jobs in a new coal field not too far distant. In addition, the new coal field would be capable of being strip-mined, so the new mining jobs would be free from the accident and health hazards that had become increasingly serious in the old and worked-out mines of the area. Union Carbide top management came to the conclusion that social responsibility demanded building the new plant, despite its marginal economics.

The plant was built with the most up-to-date antipollution equipment known at the time. Whereas even big-city power stations were then content to trap half the fly ash escaping their smokestacks, the Vienna plant installed scrubbers to catch 75 percent — though there was little anyone could do about the sulfur dioxide fumes emitted by the high-sulfur coal.

When the plant was opened in 1951, Union Carbide was the hero. Politicians, public figures, educators, all praised the company for its social responsibility. But ten years later the former savior was fast becoming the public enemy. As the nation became pollution-conscious, the citizens of Vienna began to complain more and more bitterly about the ash, the soot, and the fumes that floated across the river into their town and homes. About 1961 a new mayor was elected on the platform "fight pollution," which meant "fight Union Carbide." Ten years later the plant had become a "national scandal." Even *Business Week* — hardly a publication hostile to business — chastised Union Carbide (in February, 1971) in an article entitled "A Corporate Polluter Learns the Hard Way."

There is little doubt that Union Carbide's management did not behave very intelligently. They should have realized in the early sixties that they were in trouble, rather than delay and procrastinate, make and then break promises — until the citizens, the state government, the press, the environmentalists, and the federal government all were aiming their biggest guns at the company. It was not very smart to protest for years that there was nothing wrong with the plant and then, when governmental authorities began to get nasty, announce that the plant would have to be closed as it could not be brought up to environmental standards.

Yet this is not the basic lesson of this cautionary tale. Once the decision had been made to employ an obsolescent process and to build an economically marginal plant in order to alleviate unemployment in a bitterly depressed area, the rest followed more or less automatically. This decision meant that the plant could not make enough money to modernize its equipment. There is very little doubt that on economic reasoning alone the plant would never have been built. Public opinion forced Union Carbide to invest substantial sums in that plant to remedy the worst pollution problems — though it is questionable whether the technology exists to do more than a patch-up job. Publicity also forced Union Carbide to keep the plant open. But, once the spotlight shifts elsewhere, most of the jobs in the Vienna, West Virginia, plant are likely to disappear again, if indeed the plant remains open at all.

Swift do Argentina and Deltec

The Swift meat-packing plant in the Buenos Aires port district has been the largest meat-packing plant in Argentina for many years. It has also been a major employer in a poor area of Buenos Aires. Originally a subsidiary of Swift of Chicago, the company became independent, though still under American ownership, shortly after World War II.

But the Argentinian meat-packing industry fell on evil days after World War II — in part because of government measures that have been driving up the price of Argentinian cattle, while cutting down the supply, thus making Argentinian beef increasingly non-competitive in the world market and depriving meat-packers of their source of raw materials. Swift became increasingly unprofitable. The owners finally sold out in 1968 to a Canadian-based "multinational," Deltec, a company that is active in many parts of Latin America, primarily in financial service businesses. Deltec promptly started to modernize the Swift plant to make it competitive again. But the Argentinian meat-packing industry continued on its decline.

Swift's two major competitors, both foreign-owned, decided in the late sixties to close down. They paid off the workers according to Argentinian law and went out of business. Deltec, however, decided that it could not afford to do this in view of its many other interests in Latin America. It had to maintain employment in an area where unemployment was far too high anyhow. Deltec worked out an agreement with the labor unions under which employment was substantially cut and productivity greatly improved. The company poured substantial amounts of money into the plant and used its financial connections to obtain foreign bank loans for it. Still the meat business in Argentina did not improve.

By 1971 Swift had used up all the capital Deltec could make available to it and was still not back on a profitable and competitive basis. Thereupon Swift worked out a voluntary agreement with the creditors, including the company's workers, for full repayment of all debts over an extended period — with Deltec being the last creditor to receive any payment. Eighty-six percent of the creditors, far more than required by law, accepted this agreement. But to everyone's surprise the Argentinian judge, whose approval had been expected as a mere formality, turned the agreement down. He decided that Deltec had obtained it improperly, declared Swift do Argentina bankrupt, ordered its liquidation, and asked the Argentinian government to appoint a liquidator. In effect he expropriated the company and its property. He not only refused to recognize any rights of Deltec as a creditor but decided that all Deltec holdings in other Argentinian companies be impounded as security for Swift's debts to Argentinian creditors.

There was no public pressure for such an action — and no legal pressure either. The Swift workers, although members of the most militant of Argentinian unions, fully supported Deltec. Yet the decision found tremendous approval in Argentina, even among people who by no stretch of the imagination could be considered antibusiness or even anti-American. "The other foreign-owned meat-packers," a good many people said, "did the right thing in closing down their plants and paying off their workers when they could no longer operate economically. Deltec, by trying to keep going, raised expectations which it then cruelly had to disappoint."

Civil Rights and the Quaker Conscience

In the late 1940s a major American steel company appointed a new general manager for its large southern division, located in one of the most strongly "white supremacy" areas in the South. Traditionally, all top-management postitions in that division had been held by Southerners. The new appointee was a Northerner. Moreover, he was a scion of one of the old Philadelphia Quaker families and had been active in several civil rights organizations.

Upon his appointment top management called him in and said, "We know what we are doing and why we are appointing you. To be sure, your performance has earned this promotion. But you are also a Northerner and committed to employment equality for the Black people. And this, of course, is what both the laws of the United States and our union contract demand of us. Yet, as we all know, our southern division has never given employment opportunities to Blacks. No Black, however skilled, no matter what his or her job, has ever been paid more than 'helper's' wages. We have never been able to make a dent in this down south. But we know that we will not be able much longer to defend and to keep up these practices. We expect you, therefore, to move as fast as you can for civil rights for our Negro employees, as the laws of the country and our union contract demand. Try to get the support and cooperation of the top people in the union which represents our workers. We know that you have been working with them in several civil rights organizations."

The new general manager spent about a year getting accepted by his new associates, getting known in the local community, and establishing friendly relations with the union leaders in the mill. Then he saw his opportunity. A new major extension to the mill was about to be opened, and a number of new furnaces had to be staffed. The new general manager strictly applied the hiring provisions of the union contract. As a result, a small but still substantial number of Black workers with high job skills and considerable seniority got positions on the new crews. In no case was a white worker deprived of his seniority rights or put under a Black supervisor.

The morning after the new staffing tables had been posted, as required by the union contract, a delegation of local union leaders called on the general manager. "You know that there are several hundred grievances," they said, "which have been pending for far too long a time without a settlement. The patience of our men is exhausted. We are going out on strike in thirty-six hours. But we don't want to be unreasonable. If the company makes even a token gesture of goodwill, we will postpone this strike. All you have to do is to suspend those staffing tables you just posted, and let us, together with the supervisors, work out the composition of the crews for the new furnaces. In the meantime, here is the official strike notice as required by our contract."

The general manager first tried to reach the president and the general counsel of the union. Unaccountably, neither could be found, nor did their secretaries know where they could be reached or when they would return. Then the general manager bethought himself of an old friend, one of the "sages" of the Quakers and a "radical" on race relations, and especially on employment opportunities for Blacks. But to the general manager's immense surprise, the "sage" was not one bit sympathetic with his plight. "I fully agree with you, as you know, in considering employment discrimination against the Negro to be illegal, immoral, and sinful," the sage said. "But what you have done, while legal, is just as immoral. You have used the economic muscle of a big company to impose your mores and values on the community in which you operate. Yours are the right mores and the right values. But still, you are using the economic power of a business, the power of the employer, and the authority of your office to dictate to the community. This is 'economic imperialism' and it cannot be condoned, no matter how good the cause."

The general manager resigned and took another job up north. The company quietly dropped the staffing tables. The mills remained open. And a few years later, needless to say, the company came under bitter attack — in which the union's general counsel joined loudly — for its failure to take leadership in race matters. As the biggest employer in the community, the critics charged, the company had a social responsibility not to condone practices which it must have known to be both illegal and immoral.

Managers: The Leadership Group for Social Responsibility

Clearly, the demand for social responsibility is not as simple as most books, articles, and speeches on the subject make it out to be. But it is not possible to disregard it, as such distinguished economists as Milton Friedman of Chicago have urged. To be sure, Friedman's argument that business is an economic institution and should stick to its economic task is well taken. There is danger that social responsibility will undermine economic performance and with it society altogether. There is surely an even greater danger that social responsibility will mean usurpation of power by business managers in areas in which they have no legitimate authority.

But it is also clear that social responsibility cannot be evaded. It is not only that the public demands it. It is not only that society needs it. The fact remains that in modern society there is no other leadership group but managers. If the managers of our major institutions, and especially of business, do not take responsibility for the common good, no one else can or will. Government is no longer capable, as political theories still have it, of being the "sovereign" and the "guardian of the common good" in a pluralist society of organizations. The leadership groups in this society, and this means the managers of the key institutions, whether they like it or not — indeed whether they are competent or not — have to think through what responsibilities they can and should assume, in what areas, and for what objectives.

If there is one moral to these cautionary tales, it is not that social responsibility is both ambiguous and dangerous. It is that social impacts and social responsibilities are areas in which business — and not only big business — has to think through its role, has to set objectives, has to perform. *Social impacts and social responsibilities have to be managed.*

Social Impacts and Social Problems

Chapter 29

Responsibility for Impacts
The High Price of Neglect
Anticipating Impacts
"Technology Assessment" or "Technology Monitoring"
How to Deal with Impacts
Their Elimination as a Business Opportunity
When Regulation is Needed
The Trade-Offs
Impacts as Business Responsibility
Social Problems as Business Opportunities
Solving a Social Problem
Sears, Ford, IBM
Second Careers for the Middle-Aged Knowledge Worker
The "Degenerative Diseases" of Society
Are There Limits to Social Responsibility?

*S*ocial responsibilities — whether of a business, a hospital, or a university — may arise in two areas. They may emerge out of the social impacts of the institution. Or they arise as problems of the society itself. Both are of concern to management because the institution which managers manage lives of necessity in society and community. But otherwise the two areas are different. The first deals with what an institution does *to* society. The second is concerned with what an institution can do *for* society.

The modern organization exists to provide a specific service to society. It therefore has to be in society. It has to be in a community, has to be a neighbor, has to do its work within a social setting. But also it has to employ people to do its work. Its *social impacts* inevitably go beyond the specific contribution it exists to make.

The purpose of the hospital is not to employ nurses and cooks. It is patient care. But to accomplish this purpose, nurses and cooks are needed. And in no time at all they form a work community with its own community tasks and community problems.

The purpose of a ferroalloy plant is not to make noise or to release noxious fumes. It is to make high-performance metals that serve the customer. But in order to do this, it produces noise, creates heat, and releases fumes.

Nobody wants to create a traffic jam. But if a lot of people are employed in one place and have to enter and leave at the same time, a traffic jam will be a totally unintended and yet inescapable by-product.

These impacts are incidental to the purpose of the organization. But in large measure they are inescapable by-products.

Social problems, by contrast, are dysfunctions of society rather than impacts of the organization and its activities.

The steel company discussed in the preceding chapter did, of course, practice racial discrimination. But racial discrimination was not caused by its activities; it was not an impact. On the contrary, the racial problem of the old South has all along been considered by business a major obstacle to industrialization and economic development. It had been an external condition to which any institution operating in southern society had to conform. Similarly, Swift do Argentina — or the Argentinian meat-packers as a whole — did not cause the long-time secular decline of the Argentinian livestock industry and the resulting unemployment in the Port of Buenos Aires. On the contrary, they fought the government policies responsible for the decline.

Still, both the U.S. steel company operating in the South and Swift do Argentina could not escape concern. Such problems are the degenerative diseases or the toxic wastes of the society and community in which a business exists. Since the institution can exist only within the social environment, is indeed an organ of society, such social problems affect the institution. They are of concern to it even if, as in the steel company's case, the community itself sees no problem and resists any attempt to tackle it.

A healthy business, a healthy university, a healthy hospital cannot do well in a sick society. Management has a self-interest in a healthy society, even though the cause of society's sickness is none of management's making.

Responsibility for Impacts

One is responsible for one's impacts, whether they are intended or not. This is the first rule. There is no doubt regarding management's responsibility for the social impacts of its organization. They are management's business.

In the Union Carbide story in the preceding chapter, the main reason why the community became so incensed against the company was probably not the pollution it caused. The community knew as well as Union Carbide that the pollution was incidental to production, and thereby to the jobs on which the community depended. But what the community bitterly resented, and with reason, was Union Carbide's refusal for long years to accept responsibility. This is indeed irresponsible.

Because one is responsible for one's impacts, one minimizes them. The fewer impacts an institution has outside of its own specific purpose and mission, the better does it conduct itself, the more responsibly does it act, and the more acceptable a citizen, neighbor, and contributor it is. Impacts which are not essential, and which are not part of the discharge of one's own specific purpose and mission, should be kept to the absolute minimum. Even if they appear to be beneficial, they are outside the proper boundaries of one's function and will, therefore, sooner or later be resented, be resisted, and be considered impositions.

One of the main reasons why management should, in its own self-interest, foster self-government of the work community is precisely that the community functions of the plant are incidental to the purpose of the business. They are not essential to it. The business exists to produce shoes or candy, or to turn out insurance policies. Any control that goes beyond what is strictly necessary to get the work done is incidental to the main function. It is an impact. And it should, therefore be minimized, if it cannot be eliminated.

Impacts are at best a nuisance. At worst they are harmful. They are never beneficial. Indeed they always carry with themselves a cost and a threat. Impacts use up resources, burn up or waste raw materials, or at the least tie up management efforts. Yet they add nothing to the value of the product or to the customer's satisfaction. They are "friction," that is, non-productive cost.

But even minor impacts are likely to become "crises" and "scandal" and to result in serious damage to business — or to any other institution that disregards its impacts. What only yesterday seemed harmless — and indeed even popular — suddenly becomes offense, a public outcry, a major issue. Unless management has taken responsibility for the impact, thought it through, and worked out the optimal resolution, the result will be punitive or restrictive legislation and an outcry against the "greed of business" or the "irresponsibility of the university."

It is not enough to say, "But the public doesn't object." It is, above all, not enough to say that any action to come to grips with such a problem is going to be "unpopular," is going to be "resented" by one's colleagues and one's associates, and is not required. Sooner or later society will come to regard any such impact as an attack on its integrity and will exact a high price from those who have not responsibly worked on eliminating the impact or on finding a solution to the problem.

Here are some examples.

In the late forties and early fifties, one American automobile company tried to make the American public safety-conscious. Ford introduced cars with seat belts. But sales dropped catastrophically. The company had to withdraw the cars with seat belts and abandon the whole idea. When, fifteen years later, the American driving public became safety-conscious, the car manufacturers were sharply attacked for their "total lack of concern with safety" and for being "merchants of death." And the resulting regulations were written as much to punish the companies as to protect the public.

Several large electric-power companies had tried for years to get the various state utility commissions to approve low-sulfur fuels and cleaning devices in smokestacks. The commissions discouraged them again and again with the argument that the public was entitled to power at the lowest possible cost. They pointed out that neither a more expensive fuel nor capital investment to clean the smoke could be permitted in the rate base as a legitimate cost under the state laws. Yet when eventually air pollution became a matter of public concern, the same power companies were roundly berated for "befouling the environment."

Public-service institutions similarly pay the price of neglecting impacts or of dismissing them as trivial. Columbia University was almost destroyed because it did not take responsibility for an impact but had comforted itself with the notion that the impact was trivial. The explosion which rocked Columbia to its foundation in 1968 came over a perfectly harmless and minor matter: a plan to build a new university gymnasium which would be available equally to university students and to the residents of the Black ghetto which abuts Columbia. But the causes for the explosion lay much deeper. They were the conviction on the part of Columbia and of its faculty that a liberal educational institution does not have to concern itself with its relations with its Black ghetto neighborhood.

Another example of impact is the business that is "too big" for its own good and that of the community. The business that is too big, especially the business that is too big for the local community, is a threat to its community but, above all, to itself. It is incumbent on management to correct the situation in the interest of the business (or of the university or hospital). To ignore the problem is to put ego, desire for power, and vanity ahead of the good of the institution and of the community. And this is irresponsible.

Identifying Impacts

The first job of management is, therefore, to identify and to anticipate impacts — coldly and realistically. The question is not "Is what we do right?" It is "Is what we do what society and the customer pay us for?" And if an activity is not integral to the institution's purpose and mission, it is to be considered as a social impact and as undesirable.

This sounds easy. It is actually very difficult. The best illustration is the problem of "technology assessment," that is, the identification of social and economic impacts of new technology at the time of its introduction.

There is, these days, great interest in technology assessment, that is in anticipating impact and side effects of new technology *before* going ahead with it. The U.S. Congress has actually set up an Office of Technology Assessment. This new agency is expected to predict what new technologies are likely to become important, and what long-range effects they are likely to have. It is then expected to advise government what new technologies to encourage and what new technologies to discourage, if not to forbid altogether.

This attempt can end only in fiasco. Technology assessment of this kind is likely to lead to the encouragement of the wrong technologies and the discouragement of the technologies we need. For *future* impacts of *new* technology are almost always beyond anybody's imagination.

DDT is an example. It was synthesized during World War II to protect American soldiers against disease-carrying insects, especially in the tropics. Some of the scientists then envisaged the use of the new chemical to protect civilian populations as well. But not one of the many people who worked on DDT thought of applying the new pesticide to control insect pests infesting crops, forests, or livestock. If DDT had been restricted to the use for which it was developed, that is, to the protection of humans, it would never have become an environmental hazard; use for this purpose accounted for no more than 5 or 10 percent of the total at DDT's peak, in the mid-sixties. Farmers and foresters, without much help from the scientists, saw that what killed lice on soldiers would also kill lice on plants and made DDT into a massive assault on the environment.

Another example is the population explosion in the developing countries. DDT and other pesticides were a factor in it. So were the new antibiotics. Yet the two were developed quite independently of each other; and no one "assessing" either technology could have foreseen their convergence — indeed no one did. But more important as causative factors in the sharp drop in infant mortality which set off the population explosion were two very old "technologies" to which no one paid any attention. One was the elementary public-health measure of keeping latrine and well apart — known to the Macedonians before Alexander the Great. The other one was the wire-mesh screen for doors and windows invented by an unknown American around 1860. Both were suddenly adopted even by backward tropical villages after World War II. Together they were probably the main causes of the population explosion.

At the same time, the technology impacts which the experts predict almost never occur. One example is the "private flying boom," which the experts predicted during and shortly after World War II. The private plane, owner-piloted, would become as common, we were told, as the Model T automobile had become after World War I. Indeed, experts among city planners, engineers, and architects advised New York City not to go ahead with the second tube of the Lincoln Tunnel, or with the second deck on the George Washington Bridge, and instead build a number of small airports along the west bank of the Hudson River. It would have taken fairly elementary mathematics to disprove this particular technology assessment — there just is not enough airspace for commuter traffic by air. But this did not occur to any of the experts; no one realized how finite airspace is. At the same time, almost no experts foresaw the expansion of commercial air traffic and anticipated, at the time the jet plane was first developed, that it would lead to mass transportation by air, with as many people crossing the Atlantic in jumbo jets in one day as used to go in a week in the big passenger liners. To be sure, transatlantic travel was expected to grow fast — but of course it would be by ship. These were the years in which all the governments along the North Atlantic heavily subsidized the building of new super-luxury liners, just when the passengers deserted the liner and switched to the new jet plane.

A few years later, we were told by everyone that automation would have tremendous economic and social impacts — it has had practically none. The computer offers an even odder story. In the late forties nobody predicted that the computer would be used by business and governments. While the computer was a "major scientific revolution," everybody "knew" that its main use would be in science and warfare. As a result, the most extensive market research study undertaken at that time reached the conclusion that the world computer market would, at most be able to absorb 1,000 computers by the year 2000. Now, only thirty years later, there are some 250,000 computers installed in the world, most of them doing the most mundane bookkeeping work. Then a few years later, when it became apparent that business was buying computers for payroll and billing, the experts predicted that the computer would displace middle management, so that there would be nobody left between the chief executive officer and the first line supervisor. *"Is middle management obsolete?"* asked a widely quoted *Harvard Business Review* article in the early fifties; and it answered this rhetorical question with a resounding "Yes." At exactly that moment, the tremendous expansion of middle-management jobs began. In every developed country middle-management jobs, in business as well as in government, have grown three times as fast as total employment in the last twenty-five years; and their growth has been parallel to the growth of computer usage. Anyone depending on technology assessment in the early 1950s would have abolished the graduate business schools as likely to produce graduates who could not possibly find jobs. Fortunately, the young people did not listen and flocked in record numbers to the graduate business schools so as to get the good jobs which the computer helped create.

But while no one foresaw the computer impact on middle-management jobs, every expert predicted a tremendous computer impact on business strategy, business policy, planning, and top management — on none of which the computer has, however, had the slightest impact at all. At the same time, no one predicted the real revolution in business policy and strategy in the fifties and sixties: the merger wave and the conglomerates.

It is not only that a human being has the gift of prophecy no more with respect to technology than with respect to anything else. The impacts of technology are actually more difficult to predict than most other developments. In the first place, as the example of the population explosion shows, social and economic impact are almost always the result of the convergence of a substantial number of factors, not all of them technological. And each of these factors has its own origin, its own development, its own dynamics, and its own experts. The expert in one field — e.g., the expert on epidemiology — never thinks of plant pests. The expert on antibiotics is concerned with the treatment of disease, whereas the actual explosion of the birthrate resulted largely from elementary and long-known public health measures.

But equally important, what technology is likely to become important and have an impact, and what technology either will fizzle out — like the "flying Model T" — or will have minimal social or economic impacts — like automation — is impossible to predict. And which technology will have social impacts and which will remain just technology is even harder to predict. The most successful prophet of technology, Jules Verne, predicted a great deal of twentieth-century technology a hundred years ago (though few scientists or technologists of that time took him seriously). But he anticipated absolutely no social or economic impacts, only an unchanged mid-Victorian society and economy.

Economic and social prophets, in turn, have the most dismal record as predictors of technology.

The one and only effect an Office of Technology Assessment is therefore likely to have would be to guarantee full employment to a lot of fifth-rate science-fiction writers.

The Need for Technology Monitoring

The major danger is, however, that the delusion that we can foresee the impacts of new technology will lead us to slight the really important task. For technology does have impacts and serious ones, beneficial as well as detrimental. These do not require prophecy. They require careful monitoring of the actual impact of a technology once it has become effective. In 1948, practically no one correctly saw the impacts of the computer. Five or six years later, one could and did know. Then one could say, "Whatever the technological impact, *socially* and *economically* this is not a major threat." In 1943, no one could predict the impact of DDT. Ten years later, DDT had become worldwide a tool of farmer forester, and livestock breeder, and as such, a major ecological factor. Then thinking as to what action to take should have begun, work should have been started on the development of pesticides without the major environmental impact of DDT, and the difficult trade-offs should have been faced between food production and environmental damage — which neither the unlimited use nor the present complete ban on DDT sufficiently considers.

Technology monitoring is a serious, an important, indeed a vital task. But it is not prophecy. The only thing possible with respect to *new* technology is *speculation* with about one chance out of a hundred of being right — and a much better chance of doing harm by encouraging the wrong, or discouraging the most beneficial new technology. What needs to be watched is "developing" technology, that is, technology which has already had substantial impacts, enough to be judged, to be measured, to be evaluated.

And monitoring a developing technology for its social impacts is, above all, a managerial responsibility.

But equally important — and totally overloked by the advocates of technology assessment — are the impacts of nontechnological, that is social and economic innovations and developments. They are just as hard to predict until they have emerged and can be identified, evaluated, and measured. They too, therefore, need being monitored. And that too is a management responsibility.

How to Deal with Impacts

Identifying incidental impacts of an institution is the first step. But how does management deal with them? The objective is clear: impacts on society and economy, community, and individual that are not in themselves the purpose and mission of the institution should be kept to the minimum and should preferably be eliminated altogether. The fewer such impacts the better, whether the impact is within the institution, on the social environment, or on the physical environment.

Wherever an impact can be eliminated by dropping the activity that causes it, this is therefore the best — indeed the only truly good — solution.

Managerial authority over, and control of, work-community affairs is perhaps the one area where this can be done — and with direct benefit to institution and management themselves.

In most cases the activity cannot, however, be eliminated. Hence there is need for systematic work at eliminating the impact — or at least at minimizing it — while maintaining the underlying activity itself.

The ideal approach is to make the elimination of impacts into a profitable business opportunity. One example is the way Dow Chemical, one of the leading U.S. chemical companies, has for almost twenty years tackled air and water pollution. Dow decided, shortly after World War II, that air and water pollution was an undesirable impact that had to be eliminated. Long before the public outcry about the environment, Dow adopted a zero-pollution policy for its plants. It then set about systematically to develop the polluting substances it removes from smokestack gases and watery effluents into salable products and to create uses and markets for them.

A variant is the Du Pont Industrial Toxicity Laboratory. Du Pont, in the 1920s, became aware of the toxic side effects of many of its industrial products, set up a laboratory to test for toxicity and to develop processes to eliminate the poisons. Du Pont started out to eliminate an impact which at that time every other chemical manufacturer took for granted. But then Du Pont decided to develop toxicity control of industrial products into a separate business. The Industrial Toxicity Laboratory works not only for Du Pont but for a wide variety of customers for whom it develops nonpoisonous compounds, whose products it tests for toxicity, and so on. Again, an impact has been eliminated by making it into a business opportunity.

When Regulation is Needed

To make elimination of an impact into a business opportunity should always be attempted. But it cannot be done in many cases. More often eliminating an impact means increasing the costs. What was an "externality" for which the general public paid becomes business cost. It therefore becomes a competitive disadvantage unless everybody in the industry accepts the same rule. And this, in most cases, can be done only by regulation — that means by some form of public action.

Whenever an impact cannot be eliminated without an increase in cost, it becomes incumbent upon management to think ahead and work out the regulation which is most likely to solve the problem at the minimum cost and with the greatest benefit to public and business alike. And it is then management's job to work at getting the right regulation enacted.

Management — and not only business management — has shunned this responsibility. The traditional attitude has always been that "no regulation is the best regulation." But this applies only when an impact can be made into a business opportunity. Where elimination of an impact requires a restriction, regulation is in the interest of business, and especially in the interest of responsible business. Otherwise it will be penalized as "irresponsible," while the unscrupulous, the greedy, the stupid, and the chiseler cash in.

And to expect that there will be no regulation is willful blindness.

Whenever there has been the kind of crisis which the automobile industry ran into with respect to automotive safety or the public utilities with respect to air pollution, the penalty imposed on business in the end has been high. Such a crisis always leads to a scandal. It leads to governmental inquisition, to angry editorials, and eventually to loss of confidence in an entire industry, its management, and its products by broad sectors of the public. Finally, there is punitive legislation.

The fact that the public today sees no issue is not relevant. Indeed it is not even relevant that the public today — as it did in every single one of the examples above — resists actively any attempts on the part of farsighted business leaders to prevent a crisis. In the end, there is the scandal.

One example is the failure of the international petroleum companies to think ahead and develop the successor to the "petroleum concession," the impacts of which could clearly be anticipated at the end of World War II. Another example is the failure of U.S. industry to think through the regulation of foreign investment which Canada might adopt to preserve both political identity and access to capital.

The American pharmaceutical industry knew, as early as 1955, that the existing rules and procedures to test new drugs needed critical review and updating. They had been written long before the arrival of the modern potent wonder drugs and their — equally potent — side effects. The U.S. had all along had the most stringent drug regulations among major nations. But were they still appropriate to a very different situation in pharmacology and in the use of drugs by the physicians? Yet any pharmaceutical company that tried to get the industry to face up to the problem was shushed by the other members of the club. "Don't rock the boat," the prospective innovator was told. One company, it is reported, actually worked up a comprehensive new approach and new regulatory procedures. It was prevailed upon to bury them in its archives.

And then came the Thalidomide scandal. It actually *proved* the effectiveness of the American control system; for while Thalidomide was approved for medical practice in the European countries, the U.S. regulatory authorities became concerned very early about the drug's toxic side effects and withheld approval. As a result there are no deformed Thalidomide babies in the U.S. as there are in Germany, Sweden, and England. Still, the scandal released an enormous tidal wave of anxiety about drug testing and drug safety in the U.S. And because industry had not faced up to the problem and had not thought through and agitated for the right solution, Congress panicked into passing legislation that threatens seriously to impair the development and market introduction of new medicines — and yet, pradoxically, would probably not prevent another Thalidomide.

The Trade-Offs

Any solution to an impact problem requires trade-offs. Beyond a certain level elimination of an impact costs more in money or in energy, in resources or in lives, than the attainable benefit. A decision has to be made on the optimal balance between costs and benefits. This is something people in an industry understand, as a rule. But no one outside does — and so the outsider's solution tends to ignore the trade-off problem altogether.

Where is the trade-off between the overdue concern for a natural environment threatened by the strip-mining of coal and the lives saved in switching from underground mining to strip-mining? Underground mining can never be truly safe. It will always remain a health hazard because of the coal dust and the contaminated air in which underground work has to be performed. Strip-mining, on the other hand, should be a fairly safe occupation and has few health hazards. But where is the trade-off between lives and natural beauty and clean, unpolluted streams?

But there is, in the strip-mining issue, also a trade-off between the costs of environmental damage and the cost in jobs, living standards, and in the health hazard of cold homes and the safety of dark streets implicit in dear and scarce energy.

What happens when management fails to face up to an impact and to think through the trade-off is shown by the American experience with automotive emissions.

That such controls would be needed has been known since the end of World War II when smog first became a houshold word in Los Angeles. The automobile industry, however, relied on public relations, which told it that the public was not concerned about smog. Then, suddenly, in the sixties, the public panicked and forced through drastic emission control legislation. Whether the new controls will actually cut pollution is quite doubtful. For while they cut down on emission of old pollutants — provided the control euipment is maintained carefully — the new controls also cause substantial new pollution. They greatly increase the energy needed to drive the car and will therefore have to use more gasoline. This will require more petroleum refining — one of the most polluting of industrial activities. At the same time, they add substantially to the cost of the car and of automotive service. What the right trade-offs would have been we do not know — for industry did not do its work. But both industry and public will pay and suffer.

The public welcomes an intelligent solution for such a problem if management presses for one before the scandal. This has been the experience of the Committee for Economic Development (CED) in its twenty years of existence, and of any other business or industry group which took responsibility for an impact and brought to bear on it the knowledge, competence, and seriousness of its best people.

Most managers know this. And yet they hope against hope that the problem will go away. They postpone thinking about it, let alone taking action. At the most they make speeches. And they fight a rearguard action after they have lost.

Responsibility for social impacts is a management responsibility — not because it is a social responsibility, but because it is a business responsibility. The ideal is to make elimination of such an impact into a business opportunity. But wherever that cannot be done, the design of the appropriate regulation with the optimal trade-off balance — and public discussion of the problem and promotion of the best regulatory solution — is management's job.

Social Problems as Business Opportunities

Social problems are dysfunctions of society and — at least potentially — degenerative diseases of the body politic. They are ills. But for the management of institutions, and, above all, for business management they represent challenges. They are major sources of opportunity. For it is the function of business — and to a lesser degree of the other main institutions – to satisfy a social need and at the same time serve their institution, by making resolution of a social problem into a business opportunity.

It is the job of business to convert change into innovation, that is, into new business. And it is a poor business manager who thinks that innovation refers to technology alone. Social change and social innovation have throughout business history been at least as important as technology. After all, the major industries of the nineteenth century were, to a very large extent, the result of converting the new social environment – the industrial city – into a business opportunity and into a business market. This underlay the rise of lighting, first by gas and then by electricity, of the streetcar and the interurban trolley, of telephone, newspaper, and department store – to name only a few.

The significant opportunities for converting social problems into business opportunities may therefore not lie in new technologies, new products, and new services. They may lie in *solving* the social problem, that is, in social innovation which then directly and indirectly benefits and strengthens the company or the industry.

The success of some of the most successful businesses is largely the result of such social innovation. Here are some American examples:

Julius Rosenwald, the "city slicker" who built Sears, Roebuck, invented and for many years financed the County Farm Agent. The social problem he identified was the poverty, ignorance, and isolation of the American farmer who still, in the early years of this century, constituted half the U.S. population. Knowledge to enable the farmers to produce more, to produce the right things, and to get more for their efforts was available. But it was inaccessible to the farmer. The County Farm Agent – rather than new technology, new machines, or new seeds – became a main force behind the "productivity explosion" on the American farm. Rosenwald saw a genuine social problem. But he also saw a genuine business opportunity. For the farmer's poverty, ignorance, and isolation were major obstacles to Sears. As the farmer's position and income grew, so did the Sears market. And Sears came to be identified by the farmers as the "farmer's friend."

Tackling a social problem as a business opportunity also played a substantial part in the meteoric rise of Ford in its early days.

The years immediately prior to World War I were years of great labor unrest in the United States, growing labor bitterness, and high unemployment. Hourly wages for skilled workers ran as low as 15 cents in many cases. It was against this background that the Ford Motor Company, in the closing days of 1913, announced that it would pay a guaranteed $5-a-day wage to every one of its workers – two to three times what was then standard. James Couzens, the company's general manager, who had forced this decision on his reluctant partner, Henry Ford, knew perfectly well that his company's wage bill would almost triple overnight. But he became convinced that the workers' sufferings were so great that only radical and highly visible action could have an effect. Couzens also expected that Ford's actual labor cost, despite the tripling of the wage rate, would go down – and events soon proved him right. Before Ford changed the whole labor economy of the United States with one announcement, labor turnover at the Ford Motor Company had been so high that, in 1912, 60,000 workers had to be hired to retain 10,000 of them. With the new wage, turnover almost disappeared. The resulting savings were so great that, despite sharply rising costs for all materials in the next years, Ford could produce and sell its Model T at a lower price and yet make a larger profit per car. It was the saving in the labor cost produced by a drastically higher wage that gave Ford market domination. At the same time Ford's action transformed American industrial society. It established the American worker as fundamentally middle class.

IBM also owes its rise largely to a frontal attack on a social problem. During the years of the Great Depression IBM was a very small company and had little visibility. Hence its action had none of the impact of Ford's $5-a-day wage twenty years earlier. Yet in giving workers employment security and then putting them on a salary instead of an hourly wage IBM was as bold and innovative as Ford had been. IBM's action too was aimed at a major social problem of the time, the fear, insecurity, and loss of dignity that the Depression inflicted on workers in America. It too turned a social disease into a business opportunity. It was this action, above all, which created the human potential for IBM's rapid growth and, then, a decade later, for its aggressive move into the totally new computer technology.

And here is a European example.

The growth of Olivetti into one of the world's leading producers of office equipment rests on two insights of the late Adrian Olivetti, who in the 1920s, inherited a small, unknown, and barely viable family company in the small town of Ivrea in northern Italy. Adriano Olivetti saw the opportunity to give his company and his products distinction through good design. Olivetti's design gave him market recognition within a decade. He also saw in Italy's corrosive class hatred an opportunity. The community in which he tried to fuse management and worker in Ivrea gave him exceptional labor productivity, high-quality production, and a work force willing to accept new technology and changes — and with it competitive strength and profitability.

In present-day society one area where a serious social problem might be solved by making it into an opportunity could well be the fatigue, frustration, and "burning-out" of middle-aged knowledge workers and their need for a second career. The hidden cost of the middle-aged knowledge workers — managers and knowledge professionals — who have "retired on the job," have lost interest, and just go through the motions, may well be larger than that of Ford's labor turnover in 1913. At the same time, the frustration and silent despair of these men and women may pose as great a social danger to society as the misery, bitterness, and despair of the suffering manual worker of yesterday. Nothing is as corrosive as success turned into frustration. The first company which tackles this problem as both a social problem and an opportunity might well reap benefits fully as great as those reaped by Ford sixty-five years ago and Olivetti and IBM fifty years ago.

To cure social ills by making them into opportunities for contribution and performance is by no means a challenge to business enterprise alone. It is the responsibility as well of all the other institutions of our society of organizations.

There is a great deal of talk today about the crisis of the university; and the crisis is real. In some places, however, it has been seized as an opportunity. In Great Britain there is the Open University, which uses television to make university education available to anyone who is willing to do the work. In California the medium-sized and little-known University of the Pacific, in Stockton, is building a new kind of university. It utilizes the desire of young people to learn but also to be responsible participants in their learning.

Rosenwald, Ford, IBM's Watson, and Olivetti were all initially ridiculed as visionaries. No one could solve the problems they tackled, they were told. Ten or fifteen years later, their solutions were dismissed as "obvious." The right solution is always obvious in retrospect. What matters is that these men and their companies identified a major social problem and asked, "How can it be solved as a business opportunity?"

Any business, and indeed any institution, needs to organize innovative efforts to convert social problems into opportunities for performance and contribution.

In the last quarter century organized technological research has become commonplace. Social innovation is still largely left to chance and to the individual entrepreneur who stumbles upon an opportunity. This is no longer adequate. In the society of organizations, every institution needs to organize its R & D for society and community fully as much as it had been organizing it for technology. Management has to organize to identify the issues, the crises, the problems in society and community, and to work at the innovations that will make their solution into a profitable opportunity.

The "Degenerative Diseases" of Society

Social problems that management action converts into opportunities soon cease to be problems. The others, however, are likely to become "chronic complaints," if not "degenerative diseases."

Not every social problem can be resolved by making it into an opportunity for contribution and performance. Indeed, the most serious of such problems tend to defy this approach.

No business could, for instance, have done much about America's most serious degenerative disease throughout our history — the racial problem. It could not even be tackled until the whole society had changed awareness and convictions — by which time it was very late, if not altogether too late. And even if one management solves such a problem, the rest may not follow. There may be a solution; but while known and visible, it is not being used. The problem stays acute and unresolved.

America's business had to follow Ford's lead between 1914 and 1920 — though the labor shortage of World War I had as much to do with this as Ford's example. But few American companies imitated IBM and even fewer Italian companies imitated Olivetti, despite their visible success.

What then is the social responsibility of management for these social problems that become chronic or degenerative diseases?

They are management's problems. The health of the enterprise is management's responsibility. A healthy business and a sick society are hardly compatible. Healthy businesses require a healthy, or at least a functioning, society. The health of the community is a prerequisite for successful and growing business.

And it is foolish to hope that these problems will disappear if only one looks the other way. Problems go away because someone does something about them.

With any such problem, management had better find out whether someone has, in fact, done something that works. That few, if any, U.S. businesses have followed IBM, and few Italian businesses have followed Olivetti, is management failure. It is basically not too different from the management failure to keep technology and products competitive. And the reasons are not too different either; they are shortsightedness, indolence, and incompetence.

Yet there remain the big, tough, dangerous dysfunctions of society, the social problems for which no one has worked out a solution, and which cannot, it seems, be resolved, or perhaps not even assuaged, by being made performance opportunities.

To what extent should business — or any other of the special-purpose institutions of our society — be expected to tackle such a problem which did not arise out of an impact of theirs and which cannot be converted into an opportunity for performance of the institution's pupose and mission? To what extent should these institutions, business, university, or hospital, even be permitted to take responsibility?

Today's rhetoric tends to ignore that question. "Here is," former Mayor Lindsay of New York said, "the Black ghetto. No one knows what to do with it. Whatever government, social workers, or community action try, things seem only to get worse. *Therefore* big business better take responsibility."

That Mayor Lindsay frantically looked for someone to take over is understandable; and the problem that is still unsolved is indeed desperate and a major threat to this city, to American society, and to the Western world altogether. But is it enough to make the problem of the Black ghetto the social responsibility of management? Or are there limits to social responsibility? And what are they?

The Limits of Social Responsibility

Chapter 30

Management's First Responsibility: Its Own Institution
The Need to Know Minimum Profitability Requirements
To "Do Good" and to "Do Well"
The Limits of Competence
The Limits of Authority
No Responsibility Without Authority
When to Say No
The Commitment to Working Out Alternatives
*The Limits of Social Responsibility as a Central Problem to
    Management and to the Society of Organizations*

*T*he manager is a servant. As a manager your master is the institution you manage and your first responsibility must therefore be to it. The first task is to make the institution, whether business, hospital, school, or university, perform the function and make the contribution for the sake of which it exists. Anyone who uses the position at the head of a major institution to become a public figure and to take leadership with respect to social problems, while his company or university erodes through neglect, is not a leader. Such managers are irresponsible and false to their trust.

The institution's performance of its specific mission is also society's first need and interest. Society does not stand to gain but to lose if the performance capacity of the institution in its own specific task is diminished or impaired. Performance of its function is the institution's first social responsibility. Unless it discharges its performance responsibly, it cannot discharge anything else. A bankrupt business is not a desirable employer and is unlikely to be a good neighbor in a community. Nor will it create the capital for tomorrow's jobs and the opportunities for tomorrow's workers. A university which fails to prepare tomorrow's leaders and professionals is not socially responsible, no matter how many "good works" it engages in.

The first "limitation" on social responsibility is, therefore the higher responsibility for the specific performance of the institution which is the manager's master. This needs particular stress with respect to the business enterprise, the economic institution of society. Any solution of a social impact or of a social problem except to make it into an opportunity for performance and results creates social overhead costs. These costs cannot be borne out of profits, no matter what popular rhetoric may say. They are paid for either out of current costs — that is, by consumer or taxpayer — or they are paid for out of capital — that is, by fewer and poorer jobs tomorrow and impaired standards of living. The only way to cover costs and to accumulate capital is through economic performance. All other satisfactions of society are being paid for, one way or another, out of the surplus between current production and current consumption, that is, out of the surplus of the economy.

This again underscores the responsibility of managers to anticipate problems and to think through the trade-offs involved in their solutions. At what point does a solution become prohibitively expensive for society because it impairs the performance capacity of existing and needed institutions, whether of the economy, of health care, of education, or of the military? What is the optimal balance between the need to take care of a social problem and the need to preserve the performance capacity of the existing social institutions? And at what point does one risk losing social performance — and thereby creating new and bigger problems — by overloading the existing institutions? At what point do we achieve the best balance between the old costs and the new benefits?

Managers need to be able to think through the limits on social responsibility set by their duty to the performance capacity of the enterprises in their charge.

In the case of the business enterprise this requires knowing the objectives in the key areas. For these objectives set the *minimum* performance goals for the attainment of the enterprise's mission. As long as they can be attained, the enterprise can perform. If the objective in any one area is seriously jeopardized, the performance capacity of the entire business is endangered.

Above all, management needs to know the *minimum profitability* required by the risks of the business and by its commitments to the future. It needs this knowledge for its own decisions. But it needs it just as much to explain its decisions to others — the politicians, the press, the public. As long as managements remain the prisoners of their own ignorance of the objective need for, and function of, profit — i.e., as long as they think and argue in terms of the "profit motive" — they will be able neither to make rational decisions with recept to social responsibilities, nor to explain these decisions to others inside and outside the business.

A popular pun these days says, "It is not enough for business do do well; it must also do good." But in order to "do good," a business must first "do well" (and indeed "do very well").

Whenever a business has disregarded the limitation of economic performance and has assumed social responsibilities which it could not support economically it has soon gotten into trouble.

Union Carbide was not socially responsible when it put its plant into Vienna, West Virginia, to alleviate unemployment there. It was, in fact, irresponsible. The plant could barely keep its head above water. And this, inevitably, meant a plant unable to take on social resesponsibility, even for its own impacts. Because the plant was uneconomical to begin with, Union Carbide resisted so long all demands to clean it up. This particular demand could not have been foreseen in the late 1940s when concern with jobs far outweighed any concern for the environment. But demands of some kind can always be expected. To do something out of social responsibility which is economically irrational and untenable is therefore never responsible. It is sentimental. The result is always greater damage.

Similarly, Deltec in Buenos Aires may be vulnerable to the charge that to keep a plant open when every other major meat-packer had reached the conclusion that the business could not survive was sentimentality rather than social responsibility. It was an assumption of responsibility beyond tenable limits. The intentions were good and honorable — as in Union Carbide's case. It may be argued that Deltec took a calculated risk. Also, the outcome was far more the result of internal Argentinian politics than of anything Deltec did or omitted to do. Yet Deltec management took a greater risk than might be compatible with true social responsibility.

The same limitation on social responsibility applies to noneconomic institutions. There, too managers are duty-bound to preserve the performance capacity of the institutions in their care. To jeopardize it, no matter how noble the motive, is irresponsibility. These institutions too are capital assets of society on the performance of which society depends.

This, to be sure, is a very unpopular position to take. It is much more popular to be "progressive." But managers, and especially managers of key institutions of society, are not being paid to be heroes to the popular press. They are being paid for performance and responsibility.

The Limits of Competence

To take on tasks for which one lacks competence is irresponsible behavior. It is also cruel. It raises expectations which will then be disappointed.

An institution, and especially a business enterprise, has to acquire whatever competence is needed to take responsibility for its impacts. But in areas of social responsibility other than impacts, right and duty to act are limited by competence.

In particular an institution better refrain from tackling tasks which do not fit into its value system. Skills and knowledge are fairly easily acquired. But one cannot easily change personality. No one is likely to do well in areas which he or she does not respect. If a business or any other institution tackles such an area because there is a social need, it is unlikely to put its good people on the task and to support them adequately. It is unlikely to understand what the task involves. It is almost certain to do the wrong things. As a result, it will do damage rather than good.

What not to do was demonstrated when the American universities in the sixties rushed into taking social responsibility for the problems of the big city. These problems are real enough. And within the university were to be found able scholars in a variety of areas with relevance to the problems. Yet the tasks were primarily political tasks. The values involved were those of the politician rather than the scholar. The skills needed were those of compromise, of mobilizing energies, and above all, of setting priorities. And these are not skills which the academician admires and respects, let alone excels in. They are almost the opposite of the objectivity and the "finding of truth" which constitute excellence in academia. These tasks exceeded the competence of the university and were incompatible with its value system.

The result of the universities' eager acceptance of these tasks was therefore, inevitably, lack of performance and results. It was also damage to the prestige and standing of the university, and to its credibility. The universities did not help the problems of the city; but they seriously impaired their own performance capacity in their own area.

The major corporations in New York City would have acted totally irresponsibly had they responded to Mayor Lindsay's call to "adopt the Black ghetto." All they could have done (as they apparently realized) was damage — to the ghetto and to themselves.

What the limits of competence are depends in part on circumstances. If a member of a climbing team develops acute appendicitis in the high Himalayas and is almost certain to die unless operated on, any medical doctor in the group will operate, even though the doctor may be a dermatologist who has never done a single operation. The dermatologist, though a qualified physician, will be considered irresponsible and vulnerable to both a malpractice suit and a conviction for manslaughter, should he or she operate on an appendix in a place where a qualified surgeon, or even a general practitioner, are within reach.

Management therefore needs to know at the very least what it and its institution are truly *incompetent* for. Business, as a rule, will be in the position of absolute incompetence in an "intangible" area. The strength of business is accountability and measurability. It is the discipline of market test, productivity measurements, and profitability requirement. Where these are lacking businesses are essentially out of their depths They are also out of fundamental sympathy, that is, outside their own value systems. Where the criteria of performance are intangible, such as "political" opinions and emotions, community approval or disapproval, mobilization of community energies and structuring of power relations, business is unlikely to feel comfortable. It is unlikely to have respect for the values that matter. It is, therefore, most unlikely to have competence.

In such areas it is, however, often possible to define goals clearly and measurably for *specific partial tasks.* It is often possible to convert parts of a problem that by itself lies outside the competence of business into work that fits the competence and value system of the business enterprise.

No one in America has done very well in training hard-core unemployable Black teenagers for work and jobs. But business has done far less badly than any other institution:

schools, government programs, community agencies. This task can be identified. It can be defined. Goals can be set. And performance can be measured. And then business can perform.

Before acceding to the demand that it take this or that social responsibility, and go to work on this or that problem, management better think through what, if any, part of the task can be made to fit the competence of its institution. Is there any area which can be defined in terms of tangible goals and measurable performance — as business managers understand these slippery terms? If the answer is yes, one is justified in thinking seriously about one's social responsibility. But when the answer is no — and this will be the answer in a good many areas — business enterprise better resist, no matter how important the problem and how urgent the demand for business to take over. It can only do harm to society and to itself. It cannot perform and therefore cannot be responsible.

Limits of Authority

The most important limitation on social responsibility is the limitation of authority. The constitutional lawyer knows that there is no such word as "responsibility" in the political dictionary. The term is "responsibility *and* authority." Whoever claims authority thereby assumes responsibility. But whoever assumes responsibility thereby claims authority. The two are but different sides of the same coin. To assume social responsibility therefore always means to claim authority.

Again, the question of authority as a limit on social responsibility does not arise in connection with the impacts of an institution. For the impact is the result of an exercise of authority, even though purely incidental and unintended. And then responsibility follows.

But where business or any other institution of our society of organizations is asked to assume social responsibility for one of the problems or ills of society and community, management needs to think through whether the authority implied in the responsibility is legitimate. Otherwise it is usurpation and irresponsible.

Every time the demand is made that business take responsibility for this or that, one should ask, "Does business have the authority and should it have it?" If business does not have and should not have authority — and in a great many areas it should not have it — then responsibility on the part of business should be treated with grave suspicion. It is not responsibility; it is lust for power.

The position of the Chicago economist, Milton Friedman, that business should stick to its business, that is, to the economic sphere, is not a denial of responsibility. It can be argued with great force that any other position can only undermine and compromise a free society. Any other position can only mean that business will take over power, authority, and decision-making in areas outside of the economic sphere, in areas which are or should be reserved to government or to the individual or to other institutions. For, to repeat, whoever assumes responsibility will soon have to be given authority. History amply proves this.

From this point of view the present "critics" of big business can rightly be accused of pushing big business into becoming our master.

Ralph Nader, the American consumerist, sincerely considers himself a foe of big business and is accepted as such by business and by the general public. Insofar as Nader demands that business take responsibility for product quality and product safety, he is surely concerned with legitimate business responsibility, i.e., with responsibility for performance and contribution. The only question — apart from the accuracy of his facts and the style of his campaign — would be whether Nader's demand for perfection is not going to cost the consumer far more than the shortcomings and deficiencies which Nader assails. The only questions are the trade-offs.

But Ralph Nader demands, above all, that big business assume responsibility in a multitude of areas beyond products and services. This, if acceded to, can lead only to the emergence of the managements of big corporations as the ultimate power in a vast number of areas that are properly some other institution's field.

And this is, indeed, the position to which Nader — and other advocates of unlimited social responsibility — are moving rapidly. One of the Nader task forces published in 1972 a critique of the Du Pont Company and its role in the small state of Delaware, where Du Pont has its headquarters and is a major employer. The report did not even discuss economic performance; it dismissed as irrelevant that Du Pont, in a period of general inflation, consistently lowered the prices for its products, which are, in many cases, basic materials for the American economy. Instead it sharply criticized Du Pont for not using its economic power to force the citizens of the state to attack a number of social problems, from racial discrimination to health care to public schools. Du Pont, for not taking responsibility for Delaware society, Delaware politics, and Delaware law, was called grossly remiss in its social responsibility.

One of the ironies of this story is that the traditional liberal or left-wing criticism of the Du Pont Company for many years has been the exact opposite, i.e., that Du Pont, by its very prominence in a small state, "interferes in and dominates" Delaware and exercises "illegitimate authority."

The Nader line is only the best-publicized of the positions which, under the cover of antibusiness rhetoric, actually plead for a society in which big business is the most powerful, the dominant, the ultimate institution. Of course such an outcome is the opposite of what Nader intends. But it would not be the first time that a demand for social responsibility has had results opposite from those intended.

The most likely result of the Nader line neither he nor management would want. It is either a destruction of all authority, that is, complete irresponsibility. Or it is totalitarianism — another form of irresponsibility.

Yet Milton Friedman's "pure" position — to shun all social responsibility — is not tenable either. There are big, urgent, desperate problems. Above all, there is the "sickness of government" which is creating a vacuum of responsibility and performance — a vacuum that becomes stronger the bigger government becomes. Business and the other institutions of our society of organizations cannot be pure, however desirable that may be. Their own self-interest alone forces them to be concerned with society and community and to be prepared to shoulder responsibility beyond their own main areas of task and responsibility.

But in doing this they have to be conscious of the danger — to themselves and to society. They have to be conscious of the risk. No pluralist society such as ours has become, has ever worked unless its key institutions take responsibility for the common good. But at the same time, the perennial threat to a pluralist society is the all-too-easy confusion between the common good and one's own lust for power.

In a few areas guidelines can be developed. It is not the task of business (or of the university) to substitute its authority for that of the duly constituted political sovereign, the government, in areas that are clearly national policy. In a free society a business is, of course, entitled not to engage in activities, even though they are sanctioned and even encouraged by governmental policy. It can stay out. But it is surely not entitled to put itself in the place of government. And it is not entitled to use its economic power to impose its values on the community.

By these criteria, the Quaker sage who chided his friend the steel-mill manager for using the economic power of a big company to impose a little racial justice on a southern U.S. city in the 1940s was right. That the end was surely right and moral does not sanction the means, that is, the exercise of an authority which a business does not possess. This is as much "imperialism" as any which the most fervent believer in racial equality denounces. The steel company can be faulted — deservedly so, I would say — for having done nothing for long years to work toward the racial justice in which it professed to believe. It can be faulted, and with cause, for not finding whatever possibilities for racial justice could have been put into practice. But two wrongs do not make a right, two examples of irresponsibility do not add up to responsibility.

When to Say No

Demands for social responsibility which in effect ask of business — or any other institution — that it usurp authority are to be resisted. They are to be resisted in business's own self-interest; the usurper's power is always shaky. They are to be resisted on grounds of true social responsibility. For they are, in effect, demands for irresponsibility. Whether they are made sincerely and out of honest anguish, or whether they are rhetoric to cloak the lust for power, is irrelevant. Whenever business, or any other of our institutions, is being asked to take social responsibility beyond its own area of performance and its own impact, it better ask itself, "Do we possess authority in the area and should we have it?" And if the answer is no, then the socially responsible thing is not to accede to the demand.

Yet in many cases it may not be enough to say no. Management must resist responsibility for a social problem that would compromise or impair the performance capacity of its business (or its university or its hospital). It must resist when the demand goes beyond the institution's competence. It must resist when responsibility would, in fact be illegitimate authority. But then, if the problem is a real one, it better think through and offer an alternative approach. If the problem is serious, something will ultimately have to be done about it. And if management then has been purely obstructionist and has blocked any approach — even though its objection to any one proposed course of action was legitimate and indeed reponsible — the ultimate solution is likely to do even more damage.

In a pluralist society responsibility for the common good is a central problem that is never solved. The only way concern for social responsibility could disappear would be for society to become totalitarian. For it is the definition of a totalitarian government that it has authority over everything and responsibility for nothing.

For this reason managements of all major institutions, including business enterprise, need too to concern themselves with serious ills of society. If at all possible they convert solution of these problems into an opportunity for performance and contribution. At the least they think through what the problem is and how it might be tackled. They cannot escape concern; for this society of organizations has no one else to be concerned about real problems. In this society managers of institutions are the leadership group.

But we also know that a developed society needs performing institutions with their own autonomous management. It cannot function as a totalitarian society. Indeed, what characterizes a developed society — and indeed makes it a developed one — is that most of its social tasks are carried out in and through organized institutions, each with its own autonomous management. These organizations, including most of the agencies of our government, are special-purpose institutions. They are organs of our society for specific performance in a specific area. The greatest contribution they can make, their greatest social responsibility, is performance of their function. The greatest social irresponsibility is to impair the performance capacity of these institutions by tackling tasks beyond their competence or by usurpation of authority in the name of social responsibility.

The Ethics
of Responsibility

Chapter 31

The Ethics of Businessmen: The Wrong Question?
Leadership Groups but Not Leaders
What Being a Professional Means
An Ethic of Responsibility
Primum non nocere
Social Responsibility vs. "Club Membership"
Executive Compensation and Income Inequality
The "Golden Fetters"
The Rhetoric of the Profit Motive
Private Function and Public Character

*C*ountless sermons have been preached and printed on the ethics of business or the ethics of business people. Most have nothing to do with business and little to do with ethics.

One main topic is plain, everyday honesty. People in business, we are told solemnly, should not cheat, steal, lie, bribe, or take bribes. But nor should anyone else. Men and women do not acquire exemption from ordinary rules of personal behavior because of their work or job. Nor, however, do they cease to be human beings when appointed vice-president, city manager, or college dean. And there has always been a number of people who cheat, steal, lie, bribe, or take bribes. The problem is one of moral values and moral education, of the individual, of the family, of the school. But there neither is a separate ethics for business, nor is one needed.

All that is needed is to mete out stiff punishments to those — whether business executive or others — who yield to temptation. In England a magistrate still tends to hand down a harsher punishment in a drunken-driving case if the accused has gone to one of the well-known public schools or to Oxford or Cambridge. And the conviction still rates a headline in the evening paper: "Eton graduate convicted of drunken driving." No one expects an Eton education to produce temperance leaders. But it is still a badge of distinction, if not of privilege. And not to treat a wearer of such a badge more harshly than an ordinary working person who has had one too many would offend the community's sense of justice. But no one considers this a problem of the "ethics of the Eton graduate,"

The other common theme in the discussion of ethics in business has nothing to do with ethics.

Such things as the employment of call girls to entertain customers are not matters of ethics but matters of esthetics. "Do I want to see a pimp when I look at myself in the mirror while shaving?" is the real question.

It would indeed be nice to have fastidious leaders. Alas, fastidiousness has never been prevalent among leadership groups, whether kings or counts, priests or generals, or even "intellectuals" such as the painters and humanists of the Renaissance, or the "literati" of the Chinese tradition. All a fastidious person can do is withdraw personally from activities that violate his or her self-respect and sense of taste.

Lately these old sermon topics have been joined, especially in the U.S., by a third one: managers, we are told, have an "ethical responsibility" to take an active and constructive role in their community, to serve community causes, give of their time to community activities, and so on.

There are many countries where such community activity does not fit the traditional mores; Japan and France would be examples. But where the community has a tradition of "volunteerism" — that is, especially the U.S. — managers should indeed be encouraged to participate and to take responsible leadership in community affairs and community organizations. Such activities should, however, never be forced on them nor should they be appraised, rewarded, or promoted according to their participation in voluntary activities. Ordering or pressuring managers into such work is abuse of organizational power and illegitimate.

An exception might be made for managers in businesses where the community activities are really part of their obligation to the business. The local managers of the telephone company, for instance, who take part in community activities, do so as part of their managerial duties and as the local public-relations representatives of their company. The same is true of the manager of a local Sears Roebuck store. And the local realtors who belong to a dozen different community activities and eat lunch every day with a different "service club" know perfectly well that they are not serving the community but promoting their own business and hunting for prospective customers.

But, while desirable, community participation of managers has nothing to do with ethics, and not much to do with responsibility. It is the contribution of an individual in his or her capacity as a neighbor and citizen. And it is something that lies outside their job and outside their managerial responsibility.

Leadership Groups but Not Leaders

A problem of ethics that is peculiar to the manager arises from the fact that the managers of institutions are *collectively* the leadership groups of the society of organizations. But *individually* a manager is just another fellow employee.

This is clearly recognized by the public. Even the most powerful head of the largest corporation is unknown to the public. Indeed most ot the company's employees barely know his name and would not recognize his face. He may owe his position entirely to personal merit and proven performance. But he owes his authority and standing entirely to his institution. Everybody knows GE, the Telephone Company, Mitsubishi, Siemens, and Unilever. But who heads these great corporations — or for that matter, the University of California, the École Polytechnique or Guy's Hospital in London — is of direct interest and concern primarily to the management group within these institutions.

It is therefore inappropriate to speak of managers as leaders. They are "members of the leadership group." The group, however, does occupy a position of visibility, of prominence, and of authority. It therefore has responsibility.

But what are the responsibilities, what are the ethics of the individual manager, as a member of the leadership group?

Essentially being a member of a leadership group is what traditionally has been meant by the term "professional." Membership in such a group confers status, position, prominence, and authority. It also confers duties. To expect every manager to be a leader is futile. There are, in a developed society, thousands, if not millions, of managers — and leadership is always the rare exception and confined to a very few individuals. But as a member of a leadership group a manager stands under the demands of professional ethics — the demands of an ethic of responsibility.

Primum Non Nocere

The first responsibility of a professional was spelled out clearly, 2,500 years ago, in the Hippocratic oath of the Greek physician: *primum non nocere* — "Above all, not knowingly to do harm."

Professionals, whether doctor, lawyer, or manager, cannoτ promise to do good for a client. All they can do is try. But they can promise that they will not knowingly do harm. And the client, in turn, must be able to trust that the professional will not knowingly do him harm. Otherwise the client cannot trust the professional at all. Professionals have to have autonomy. They cannot be controlled, supervised, or directed by the client. The professional has to be private in that his or her knowledge and judgment have to be entrusted with the decision. But it is the foundation of this autonomy, and indeed its rationale, that the professional sees himself as "affected with the public interest." Professionals, in other words, are private in the sense that they are autonomous and not subject to political or ideological control. But they are public in the sense that the welfare of their clients sets limits to their deeds and words. And *Primum non nocere*, "not knowingly to do harm," is the basic rule of professional ethics, the basic rule of an ethics of public responsibility.

There are important areas where managers, and especially business managers, still do not realize that in order to be permitted to remain autonomous and private they have to impose on themselves the responsibility of the professional ethic. They still have to learn that it is their job to scrutinize their deeds, words, and behavior to make sure that they do not knowingly do harm.

Managers who fail to think through and work for the appropriate solution to an impact of their business because it makes them "unpopular in the club" knowingly do harm. They knowingly abet a cancerous growth. That this is stupid has been said. That this always in the end hurts the business or the industry more than a little temporary "unpleasantness" would have hurt has been said too. But it is also gross violation of professional ethics.

But there are other areas as well. American managers, in particular, tend to violate the rule not knowingly do do harm with respect to:

- executive compensation;
- the use of benefit plans to impose "golden fetters" on people in the company's employ; and
- in their profit rhetoric.

Their actions and their words in these areas tend to cause social disruption. They thend to conceal healthy reality and to create disease, or at least social hypochondria. They tend to misdirect and to prevent understanding. And this is grievous social harm.

Executive Compensation and Economic Inequality

Contrary to widespread belief, incomes have become far more equal in all developed countries than in any society of which we have a record. And they have tended to become steadily more equal as national and personal incomes increase. And, equally contrary to popular rhetoric, income equality is greatest in the United States. No only is the distance between net after-tax income of the top earners, e.g., the managers in a business, and both the average and the bottom incomes smaller in the U.S. than in any other developed country — let alone than in any developing country. The proportion of income recipients in extreme income brackets at top and bottom is far smaller compared to the middle income group.

The most reliable measure of income equality is the so-called Gini co-efficient in which an index of zero stands for complete equality of income and an index of 1 for total inequality in which one person in the population receives all the income. The lower the Gini co-efficient, the closer a society is to income equality. In the U.S. the Gini in the early 1970s stood around 0.35 — with about the same figure in Canada, Australia, and Great Britain, and probably also in Japan. West Germany and the Netherlands are about 0.40. France and Sweden are around 0.50

Specifically, in the typical American business the inequality of income between the lowest-paid people and the people in charge — that is, between the machine operator and the manager of a large plant — is at most one to four, if taxes are taken into account. The take-home pay of the machine operator after taxes in 1975 was around $8,000 a year; the after-tax income of very few plant managers was larger than $28,000, all bonuses included. If fringe benefits are included, the ratio is even lower, i.e., one to three (or $14,000 to $38,000 maximum). And similar ratios prevail in other developed countries, e.g., Japan. This, it should be said, is far greater income equality than in any communist country for the simple reason that the economic level of a communist country is lower.

In Soviet Russia, where there are practically no income taxes, the income differential between industrial worker and plant manager runs around 1 to 7, without taking into account the noncash benefits of the Russian manager. And Russian managers operate at an extreme of profit maximization; their profit-based bonus system of compensation so directs them. In China, the differential between workers and plant managers seems to run around 1 to 6 or so.

Whether the degree of inequality of incomes that actually prevails in the U.S. economy is "too high" or "too low" is a matter of opinion. But clearly it is much lower than the great majority of the American public accepts or even considers desirable. Every survey shows that an "income ratio of 1 to 10 or 12" between the blue-collar worker in the factory and the "big boss" would be considered "about right." That would make the "after-tax take-home pay" of the "big boss" somewhere around $75,000 to $100,000 a year, which would be equal to a pre-tax salary of at least $200,000. And only a mere handful of executives earn that much, bonuses included. If the comparison is made — as it should be — between total incomes including fringes, deferred compensation, stock options, and all other forms of extra compensation, a 1 to 12 ratio would work out to an after-tax top figure of $150,000. And no more than a dozen or so top executives in the very largest companies have a pre-tax "total compensation package" of $300,000 and up, which is needed to produce an after-tax value of $150,000. The "extremely rich" are not employed executives — the tax system takes care of those (as it should); they are either a few heirs of the millionaires of pre-tax days or owners of small businesses.

And relative to the incomes of manual and clerical workers, after-tax executive compensation, and especially the income of the executives at the very top, has been going down steadily for fifty years or more.

The facts of increasing income equality in U.S. society are quite clear. Yet the popular impression is one of rapidly increasing inequality. This is illusion; but it is a dangerous illusion. It corrodes. It destroys mutual trust between groups that have to live together. It can only lead to political measures which, while doing no one any good, can seriously harm society, economy, and the manager as well.

In some considerable measure, the belief in growing income inequality in the U.S. reflects, of course, America's racial problem. The emergence into visibility, that is, into the big cities, of a disenfranchised nonworking population of Blacks has created a marginal but highly visible group suffering from extreme inequality of incomes. That the income of the employed Negro has been going up rapidly and is likely, within a decade or so, to be equal to that of the employed white doing the same kind of work — and that four-fifths of the American Negroes are employed and working — tends to be obscured by the dire poverty of the much smaller but highly concentrated groups of unemployed or un-employables in the Black ghettos of the core cities.

Another reason for the widespread belief in growing inequality is inflation. Inflation is a corrosive social poison precisely because it makes people look for a villain. The economists' explanation that no one benefits by inflation, that is, that no one gets the purchasing power that inflation takes away from the income recipients, simply makes no sense to ordinary experience. Somebody must have benefited, somebody "must have stolen what is rightfully mine." Every inflation in history has therefore created class hatred, mutual distrust, and beliefs that, somehow, "the other fellow" gains illicitly at "my" expense. It is always the middle class which becomes paranoid in an inflationary period and turns against the "system." The inflations of the sixties in the developed countries were no exceptions.

But the main cause of the dangerous delusion of increasing inequality of income is the widely publicized enormous *pre-tax* incomes of a few people at the top of a few giant corporations, and the — equally widely publicized — "extras" of executive compensation, e.g., stock options.

The $500,000 a year which the chief executive of one of the giant corporations is being paid is largely "make believe money." Its function is status rather than income. Most of it, whatever tax loopholes the lawyers might find, is immediately taxed away. And the "extras" are simply attempts to put a part of the executive's income into a some-what lower tax bracket. Economically, in other words, neither serves much purpose. But socially and psychologically they "knowingly do harm." They cannot be defended.

One way to eliminate the offense is for companies to commit themselves to a maximum range of *after-tax* compensation. The 1 to 10 ratio that the great majority of Americans would consider perfectly acceptable, would, in fact, be wider than the actual range of most companies. (There should, I would argue, be room, however, for an occasional exception; the rare, "once-in-a-lifetime," very big, "special bonus" to someone, a research scientist, a manager, or a salesperson, who has made an extraordinary contribution.)

But equally important is the acceptance of social responsibility on the part of managers to work for a rational system of taxation, which eliminates the temptation of "tax gimmicks" and the need for them. We know the specifications of such a system — and they are simple: *no* preferential tax rates for *any* personal income, whether from salaries or from capital gains, and a limit on the maximum tax — say 50 percent of total income received.

There is a strong case for adequate incentives for performing executives. And compensation in money is far preferable to hidden compensation such as perquisites. The recipient can choose what to spend the money on rather than, as in the case of "perks," taking whatever the company provides, be it a chauffeur-driven car, a big house, or (as in the case of some Swedish companies) a governess for the children. Indeed it may well be that the compression of income differentials in the years since 1950 has been socially and economically detrimental.

What is pernicious, however, is the delusion of inequality. The basic cause is the tax laws. But the managers' willingness to accept, and indeed to play along with, an antisocial tax structure is a major contributory cause. And unless managers realize that this violates the rule "not knowingly to do damage," they will, in the end, be the main sufferers.

The Danger of "Golden Fetters"

A second area in which the manager of today does not live up to the commitment of *Primum non nocere* is closely connected with compensation.

Since World War II compensation and benefits have been increasingly misused to create "golden fetters."

Retirement benefits, extra compensation, bonuses, and stock options are all forms of compensation. From the point of view of the enterprise — but also from the point of view of the economy — these are "labor costs" no matter how they are labeled. They are treated as such by managements when they sit down to negotiate with the labor union. But increasingly, if only because of the bias of the tax laws, these benefits are being used to tie an employee to his or her employer. They are being made dependent on staying with the same employer, often for many years. And they are structured in such a way that leaving the company's employ entails drastic penalties and actual loss of benefits that have already been earned and that, in effect, constitute wages relating to past employment.

This may be proper in a society which, like that of Japan, is built on lifetime employment and excludes mobility. Even in Japan, however, "golden fetters" are no longer acceptable to professional and technical employees who increasingly should have mobility in their own interest, in that of the Japanese economy, and even in that of the Japanese company. In the West, and especially in the United States, such golden fetters are clearly antisocial.

Golden fetters do not strengthen the company. They lead to "negative selection." People who know that they are not performing in their present employment — that is, people who are clearly in the wrong place — will often not move but stay where they know they do not properly belong. But if they stay because the penalty for leaving is too great, they resist and resent it. They know that they have been bribed and were too weak to say no. They are likely to be sullen, resentful, and bitter the rest of their working lives.

The fact that the employees themselves eagerly seek these benefits is no excuse. After all, medieval serfdom also began as an eagerly sought "employee benefit."

It is incumbent, therefore, on the managers to think through which of these benefits should properly — by their own rationale — be tied to continued employment. Stock options might, for instance, belong here. But pension rights, performance bonuses, participation in profits, and so on, have been "earned" and should be available to employees without restricting their rights as a citizen, an individual, and a person. And, again, managers will have to work to get the tax law changes that are needed.

The Rhetoric of the Profit Motive

Managers, finally, through their rhetoric, make it impossible for the public to understand economic reality. This violates the requirement that managers, being leaders, not knowingly do harm. This is particularly true of the United States but also of Western Europe. For in the West, managers still talk constantly of the profit motive. And they still define the goal of their business as profit maximization. They do not stress the objective function of profit. They do not talk of risks — or very rarely. They do not stress the need for capital. They almost never even mention the cost of capital, let alone that a business has to produce enough profit to obtain the capital it needs at minimum cost.

Managers constantly complain about the hostility to profit. They rarely realize that their own rhetoric is one of the main reasons for this hostility. For indeed in the terms management uses when it talks to the public, there is no possible justification for profit, no explanation for its existence, no function it performs. There is only the profit motive, that is, the desire of some anonymous capitalists — and why that desire should be indulged in by society any more than bigamy, for instance, is never explained. But profitability is a crucial *need* of economy and society.

Managerial practice in most large American companies is perfectly rational. It is the rhetoric which obscures, and thereby threatens to damage both business and society. To be sure, few American companies work out profitability as a *minimum* requirement. As a result, most probably underestimate the profitability the company truly requires, let alone the inflationary erosion of capital. But they, consciously or not, base their profit planning on the twin objectives of ensuring access to captial needed and minimizing the cost of capital. In the American context, if only because of the structure of the U.S. capital market, a high "price/earnings ratio" is indeed a key to the minimization of the cost of capital; and "optimization of profits" is therefore a perfectly rational strategy which tends to lower, in the long run, the actual cost of capital.

But this makes it even less justifiable to keep on using the rhetoric of the profit motive. It serves no purpose except to confuse and embitter.

These examples of areas in which managers do not hold themselves to the rule "not knowingly to do harm" are primarily American examples. They apply to some extent to Western Europe. But they hardly apply to Japan. The principle, however, applies in all countries, and in the developing countries as much as in developed ones. These cases are taken from business management. The principle, however, applies to managers of all institutions in the society of organizations.

In any pluralist society responsibility for the public good has been the central problem and issue. The pluralist society of organizations will be no exception. Its leaders represent "special interests," that is, institutions designed to fulfill a specific and partial need of society. Indeed the leaders of this pluralist society of organizations are the servants of such institutions. At the same time, they are the major leadership group such as society knows or is likely to produce. They have to serve both their own institution and the common good. If the society is to function, let alone if it is to remain a free society, the people we call managers will remain "private" in their institutions. No matter who owns them and how, they will maintain autonomy. But they will also have to be "public" in their ethics.

In this tension between the private functioning of the manager: the necessary autonomy of the manager's institution and its accountability to its own mission and purpose, and the public character of the manager, lies the specific ethical problem of the society of organizations. *Primum non nocere* may seem tame compared to the rousing calls for "statesmanship" that abound in today's manifestos of social responsibility. But, as the physicians found out long ago, it is not an easy rule to live up to. Its very modesty and self-constraint make it the right rule for the ethics managers need, the ethics of responsibility.

Multinationals and Developing Countries: Myths and Realities

Chapter 32

*Four False Assumptions: Corporate Capitalism; The Resource Is
Foreign Capital; Global Exploitation; and The Form and
Ownership of the Multinational Organization
Developing Countries Are Not a Significant Source of Profit
Resources Can't Be Imported, They Must Be Developed Within the
Developing Country
Productive Integration Across National Boundaries
Local Participation in Ownership Favors, Does Not Limit, the Foreign
Investor
Response to an Emerging Genuine World Economy*

*F*our assumptions are commonly made in the discussion of multinationals and the developing countries — by friends and enemies alike of the multinational company. These assumptions largely inform the policies both of the developing countries and of the multi-national companies. Yet, all four assumptions are false, which explains in large measure both the acrimony of the debate and the sterility of so many development policies.

These four false but generally accepted assumptions are:

1. the developing countries are important to the multinational companies and a major source of sales, revenues, profits and growth for them, if not the mainstay of "corporate capitalism";

2. foreign capital, whether supplied by governments or by businesses, can supply the resources, and especially the capital resources required for economic development;

3. the ability of the multinational company to integrate and allocate productive resources on a global basis and across national boundaries, and thus to substitute transnational for national economic considerations, subordinates the best national interests of the developing country to "global exploitation";

4. the traditional nineteenth century form of corporate organization, that is, the "parent company" with wholly owned "branches" abroad, is the form of organization for the twentieth-century multinational company.

What are the realities?

Developing Countries Are Not A Significant Source of Profit

Extractive industries have to go wherever the petroleum, iron, or copper ore or bauxite is to be found, whether in a developing or in a developed country. But for the typical twentieth-century multinational, that is a manufacturing, distributing or financial company, developing countries are important neither as markets nor as producers of profits. Indeed it can be said bluntly that the major manufacturing, distributive and financial companies of the developed world would barely notice it, were the sales in and the profits from the developing countries suddenly to disappear.

Confidential inside data in my possession on about 45 manufacturers, distributors and financial institutions among the world's leading multinationals, both North American and European, show that the developed two-thirds of Brazil — from Bello Horizonte southward — is an important market for some of these companies, though even Brazil ranks among the first 12 sales territories, or among major revenue producers, for only two of them. But central and southern Brazil, while still "poor," are clearly no longer "underdeveloped." And otherwise not even India or Mexico — the two "developing" countries with the largest markets — ranks for any of the multinational companies in my sample ahead even of a single major sales district in the home country, be it the Hamburg-North Germany district, the English Midlands or Kansas City.

On the worldwide monthly or quarterly sales and profit chart, which most large companies use as their most common top-management tool, practically no developing country even appears in my sample of 45 major multinationals except as part of a "region," e.g., "Latin America," or under "Others."

The profitability of the businesses of these companies in the developing countries is uniformly lower by about two percentage points than that of the businesses in the developed countries, except for the pharmaceutical industry where the rate of return, whether on sales or on invested capital, is roughly the same for both. As a rule, it takes longer — by between 18 months to three years — to make a new operation break even in a developing country. And the growth rate — again excepting the pharmaceutical industry — is distinctly slower. Indeed, in these respresentative 45 businesses, 75 to 85 percent of all growth, whether in sales or in profits, in the last 25 years, occurred in the developed countries. In constant dollars the business of these 45 companies in the developed world doubled — or more than doubled — between 1955 and 1970. But their business in the developing countries grew by no more than one-third during that period if the figures are adjusted for inflation.

Published data, while still scarce and inadequate, show the same facts. Only for the extractive industries have the developing countries — and then only a very few of them — been of any significance whether as a source of profits, as loci of growth, or as areas of investment.

The reason is, of course, that — contrary to the old, and again fashionable, theory of "capitalist imperialism" — sales, growth and profits are where the market and the purchasing power are.

To the developing country, however, the multinational is both highly important and highly visible.

A plant employing 750 people and selling eight million dollars worth of goods is in most developing countries a major employer — both of rank and file and of management — and a big business. For the multinational parent company, employing altogether 97,000 people and selling close to two billion dollars worth of goods a year, that plant is, however, at best marginal. Top management in Rotterdam, Munich, London or Chicago can spend practically no time on it.

Neglect and indifference rather than "exploitation" is the justified grievance of the developing countries in respect to the multinationals. Indeed, top management people in major multinationals who are personally interested in the developing countries find themselves constantly being criticized for neglecting the important areas and for devoting too much of their time and attention to "outside interests." Given the realities of the business, its markets, growth opportunities and profit opportunities, this is a valid criticism.

The discrepancy between the relative insignificance of the affiliate in a developing country and its importance and visibility for the host country poses, however, a major problem for the multinationals as well. Within the developing country the manager in charge of a business with 750 employees and eight million dollars in sales has to be an important person. While this business is minute compared to the company's business in Germany, Great Britain or the United States, it is just as difficult for the manager to manage — indeed it is likely to be a good deal more difficult, risky and demanding. And the manager has to treat as an equal with the government leaders, the bankers and the business leaders of his country — people whom the district sales manager in Hamburg, Rotterdam or Kansas City never even sees. Yet the manager's sales and profits are less than those of the Hamburg, Rotterdam or Kansas City sales district. And the growth potential is, in most cases, even lower.

This clash between two realities — the personal qualifications and competence, the position, prestige and power needed by the affiliate's top management people to do their job in the developing country, and the reality of a "sales district" in absolute, quantitative terms — the traditional corporate structure of the multinationals cannot resolve.

Resources: Not Imported But Developed Within

The second major assumption underlying the discussion of multinationals and developing countries is the belief that resources from abroad, and especially capital from abroad, can "develop" a country.

But in the first place no country is "underdeveloped" because it lacks resources. "Underdevelopment" is inability to obtain full performance from resources; indeed we should really be talking of countries of higher and lower productivity rather than of "developed" or "underdeveloped" countries. In particular, very few countries — Tibet and New Guinea may be exceptions — lack *capital*. Developing countries have, almost by definition, more capital than they productively employ. What "developing" countries lack is the full ability to mobilize their resources, whether human resources, capital or the physical resources. What they need are "triggers," stimuli from abroad and from the more highly developed countries, that will energize the resources of the country and will have a "multiplier impact," that is mobilize several units of local energies and resources for every unit brought in.

The two success stories of development in the last hundred years — Japan and Canada — show this clearly. In the beginning, Japan imported practically no capital except small sums for early infrastructure investments, such as the first few miles of railroad. Japan organized, however, quite early, what is probably to this day the most efficient system for gathering and putting to use every drop of capital in the country. And she imported — lavishly and without restraints — technology with a very high multiplier impact and has continued to do so to this day.

Canada, in the mid-1930s, was far less "developed" a country than most Latin American countries are today. Then the Liberal governments of the 1930s decided to build an effective system for collecting domestic capital and to put it into infrastructure investments with a very high "multiplier" effect — roads, health care, ports, education and effective national and provincial administrations. Foreign capital was deliberately channeled into manufacturing and mining. Domestic capital and entrepreneurs were actually discouraged in the extractive and manufacturing sectors. But they were strongly encouraged in all tertiary activities such as distribution, banking, insurance and in local supply and finishing work in manufacturing. As a result a comparatively small supply of foreign capital — between a tenth and a twentieth of Canada's total capital formation — led to very rapid development within less than two decades.

There is a second fallacy in the conventional assumption, namely that there is unlimited absorptive capacity for money and especially for money from abroad. But in most developing countries there are actually very few big investment opportunities. There may be big hydroelectric potential; but unless there are customers with purchasing power, or industrial users nearby, there is no economic basis for a power plant. Furthermore, there is no money without strings. To service foreign capital, even at a minimal interest rate, requires foreign exchange. At that, loans or equity investments as a rule constitute a smaller (and, above all, a clearly delimited) burden than grants and other political subsidies from abroad. The latter always create heavy obligations, in terms of both, foreign and domestic policy, no matter where they come from.

A developing country will therefore get the most out of resources available abroad, especially capital, if it channels capital where it has the greatest "multiplier impact." Moreover, it should channel it where one dollar of imported capital will generate the largest number of domestic dollars in investment, both in the original investment itself and in impact-investment (e.g., the gas stations, motels and auto repair shops which an automobile plant calls into being), and where one job created by the original investment generates the most jobs directly and indirectly (again an automobile industry is a good example). Above all, the investment should be channeled where it will produce the largest number of local managers and entrepreneurs and generate the most managerial and entrepreneurial competence. For making resources fully effective depends on the supply and competence of the managerial and entrepreneurial resource.

According to all figures, government money has a much lower multiplier impact than private money. This is, of course, most apparent in the Communist-bloc countries; low, very low, productivity of capital is the major weakness of the Communist economies, whether that of Russia or of her European satellites. But it is true also of public (e.g., World Bank) money elsewhere; it generates little, if any, additional investment either from within or from without the recipient country. And "prestige" investments, such as a steel mill, tend to have a fairly low multiplier impact — both in jobs and in managerial vigor — as against, for instance, a department store which brings into existence any number of small local manufactureres and suppliers and creates a major managerial and entrepreneurial cluster around it.

For the multinational in manufacturing, distribution, or finance locating in a developing country, rapid economic development of the host country offers the best chance for growth and profitability. The multinational thus has a clear self-interest in the "multiplier" impact of its investment, products and technology. It would be well advised to look on the capital it provides as "pump priming" rather than as "fuel." The more dollars (or pesos or cruzeiros) of local capital each of its own dollars of investment generates, the greater will be the development impact of its investment, and its chance for success. For the developing country the same holds true: to maximize the development impact of each imported dollar.

The Canadian strategy was carried on too long; by the early 1950s, Canada had attained full development and should have shifted to a policy of moving its own domestic capital into "superstructure" investments. But though the Canadian strategy is certainly not applicable to many developing countries today — and though, like any strategy, it became obsolete by its very success — nevertheless it was highly successful, very cheap and resulted in rapid economic growth while at the same time ensuring a high degree of social development and social justice.

What every developing country needs is a strategy which looks upon the available foreign resources, especially of capital, as the "trigger" to set off maximum deployment of a country's own resources and to have the maximum "multiplier effect." Such a strategy sees in the multinational a means to energize domestic potential — and especially to create domestic entrepreneurial and managerial competence — rather than a substitute for domestic resources, domestic efforts and, even, domestic capital. To make the multinationals effective agents of development in the developing countries therefore requires, above all, a policy of encouraging the domestic private sector, the domestic entrepreneur and the domestic manager. If they are being discouraged the resources brought in from abroad will, inevitable, be wasted.

For by themselves multinationals cannot produce development; they can only turn the crank but not push the car. It is as futile and self-defeating to use capital from abroad as a means to frighten and cow the local business community — as the bright young men of the early days of the Alliance for Progress apparently wanted to do — as it is to mobilize the local business community against the "wicked imperialist multinational."

Productive Integration Across National Boundaries

The multinational, it is said, tends to allocate production according to global economics. This is perfectly correct, though so far very few companies actually have a global strategy. But far from being a threat to the developing country, this is potentially the developing country's one trump card in the world economy. Far from depriving the governments of the developing countries of decision-making power, the global strategy of the multinationals may be the only way these governments can obtain some effective control and bargaining leverage.

Short of attack by a foreign country the most serious threat to the economic sovereignty of developing countries, and especially of small ones, i.e., of most of them, is the shortage of foreign exchange. It is an absolute bar to freedom of decision. Realizing this, many developing countries, especially in the 1950s and early 1960s, chose a deliberate policy of "import substitution." They granted subsidies and high protective tariffs to investors — mostly from abroad — who would manufacture something in the country, e.g., refrigerators, that formerly had to be imported and paid for with foreign exchange.

By now we have learned that in the not-so-very-long run this creates equal or worse import-dependence and foreign-exchange problems. Now a variant of "import substitution" has become fashionable: a "domestic-content" policy which requires the foreign company to produce an increasing proportion of the final product in the country itself. This, predictably, will eventually have the same consequences as the now discredited "import substitution," namely, greater dependence on raw materials, equipment and supplies from abroad. And in all but the very few countries with already substantial markets (Brazil is perhaps the only one — but then Brazil is not, after all, "developing" any longer in respect to the central and southern two-thirds of the country) such a policy must, inevitably, make for a permanently high-cost industry unable to compete and to grow. The policy creates jobs in the very short run, to be sure; but it does so at the expense of the consumer, that is of the poor and of the country's potential to generate jobs in the future and to grow.

What developing countries need are *both* — foreign-exchange earnings and productive facilities large enough for efficient and economical production and distribution and with them substantial employment. This they can obtain only if they can integrate their emerging productive facilities — whether in manufactured goods or in such agricultural products as fruits and wine — with the largest and the fastest-growing economy around, i.e., the world market.

But exporting requires market knowledge, marketing facilities and marketing finance. It also requires political muscle to overcome strongly entrenched protectionist forces, and especially labor unions and farm blocs in the developed countries. Exporting is done most successfully, most easily and most cheaply if one has an assured "captive" market, at least for part of the production to be sold in the world market. This applies particularly to most of the developing countries, whose home market is too small to be an adequate base for an export-oriented industry.

The multinational's capacity to allocate production across national boundary lines and according to the logic of the world market should thus be a major ally of the developing countries. The more rationally and the more "globally" production is being allocated, the more they stand to gain. A multinational company, by definition, can equalize the cost of capital across national lines (to some considerable extent, at least). It can equalize to a large extent the managerial resource, that is, it can move executives, can train them, etc. The only resource it cannot freely move is labor. And that is precisely the resource in which the developing countries have the advantage.

This advantage is likely to increase. Unless there is a world-wide prolonged depression, labor in the developed countries is going to be increasingly scarce and expensive, if only because of low birthrates, while a large-scale movement of people from pre-industrial areas into developed countries, such as the mass-movement of American Blacks to the Northern cities or the mass-movement of "guest workers" to Western Europe, is politically or socially no longer possible.

But unless the multinationals are being used to integrate the productive resources of the developing countries into the productive network of the world economy — and especially into the production and marketing system of the multinationals themselves — it is most unlikely that major export markets for the production of the developing countries will actually emerge very quickly.

Thus, the most advantageous strategy for the developing countries would seem to be to replace — or, at least to supplement — the policy of "domestic content" by a policy that uses the multinationals' integrating ability to develop large productive facilities with access to markets in the developed world. A good idea might be to encourage investment by multinationals with definite plans — and eventually firm commitments — to produce for export, especially within their own multinational system. As Taiwan and Singapore have demonstrated, it can make much more sense to become the most efficient large supplier worldwide of one model or one component than to be a high-cost small producer of the entire product or line. This would create more jobs and provide the final product at lower prices to the country' own consumers.   And it should result in large foreign-exchange earnings

I would suggest a second integration requirement. That developing countries want to limit the number of foreigners a company brings in is understandable. But the multinational can be expected to do that anyhow as much as possible — moving people around is expensive and presents all sorts of problems and troubles. Far more important would be a requirement by the developing country that the multinational integrate the managerial and professional people it employs in the country within its worldwide management development plans. Most especially it should assign an adequate number of the younger, abler people for its affiliate in the developing country to from three to five years of managerial and professional work in one of the developed countries. So far, to my knowledge, this is being done systematically only by some of the major American banks, by

Alcan, the Canada-based aluminum company, and by Nestle, the Swiss food-products giant. Yet it is people and their competence who propel development; and the most important competence needed is not technical, i.e., what one can learn in a course, but management of people, marketing and finance, and first-hand knowledge of developed countries.

In sum, from the point of view of the developing countries the best cross-national use of resources which the multinational is — or should be — capable of may well be the most positive element in the present world economy. A policy of self-sufficiency is not possible even for the best-endowed country today. Development, even of modest proportions, cannot be based on uneconomically small, permanently high-cost facilities, either in manufacturing or in farming. Nor is it likely to occur, let alone rapidly, under the restraint of a continuous balance-of-payments crisis. The integration of the productive capacities and advantages of developing countries into the world economy is the only way out. And the multinational's capacity for productive integration across national boundaries would seem the most promising tool for this.

Local Ownership Favors Not Limits the Foreign Investor

That 100-percent ownership on the part of the "parent company" is *the* one and only corporate structure for the multinational, while widely believed, has never been true. In so important a country as Japan it has always been the rather rare exception, with most non-Japanese companies operating through joint ventures. Sears, Roebuck is in partnership throughout Canada with a leading local retail chain, Simpson's. The Chase Manhattan Bank operates in many countries as a minority partner in and with local banks. Adela, the multinational venture-capital firm in Latin America, and by far the most successful of all development institutions in the world today, has confined itself from its start, in the mid-sixties, to minority participation in its ventures, and so on.

But it is true that, historically, 100-percent ownership has been considered the preferred form, and anything else as likely to make unity of action, vision and strategy rather difficult. Indeed, restriction of the foreign investor to less than 100-percent control or to a minority participation, e.g., in the Andean Pact agreements or in Mexico's legislation regarding foreign investments, is clearly intended as restraint on the foreigner, if not as punitive action.

But increasingly the pendulum is likely to swing the other way. (Indeed, it may not be too far-fetched to anticipate that, a few years hence, "anti-foreign" sentiment may take the form of demanding 100-percent foreign-capital investment in the national company in the developing country, and moving toward outlawing partnerships or joint ventures with local capital as a drain on a country's slender capital resources.) The multinational will find it increasingly to its advantage to structure ownership in a variety of ways, and especially in ways that make it possible for it to gain access to both local capital and local talent.

Capital markets are rapidly becoming "polycentric." The multinationals will have to learn so to structure their businesses as to be able to tap any capital market — whether in the United States, Western Europe, Japan, Brazil, the Middle East or wherever. This the monolithic "parent company" with wholly-owned branches is not easily capable of. Europeans, for instance, much prefer to buy convertible debentures rather than common shares. But a purely American company is likely to be unable to offer their preferred security to the Europeans; neither the U.S. capital market nor U.S. laws favor it. There is also more and more evidence that the capital-raising capacity of a huge multinational, especially for medium-term working capital, can be substantially increased by making major segments of the system capable of financing themselves largely in their own capital markets and with their own investing public and financial institutions.

But capital is also likely to be in short supply for years to come, barring a major global depression. And this might well mean that the multinationals will only be willing and able to invest in small, less profitable and more slowly growing markets, i.e., in developing countries, if these countries supply a major share of the needed capital rather than have the foreign investor put up all of it.

That this is already happening, the example of Japan shows. Lifting restrictions on foreign investment was expected to bring a massive rush of take-over bids and 100 percent foreign-owned ventures. Instead it is now increasingly the Western investor, American as well as European, who presses for joint ventures in Japan and expects the Japanese partner to supply the capital while he supplies technology and product knowledge.

Perhaps more important will be the need to structure for other than 100-percent ownership to obtain the needed managerial talent in the developing country. If the affiliate in the developing country is not a "branch" but a separate company with substantial outside capital investment, the role and position of its executives becomes manageable. They are then what they have to be, namely, truly "top management," even though in employment and sales their company may still be insignificant within the giant concern.

And if the multinational truly attempts to integrate production across national boundaries, a "top management" of considerable stature becomes even more necessary. For then, the managers of the affiliate in a developing country have to balance both a national business and a global strategy. They have to be "top management" in their own country and handle on the local level highly complex economic, financial, political and labor relations as well as play as full members on a worldwide "systems management" team. To do this as a "subordinate" is almost impossible. One has to be an "equal," with one's own truly autonomous command

Domestically, we long ago learned that "control" has been divorced from "ownership" and, indeed, is rapidly becoming quite independent of "ownership." There is no reason why the same development should not be taking place internationally — and for the same reasons: (1) "ownership" does not have enough capital to finance the scope of modern business; and (2) management, i.e., "control," has to have professional competence, authority and standing of its own. Domestically the divorce of "control" from "ownership" has not undermined "control." On the contrary, it has made managerial control and direction more powerful, more purposeful, more cohesive.

There is no inherent reason why moving away from "100-percent ownership" in developing countries should make impossible maintenance of common cohesion and central control. On the contrary, both because it extends the capital base of the multinational in a period of worldwide capital shortage and because it creates local partners, whether businessmen or government agencies, the divorce between control and direction may well strengthen cohesion, and may indeed even be a prerequisite to a true global strategy.

At the same time such partnership may heighten the development impact of multinational investment by mobilizing domestic capital for productive investment and by speeding up the development of local entrepreneurs and managers.

Admittedly, mixed ownership has serious problems; but they do not seem insurmountable, as the Japanese joint-venture proves. It also has advantages; and in a period of worldwide shortage of capital it is the multinational that would seem to be the main beneficiary. Indeed one could well argue that developing countries, if they want to attract foreign investment in such a period, may have to *offer* co-investment capital, and that provisions for the participation of local investment in ownership will come to be seen (and predictably to be criticized) as favoring the foreign investor rather than as limiting him.

Multinationals: A Response to an Emerging World Economy

The multinational, while the most important and most visible innovation of the postwar period in the economic field, is primarily a symptom of a much greater change. It is a response to the emergence of a genuine world economy. This world economy is not an agglomeration of national economies as was the "international economy" of nineteenth-century international trade theory. It is fundamentally autonomous, has its own dynamics, its own demand patterns, its own institutions — and even its own money and credit system in embryonic form, the so-called "Special Drawing Rights" (SDR). For the first time in 400 years — since the end of the sixteenth century when the word "sovereignty" was first coined — the territorial political unit and the economic unit are no longer congruent.

This, understandably, appears as a threat to national governments. The threat is aggravated by the fact that no one so far has a workable theory of the world economy. As a result there is today no proven, effective, predictable economic policy: witness the impotence of governments in the face of worldwide inflation.

The multinationals are but a symptom. Suppressing them, predictably, can only aggravate the disease. But to fight the symptoms in lieu of a cure has always been tempting. It is therefore entirely possible that the multinationals will be severely damaged and perhaps even destroyed within the next decade. If so, this will be done by the governments of the developed countries, and especially by the governments of the multinationals' *home* countries, the United States, Britain, Germany, France, Japan, Sweden, Holland and Switzerland — the countries where 95 percent of the world's multinationals are domiciled and which together account for at least three-quarters of the multinationals' business and profits. The developing nations can contribute emotionalism and rhetoric to the decisions, but very little else. They are simply not important enough to the multinationals (or to the world economy) to have a major impact.

But at the same time the emergence of a genuine world economy is the one real hope for most of the developing countries, especially for the great majority which by themselves are too small to be viable as "national economies" under present technologies, present research requirements, present capital requirements and present transportation and communications facilities. The next ten years are the years in which they will both most need the multinationals and have the greatest opportunity of benefiting from them. For these will be the years when the developing countries will have to find jobs and incomes for the largest number of new entrants into the labor force in their history while, at the same time, the developed countries will experience a sharp contraction of the number of new entrants into their labor force — a contraction that is already quite far advanced in Japan and in parts of Western Europe and will reach the United States by the late 1970s. And the jobs that the developing countries will need so desperately for the next ten years will to a very large extent require the presence of the multinationals — their investment, their technology, their managerial competence, and above all their marketing and export capabilities.

The best hope for developing countries, both to attain political and cultural nationhood and to obtain the employment opportunities and export earnings they need, is through the integrative power of the world economy. And their tool, if only they are willing to use it, is, above all, the multinational company — precisely because it represents a global economy and cuts across national boundaries.

The multinational, if it survives, will surely look different tomorrow, will have a different structure, and will be "transnational" rather than "multinational." But even the multinational of today is — or at least should be — a most effective means to constructive nationhood for the developing world.

Definitions of Key Terms

Accountability Responsibility for results.

Accounting The system of keeping records of financial transactions and of summarizing these data in appropriate reports for management, financial institutions, or government agencies.

Administer To manage, especially in a setting that emphasizes the application of fixed procedures and minimal environmental turbulence.

Administrators Persons who administer. Also a title used for some managerial positions such as the administration of a hospital.

Advertising and promotion specialist A person well-versed in the cost and appropriateness of different modes of advertising and promoting a product or service and thereby able to advise on the best means to use in generating interest in that product or service.

Affiliate A company that works closely with another company in serving a particular market. A subsidiary of a multinational corporation that serves a country other than the larger company's home country is an affiliate.

Allocate To divide resources among competing interests. Allocating financial resources through a budgetary process is a prime example of such division. Other resources such as people and time are allocated by some mechanism if there are varying ways to employ them.

Allocation A quantity of a resource allocated for a particular item. In speaking about money, a travel allocation would be an amount of money set aside for travel.

Analytical methods Methods of analysis that use mathematics and logic to resolve managerial problems. Financial ratio analysis and operations research analysis are prime examples of analytical methods.

Antitrust legislation Laws that prohibit the formation and operation of business monopolies. The Sherman Antitrust Law is the base of American antitrust law.

Appraise To assess the value of a property, a person's job performance, or other item of value.

341

Assessment center A method of evaluating candidates for a managerial position that involves bringing the candidates to a central location for a series of tests, interviews, and exercises. Assessors evaluate the candidates' performance and make recommendations to the person or persons who will make the final choice.

Assets The items of value owned by a company or person. Also the items fitting this description that appear on the left-hand side of a balance sheet opposite the liabilities.

Authority The right to use assigned resources within one's discretion to accomplish an assigned task, including the right to direct people and other resources. Authority is always limited by the organization's policies and procedures and the rules of the larger society.

Automation The system of production that uses self-controlled machines to accomplish the task at hand. When further self-controlled devices are incorporated, one says that there is greater automation in the process.

Autonomy The ability to operate independently of other units. A manager may have great autonomy in his job, or one can speak of a subsidiary of a conglomerate having limited autonomy.

Balance of payments The payments due a country for exports less the payments it owes for imports during a particular time period. The notion can be applied to a single pair of countries or to one country versus all others. The term "balance of trade" is also used.

Bankrupt A legal or economic term that means insolvency or inability to pay one's debts.

Basic strategy objective A company or organization's central aim in trying to achieve its overall financial or other objectives. For example, Sears and Roebuck's basic strategy objective during its early decades was to merchandise true values to farmers and their families through mail-order merchandising.

Behavioral psychology The school of psychology that relies exclusively on the analysis of empirically observed behavior in accounting for why people act as they do.

Behavioral science approach to management The school of thought that gives primary importance to the disciplines of psychology, sociology, and anthropology in explaining management and in trying to improve the practice of management.

Billing The business function of giving customers or clients formal notice that payment is due on a certain date for goods or services provided.

Boss The person in charge or holding final authority.

Brand name product A product sold with a company's name or other specific name attached to it rather than being sold with only a generic name.

Break-even point The level of sales or production that is necessary to break even — that is, to lose no money and to make no money. Analysis whose objective is to determine this level is called break-even analysis.

Budget An approved scheme that specifies how much is to be spent on each category of expenditure during a given time period. The scheme is usually compiled in a document referred to as the budget.

Budget allocation The amount to be spent in a particular category as specified in a budget.

Budgeting The process of developing a budget.

Budget-based institution An organization that receives relatively assured income rather than being subject to an immediately responsive market. Government agencies and nonprofit organizations are examples of such institutions.

"Buying-in" The process of getting approval to provide a product or service by underestimating the total cost.

By-product A substance, product, or condition produced by a production process in addition to the primary item produced.

Capacity   The maximum amount of product or service that could be provided by a given mechanism.

Capital   Wealth that an organization possesses to employ in achieving its aims.

Capital equipment   A company or organization's equipment or buildings whose purchase required the expenditure of substantial capital.

Capital formation   The process by which capital is created in an economy.

Capital-intensive industry   An industry that in comparison to other industries requires large investments of capital per dollar of sales or production. Frequently contrasted with labor-intensive industry.

Capital investment   An investment or an employing of a company's capital in a specific project.

Capital investment decisions   Decisions regarding the employment of a firm's capital. Since capital is usually invested in plant or equipment for long periods, it is of utmost importance that decisions be made with as much knowledge as possible about the expected rate of return on the capital. Thus there is a vast body of literature on this kind of analysis and decision making.

Carrying costs   The costs incurred by holding inventory.

Centralization   A method of organizing that concentrates decision making at the top of an organization's hierarchy.

Client   A customer for a service-producing enterprise.

Commander   A person empowered to give orders and expect results, most frequently in a military context.

Committee   A group of people assigned to perform a given task as a group.

Common Market   The group of Western European countries banded together to provide a larger market open to all members, or any market formed in this manner.

Communication   The transfer of meaning from one (the sender) to another (the receiver). The sender and receiver may be persons, corporate entities, or other groups of people.

Compensation   That which is given in exchange for work performed. Compensation is usually money but may include other items such as privileges.

Competition   The companies that are alternative sources of supply for a given company's customers or clients.

Computer   Electronic device that can perform multiple complex calculations or logic operations.

Computer program   An integrated set of instructions for a computer to use in performing a particular task.

Computer programmer   A person who creates computer programs.

Conflict   Disagreements or clashes in feelings within an organization.

Conglomerate   A company made up of many other companies in a wide variety of industries. Many such companies were formed in the late 1960s.

"Conscience" activities   The activities directed to giving vision and to setting standards and auditing performance against them.

Constituencies   The various interest groups who vie for the attention of an organization. Faculty, students, parents, foundations, and government agencies each constitute a constituency for a university.

Consumer   The person who is the user of the product or service produced.

Consumerism   The social movement that insists that products and services be of unassailable quality and without any possible hazardous side effects.

Control   The management function that aims to keep activities directed in such a way that desired results are achieved. Monitoring of performance is the starting point of all control. In case performance deviates from what is expected, corrective action must be taken to get the process back on the track.

Cooperation   Joint effort to achieve a desired result.

Coordinate   To integrate one's own efforts with those of others to achieve a desired result.   Frequently one speaks of coordination of efforts in various parts of the organization so that a manager is coordinating his efforts with those of people in other departments.

Corporation   A legal entity formed by persons to enter a business while limiting their liability to the monies they have contributed to the enterprise.

Cost accountant   An accountant whose primary responsibility is to determine the cost of goods or services.   The cost figures are to be used in determining profit levels and in meeting other demands for judgments on what the costs are.

Cost center   In a business, costs are either assigned exclusively to the business as a whole, or the business is broken into parts each of which is responsible for certain costs.   In the latter event, the parts are the cost centers.   In a multidivision company, the divisions may be the cost centers.

Cost effectiveness analysis   The method of analysis that compares the cost of alternative solutions for a problem with the relative benefits provided by each.

Cost of capital   The rate of return that should be used as the minimum acceptable for considering a given capital expenditure;   the "rental" cost of money.   Thus, projects must pay more than it would cost to "rent" the money required, or no financial benefit has been produced.

Credit   Ability to borrow funds, or the funds so borrowed.

Critical path analysis   A method of analyzing the scheduling of a project with multiple subactivities.   The method uses network diagrams that represent the component activities.   Time required to complete each activity is analyzed, and the earliest and latest beginning date for each activity is specified.   Finally the longest path through the sequence of activities (the critical path) is identified, and that path receives special attention so that the project will be completed on time.

Customers   The persons or organizations that consume the product or services provided by another company.

Data processing   The function of handling the masses of data involved in the multiple transactions related to a firm's business.   Since most large firms use computers in this function, the department in charge of the computing is frequently called the data processing department.   Similarly, the function is often referred to as electronic data processing (EDP).

Decentralization   A method of organizing that disburses decision making to multiple locations and levels rather than concentrating it at the top of the organization's hierarchy.

Decision   A determination to take a particular action.

Decision making   The process of arriving at decisions.

Decision theory   A body of analytical tools including logic, mathematical models (especially models that use probability theory), and diagrams to be used in decision making.

Decision tree   From decision theory, a diagram that looks very much like a tree and that allows alternative decisions to be pictured in an orderly fashion.

Deficit   The amount by which expenses exceed the funds available (or allocated) to cover them.

Delegation   The process a manager uses to assign a task or part of a task to one of his subordinates.

Demand pattern   The relative distribution of demand among the various markets served or that could be served.

Demographics   The study of populations as regards their numbers, births, deaths, etc., and the statistics so produced.

Department   A basic subunit of an organization, frequently used in the formal title of some subunits.

Departmentalization The process of grouping organizational activities into basic sub-units, usually done using a common characteristic such as function, product, or geography.

Depreciate The process by which the worth or equipment or buildings are assigned decreased values due to deterioration, obsolescence, or other considerations.

Depression A period of extremely low business activity, marked by high unemployment and extreme declines in demand.

Developed countries Those countries with the highest standards of living, generally the industrialized nations.

Developing countries Nations that have begun to industrialize but whose economies are still dominated by small farms and low personal-income levels.

Direct labor cost The cost that is attributable to the production process itself and that is so ascribed in accounting for the results of the business. Direct labor costs are frequently contrasted with indirect labor costs, which are costs counted in determining results but are not part of the production payroll.

Direct To indicate that a certain action should be taken; to command.

Discounted cash flow analysis A method of allowing a stream of fund flows that are to occur over a period of years to be summarized into a single number so that alternative streams can be compared.

Distribution The function of dispensing the goods manufactured or warehoused to the locations where they will be consumed or received by customers. Choices of modes of transportation to be used and their timeliness and cost are important elements of the distribution function.

Distributive system The mechanism set up to accomplish the distribution task.

Distributor A company or business agent who is the middleman between the manufacturer and the end user.

Dividend The amount of profit for a given period returned to the owner of one share of a company's stock.

Division of labor The method of dividing a task into specialized subtasks with different people doing different subtasks so that they may become very efficient at performing their subtask and thereby contribute to accomplishing the overall job at least cost.

Economic development The process by which a nation's economy grows and moves toward providing its people a higher standard of living.

Econometric methods Methods used by a branch of economics that makes extensive use of mathematical modeling and simulation.

EDP (electronic data processing) Data processing using computers.

Effective demand The demand that will be realized if the product or service is made available.

Effectiveness The extent to which the desired result is realized. Frequently compared with efficiency.

Efficiency Output divided by input, or the extent to which the result produced was produced at least cost.

Employee satisfaction The degree to which employee needs are met, a relative measure.

Entrepreneur A person who starts and develops a business.

Environment The external setting in which a business operates. Of special importance are the factors that may have a large impact on the business's success — such factors as competition, labor market conditions, the general economic climate, government regulation, etc.

Equipment Machinery and devices that can be employed in producing the results the firm desires.

Executive A manager. Most frequently used to refer to middle and upper levels of the organizational hierarchy.

Exports Goods and services provided from one country to another. Generally contrasted with imports, goods consumed in a home country but produced abroad.

Extrapolation A method of forecasting that assumes that the future will continue to reflect already established trends.

Facilities Buildings and structures that can be used in a firm's operations.

Factors of production The elements necessary in order to produce goods and services in an economy, for example capital and labor.

Federal decentralization A mode of organizing a large multidivision company by decentralizing authority and centralizing control.

Feedback mechanism A mechanism to allow recognition of unexpected deviations in a process and prompt corrective action so that the process will stay at the level needed to obtain the desired results.

First-line supervisor A manager who supervises other employees at the lowest managerial level in the organizational hierarchy. These people are also referred to as first-line management.

Fixed capital Money invested permanently in buildings, machinery, and equipment.

Fixed Costs Costs that are incurred regardless of the level of production. Frequently contrasted with variable costs, which depend on the amount produced.

Forecasting Estimating the value of a certain variable in the future, such as sales for the coming year.

Foreman A manager who is in charge of one of the basic units of a production facility.

Formal organization The structure that indicates to whom each person in the hierarchy reports, frequently diagramed in an "organization chart."

Free enterprise system The economic system that has private ownership of property and business units operated with a minimum of governmental interference.

Functional authority Authority based on a business function whose exercise may require compliance by persons who are not subordinates of the person exercising the authority. For example, a purchasing department may require persons in another department to follow its procedures for ordering equipment.

Function organization A mode of organizing a business that makes the manufacturing, selling, engineering, accounting, and other departments defined by business functions the basic subunits of the organization.

Gantt Chart A chart to be used in planning and coordinating an activity that involves several parallel subactivities. A time line is depicted horizontally at the top of the chart. Below the time line are horizontal bars for each activity, with the length of each bar representing its duration and the left-end border representing the beginning time of the activity.

Goals The basic aims of an enterprise.

Gross national product (GNP) The sum of the values of all the products and services produced by a national economy during a single year.

Hierarchy of needs A construct in Maslow's theory of motivation. The theory postulates that human needs consist of the hierarchy: physiological, security, affiliation, esteem, and self-actualization needs. The theory suggests that the lower-level needs must be satisfied before higher-order needs come into play and that once lower-level needs are satisfied, they lose their motivational importance.

Human asset accounting A set of methods for trying to value a firm's human resources.

Human relations approach to management An approach to management thought and practice that insists on the primacy of the relations among a firm's employees as the determinant of success.

Hygiene and housekeeping activities Activities that do not contribute to the basic results of the business but that if done poorly could damage the business, for example keeping the premises clean, the employees fed, reporting to the government, etc.

Hygiene factors   A construct in Herzberg's theory of motivation, factors that do not motivate positively but that could demotivate if handled poorly.

Impact   The consequences an action has in addition to those that constitute its raison d'etre, for example an action taken in one department may have consequences far beyond that department, or a production process may have polluting wastes as an impact.

Incentives   The items provided as "carrots" using a carrot-stick theory of motivation.

Industrial anthropology   The science of man in the work place. Concepts of sociology, psychology, and physiology are applied to understanding life in an industrial setting.

Industrial engineer   An engineer who applies scientific methods to solving work-related problems, especially in a factory or production setting.

Industrial engineering   The discipline that includes the scientific principles and research the industrial engineer applies in the work place.

Industrial physiology   The subdivision of physiology that is concerned with the impact of specific industrial practices on the human body and its functioning.

Industrial psychology   The branch of psychology that studies human behavior in organizational settings, with special attention being given to behavior in business firms.

Industrial relations   An approach to management promoted by some behavioral scientists. The central theme is the relief or prevention of dissatisfaction among employees.

Industrial sociology   The study of human institutions and groups and their operating characteristics in an industrial setting.

Information   Facts or data that can be communicated.

Inflation   The process by which money loses some of its value.

Inflationary pressures   Economic conditions that if left unchecked will bring on inflation, for example continued wage increases unmatched by productivity improvements.

Individual professional contributors   Managerial personnel who may supervise no one (except possibly a secretary and an assistant) but who make major contributions to the results of the firm by applying their professional competence, for example an advertising specialist.

Informal organization   The set of relationships that reflect actual interactions within an organization as contrasted with the formal organization structure.

Innovation   Activity or developments in a firm that result in the adoption of a new product, business, or way of doing things.

Installment credit   Credit extended in exchange for the promise to repay the money with interest in equal payments at specified intervals until the money is repaid.

Institutional investors   Investors who represent large organizations and as a consequence buy and sell very large blocks of stocks and bonds, for example, mutual funds, pension funds, university endowment funds. Since the late 1960s such investors have come to dominate the market, whereas individual investors were once a large part of the market.

Insurance   A method of protecting individuals against the effects of a specific kind of loss by having each individual in the insured group pay a fee in exchange for a promise to be compensated in the event the loss occurs.

Integrate   A process by which a manager meshes his work with that of others (in his unit, in other units, above him, below him, and laterally) in order to insure performance.

Interest group   A group banded together in order to pursue a particular objective.

Intermediate product   A product made to be used in making another product rather than to be used by an end user, for example a basic chemical product such as carbon dioxide.

Interpersonal relations   Relations among people, based on continued face-to-face interactions.

Invention   A technological advance, either a product or a means of doing something.

Inventor   A person who creates or produces an invention.

Inventory   The supply of goods or resources on hand at one time.

Inventory models   Models that may be used to determine when inventories should be re-supplied.

Investment   An application of a firm's resources (especially money) in a means that is expected to pay off in future results.

Investment banking   The function performed by financial institutions that underwrite and sell new isssues of stocks and bonds of a company and advise the company on such matters.

Investment decision   A decision about how to employ substantial portions of a firm's resources, especially capital.

Investment instruments   Vehicles that may be used to invest funds, for example stocks, bonds, mutual funds, certificates of deposit.

Irreversible decision   A decision whose impact cannot be removed or reversed, for example introducing a completely new technology (the secret of the technology cannot be reinstated).

Job description   An exposition of the duties and responsibilities that are inherent in a particular job.

Job enlargement   Including more tasks or more kinds of tasks in a given job in order to make the job more satisfying.

Job enrichment   Changing some aspects of a job in order to have it satisfy more of a person's higher-order needs.

Joint venture   A business venture that is funded by more than one company. For example, the European SST was a joint venture of British and French companies.

Key activities   Activities in the most important business areas: marketing, innovation, human organization, financial resources, physical resources, productivity, social responsibility, and profit requirements.

Knowledge worker   An employee whose major contribution depends on his employing his knowledge rather than his muscle power and coordination, frequently contrasted with production workers who employ muscle power and coordination to operate machines.

Labor economics   The branch or discipline of economics that concentrates its studies on the supply and demand of labor in an economy.

Labor-intensive industry   An industry that, in comparison to other industries, requires large expenditures for labor per dollar of sales or production. Frequently contrasted with capital-intensive industry.

Labor unions   Organizations of workers banded together to promote worker interests, especially higher wages and better fringe benefits and working conditions.

Large-scale organizations   Organizations that require huge investments or employ thousands of workers, as contrasted with small businesses, proprietorships, or businesses with limited managerial employees.

Lateral mobility   Ability to move from one area of a business to another, as from production to sales. Frequently compared to vertical mobility.

Leadership   The managerial function of providing guidance in setting business goals or quality standards.

Lead time   The time that must pass between a decision and its coming to fruition, for example the number of years between the decision to build a new steel mill and the time when it can be placed in operation.

Limited liability insurance   Insurance that covers only certain kinds of losses or only losses of a particular size.

Linear programming   An operations research technique that can be used to determine the proper mix of products or ingredients to maximize profits or some other dimension of interest to management.

Line management job   A managerial job that includes supervision and one of the central business functions such as selling or production. Frequently contrasted with staff jobs.

Liquidate   To terminate an operation by disposing of all assets and inventory, returning the proceeds to the owners of the operation.

Long-range planning   Planning with a multi-year time horizon. Contrasted with yearly plans and other short-range plans.

Logistics   The function of moving, storing, and distributing resources and goods.

Manage   In an organizational setting, to mobilize resources for the achievement of a human purpose.

Manageability   The characteristic inherent in an organization that can be managed, believed to be related to complexity and size. For example, some commentators have questioned the manageability of large cities.

Management   The group of persons who manage an organization. Also the discipline concerned with understanding and improving the knowledge of how to manage.

Management by objective (MBO)   The approach to management that emphasizes the central role of objectives for each unit of an organization and for each individual contributor. The approach emphasizes self-control as a consequence of having clear objectives for each individual.

Management development   The means by which an organization contributes to the development of the managerial abilities of its management group.

Management science   The approach to management that emphasizes the application of scientific methods for the improved understanding and practice of management.

Managers   The people in an organization whose jobs include managing responsibilities.

Managerial accounting   The accounting done in a firm to produce reports that will contribute to management decisions. Contrasted with tax accounting or financial accounting.

Managerial economics   The subdivision of economics that emphasizes notions of direct relevance to managers; decisions such as investment and pricing decisions receive special attention.

Manual worker   A worker whose primary contribution is a result of his or her muscle power and coordination.

Manufacturing business   A business whose central role is to produce an item, the chemical industry for example. Manufacturing is frequently contrasted to retailing or to other service industries.

Marginal cost   The cost of producing and selling an additional unit.

Marginal efficiencies   Efficiencies that if adopted would make very small changes in overall results.

Marginal revenue   The revenue that would be produced by producing and selling an additional unit.

Market   An area in which buyers and sellers may come together or an area of demand (however defined).

Market analysts   Specialists who attempt to define, map, quantify, and develop information about markets.

Market standing   The relative ranks of various firms in a single market, for example first, second, etc.

Market research   The research produced by market analysts.

Mass-distribution system   A system for distributing goods or services to large numbers of customers who are dispersed within an area.

Mass-production system   A system of production that is geared to produce large numbers of units.

Matrix organization   A mode of organizing, especially of large technological projects, that includes persons having both task and function assignments and as a consequence being attached to two units of the organization at one time (with the possibility of having two bosses). The "matrix" is suggested by a diagram that has functional units across the top and task units down the side with entries indicating persons from various functions assigned to a given task.

Media   Vehicles for communication, for example television, radio, newspapers, etc.

Middle managers   Managers who occupy positions in the formal organization above first-line supervisors and below top management.

Minimum profitability   The least level of profitability a particular industry should accept in order to take the risk inherent in that industry.

MIS (management information system)   A term created to describe a management's mechanisms for obtaining, processing, storing, retrieving, and using information, frequently suggesting the use of computers.

Mission   An organization's paramount objective for its intermediate future.

Model   A simplified replication of a problem situation that can be manipulated to explore the range and quality of solutions to the problem.

Motivation   Personal mechanisms that move an individual to action.

Multinational corporation   A corporation that has significant production, markets, and operations in many countries.

Multiplier impact   An impact that prompts multiple other impacts, as the multiplier impact of the building of infrastructure in a developing nation.

Multiproduct, multimarket, or multitechnology company   A company that produces multiple products, operates in many markets, or employs a wide variety of technologies in its operations.

Mutual fund   An investment vehicle that allows the investor to have an interest in many companies without being the direct owner of their stocks.

Network analysis   Analysis used in planning and scheduling, for example critical path analysis.

Nonmanufacturing business   A business whose primary function is selling or some business function.

Not-for-profit organization   An organization such as a university whose mission is other than to create a profit from its operations.

Objectives   The levels of results to be sought within a specific time period.

Obsolete   No longer in use; outmoded.

Operations   The activities associated with the production of current results. Frequently contrasted with the preparations for future business opportunities.

Operations manager   A manager whose prime responsibility is in operations.

Operations research   The discipline that studies the application of mathematical tools and logic to the solution of industrial problems.

Optimal solution   A solution to a problem that is the best one possible.

Optimization   The process of finding the optimal solution to a management problem, usually using an operations research model.

Organization chart   The pictorial representation of the formal organization.

Organization design   The design principles incorporated in the formal organization of a company or the discipline that studies alternative ways to design organizations.

Organizational psychology   The branch of psychology that studies human behavior in organizations; includes industrial psychology.

Organizing   The process of creating a formal organization structure or of breaking a task to be performed into subtasks.

Output   That which results from a production process.

Participative management   An approach to improving management practice that emphasizes participation of all impacted parties in decisions.

Partnership   A mode of legally structuring a business that includes specifications of each partner's role and responsibility.

Payback period The period required for the proceeds from an investment to equal the amount invested.

Payroll The business function that calculates the amount due each employee and conveys those funds to the employee by check or alternative means.

Pension A regular amount received by a retired employee based on certain payments made by employer and/or employee during the employee's working years.

Pension fund The invested proceeds of the funds contributed by an employer and/or employees for the purpose of paying pensions.

Performance Actual results obtained. Sometimes used to denote the achievement of positive results.

Personal income Wages and salaries paid to individuals. Frequently contrasted with investment income.

Personnel administration The management role concerned with the hiring and training of employees and with keeping employee records.

Personnel appraisal The evaluation of employees' performance and interaction between a boss and subordinate to discuss the subordinate's performance and future objectives, a process frequently discussed in conjunction with MBO.

Personnel department The unit of an organization that performs the personnel administration role.

Personnel management The management of the firm's human resources. Sometimes called human resources management.

PERT Chart (Program Evaluation Review Technique) A planning technique that uses charts, created by the Navy to aid in planning a project and in evalutating progress after it is under way.

Pilot-plant A plant built to test a new process, usually on a scale much less than that proposed for subsequent implementation. Frequently a pilot-plant test of a process, if successful, will suggest ways to improve the larger facility to be built later.

Planned obsolescence An approach to design that utilizes the expectation that the product design will become out of vogue before the product itself is physically unuseable; the approach includes subsequent designs that are intended to make previous designs unfashionable. Also, the design of products to become obsolete earlier than necessary in order to be able to introduce new designs.

Planning The management function that includes decisions and actions to insure future results.

Planning assumptions or hypotheses Assumptions or hypotheses used in plans.

Plans The view of the future as specified in the decisions resulting from planning.

Plant The facilities that a firm can use for production.

Policy A specified mode of approaching a particular area in the future, for example a marketing policy.

Power Ability to influence, to make others act in a way desired by the holder of the power.

PPBS (Planning Programming Budgeting System) A comprehensive planning methodology utilized by some public agencies.

Priorities The relative order in which an organization intends to address a list of issues or areas.

Probability mathematics A subdivision of mathematics that is concerned with modeling situations with outcomes that have relative likelihoods of occurence.

Procedures Specified ways to approach narrowly defined situations, for example procedures for recording a sale.

Process industry An industry that neither manufactures nor provides an intangible service; rather it subjects certain resources to a process, for example the oil refining industry.

Producing capital Capital invested in the land, buildings, and equipment used to produce the product or service.

Product lines The various basic categories and subcategories of products produced or provided.

Product manager A managerial role that has responsibility for coordinating all of the activities that affect the results produced from the assigned product. Such a manager might coordinate all of production, advertising, selling and distributing.

Product mix The variety of products offered by one company.

Productivity The relative output for given levels of input, especially the production per production employee. The continuing challenge is to improve productivity.

Profit The difference between income and costs.

Profit centers In large multidivision companies, profits may be calculated in various subdivisions of the company to add up to the overall profit, compare with cost centers. A manager in charge of a profit center (one of the subdivisions) has profit and loss responsibility.

Programmer A person who creates computer programs.

Proprietor The sole owner and manager of a small business.

Prototype A model of a potential new product, used to evaluate the product's prospects.

Public-service institutions Institutions such as government and nonprofit institutions which exist to provide a service in a nonprofit manner.

Purchasing power The ability a person or a group of people has to purchase goods and services because of their income.

Qualitative factors Factors to be incorporated in decisions that cannot be quantified, such as values and beliefs.

Quality control The production function that sets quality standards and monitors the production process to insure that the process yields goods meeting the established standards.

Quality of life The qualitative assessment of the relative quality of living conditions, including attention to pollutants, noise, aesthetics, complexity, etc.

Queing theory The branch of management science that uses models of waiting-lines to approximate certain industrial problem situations.

Receivables An accounting term denoting the amounts owed the company.

Regulation Governmental action sanctioned by law to control business behavior.

Reserves Monies held out of use by a company to meet certain demands or serve designated purposes, for example reserves for the replacement of worn out equipment.

Responsibility Performance areas in which a person or unit is expected to produce results.

Result-producing activities Activities that produce measurable results that can be related, directly or indirectly, to the results and performance of the entire enterprise. Among result-producing activities are revenue-producing activities such as selling, nonrevenue activities such as manufacturing (result contributing activities), and information activities.

Return on investment (ROI) The ratio of the amount earned per year to the amount invested in a particular project or business (stated as a percentage).

Risk The likelihood of success versus the likelihood of failure for any undertaking. Assessing a risk is the process of trying to quantify or judge which likelihood is the larger and by how much.

Scientific management The approach to management fathered by Frederick W. Taylor. Its core is the organized study of work, the analysis of work into its simplest elements, and the systematic improvement of the worker's performance of each of these elements, resulting in higher levels of output per worker.

Service institutions Organizations constituted to perform a public task not involving the production of a product. The service is provided in a nonprofit mode. Examples include the postal service, educational institutions, and utility districts.

Service industries   Industries whose primary output is not the provision of a manufactured product. Such industries are generally contrasted with manufacturing industries.

Simulation   An abstract replication of certain of the dynamics of a problem situation. The replication usually involves the manipulation of a model using a computer.

Simulated decentralization   A mode of organizing large companies that are too big to remain functionally organized and too integrated to be genuinely decentralized. One function or segment is treated as if it were an autonomous business relating to other units as if in an actual marketplace. The mode is typical in the materials, computer, chemical, and pharmaceutical industries.

Social impacts   The societal consequences of actions that go beyond the consequences that are the action's *raison d'etre.*

Social psychology   The branch of psychology concerned with human behavior in groups. The behavior of the individual in the group and the behavior of the group as a group are studied with the expectation that the results may be applied to improve individual and group performance.

Social responsibility   An institution's obligations to the society in which it resides. Recent discussion has highlighted differing points of view about what these obligations are.

Span of control   A number of persons who report directly to a given manager. In decades past, the question of whether this number had an upper limit or an ideal received much attention.

Speculation   Investments that have high likelihoods of failure but promise huge returns if successful.

Staff   Individual contributors who advise or counsel rather than directly manage a group of people. Such persons are often contrasted with line managers.

Staffing   The management function that recruits, places, and trains the firm's resources.

Stock   Units of ownership of a corporation.

Stockholders   The owners of the stock of a particular company. The stockholders are generally a very large group, but theoretically they exercise control over the company through a smaller board of directors.

Strategic planning   The planning for a company's long-term future that includes the setting of major overall objectives, the determination of the basic approaches to be used in pursuing these objectives, and the means to be used in obtaining the necessary resources to be employed.

Strategy   A company's basic approach to achieving its overall objectives. For example, Sears' early strategy was to become a major supplier of products to the rural population by means of mail-order sales utilizing attractive catalogues and efficient "mail-order factories" (order processing and shipping facilities).

Structure   The arrangement of processes and functions within the company as regards their relationships to each other. The methods used vary including the functional approach, decentralization, simulated decentralization, and matrix forms.

Suboptimization   Producing ideal performance in one area of a business and thereby being unable to produce ideal or optimum performance for the business as a whole.

Subordinate   A person who reports to a particular manager is said to be one of that manager's subordinates. Thus each line manager except the chief executive both has subordinates and is a subordinate.

Successor   The person who is appointed to a managerial position immediately after another person leaves the position is called the departing person's successor. The question of who the successors for top positions are to be frequently has great impact on a company's chances of success.

Supervisor   A person who has responsibility for directing the activities of a group of employees.

Support activities Support activities include "conscience" activities (staff), and such functions as legal counsel, labor-relations activities. They are compared to result-producing activities, hygiene and housekeeping activities, and top-management activities.

Supporting capital Working capital, that is, capital used to bring goods and services to market or to finance the time between their production and the time the buyer pays. Frequently contrasted with "producing" capital.

Surplus Profits and other savings that successful performance can produce.

System A set of interrelated parts. For example, one can speak about a distribution system, which might consist of a network of warehouses to be served in a particular manner by a number of plants and which, in turn, would ship to customers according to prescribed procedures.

System thinking Analysis that uses systems and their dynamics to examine problems and possible solutions.

Tactics Basic approaches to be used in carrying out a predetermined strategy.

Task force A group assigned to accomplish a task. Committees may limit their attentions to making recommendations, while task forces are expected to perform a job.

Tax accounting The subdivision of accounting that attends to keeping and summarizing records for tax purposes.

Team A group of people who are expected to work together on a project.

Team organization A mode of organization that creates and disbands teams for a succession of projects that constitute the majority of a firm's business.

Technology A way or means to accomplish a task. The technology may or may not include the use of machines.

Technology assessment The function of trying to determine the impacts of utilizing a particular technology in advance of its introduction. Proponents argue that technology assessment is possible, and Congress has established an office to do technology assessment. Opponents argue that it is impossible to assess technology in advance of its introduction.

Technology monitoring Following the impacts of a technology as it is introduced in order to identify and combat the harmful impacts, if any. This process is recommended by some who think that technology assessment is difficult if not impossible.

Theroy X and Theroy Y Theories about human behavior formulated by Douglas McGregor. Theory X assumes that people are lazy, dislike and shun work, have to be driven, and need both carrot and stick. It assumes that most people are incapable of taking responsibility for themselves and have to be looked after. Theory Y assumes that people have a psychological need to work and that they desire achievement and responsibility and will find them under the right conditions.

Time and motion studies Methods first promoted by the scientific management school. They include the study of physical work using stopwatches in order to break a task into segments that are redesigned in order to be performed more readily so that the productivity of the job is improved.

Time-sharing A method of arranging the operating characteristics of a computer so that several users can be working on it at the same time. The term also refers to computing that a person does while the computer is set up in this way.

Top management The managers who occupy the upper positions in the organizational hierarchy.

Top-management activity Activity that is to accomplish the top management tasks, which include thinking through the mission of the business, standard setting, building and maintenance of the human organization, major relations that only the people at the top of a business can establish and maintain, "ceremonial" functions, and the provision of an organ to respond to major crises.

Trade associations Organizations that bring the companies of an industry together for the purpose of exchanging information and jointly promoting the interests of the industry.

Union relations The business function of conducting interactions with the unions to which a company's employees belong.

Union An organization that brings workers in a trade or industry together for the purpose of bargaining collectively for improved wages, benefits, and working conditions.

Unity of command A management notion emphasized by early thinkers. The concept states that each employee should have one and only one boss.

Utility The usefulness or inherent value of something as perceived by an individual or an organization. A branch of economics tries to empirically measure and compare utilities.

Variable costs Costs of a production process that vary with the level of production.

Wage and salary administration The business function that determines wage and salary rates and adjusts them in response to market conditions and changed assignments.

Wealth The sum total of economic valuables owned by an individual, a country, or a society.

Wholly-owned subsidiaries Subsidiaries all of whose stock is owned by the parent company, as contrasted with a subsidiary that is controlled because of the parent's being the largest, but not the only, holder of stock in the subsidiary company.

Working capital Supporting capital.

Yardsticks Means of measuring results in key areas of a business.

Zero-based budgeting Budgeting that assumes that each project or activity must justify again any expenditures (above zero) for each new year even if the project or activity was justified previously.

Zero-sum games Games in which the total of all winnings equals what is lost, that is, in which anything won resulted from a loss of one of the participants.

Index

Abilities and skills, knowledge workers, 274–275
Achievement and productive work, 28
Activities
    conscience, 181–182
    contributions analysis, 179–180
    key, 177–179
Adela, 336
Administration and entrepreneurship, 32–34
Agriculture Department and farm policy, 136–137
American Telephone and Telegraph Co., 164
Andean Pact, 336
Argyris, Chris, 165, 244
ASEA, 149
Assignment control, knowledge workers, 273–274
Attitude, innovative, 157–159
Authority
    decision making, knowledge organizations's need for, 76–77
    over economic shares, 244
    limits of, 316–318
    problem of, 25
    and redistribution, 245

Bank of America, 149
Baruch, Bernard, 154, 157
Bell Laboratories, 149–150
Bell System, 138–139
    as multinational, 215
Bennis, Warren, 165, 250
Betriebswissenschaft (science of enterprise), 17, 20
Blacks
    and economic inequality, 324 325
    civil rights and Quaker conscience, 295–296
    and social responsibility of business, 288–289, 290
Booth, Charles, 290
Boulding, Kenneth, 15
Brown, Wilfred, 251
Budget
    and measurement, innovation, 155–156
    misdirection by, 135–137
Burt, Cyril, 235
Business. *See also* Enterprise; Management; Multinationals; Organization; Service institution
    economic task, 101–102

Business (*Continued*)
  efforts and cost, 104–107
  entrepreneurial functions, 90–91
  innovation as, 161–163
  productivity, 94–97
  profit functions, 97–99
  and profit motive, 88–89
  purpose of, 89–90
  results and resources outside of, 102
  social problems as opportunities for,
    307–310
  social responsibility, 287–291
Businessmen, ethics of, 320–322
Business society, to pluralist society,
    11–13
Butler, Nicholas Murray, 139, 140

Cahn, Edmond, 255
Capital
  cost of, 122–123
  in developing countries, 332
  fixed vs. working, 128–129
  productivity of, 117, 127–128
  and time, 129–130
  turnover, 127
Capital formation and productivity, 94
Capital fund, 242
Career professional, 51–52
  title, function, and pay, 52–53
Carnegie, Andrew, 7
Carrot and stick, 251
  replacing, 257–260
Carrothers, Dr., 156
CERN, 149, 161
Chase Manhattan Bank, 336
Civil rights and Quaker conscience,
    295–296
Clay, Henry, 15, 214
Columbia University, social impact and
    responsibility, 289, 301
Committee for Economic Development,
    307
Common Market, 196
Communication
  as basic employee skill, 262–263
  manager's use of time in, 57
  as manager's work, 55, 56
  upward, 2
Community activities, participation of
    managers in, 321
Community bond, work as, 240–241
Compensation. *See* Executive compen-
    sation; Pay

Competence, limits of, 314–316
Computer
  basic skills, 277–278
  control, 279
  decision-making, 279–280
  in designing physical structures,
    278–279
  indigestible information, 280–281
  and information as public resource, 283
  in making better middle managers,
    281–282
  and middle management obsolescence,
    303
  in multiplying human capacity, 277
  programmers, reduced dependence on,
    283–284
  time sharing, 282–283
Concentration and results, 106
The Conditions of the Working Classes in
    England (Engels), 290
Conscience activities, 181–182
Consortium banks, 197
Consumerism and marketing, 91–92
Consumer research, Marks & Spencer,
    115
Contribution(s)
  analysis, organization, 179–180
  of knowledge workers, 272–273
  management responsibility for, 50
Control
  of assignments for knowledge workers,
    273–274
  computer, 279
  knowledge work, 236–237
Corporation. *See* Business; Enterprise;
    Management; Multinationals; Or-
    ganization
Cost
  business efforts and, 104–107
  of capital, 122–123
  of future jobs and pensions, 124
  vs. risk and uncertainty, 123–124
Couzens, James, 308
CPC, 204, 219
Customer, and purpose of business,
    89–90

Dana, Richard Henry, 239
DDT, 302, 304
Dean, Joel, on profit maximization, 88
Decentralization
  federal, 169, 170
  need to go beyond, 38

simulated, 169, 170
Decision, and organization, 170, 188–190
Decision analysis, 181–182
Decision-making
    computer, 279–280
    knowledge organization, need for authority in, 76–77
    problem of, 22–23
Deltec, and social responsibility, 294–295, 314
Deutsche Bank, 11, 16
Developing countries
    development of resources, 331–334
    and local ownership, 336–338
    and multinationals, 212–216
    productive integration across boundaries, 334–336
    as profit source, 330–331
Development of people, as manager's work, 55, 56
Doering, Otto, 110
Douglas, Paul, 242
Dow Chemical Co., 305
du Pont, Pierre S., 7, 53
du Pont de Nemours (E. I.) & Co., 7, 164, 189, 192
    Industrial Toxicity Laboratory, 305
    innovation measurement and budgets, 155–156
    and social responsibility, 317
    structure for innovation, 160, 162

Economic development, 24
    and growth, enterprise as organ of, 92–94
Economic dimension of working, 241–242
Economic incentives, as rights, 254
Economic inequality, and executive compensation, 323–326
Economics, power dimension of, 244–245
Economic shares, authority over, 244
Economy, international, 338–339
Edison, Thomas A., 31
Effectiveness
    vs. efficiency, 32–33
    service institution, 136
    of service staff, 182–184
Effectiveness centers, 24
Efficiency
    vs. effectiveness, 32–33

service institution, 136
Eliot, Charles W., 139, 140
Employee(s)
    choice of big or small company, 265–266
    communication as basic skill of, 262–263
    importance of being fired, 267–268
    kinds of, 263–264
    life off the job, 269
    personality and security need, 264–265
    promotion, 269
    society of, 10–11, 261–262
    as specialist or generalist, 266–267
    starting at the bottom, 266
    when to quit, 268–269
Employee benefits, as golden fetters, 326
Engels, Friedrich, 290
"The Engineer as Economist" (Towne), 16
Enterprise. *See also* Business; Management; Multinationals; Organization; Service institution
    and economic growth and development, 92–94
    manageability problem, 22
    social impacts and responsibilities, 29–31
    worker ownership, 243
Entrepreneur, 15, 19
    manager as, 39–40
    partnership with, 162
Entrepreneurial decisions, 23
Entrepreneurship, and innovation, 34
Environment, and multinationals, 209–212
Ethics
    basic rule, 322–323
    of businessmen, 320–322
    of leadership groups, 322
Executive compensation
    and economic inequality, 323–326
    and golden fetters, 326
    multinationals, 208–209
Expectations, rising tide of, 37

Factors of production
    balancing, 130
    integration, multinationals, 200–201
Failure, and innovation, 156–157

Fayol, Henri, 16, 20, 166, 168, 172
Fear
    and motivation, 251–253
    and production of knowledge, 256
Federal decentralization, 169, 170
Fiat, 149
Financial dimension, working, 242–244
First-line supervisor, job of, 50
Fixed capital, 128–129
    and time, 129–130
Ford, Henry, 4–6, 232, 257, 308
Ford, Henry II, 5–6
Ford Motor Co.
    guaranteed daily wage, 308–309
    vs. GM, management at, 4–6
    as multinational, 200
Fourier, François, 15
Freybey, Berthold, 204
Friedman, Milton, 297, 316, 317
Function
    of career professional, 52–53
    innovation as, 90–91
    as management criterion, 50
    of profit, 97–99

Galbraith, John Kenneth, 88
Gantt, Henry, 20, 236
Gantt Chart, 236
General Electric Co., 153, 164, 172
    structure for innovation at, 160, 162
Generalist vs. specialist, 266–267
General Motors Corp., 53, 117, 164, 192
    management team under Sloan, 5–6
    organization model vs. present realities,
        166–168, 172
    study of worker attitudes, 249, 255
Giannini, A. P., 150
Gilbreth, Lillian, 229
Gilman, Daniel Coit, 139, 140
Gino coefficient, 323
Goals, measurable, and intangible objec-
    tives, 134–135
Gompers, Samuel, 253–254
The Good Soldier Schweik (Hasek), 256
Government
    disenchantment with, 291
    multiplier effect of money, 333
Grant, U. S., 79

Hamilton, Alexander, 15
Harper, William Rainey, 139, 140
Harvard Business School, 13, 26

Hasek, Jaroslav, 256
Hawthorne studies, 225
Herzberg, Frederick, 246, 249
Honeywell, Inc., 200, 212
Hoover, Herbert, 26
Hopf, Harry, 229
Hospital, as service institution, 140–141
Hughes, Howard, 6
Hughes Aircraft Co., 6
Human relations
    insight and limitations of, 227–228
    and personnel administration, 224–225
The Human Side of Enterprise (McGreg-
    gor), 249
Hygiene and housekeeping activities,
    185–186

ICL, 200, 212
Imperial Chemicals, 164, 172
Income equality, and executive compen-
    sation, 323–326
Industrial physiology, 325
Industrial psychology, 235
Inflation
    and income inequality, 325
    and material rewards, 255
Information, as manager's tool, 56–57
Information activities, 184–185
Innovation
    attitude, 157–159
    background, 146–149
    as business, 161–163
    as business function, 90–91
    dynamics of, 151–152
    and entrepreneurship, 34
    examples, 149–150
    vs. invention, 92–94
    meaning of, 150–151
    measurements and budgets, 155–156
    objectives, Marks & Spencer, 117
    and risk of failure, 156–157
    at Sears, 111, 112
    social vs. technical, 40
    strategy, 152–155
    structure for, 159–161
Installment credit, and economic growth
    and development, 93
Institution. *See also* Business; Enterprise;
    Management; Multinationals; Or-
    ganization; Service institution
    manager's responsibility to, 312–314
    nonbusiness, 12–13

society of, 9–10
Insurance, and economic growth and
    development, 93
International Business Machines Corp.,
    72, 203, 216
    employment security at, 309
    marketing approach, 91
International Management Movement,
    25–26
International Monetary Fund, 195
International Telephone & Telegraph
    Corp., 211
Invention vs. innovation, 92–94
Iron law of wages, 16

Jaques, Elliott, 251
Jobs, future, cost of, 124
Jordan, David Starr, 139

Kami, Michael J., 153
Kennedy, Robert, 291
Key activities, and organization,
    177–179
Knowledge, productivity of, 40–41
Knowledge organization
    need for decision authority, 76–77
    top management's role in, 77–78
Knowledge work
    analysis, synthesis, and control,
        236–237
    and productivity, 95–96
Knowledge workers
    assignment control, 273–274
    contribution, 272–273
    doing what they're paid for, 273
    growth of group, 271–272
    junior, pay of, 52
    middle managers as, 74
    and productivity of knowledge, 40–41
    productivity and satisfaction, 272
    as real labor force, 23–24
    and second careers, 309
    skills and abilities, 274–275
    and Theory X, 256
Kuznets, Simon, 242

Labor, manual, and productivity, 94
Labor cost
    and employee benefits, 326
    and turnover, 308–309
Labor force, professionals in, 23–24

Land, Edwin H., 150
Language, as manager's tool, 57
Laski, Norman, 116
Leadership
    from personnel management to,
        38–39
    and results, 103
Leadership groups
    vs. leaders, 322
    management, 292
    and social responsibility, 297
Lee, R. E., 80
Lincoln, A., 79
Lindsay, John, 288, 311
List, Friedrich, 214

Malorganization, 190–193
Manageability
    problem of, 22
    of service institutions, 132–133
Management. *See also* Business; Enter-
        prise; Manager; Middle manage-
        ment; Multinationals; Organiza-
        tion; Service institution; Top
        management
    authority problem, 25
    basic themes, 19–20
    of boss, 83–84
    as change of phase, 7–8
    conceptual foundations, 36–37
    decision-making problem, 22–23
    differences in levels of, 63–64
    by drives, 65
    and employee society, 10–11
    as focus, 13–14
    Ford vs. GM, 4–6
    of future multinationals, 217–220
    history and roots, 14–15
    legitimacy, 25
    in making work productive and worker
        achieving, 28–29
    and malorganization, 191
    multi-institutional, 40
    multinational and multicultural,
        41–42
    need for new knowledge in, 37–38
    new themes, 20–21
    in nonbusiness institutions, 12–13
    philosophy of, 70
    professionals in, 48–49
    purpose and mission, 28

Management (*Continued*)
  and quality of life, 42–43
  of Sears, 108–114
  social and political problems, 23–24
  as supernational function, 25–26
  time dimension, 31–32
Management by objectives, 61
Management group, 50–51
Management science, in dealing with
    people vs. things, 23
Manager. *See also* Management; Middle
    management; Top management
  of career professional, 51–52, 53
  and computer, 282
  danger of golden fetters, 326
  defined, 59
  entrepreneurial, 39–40
  functional, 61–62
  information tool, 56–57
  leadership groups, 292, 297
  of multinationals, 205–208
  new definition, 49–51
  reality of, 251–253
  responsibility to institution, 312–
    314
  setting objectives, 64–67
  tasks, 53–54
  traditional definition, 47–49
  and upward communication, 2
  use of time, 57–58
  work of, 34–35, 54–56
Manager's letter, 57, 66–67
Manhattan Project, 149, 161
Manual labor, and productivity, 94
Mao Tse-tung, 254
Marketing
  as business function, 90–91
  and consumerism, 92–93
  objectives, Marks & Spencer, 115
  vs. selling, 91–92
Marks, Simon, 116
Marks & Spencer, 108
  laboratory, 177–178
  objectives at, 115–121
Marshall, Alfred, 15
Marx, Karl, 15, 126, 246
Masaryk, Thomas, 26
Maslow, Abraham H., 246
  criticism of McGregor's theory, 250–
    251
Material rewards, potency of, 253–256
Matrix organization, 149

Mayo, Elton, 20, 225, 235, 246
McClelland, David C., 251
McCormick, Cyrus H., 90
McGregor, Douglas, Theory X and
    Theory Y, 165, 249
Measurement
  and budgets, innovation, 155–156
  as manager's work, 55, 56
  and self-control, 67–68
Meetings, and malorganization, 192
Melville, Herman, 239
Merrill Lynch, Pierce, Fenner and Smith,
    178
Middle management. *See also* Manage-
    ment; Manager; Top management
  computer in making better, 281–282
  decision impact of, 75–76
  growth, 71–72, 74–75
  as knowledge organization, 76
  need for decision authority, 76–77
  overstaffing, 73–74
Mill, John Stuart, 14
Misdirection, by managers, 62–63
Mobil Oil Corp., 10
Motivation
  and fear, 251–253
  as manager's work, 55, 56
  of material rewards, 254–255
  and overstaffing, 73
Muensterberg, Hugo, 17, 235
Multinationals
  and developing countries, 212–216
  and environment, 209–212
  executive compensation, 208–209
  future of, 216–217
  and local ownership, 336–338
  management structures of future,
    217–220
  manager, 205–208
  myths about, 195–197
  productive integration across national
    boundaries, 334–336
  profit from developing countries,
    330–331
  and resources of developing countries,
    331–334
  strategy problems, 201–203
  top-management teams, 203–205
  as transnationals, 201
  and world economy, 338–339
  and world market, 198–201
  and world trade, 197–198

Nader, Ralph, 317
The New Industrial State (Galbraith), 88

Objectives
    how set and by whom, 65–67
    intangible, and measureable goals,
        134–135
    manager's work in setting, 55, 56
    at Marks & Spencer, 115–121
    what they should be, 64
Office of Technology Assessment, 301
Olivetti, Adrian, 309
Opportunities
    for promotion, 268–269
    resources to, 102
    results from, 102
    social problems as, 307–310
Organization. *See also* Business; Enter-
        prise; Multinationals; Organization
        structure; Service institution
    and alienation, 244
    conscience activities, 181–182
    contribution analysis, 179–180
    decision analysis, 187–190
    design logics, 170–171
    design principles, 168–169
    early models, 166
    GM model, 166–168, 172
    hygiene and housekeeping activity,
        185–186
    information activities, 184–185
    large-scale, 16–17
    and malorganization, 190–193
    organizitis, 193
    relations analysis, 190
    service staff, 182–184
Organization of Petroleum Exporting
        Countries (OPEC), 122
Organization structure. *See also* Organi-
        zation
    building new, 172–174
    for innovation, 159–161
    integral parts of, 171–172
    key activities, 177–179
    multinationals, 204–205
    and productivity, 96–97
    and strategy, 173, 182
    surveying, 172
Organizing, as manager's work, 55, 56
Organizitis, 193
Overstaffing, danger of, 73–74

Owen, Robert, 15, 18, 19

Partnership with entrepreneur, 162
Pay. *See also* Executive compensation
    of career professional, 52–53
    dissatisfaction over, 255
    iron law of wages, 16
Pensions, cost of, 124
People
    first-line supervisor as manager of, 50
    leadership of, 38–39
    as manager's resource, 58–59
    manager's work in developing, 55, 56
    and performance, 134
    vs. things, management science in
        dealing with, 23
Performance
    economic, as management task, 28
    and organization, 170
    and overstaffing, 73
    and people, 134
    and profit, 99
    in service institution, 131–132,
        133–134
Personality
    and security need, employee,
        264–265
    staffing to suit, 81–83
Personnel administration
    and human relations, 224–225
    misconceptions, 226–227
    survey of, 225–226
Personnel management
    analysis vs. action, 229–230
    blind spots, 229–232
    to leadership of people, 38–39
    and scientific management, 228–229
Philips, as multinational, 203
Physiological dimension of working,
        237–238
Pluralist society, from business society to,
        11–13
Port of New York Authority, 133–134
Poverty, and social responsibility of busi-
        ness, 289–290
Power dimension
    of economics, 244–245
    of working, 244
"Principles and Methods of Scientific
        Management" (Taylor), 19–20
Priorities, setting, 138–139

Procedures and reports, 68–70
Process mix and productivity, 96
Production
    balancing factors of, 130
    integration across national boundaries,
        334–336
    principles of, 236
Productivity
    of knowledge, 40–41
    need for new knowledge on, 37–38
    problem of, 24
    and satisfaction, knowledge workers,
        272
    in utilizing resources, 94–97
Product mix and productivity, 96
Professional(s)
    career, 51–53
    in labor force, 23–24
    in management, 48–49
Profit
    and cost against risk and uncertainty,
        123–124
    and cost of capital, 122–123
    and cost of future jobs and pension,
        124
    developing countries as source of,
        330–331
    functions of, 97–99
    at Marks & Spencer, 118–119
    and worker ownership, 243
Profitability
    and capital productivity, 127
    minimum, 313
Profit maximization, 88–89
Profit motive
    and profit maximization, 88–89
    rhetoric of, 326–328
Programmers, reduced dependence on,
    283–284
Promotion
    opportunities, 268–269
    who is chosen, 269
Psychological despotism, 257–259
Psychological dimension of working,
    238–239
Psychology, industrial, 235
Public service institution. *See* Service in-
    stitution

Quaker conscience, and civil rights,
    295–296
Quality of life, management and, 42–43

Rathenau, Emil, 17
Rathenau, Walther, 16–17, 20, 98
Redistribution, 245
Redistributive system, institution as, 245
Regulation of social impact, 305–306
Relations analysis, 190
Relationships, and organization, 170
Renault, 149
Reports and procedures, 68–70
Resources
    allocation of, 138
    of developing countries, development
        of, 331–334
    to opportunites, 102
    outside of business, 102
    productivity in utilizing, 94–97
Responsibility. *See also* Social responsi-
        bility
    of manager to institution, 312–314
    for social impacts, 299–301
Results
    and costs, 104–105
    and leadership position, 103
    from opportunities, 102
    and organization, 170
    outside of business, 102
Results-producing activities, 179, 180
Revenue vs. cost, 105
Ricardo, David, 14
Risk
    and decision making, 23
    and innovation, 156–157
    and uncertainty vs. cost, 123–124
Rockefeller, John D. Jr., 7
Root, Elihu, 20
Rosenwald, Julius, 110, 112, 308
Royal Dutch/Shell, 196

Sacher, Harry, 116
Saint-Simon, Comte de, 15, 18, 19
Satisfaction and productivity, knowledge
    workers, 272
Say, J. B., 15
Schmalenbach, Eugen, 17, 20
Schumpeter, Joseph, 20
Science of enterprise, 17
Scientific management, 228–229
    and new technology, 232–233
    and resistance to change, 232
Sears, Richard, 110
Sears, Roebuck and Co., 164, 172

laboratory in, 177
management of, 108–114
as multinational, 197, 336
Security need and personality, 264–265
Self-control and measurements, 67–68
Selling vs. marketing, 91–92
Service institution. *See also* Organization; Organization structure
budget-based achievement, 137–138
goals and objectives, 134–135
hospital, 140–141
making staff effective in, 182–184
manageability of, 132–133
misdirection by budget, 135–137
performance in, 131–132, 133–134
requirements for success, 141–142
setting priorities and allocating resources in, 138–139
university as, 139–140
Service staff, effectiveness of, 182–184
Shibusawa, Eiichi, 16
Sieff, Israel, 116
Siemens, Georg, 11, 16, 17
Siemens, Werner von, 150
Simulated decentralization, 169
Simulation, computer, 280
Singer Co., 199–200
Skills and abilities, knowledge workers, 274–275
Sloan, Alfred P. Jr., and GM organization, 5, 6, 7, 53, 166, 169, 172
Smith, Adam, 14, 15
Social bond, work as, 240–241
Social dimension of working, 240–241
Social impacts
dealing with, 304–305
of enterprise, 29–31
identifying, 301–304
regulation need, 305–306
responsibility for, 299–301
trade-offs, 306–307
Social problems as business opportunities, 307–310
Social responsibility
of business, 287–291
civil rights and Quaker conscience, 295–296
limitations on, 303
and limits of authority, 316–318
and limits of competence, 314–316
management's leadership group for, 297

and social impacts, 29–31, 299–301
Swift do Argentina and Deltec, 294–295
Union Carbide, 293–294, 300
when to say no, 318–319
Society
business to pluralist, 11–13
"degenerative diseases," 310–311
employee, 10–11, 261–262
of institutions, 9–10
managers as new leadership groups, 292
Sony, 149, 203
Spates, Thomas, 225
Specialist
vs. generalist, 266–267
misdirection of, 62
Staffing
to build strength, 79–81
to suit personality, 81–83
Stalin, Josef, 254
Standard Oil Co. (N. J.), 10, 192
Standard Oil Co. of California, 10
Standard Oil Trust, 10
Strategy
innovative, 152–155
multinationals, 201–203
and structure, 173, 182
Structure. *See* Organization structure
Suboptimization, 189, 190
Swift do Argentina, 294–295
Systems structure, 169, 170

Tannenbaum, Frank, 291
Taylor, Frederick W., and scientific management, 19–20, 40–41, 229, 231, 235, 236
Team organization, 149, 169, 170
Technology
identifying impacts of, 301–304
need for monitoring of, 304
and scientific management, 232–233
Thalidomide scandal, 306
"Theory of Economic Development" (Schumpeter), 20
Theory X and Theory Y, 249
and knowledge worker, 256
Maslow's criticism of, 250–251
and psychological despotism, 257–259
Thompson, D'Arcy, 7
3M Co., 149

3M Co. (*Continued*)
    innovation at, 158–159, 160
Time
    and capital productivity, 129–130
    as management dimension, 31–32
    manager's use of, 57–58
    and productivity, 96
Time sharing, 282–283
Timing and innovation, 154
Title of career professional, 52–53
Top management. *See also* Management
    activities, 179, 180
    and innovation, 158
    problems of, 21–22
    role in knowledge organization,
        77–78
    teams, multinationals, 203–205
Towne, Henry, 16, 19
Transnationals, multinationals as, 201
Trans World Airways, 6–7
Turnover
    of capital, 127
    and labor cost, 308–309

Ullstein, 149
Uncertainty and risk, vs. cost, 123–124
Unilever, 164, 196, 203, 204
Union Carbide Corp., and social responsi-
    bility, 293–294, 300, 314
United Automobile Workers, 257
University
    as service institution, 139–140
    structure for innovation, 160–161

Vail, Theodore, 138–139
Verne, Jules, 303

Volkswagen, 200
Vulnerability, economic, 33–34

Wages, iron law of, 16
The Wealth of Nations (Smith), 15
Weisskopf, Victor, 149
Western Electric Co., Hawthorne studies,
    225
Westinghouse Electric Corp., 140
White, Andrew D., 139, 140
Wood, Robert E., 110, 111
Work
    analysis, synthesis, and control,
        235–237
    productive, and worker achievement,
        28–29
Worker
    achievement, and productive work,
        28–29
    professional, 23–24
Work ethic, 239
Work groups, 240–241
Working
    economic dimension, 241–242
    fallacy of dominant dimension,
        246–247
    financial dimension, 242–244
    physiological dimension, 237–238
    potency of material rewards, 253–256
    power dimension, 244
    psychological dimension, 238–239
    social dimension, 240–241
Working capital, 128–129
World Bank, 195
World market
    as integrator, 199–201
    and multinationals, 198–199